EXPERT **RESUMES** for
Managers and **Executives**

Wendy S. Enelow and
Louise M. Kursmark

Expert Resumes for Managers and Executives

© 2003 by Wendy S. Enelow and Louise M. Kursmark

Published by JIST Works, an imprint of JIST Publishing, Inc.

8902 Otis Avenue
Indianapolis, IN 46216-1033
Phone: 1-800-648-JIST   Fax: 1-800-JIST-FAX   E-mail: info@jist.com

Visit our Web site at **www.jist.com** for information on JIST, free job search tips, book chapters, and ordering instructions for our many products!

See the back of this book for additional JIST titles and ordering information. Quantity discounts are available for JIST books. Please call our Sales Department at 1-800-648-5478 for a free catalog and more information.

Acquisitions and Development Editor: Lori Cates Hand
Cover Designer: Katy Bodenmiller
Interior Designer and Page Layout: Trudy Coler
Proofreader: Jeanne Clark
Indexer: Larry Sweazy

Printed in Canada
07 06 05 04 03   9 8 7 6 5 4 3 2 1

Library of Congress Cataloging-in-Publication Data is on file with the Library of Congress

We have been careful to provide accurate information in this book, but it is possible that errors and omissions have been introduced. Please consider this in making any career plans or other important decisions. Trust your own judgment above all else and in all things.

Trademarks: All brand names and product names used in this book are trade names, service marks, trademarks, or registered trademarks of their respective owners.

ISBN 1-56370-938-4

Contents at a Glance

TABLE OF CONTENTS

About This Book

If you're a manager or executive reading this book, you're in for some really good news:

- According to the U.S. Department of Labor's Bureau of Labor Statistics, the U.S. economy should expect to see a 13.6 percent increase in the number of management and executive positions between 2000 and 2010.

- The cumulative impact of this growth will create a total of 5.1 million management and executive positions by 2010.

Despite momentous changes in the U.S. economy and the global picture since the rampant growth of the 1990s, the management and executive employment sectors continue to grow. Of course, there is more hiring activity in certain industries than in others, but overall, the Department of Labor is projecting strong and steady growth for management and executive job seekers.

As such, you've picked a great time to launch your search campaign and look for a new management opportunity. In chapter 1 you'll find more interesting statistics that will further reinforce the fact that opportunities do abound. Your challenge, then, is to be a savvy job seeker, positioning yourself distinctively in a competitive employment market and identifying new opportunities through both traditional and non-traditional search channels.

To take advantage of all of these opportunities, you must first develop a powerful, performance-based resume. To be a successful job seeker, you must know how to communicate your qualifications in a strong and effective written presentation. Sure, it's important to let employers know essential details, but a resume is more than just your job history and academic credentials. A winning resume is a concise yet comprehensive document that gives you a competitive edge in the job market. Creating such a powerful document is what this book is all about.

We'll explore the changes in resume presentation that have arisen over the past decade. In the past, resumes were almost always printed on paper and mailed. Today, e-mail has become the chosen method for resume distribution in many industries and professions. In turn, many of the traditional methods for "typing" and presenting resumes have changed dramatically. This book will instruct you in the methods for preparing resumes for e-mail, scanning, and Web site posting, as well as the traditional printed resume.

Note that the traditional printed resume is still of vital concern to management and executive candidates, who should also devote a tremendous amount of their job-search time and effort to networking and lead development. Technology-based job search is, of course, important to all job seekers, but often has less applicability if you are a senior-level search candidate. You can read more about this topic in chapter 3.

By using *Expert Resumes for Managers and Executives* as your professional guide, you will succeed in developing a powerful and effective resume that opens doors, gets interviews, and helps you land your next great opportunity!

INTRODUCTION

According to the U.S. Department of Labor's Bureau of Labor Statistics, the U.S. economy should expect to see a **13.6 percent increase in the number of management and executive positions** between 2000 and 2010. What does that mean to you? By 2010, it is estimated that there will be more than 5 million management and executive positions with U.S. companies. And, just think, all you want is *one* of those 5 million!

All too often, as we talk with our management and executive job search clients, they comment on how difficult the employment market is. They say that opportunities just don't exist. They've looked everywhere and can't find anything. But they're wrong. Consider these statistics from the U.S. Department of Labor:

- Total employment is projected to increase 15 percent between 2000 and 2010.

- Professional occupations are projected to increase the fastest with the addition of 7 million new jobs.

- Service-producing industries will continue to be the dominant employment generator, adding more than 20 million jobs by 2010. The most growth is projected in health services, business services, social services, engineering, management, and related services.

- Goods-producing industries will also experience gains in employment, although not as significant as those in the service sector.

- By a statistically significant margin, technology will be the number-one growth industry over the next 10 years and, as you would expect, technology-related positions will offer the most opportunities.

Where Are the Jobs?

The preceding facts and statistics clearly demonstrate that there are opportunities for managers and executives across a diverse spectrum of industries. Consider just this brief listing of opportunities:

- Sales, marketing, retail, and related industries/professions

- Associations, not-for-profits, social-service organizations, and government organizations

- Military, legal, emergency-services, security, and law-enforcement professions

- Human resources, organizational development, teaching, training, education, and related industries/professions

- Real estate and construction professions

- Health care and allied industries/professions

- Scientific, technology, engineering, and related industries/professions

- Accounting, corporate finance, banking, investment, and related industries/professions

- Food and beverage, hotel, travel and tourism, and related industries/professions

- Manufacturing and general business and industry

The U.S. has given birth to some of the largest and most successful companies in the world and, despite the unprecedented collapse of some major corporations in 2002, will continue to do so. The long-term prospects are excellent—for the economy, for individual companies, and for your own career.

Today's jobs are everywhere—from multinational manufacturing conglomerates to the small retail sales companies in your neighborhood; from high-tech electronics firms to 100-year-old farming operations in rural communities; from banks and financial institutions to hospitals and health-care facilities in every city and town. The jobs are everywhere.

Finding a Job in the 21st Century

An action plan will keep you moving steadily toward your goal of finding a new position. We've outlined the major steps in the job-finding process in the following sections. Use these steps to create—and follow—your own detailed action plan.

STEP 1: WRITE A POWERFUL RESUME

All job seekers in the 21st century—particularly management and executive candidates—have a unique challenge. As the workforce has grown and companies have undergone massive changes, employment has become increasingly competitive. In turn, job seekers must know how to position themselves above the crowd of other candidates applying for similar opportunities. The best way to achieve that is with a powerful resume that clearly communicates your accomplishments and the value you bring to a prospective employer. That is what this book will teach you. You must always remember:

> Your resume is a marketing tool written to sell YOU!

If you're a CEO, COO, or CFO, *sell* the fact that you've increased revenues, reduced operating costs, and improved profit margins. If you're a human resources manager, *highlight* the percentage of reduction in staffing costs that you've delivered. If you're a manufacturing manager, *focus* on your increases in product performance and reliability. If you're a controller, *sell* the fact that you've reduced operating costs by a certain percentage while contributing a specific number of dollars to bottom-line profits.

When writing your resume, your challenge is to create a picture of knowledge, action, and results. In essence, you're stating "This is who I am, this is what I know, this is how I've used it, and this is how well I've performed." Success sells, so be sure to highlight yours. If you don't, no one else will.

STEP 2: BECOME A SAVVY JOB SEEKER

Just as important, you must be an educated job seeker. This means that you must know what you want in your career, where the hiring action is, what qualifications and credentials you might need to attain your desired career goals, and how best to market your qualifications. It is no longer enough to be a successful senior executive, technology manager, administrative director, or management consultant. Now, you must be a strategic marketer, able to package and promote your experience to take advantage of this wave of employment opportunity.

There's no doubt that the employment market has changed dramatically from only a few years ago. According to the U.S. Department of Labor (2000), you should expect to hold between 10 and 20 different jobs during your career. No longer is stability the status quo. Today, the norm is movement, onward and upward, in a fast-paced and intense employment market. And to stay on top of all the changes and opportunities, you must proactively control and manage your career.

STEP 3: LAUNCH A SUCCESSFUL SEARCH CAMPAIGN

The single most important thing to remember is that **job search is marketing!** You have a product to sell—yourself—and the best way to sell it is to use all appropriate *marketing channels* just as you would for any other product.

Suppose you wanted to sell televisions. What would you do? You'd market your products using newspaper, magazine, and radio advertisements. You might develop a company Web site to build your e-business, and perhaps you'd hire a field sales representative to market to major retail chains. Each of these is a different *marketing channel* through which you're attempting to reach your audience.

The same is true for job search. You must use every marketing channel that's right for you. Unfortunately, there is no single job search marketing formula. What's right for you depends on your specific career objectives—position, industry preferences, geographic restrictions, compensation, and more.

The following is a recommended Job Search Marketing Plan for managers and executives. These items are rank ordered, from most effective to least effective, and should serve as the foundation on which you build your own search campaign.

1. **Referrals.** There is nothing better than a personal referral to a company, either in general or for a specific position. Referrals can open doors that, in most instances, would never be accessible any other way. If you know anyone who could possibly refer you to a specific organization, contact that person immediately and ask for his or her assistance.

2. **Networking.** Networking is the backbone of every successful job search and is even more important for the management candidate than for other job seekers.

Although you might consider it an arduous task, it is essential that you network effectively with your professional colleagues and associates, past employers, past co-workers, suppliers, neighbors, friends, and others who might know of opportunities that are right for you. Another good strategy is to attend meetings of trade or professional associations in your area to make new contacts and expand your network. And particularly in today's nomadic job market—where you're likely to change jobs every few years—the best strategy is to keep your network "alive" even when you're *not* searching for a new position.

3. **Responses to newspaper, magazine, and periodical advertisements (in print).** So much of job search has transitioned to the Internet and e-mail that people now often overlook a great hiring resource—the help-wanted ads. Do not forget about this "tried and true" marketing strategy. If they've got the job and you have the qualifications, it's a perfect fit. We've seen it work hundreds of times.

4. **Responses to online job postings.** One of the greatest advantages of the technology revolution is an employer's ability to post job announcements and a job seeker's ability to respond immediately via e-mail. It's a wonder! In most (but not all) instances, these are bona fide opportunities, and it's well worth your while to spend time searching for and responding to appropriate postings. However, don't make the mistake of devoting *too* much time to searching the Internet. It can consume a huge amount of your time that you should spend on other job search efforts that will yield even better results.

   Generally speaking, the higher the level of position you are seeking, the less value the Internet and electronic job search will be to you. Most very senior-level management and executive positions are filled through networking, referrals, and other person-to-person contact, as you probably well know.

   Refer to the appendix for a listing of the largest and most widely used online job posting sites. In addition, you'll find Web sites with information on interviewing and salary negotiation, along with some of our favorite sites for researching information on companies (a must-do before any interview!).

5. **Targeted e-mail campaigns (resumes and cover letters) to recruiters.** Recruiters have jobs and you want one. It's pretty straightforward. The only catch is to find the "right" recruiters who have the "right" jobs. Therefore, you must devote the time and effort to preparing the "right" list of recruiters. There are many resources on the Internet where you can access information about recruiters (for a fee) and sort that information by industry and position specialization. This enables you to identify just the "right" recruiters who would be interested in a management candidate with your qualifications. What's more, because these campaigns are transmitted electronically, they are easy and inexpensive to produce.

   When working with recruiters, it's important to realize that they *do not* work for you! Their clients are the hiring companies that pay their fees. They are not in business to "find a job" for you, but rather to fill a specific position with a qualified candidate, either you or someone else. To maximize your chances of finding a position through a recruiter or agency, don't rely on just one or two, but distribute your resume to many that meet your specific criteria.

6. **Targeted e-mail and print campaigns to employers.** Just as with campaigns to recruiters (see item 5 previously), you must be extremely careful to select just the right employers that would be interested in a management candidate with your qualifications. The closer you stick to "where you belong" in relation to your specific experience, the better your response rate will be. If you are targeting technology companies, transmit your letters and resumes via e-mail. For companies in all other industries, we believe that print campaigns (paper and envelopes mailed the old-fashioned way) are a more appropriate and effective presentation for all management and executive candidates.

7. **In-person "cold calls" to companies and recruiters.** We consider this the least effective and most time-consuming marketing strategy for management positions. It is extremely difficult to just walk in the door and get in front of the right person, or any person who can take hiring action. You'll be much better off focusing your time and energy on other, more productive channels (for example, networking, referrals, and advertisements).

8. **Online resume postings.** The 'Net is swarming with reasonably priced (if not free) Web sites where you can post your resume. It's quick, easy, and the only *passive* thing you can do in your search. All of the other marketing channels require action on your part. With online resume postings, once you've posted, you're done. You then just wait (and hope!) for some response.

What About Opportunities in Management Consulting?

Are you familiar with the term "free agent"? It's the latest buzzword for an independent contractor or consultant who moves from project to project and company to company as opportunities exist. If you are a manager or executive with a particular expertise (for example, start-up ventures, turnarounds, IPOs, new product launches, performance improvement...the list goes on and on), "free agent" status may be an avenue you might want to consider.

According to an article in *Quality Progress* magazine (November 2000), 10 years ago less than 10 percent of the U.S. workforce was employed as free agents. Currently, that number is greater than 20 percent and is expected to increase to 40 percent over the next 10 years. The demand for free agents is vast, and the market offers excellent career opportunities.

The reason for this growth is directly related to the manner in which companies are now hiring—or not hiring—their workforces. The opportunity now exists for companies to hire on a "per project" basis and avoid the costs associated with full-time permanent employees, managers, and executives. Companies hire the staff they need just when they need them. When they no longer need them, they're gone.

There are a number of Web sites where you can register as a consultant and review existing consulting opportunities. Some of our favorites are the following:

www.6figurejobs.com

www.ceweekly.com

www.chiefmonster.com

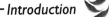

www.dice.com

www.interimexecmgmt.com

www.monster.com

www.presidentsnet.com

www.spherion.com (formerly imcor.com)

www.top-consultant.com

www.vault.com

The newest revolution in online job search has risen in response to this demand: job auction sites where employers bid on prospective employees. Individuals post their resumes and qualifications for review by prospective employers. The employers then competitively bid to hire or contract with each candidate. One of the largest and most well established job-auction Web sites is www.freeagent.com.

Conclusion

Management and executive career opportunities are on the rise, and opportunities are everywhere. It might take a bit more time than in years past to find the "right" positions, but the positions are there. What's more, it has never been easier to learn about and apply for jobs. Arm yourself with a powerful resume and cover letter, identify your most appropriate marketing channels, and start your search today. You're destined to reach the next rung on your career ladder.

PART I

Resume Writing, Strategy, and Formats

CHAPTER 1

Resume Writing Strategies for Managers and Executives

If you're reading this book, chances are you've decided to make a career move. It might be because of any of the following reasons:

- You're ready to leave your current position and move up the ladder to a higher-paying and more responsible management or executive-level position.

- The industry in which you've been working has been extremely hard-hit by economic decline, so you've decided to pursue high-level opportunities in other industries where the prospects for growth and stability are much stronger.

- You've decided on a career change and will be looking at opportunities both within and outside your current industry.

- You're unhappy with your current employer or senior management team and have decided to pursue opportunities elsewhere.

- You've been laid off, downsized, or otherwise left your position and you must find a new one.

- You've completed a contract assignment and are looking for a new "free agent" job or perhaps a permanent position.

- You've decided to resign your current position to pursue an executive-level entrepreneurial opportunity.

- You're relocating to a new area and need to find a new management opportunity.

- You're returning to the workforce after several years of unemployment or retirement and are ready for new senior-management opportunities.

- You've just earned your graduate degree and are ready to take a step upward in your career.

- You're simply ready for a change.

There might even be other reasons for your job search besides these. However, no matter the reason, a powerful resume is an essential component of your search campaign. In fact, it is virtually impossible to conduct a search without a resume. It is your calling card that briefly, yet powerfully, communicates the skills, qualifications, experience, and value you bring to a prospective employer. It is the document that will open doors and generate interviews. It is the first thing people will learn about you when you forward it in response to an advertisement, and it is the last thing they'll remember when they're reviewing your qualifications after an interview.

Your resume is a sales document and you are the product! You must identify the *features (what you know* and *what you can do)* and *benefits (how you can help an employer)* of that product and then communicate them in a concise and hard-hitting written presentation. Remind yourself over and over, as you work your way through the resume process, that you are writing marketing literature designed to sell a new product—YOU—into a new management or executive-level position.

Your resume can have tremendous power and a phenomenal impact on your job search. So don't take it lightly. Rather, devote the time, energy, and resources that are essential to developing a resume that is well-written, visually attractive, and effective in communicating *who* you are and *how* you want to be perceived.

Resume Strategies

Following are the nine core strategies for writing effective and successful resumes.

RESUME STRATEGY #1: Who Are You and How Do You Want to Be Perceived?

Now that you've decided to look for a new position, the very first step is to identify your current career interests, goals, and objectives. *This task is critical* because it is the underlying foundation for *what* you include in your resume, *how* you include it, and *where* you include it. You cannot write an effective resume without knowing, at least to some degree, what type or types of positions you will be seeking. This requires more than the simple response of "I'm looking for an executive position." You must be more specific in terms of your objectives in order to create a document that powerfully positions you for such opportunities.

There are two concepts to consider here:

- **Who you are.** This relates to what you have done professionally and/or academically. Are you a CEO, COO, CIO, CKO, or CFO? Are you a director of manufacturing, a director of purchasing, or a director of training and development? Are you the general manager of a large sales organization or the managing director of a multi-site customer-service organization? Are you a business manager, program manager, or technology manager? Have you just returned to school to complete your MBA or another advanced degree? Who are you?

- **How you want to be perceived.** This relates to your current career objectives. If you're a financial manager looking for a position as a CEO, don't focus solely on your financial skills. Put an equal emphasis on your success in general management, strategic planning, organizational leadership, joint ventures, team building, marketing, and business development. If you're a production manager seeking a promotion to the next tier of management, highlight your accomplishments in reducing operating costs, improving productivity, streamlining operations, eliminating product defects, and contributing profits to the bottom line.

The strategy, then, is to connect these two concepts by using the *Who you are* information that ties directly to the *How you want to be perceived* message to determine what information to include in your resume. By following this strategy, you're painting a picture that allows a prospective employer to see you as you want to be seen—as an individual with the qualifications for the type of position you are pursuing.

> **WARNING:** If you prepare a resume without first clearly identifying what your objectives are and how you want to be perceived, your resume will have no focus and no direction. Without the underlying knowledge of "This is what I want to be," you do not know what to highlight in your resume. In turn, the document becomes a historical overview of your career and not the sales document it is designed to be.

RESUME STRATEGY #2: *Sell It to Me...Don't Tell It to Me*

We've already established the fact that resume writing is sales. You are the product, and you must create a document that powerfully communicates the value of that product. One particularly effective strategy for accomplishing this is the "Sell It to Me...Don't Tell It to Me" strategy that impacts virtually every word you write on your resume.

If you "tell it," you are simply stating facts. If you "sell it," you promote it, advertise it, and draw attention to it. Look at the difference in impact between these examples:

> *Tell It Strategy:* Supervised customer service operations for two large sales locations.

> *Sell It Strategy:* Full strategic, operating, and P&L responsibility for the daily management of a 2,000-employee, 2-site customer-service operation supporting over $25 million in annual sales contracts for the largest automotive brake manufacturer in the world. Closed FY02 at $250,000 under budget with a 98% customer-satisfaction rating.

> *Tell It Strategy:* Managed a large-scale reorganization of one of Kodak's manufacturing facilities.

> *Sell It Strategy:* Spearheaded plant-wide reorganization of Kodak's flagship manufacturing facility, impacting 1,000 employees and over $450

million in product throughput each year. Slashed operating costs 22%, reduced waste 18%, introduced lean manufacturing techniques, and added $14+ million to bottom-line profits.

Tell It Strategy: Supervised development of next-generation voice-recognition software for IBM.

Sell It Strategy: Led 8-person technology team in design, development, prototype development, and full-scale market launch of IBM's next-generation voice-recognition software (projected to deliver $20 million in first-year sales).

What's the difference between "telling it" and "selling it"? In a nutshell...

Telling It	Selling It
Describes features.	Describes benefits.
Tells what and how.	Sells why the "what" and "how" are important.
Details activities.	Includes results.
Focuses on what you did.	Details how what you did benefited your employer, department, team members, customers, and so on.

RESUME STRATEGY #3: Use Key Words

No matter what you read or who you talk to about job search, the concept of key words is sure to come up. Key words (or, as they were previously known, buzz-words) are words and phrases specific to a particular industry or profession. For example, key words for management can include *strategic planning, organizational design, organizational leadership, team building, revenue growth, profit improvement, cost reduction, P&L management, performance optimization, productivity and efficiency improvement, business planning, operating management,* and many, many more.

When you use these words and phrases—in your resume, in your cover letter, or during an interview—you are communicating a very specific message. For example, when you include the words "marketing management" in your resume, your reader will most likely assume that you have experience in strategic market planning, market identification, market positioning, new product launch, new business development, competitor analysis, multimedia marketing, promotions, and more. As you can see, people will make inferences about your skills based on the use of just one or two individual words.

Here are a few other examples:

- When you use the words **corporate financial management,** people will assume you have experience with budgeting, tax, treasury, cash management, banking, investor reporting, financial analysis, financial reporting, and more.

- When you mention **educational services management,** readers and listeners will infer that you have experience in curriculum planning and development, instructional materials design, technology-based learning, teacher selection and training, school board relations, and more.

- By referencing **technology leadership** in your resume, you convey that you most likely have experience in identifying technology needs, developing new technologies, selecting and installing existing technologies, training technical personnel, managing technology projects and operations, and more.

- When you include **human resources leadership** as one of your areas of expertise, most people will assume you are experienced in recruitment, hiring, training and development, benefits, compensation, employee relations, employee supervision, performance evaluation, and more.

Key words are also an integral component of the resume-scanning process, whereby employers and recruiters electronically search resumes for specific terms to find candidates with the skills, qualifications, and credentials for their particular hiring needs. In organizations where it has been implemented, electronic scanning has replaced the more traditional method of an actual person reading your resume (at least initially). Therefore, to some degree, the *only* thing that matters in this instance is that you have included the "right" key words to match the company's or the recruiter's needs. Without them, you will most certainly be passed over.

Although not as prevalent in the management and executive tiers of hiring, key-word scanning is increasing in popularity because of its ease and efficiency. What's more, for those of you in technology-related industries, resume scanning and other electronic hiring systems are often the preferred method for application. Just like any other job seekers, managers and executives must stay on top of the latest trends in technology-based hiring and employment as it relates to them.

Of course, in virtually every instance your resume will be read at some point by human eyes, so it's not enough just to throw together a list of key words and leave it at that. In fact, it's not even necessary to include a separate "key-word summary" on your resume. A better strategy is to incorporate key words naturally into the text within the appropriate sections of your resume.

Keep in mind, too, that key words are arbitrary; there is no defined set of key words for a CEO, sales director, telecommunications manager, hotel manager, or vice president of engineering. Employers searching to fill these positions develop a list of terms that reflect the specifics they desire in a qualified candidate. These might be a combination of professional qualifications, skills, education, length of experience, and other easily defined criteria along with "soft skills," such as leadership, problem-solving, and communication.

NOTE: Because of the complex and arbitrary nature of key-word selection, we cannot overemphasize how vital it is to be certain that *all* of the key words that represent your experience and knowledge are included in your resume!

How can you be sure that you are including all the key words and the right key words? Just by describing your work experience, achievements, educational credentials, technical qualifications, and the like, you will naturally include most of the terms that are important in your field. To cross-check what you've written, review online or print job postings for positions that are of interest to you. Look at the precise terms used in the ads and be sure you have included them in your resume (if they are an accurate reflection of your skills and qualifications).

Another great benefit of today's technology revolution is our ability to find instant information, even information as specific as key words for managers and executives. Refer to the appendix for a listing of Web sites that list key words, complete with descriptions. These are outstanding resources.

RESUME STRATEGY #4: Use the "Big" and Save the "Little"

When deciding what you want to include in your resume, try to focus on the "big" things—revenue and profit growth, new initiatives and ventures, special projects, cost savings, productivity and efficiency improvements, new products, technology implementations, sales successes, new market launches, and more. Give a good broad-based picture of what you were responsible for and how well you did it. Here's an example:

> Senior Finance and Operating Executive with full management responsibility for all financial affairs, daily business operations, corporate administration, and all HR/employee-benefit programs. Concurrent responsibility for identifying and negotiating acquisitions to further accelerate growth and global expansion. Recruit, train, and lead a staff of 120 through 12 management reports.
>
> - Delivered strong and sustainable financial gains:
>
>   300% increase in revenues and 400% increase in bottom-line profits.
>
> $160,000 operating-cost reduction in staffing and employee costs.
>
> $1 million collected in outstanding receivables.
>
> $95,000 savings in vendor and lease costs.

Then, save the "little" stuff—the details—for the interview. With this strategy, you will accomplish two things: You'll keep your resume readable and of a reasonable length (while still selling your achievements), and you'll have new and interesting information to share during the interview, rather than merely repeating what is already on your resume. Using the preceding example, when discussing this experience during an interview you could elaborate on your specific achievements—

namely, how you increased revenues and profits so dramatically, how you were able to reduce personnel costs while still managing all operations, what you did to collect the $1 million outstanding debt, and more.

RESUME STRATEGY #5: Make Your Resume "Interviewable"

One of your greatest challenges is to make your resume a useful interview tool. After it's been determined that you meet the primary qualifications for a position (you've passed the key-word scanning test or initial review) and you are contacted for a telephone or in-person interview, your resume becomes all-important in leading and prompting your interviewer during your conversation.

Your job, then, is to make sure the resume leads the reader where you want to go and presents just the right organization, content, and appearance to stimulate a productive discussion. To improve the "interviewability" of your resume, consider these tactics:

- Make good use of Resume Strategy #4 (Use the "Big" and Save the "Little") to invite further discussion about your experiences.

- Be sure your greatest "selling points" are featured prominently, not buried within the resume.

- Conversely, don't devote lots of space and attention to areas of your background that are irrelevant or about which you feel less than positive; you'll only invite questions about things you really don't want to discuss.

- Make sure your resume is highly readable—this means plenty of white space, an adequate font size, and a logical flow from start to finish.

RESUME STRATEGY #6: Eliminate Confusion with Structure and Context

Keep in mind that your resume will be read *very quickly* by hiring authorities! You might agonize over every word and spend hours working on content and design, but the average reader will skim quickly through your masterpiece and expect to pick up important facts in just a few seconds. Try to make it as easy as possible for readers to grasp the essential facts:

- Be consistent; for example, put job titles, company names, and dates in the same place for each position.

- Make information easy to find by clearly defining different sections of your resume with large, highly visible headings.

- Define the context in which you worked (for example, the organization, your department, the specific challenges you faced) before you start describing your activities and accomplishments.

RESUME STRATEGY #7: Use Function to Demonstrate Achievement

When you write a resume that focuses only on your job functions, it can be dry and uninteresting and will say very little about your unique activities and contributions. Consider the following example:

> Responsible for all operations at the Marriott Hotel in downtown
> Washington, D.C.

Now, consider using that same function to demonstrate achievement and see what happens to the tone and energy of the sentence. It comes alive and clearly communicates that you deliver results.

> Profitably manage a 235-room luxury Marriott property that generates
> over $150 million in annual revenues. Revitalized property from loss posi-
> tion to double-digit profitability within two years through complete
> redesign of all sales, catering, front desk, and security operations.
> Currently ranked #6 for customer service out of 560 Marriott properties
> nationwide.

Try to translate your functions into achievements and you'll create a more powerful resume presentation.

RESUME STRATEGY #8: Remain in the Realm of Reality

We've already established that resume writing is sales. And, as any good salesperson does, one feels somewhat inclined to stretch the truth, just a bit. However, be forewarned that you must stay within the realm of reality. Do not push your skills and qualifications outside the bounds of what is truthful. You never want to be in a position where you have to defend something that you've written on your resume. If that's the case, you'll lose the opportunity before you ever get started.

RESUME STRATEGY #9: Be Confident

You are unique. There is only one individual with the specific combination of employment experience, qualifications, achievements, education, and technical skills that you have. In turn, this positions you as a unique commodity within the competitive job-search market. To succeed, you must prepare a resume that is written to sell *you,* and highlight *your* qualifications and *your* success. If you can accomplish this, you will have won the job search game by generating interest, interviews, and offers.

There Are No Resume-Writing Rules

One of the greatest challenges in resume writing is that there are no rules to the game. There are certain expectations about information that you will include: principally, your employment history and your educational qualifications. Beyond that, what you include is entirely up to you and what you have done in your career. What's more, you have tremendous flexibility in determining how to include the information you have selected. In chapter 2, you'll find a complete listing of each possible category you might include in your resume, the type of information that should be included in each, preferred formats for presentation, and sample text you can edit and use.

Although there are no rules, there are a few standards to live by as you write your resume. The following sections discuss these standards in detail.

CONTENT STANDARDS

Content is, of course, the text that goes into your resume. Content standards cover the writing style you should use, items you should be sure to include, items you should avoid including, and the order and format in which you should list your qualifications.

Writing Style

Always write in the first person, dropping the word "I" from the front of each sentence. This style gives your resume a more assertive and more professional tone than the passive third-person voice. Here are some examples.

First Person:

> Manage 12-person team responsible for the global market launch of new OTC pharmaceuticals for Bayer's Consumer Division.

Third Person:

> Mr. Glenwood manages a 12-person team responsible for the global market launch of new OTC pharmaceuticals for Bayer's Consumer Division.

By using the first-person voice, you are assuming "ownership" of that statement. You did such-and-such. When you use the third-person voice, "someone else" did it.

Phrases to Stay Away From

Try *not* to use phrases such as "responsible for" or "duties included." These words create a passive tone and style. Instead, use active verbs to describe what you did.

Compare these two ways of conveying the same information:

> Duties included scheduling, job assignment, and management of over 200 production workers, engineers, and maintenance support staff for a $52 million poultry-production facility.

OR

> Directed scheduling, job assignment, and daily operations for over 200 production workers, engineers, and maintenance support staff at a $52 million poultry-production facility.

Resume Style

The traditional **chronological** resume lists work experience in reverse-chronological order (starting with your current or most recent position). The **functional** style de-emphasizes the "where" and "when" of your career and instead groups similar experience, talents, and qualifications regardless of when they occurred.

Today, however, most resumes follow neither a strictly chronological nor strictly functional style; rather, they are an effective mixture of the two styles, usually known as a "combination" or "hybrid" style.

Like the chronological style, the hybrid includes specifics about where you worked, when you worked there, and what your job titles were. Like a functional resume, a hybrid emphasizes your most relevant qualifications—perhaps within chronological job descriptions, in an expanded summary section, in several "career highlights" bullet points at the top of your resume, or in project summaries. Most of the examples in this book are hybrids and show a wide diversity of organizational structures that you can use as inspiration for designing your own resume.

Resume Formats

Resumes, principally career summaries and job descriptions, are most often written in a paragraph format, a bulleted format, or a combination of both. Following are three job descriptions, all very similar in content, yet presented in each of the three different writing formats. The advantages and disadvantages of each format are also addressed.

Paragraph Format

Division Manager	2000 to 2002

National Medical Research Center, Lewiston, Maine

Created and led strategic planning, finance, accounting, administration, contracting, and partnerships for the start-up of a new entrepreneurial division launching new ventures in emerging health-care markets. Developed business plans and directed operating budgets for eight distinct profit centers worldwide.

Identified opportunity; then structured, negotiated, and closed joint venture with Central Health, the largest non-profit hospital system in the region. Created Limited Liability Corporation (LLC) to manage and market community-based health-care programs. Appointed to Board of Directors.

Created a portfolio of financial models, indices, and analyses to monitor/evaluate performance of all new ventures, new products, and new service-delivery programs.

Collaborated with business partners to create a new respiratory-care company. Won 21 contracts with projections for an additional 12 by end of year three ($2+ million in revenue).

Established program to facilitate new business-development opportunities in research, case management, and clinical services. Delivered $4 million in first-year revenue.

Negotiated joint venture with medical technology company that included a valuable insider equity position prior to IPO.

Advantages

Requires the least amount of space on the page. Brief, succinct, and to the point.

Disadvantages

Achievements get lost in the text of the second paragraph. They are not visually distinctive, nor do they stand alone to draw attention to them.

Bulleted Format

Division Manager   2000 to 2002

National Medical Research Center, Lewiston, Maine

- Created and led strategic planning, finance, accounting, administration, contracting, and partnerships for the start-up of a new entrepreneurial division launching new ventures in emerging health-care markets. Developed business plans and directed operating budgets for eight distinct profit centers worldwide.

- Identified opportunity; then structured, negotiated, and closed joint venture with Central Health, the largest non-profit hospital system in the region. Created Limited Liability Corporation (LLC) to manage and market community-based health-care programs. Appointed to Board of Directors.

- Created a portfolio of financial models, indices, and analyses to monitor/evaluate performance of all new ventures, new products, and new service-delivery programs.

- Collaborated with business partners to create a new respiratory-care company. Won 21 contracts with projections for an additional 12 by end of year three ($2+ million in revenue).

- Established program to facilitate new business-development opportunities in research, case management, and clinical services. Delivered $4 million in first-year revenue.

- Negotiated joint venture with medical-technology company that included a valuable insider equity position prior to IPO.

Advantages

Quick and easy to peruse.

Disadvantages

Responsibilities and achievements are lumped together with everything of equal value. In turn, the achievements get lost farther down the list and are not immediately recognizable.

Combination Format

Division Manager   2000 to 2002

National Medical Research Center, Lewiston, Maine

Created and led strategic planning, finance, accounting, administration, contracting, and partnerships for the start-up of a new entrepreneurial division launching new ventures in emerging health-care markets. Developed business plans and directed operating budgets for eight distinct profit centers worldwide.

- Identified opportunity; then structured, negotiated, and closed joint venture with Central Health, the largest non-profit hospital system in the region. Created Limited Liability Corporation (LLC) to manage and market community-based health-care programs. Appointed to Board of Directors.

- Created a portfolio of financial models, indices, and analyses to monitor/evaluate performance of all new ventures, new products, and new service-delivery programs.

- Collaborated with business partners to create a new respiratory-care company. Won 21 contracts with projections for an additional 12 by end of year three ($2+ million in revenue).

- Established program to facilitate new business-development opportunities in research, case management, and clinical services. Delivered $4 million in first-year revenue.

- Negotiated joint venture with medical-technology company that included a valuable insider equity position prior to IPO.

Advantages

Our recommended format. Clearly presents overall responsibilities in the introductory paragraph and then accentuates each achievement as a separate bullet.

Disadvantages

If you don't have clearly identifiable accomplishments, this format is not effective. It also might shine a glaring light on the positions where your accomplishments were less notable.

E-Mail Address and URL

Be sure to include your e-mail address prominently at the top of your resume. As we all know, e-mail has become one of the most preferred methods of communication in job search.

We advise against using your employer's e-mail address on your resume. Not only does this present a negative impression to future employers, it will become useless once you make your next career move. And because your resume might exist in cyberspace long after you've completed your job search, you don't want to direct interested parties to an obsolete e-mail address. Instead, obtain a private e-mail address that will be yours permanently. A free e-mail address from a provider such as Yahoo!, Hotmail, or NetZero is perfectly acceptable to use on your resume and has the advantage of being accessible from any Internet-connected PC.

In addition to your e-mail address, if you have a URL (Web site) where you have posted your Web resume, be sure to also display that prominently at the top of your resume. For more information on Web resumes, see chapter 3.

PRESENTATION STANDARDS

Presentation refers to the way your resume looks. It has to do with the fonts you use, the paper you print it on, any graphics you might include, and how many pages your resume should be.

Typestyle

Use a typestyle (or font) that is clean, conservative, and easy to read. Stay away from anything that is too fancy, glitzy, curly, and the like. Here are a few recommended typestyles:

Tahoma	Times New Roman
Arial	Bookman
Krone	Book Antiqua
Soutane	Garamond
CG Omega	Century Schoolbook
Century Gothic	Lucida Sans
Gill Sans	Verdana

Although it is extremely popular, Times New Roman is our least preferred typestyle simply because it is overused. More than 90 percent of the resumes we see are typed in Times New Roman. Your goal is to create a competitive-distinctive document, and, to achieve that, we recommend an alternative typestyle.

Your choice of typestyle should be dictated by the content, format, and length of your resume. Some fonts look better than others at smaller or larger sizes; some have "bolder" boldface type; some require more white space to make them readable. After you write your resume, experiment with a few different typestyles to see which one best enhances your document.

Type Size

Readability is everything! If the type size is too small, your resume will be difficult to read and difficult to skim for essential information. Interestingly, a too-large type size, particularly for senior-level professionals, can also give a negative impression by conveying a juvenile or unprofessional image.

As a general rule, select type from 10 to 12 points in size. However, there's no hard-and-fast rule, and a lot depends on the typestyle you choose. Take a look at the following examples:

Very readable in 9-point Verdana

Won the 2002 "Manager of the Year" award at Chrysler's Indianapolis plant. Honored for innovative contributions to cost reduction, product development, and profit growth.

Difficult to read in too-small 9-point Gill Sans

Won the 2002 "Manager of the Year" award at Chrysler's Indianapolis plant. Honored for innovative contributions to cost reduction, product development, and profit growth.

Concise and readable in 12-point Times New Roman

Senior Training & Development Manager specializing in the design, development, and presentation of multimedia leadership training programs for all senior managers and executives.

A bit overwhelming in too-large 12-point Bookman Old Style

Senior Training & Development Manager specializing in the design, development, and presentation of multimedia leadership training programs for all senior managers and executives.

Type Enhancements

Bold, *italics,* <u>underlining</u>, and CAPITALIZATION are ideal for highlighting certain words, phrases, achievements, projects, numbers, and other information you want to draw special attention to. However, do not overuse these enhancements. If your resume becomes too cluttered, nothing stands out.

> **NOTE:** Resumes intended for electronic transmission and computer scanning have specific restrictions on typestyle, type size, and type enhancements. We discuss these details in chapter 3.

Page Length

Our recommendation to the "average" job seeker is to keep his or her resume to one or two pages. The same is true for many managers and executives. Keep it short and succinct, giving just enough to entice your readers' interest. However, for others, it can be difficult to include all the relevant information in just two pages. In situations like this, your management career might simply warrant a longer resume, and that's okay!

There have been hundreds of situations in which we've prepared management and executive resumes that were three or four pages long (although rarely do we allow it to go any longer). Let the amount of quality information you have to share be the determining factor in the length of your resume. Do not feel as though it MUST remain on two pages. What it MUST do is attract prospective employers.

There are also other instances when a resume might be longer than two pages. For example:

- You have an extensive list of technical qualifications that are relevant to the position for which you are applying. (You might consider including these on a separate page as an addendum to your resume.)

- You have extensive educational training and numerous credentials/certifications, all of which are important to include. (You might consider including these on a separate page as an addendum to your resume.)

- You have an extensive list of special projects, task forces, and committees to include that are important to your current career objectives. (You might consider including these on a separate page as an addendum to your resume.)

- You have an extensive list of professional honors, awards, and commendations. This list is tremendously valuable in validating your credibility and distinguishing you from the competition.

- You have an extensive list of media appearances and publications. Again, this list is extremely valuable in validating your credibility and distinguishing you from the competition. It must be included.

If you create a resume that's longer than two pages, make it more reader-friendly by carefully segmenting the information into separate sections. For instance, begin with your career summary and your work experience. This will most likely take one to two pages. Then follow with education, any professional or industry credentials, honors and awards, technology and equipment skills, publications, public speaking engagements, professional affiliations, civic affiliations, volunteer experience, foreign-language skills, and other relevant information you want to include. Put each into a separate category so that your resume is easy to peruse and your reader can quickly see the highlights. You'll read more about each of these sections of your resume in chapter 2.

Paper Color

Be conservative. White, ivory, and light gray are ideal. Other "flashier" colors are inappropriate for individuals in the management and executive tiers.

Graphics

For entry-level or mid-level management positions, an attractive, relevant graphic can really add impact to your resume. When you look through the sample resumes in chapters 4 through 12, you'll see a few excellent examples of the effective use of graphics to enhance the visual presentation of a resume. Just be sure not to get carried away; be tasteful and relatively conservative.

For those of you at the senior management or executive level, we do not recommend graphics on your resume. Clean, crisp, and conservative is our motto for this level of resume.

White Space

We'll say it again: readability is everything! If people have to struggle to read your resume, they simply won't make the effort. Therefore, be sure to leave plenty of white space. It really does make a difference.

ACCURACY AND PERFECTION

The very final step, and one of the most critical in resume writing, is the proof-reading stage. It is essential that your resume be well written, visually pleasing, and free of any errors, typographical mistakes, misspellings, and the like. We recommend that you carefully proofread your resume a minimum of three times, and then have two or three other people also proofread it. Consider your resume an example of the quality of work you will produce on a company's behalf. Is your work product going to have errors and inconsistencies? If your resume does, it communicates to a prospective employer that you are careless, and this is the "kiss of death" in job search.

Take the time to make sure that your resume is perfect in all the little details that do, in fact, make a big difference to those who read it.

CHAPTER 2

Writing Your Resume

For many managers and executives, resume writing is *not* at the top of the list of fun and exciting activities! How can it compare to negotiating a joint venture, solving a major production problem, reducing corporate debt, or launching a new product? In your perception, we're sure that it cannot.

However, resume writing can be an enjoyable and rewarding task. Once your resume is complete, you can look at it proudly, reminding yourself of all that you have achieved. It is a snapshot of your career and your success. When it's complete, we guarantee you'll look back with tremendous self-satisfaction as you launch and successfully manage your job search.

The very first step in finding a new position or advancing your career, resume writing can be the most daunting of all tasks in your job search. If writing is not one of your primary job functions, it might have been years since you actually sat down and wrote anything other than notes to yourself. Even for those of you who write on a regular basis, resume writing is unique. It has its own style and a number of peculiarities, as with any specialty document.

Therefore, to make the writing process easier, more finite, and more efficient, we've consolidated it into four discrete sections:

- **Career Summary.** Think of your Career Summary as the *corporate strategy* of your resume. It is the accumulation of everything that allows your organization to work—whether your organization is an entire company or just one individual department. It is the backbone of your corporate experience and the foundation of your resume.

- **Professional Experience.** The Professional Experience section is much like the *operations* that are the foundation of your organization. It is the specifics that support your achievement of the corporate strategy. Your professional experience demonstrates how you put all your capabilities to work.

- **Education and Certifications.** Think of this section as your organization's *credentials,* the third-party validation of your qualifications, knowledge, and expertise.

- **The "Extras"** (Publications, Public Speaking, Honors and Awards, Technology Qualifications, Training and Public Speaking, Professional Affiliations, Civic Affiliations, Foreign Languages, Personal Information, and so on). These make up the *product or service features* section of your resume, the "extra stuff" that helps distinguish you from others with similar qualifications.

Step-by-Step: Writing the Perfect Resume

In the preceding section, we outlined the four core resume sections. Now we'll detail the particulars of each section—what to include, where to place it, and how to present it.

CONTACT INFORMATION

Before we start, let's briefly address the very top section of your resume: your name and contact information.

Name

You'd think writing your name would be the easiest part of writing your resume! But there are several factors you should consider:

- Although most people choose to use their full, formal name at the top of a resume, it has become increasingly more acceptable to use the name by which you prefer to be called.

- Bear in mind that it's to your advantage to have readers feel comfortable calling you for an interview. Their comfort level might decrease if your name is gender-neutral, difficult to pronounce, or very unusual; they don't know who they're calling (a man or a woman) or how to ask for you. Here are a few ways you can make it easier for them:

> Lynn T. Cowles (Mr.)
>
> (Ms.) Michael Murray
>
> Tzirina (Irene) Kahn
>
> Ndege "Nick" Vernon

Address

You should always include your home address on your resume. If you use a post-office box for mail, include both your mailing address and your physical residence address.

Telephone Number(s)

Your home telephone number should be included. If you're at work during the day, when you can expect to receive most calls, consider including a work phone number (if it's a direct line and you can receive calls discreetly). Or you can include a mobile phone number (refer to it as "mobile" rather than "cellular," to keep up with current terminology) or a pager number (this is less desirable, however, because you must call back to speak to the person who called you). You can include a private home fax number (if it can be accessed automatically), but do not include your work fax number. NEVER include your employer's toll-free number. This communicates the message that you are using your employer's resources and budget to support your own personal job search campaign—not a wise idea!

E-mail Address

Without question, if you have a private e-mail address, include it on your resume. E-mail is now often the preferred method of communication in job search, particularly in the early stages of each contact. Do not use your employer's e-mail address, even if you access e-mail through your work computer. Instead, obtain a free, accessible-anywhere address from a provider such as Yahoo!, Hotmail, or NetZero.

As you look through the samples in chapters 4 through 12, you'll see how resume writers have arranged the many bits of contact information at the top of a resume. You can use these as models for presenting your own information. The point is to make it as easy as possible for employers to contact you.

Now, let's get into the nitty-gritty of the four core content sections of your resume.

CAREER SUMMARY

The Career Summary is the section at the top of your resume that summarizes and highlights your knowledge and expertise.

You might be thinking, "But shouldn't my resume start with an Objective?" Although many job seekers still use Objective statements, we believe that a Career Summary is a much more powerful introduction. The problem with Objectives is that they are either too specific (limiting you to an "engineering management position") or too vague (doesn't everyone want a challenging opportunity with a progressive organization offering the opportunity for growth and advancement?). In addition, they can be read as self-serving because they describe what *you* want instead of suggesting what you have to offer an employer.

In contrast, an effective Career Summary allows you to position yourself as you want to be perceived and immediately "paint a picture" of yourself in relation to your career goal. It is critical that this section focus on the specific skills, qualifications, and achievements of your career that are related to your current objectives. Your summary is *not* a historical overview of your career. Rather, it is a concise, well-written, and sharp presentation of information designed to *sell* you into your next position.

This section can have various titles, such as:

Career Summary	Manufacturing Industry Summary
Career Achievements	Professional Qualifications
Career Highlights	Professional Summary
Career Synopsis	Profile
Executive Profile	Summary
Expertise	Summary of Achievements
Highlights of Experience	Summary of Qualifications
Management Profile	

Or, as you will see in the first format example below (Headline Format), your summary does not have to have any title at all.

Here are five sample Career Summaries. Consider using one of these as the template for developing your Career Summary, or use them as the foundation to create your own presentation. You will also find some type of Career Summary in just about every resume included in this book.

Headline Format

MANUFACTURING MANAGER / PRODUCTION MANAGER

Production Planning / Logistics / Multi-Site Operations

MBA — Executive Management

MS — Manufacturing Systems & Technology

Paragraph Format

CAREER SUMMARY

INSURANCE INDUSTRY MANAGER with an 18-year professional career highlighted by rapid advancement and consistent achievement in market, premium, and profit growth. Outstanding qualifications in building and managing relationships with sales producers and field management teams. Deep expertise in underwriting and policy rating. PC literate with word-processing and spreadsheet applications, email, and the Internet.

Core Competencies Summary Format

SENIOR EXECUTIVE PROFILE

Start-Up, Turnaround & High-Growth Organizations

✓ Twenty-year management career with consistent and measurable achievements in:
- Revenue & Profit Growth
- Market & Customer Expansion
- Operating Cost Reductions
- Productivity & Efficiency Improvement

✓ Successful in overcoming market, technological, financial, and competitive challenges to drive growth, profitability, and performance improvement. Expertise includes:
- Strategic Planning & Leadership
- Marketing, Sales & New Business
- New Product & New Service Launch
- Training, Development & Team Building
- Finance, Budgeting & Cost Management
- Contracts, Outsourcing & Partnerships
- Technology Optimization
- Investor & Board Relations

✓ Guest Speaker, 2002 "Leadership Innovations" Conference

✓ Winner, 2000 McKinsey Award for Leadership Excellence

Bulleted List Format

PROFESSIONAL QUALIFICATIONS

▶ **Mergers, Acquisitions, Joint Ventures, Partnerships, & IPOs.** Extensive qualifications structuring, negotiating, and transacting multi-party alliances to launch new ventures, expand market penetration, leverage business and financial resources, and improve bottom-line profitability.

▶ **Strategic Planning & Business Development.** Led high-level strategic planning for start-ups, turnarounds, high-growth companies, and Fortune 1000 corporations. Equally strong experience in marketing, sales, and public relations to drive business development and expansion initiatives.

▶ **Accounting, Financial Reporting & Financial Planning.** Hands-on responsibility for managing broad-based accounting, billing, budgeting, collections, financial analysis, financial reporting, and corporate administrative affairs.

▶ **Credit, Lending & Financial Transactions.** Managed commercial financing, leasing, and credit transactions in the capital equipment, telecommunications, and computer industries. Extensive qualifications in financial review, risk assessment, and ROI/ROA/ROE performance analysis.

Category Format

PROFESSIONAL CAREER HIGHLIGHTS

Experience	12 years as a Maintenance Director & Manager for Dow Corning and its subsidiaries
Education	Graduate Certificate in Facilities Maintenance & Engineering—University of Washington BS—Operations Management—University of Oregon
Publications	"Improving Workforce Productivity Through Maintenance Systems Design & Optimization," *American Manufacturing Association*, 2001 "Redesigning Maintenance Processes To Enhance Productivity," *National Facilities Maintenance Association*, 1999
Awards	Employee of the Year, Dow Corning, 2001 Employee of the Year, Bell Laboratories, 1996

PROFESSIONAL EXPERIENCE

Your Professional Experience is the meat of your resume—the "operations," as we discussed before. It's what gives your resume substance, meaning, and depth. It is also the section that will take you the longest to write. If you've had the same position for 10 years, how can you consolidate all that you have done into one short section? If, on the opposite end of the spectrum, you have had your current position for only 11 months, how can you make it seem substantial and noteworthy? And, for all of you whose experience is in between, what do you include, how, where, and why?

These are not easy questions to answer. In fact, the most truthful response to each question is, "it depends." It depends on you, your experience, your achievements and successes, and your current career objectives.

Here are seven samples of Professional Experience sections. Review how each individual's unique background is organized and emphasized. Consider your own background when using one of these as the template or foundation for developing your Professional Experience section.

Achievement Format

Emphasizes each position, the overall scope of responsibility, and the resulting achievements.

PROFESSIONAL EXPERIENCE

Human Resources Manager (2000 to Present)
ARNOLD & SMITH DISTRIBUTION CO., INC., Moneta, VA

Recruited by principals and given complete responsibility for defining organizational culture, developing strategic HR plans, and positioning HR as a proactive partner to operations and business units nationwide. Scope of responsibility impacts 1,500 employees in 25 operating locations and 2 NYC-based administrative office complexes. Supervise a three-person management team and 22 other HR employees.

———Achievements———

- Created best-in-class HR organizations, systems, processes, and practices as Arnold & Smith has experienced dramatic growth and expansion over the past two years. Fully integrated 150 Prestige employees, 90 US General Life Insurance employees, and others as the company has accelerated growth through acquisition.

- Introduced a focused yet flexible corporate culture to facilitate seamless integration of acquired business units, product lines, and personnel.

- Led recruitment and selection for key positions throughout the organization, including the entire legal, finance, administrative, and accounting organizations.

- Designed and implemented benefit programs, a performance-based appraisal and incentive compensation system, a system of staffing models, and a complete HR infrastructure.

- Contributed $750,000 in salary cost reductions through redesign of internal staffing patterns and management tiers.

Challenge, Action, and Results (CAR) Format

Emphasizes the challenge of each position, the action you took, and the results you delivered.

■ Professional Experience ■

WIP Systems International, Bulverde, Texas   1996 to Present

VICE PRESIDENT OF OPERATIONS (2000 to Present)
PLANT MANAGER (1996 to 2000)

Challenge: Plan and direct the turnaround and return to profitability of $42 million technology systems manufacturer plagued with cost overrides, poor productivity, dissatisfied customers, and multimillion-dollar annual losses.

Actions: Rebuilt the entire management team, introduced advanced technologies and systems to expedite production flow, retrained all operators and supervisors, and implemented team-based work culture.

Results:
- Achieved/surpassed all turnaround objectives and returned the operation to profitability in first year. Delivered strong and sustainable gains:
  - **70%** improvement in operating efficiency.
  - **250%** reduction in cycle times.
  - **75%** improvement in product quality ratings.
  - **100%** on-time customer delivery.

- Replaced obsolete equipment with state-of-the-art systems, redesigned and upgraded facility, introduced stringent standards to achieve OSHA compliance, and established in-house day-care facility (with dramatic reduction in absenteeism).

- Restored credibility with one customer generating over $30 million a year in revenues to WIP. Resolved longstanding quality and delivery issues, implemented key account management strategy, and revitalized business relationship.

- Partnered with HP, IBM, and Dell to integrate their technologies into WIP's software applications. Received over $200,000 in technology resources at no charge to the company.

- Quoted in the National Manufacturing Association's annual publication as one of 1999's *"Leaders in Manufacturing."*

Functional Format

Emphasizes the functional areas of responsibility within the job and associated achievements.

PROFESSIONAL EXPERIENCE

Vice President   STAR FINANCIAL, INC., Dayton, Ohio   1999 to Present

Recruited by former advisor to help manage Star Financial, a large private-equity investment firm operating as an incubator for emerging, undercapitalized, rapidly growing, and turnaround businesses requiring hands-on management and leadership. Challenged to identify strategic investment opportunities, develop innovative business models, conduct due diligence, structure transactions, and negotiate private placements.

New Venture Start-Up — Personally founded and invested in AAA Distributors, Inc., a privately held business-to-consumer (B2C) direct-marketing company focused on continuity-based direct marketing utilizing the Internet, direct mail, telemarketing, and television advertising. Created a portfolio of 8 consumer-based direct-marketing products, orchestrated the entire go-to-market strategy, developed best-in-class financial infrastructure and all financial systems, and launched new venture in 1999.

Organizational & Financial Infrastructure — Created a unique business/finance model leveraging outsourcing to deliver operating expertise in product development, manufacturing, packaging, media placement, inbound/outbound telemarketing, fulfillment, and customer service. Operated AAA with only 14 employees and a team of 12 core business partners/vendors. Controlled costs at less than 12% of revenue.

Financial Growth Through Strategic Marketing — Rolled out national direct-marketing campaign utilizing media to drive Internet and inbound telemarketing traffic. Generated $4.3 million in sales in first 6 months and secured 70,000+ web-based/directed customers (majority were continuity-based).

Corporate Roll-Up — Structured and negotiated sale of AAA Distributors to a large international direct marketer to achieve economies of scale, improve operating efficiencies, and increase net profitability.

Career Track Format

Emphasizes fast-track promotion, overall scope of responsibility, and notable achievements.

RYNCON AMERICA, INC., Dallas, Texas — 1993 to Present

Vice President — Marketing (2001 to Present)
Vice President of Sales — New Products Division (1998 to 2001)
Sales Director (1996 to 1998)
National Accounts Manager (1994 to 1996)
Sales Associate (1993 to 1994)

Fast-track promotion through a series of increasingly responsible positions to current role as Vice President of Marketing Operations Worldwide. Credited with building a global marketing organization that led division to 6-fold revenue growth in just 4 years. Recruited and developed a talented team of sales and marketing professionals that now serve as Ryncon's core marketing and sales management team.

☑ Built division from $20 million in annual revenues in 1998 to $120+ million in 2002.

☑ Achieved #1 market position in North America and maintained positioning for three consecutive years.

☑ Surpassed all profit goals for 10 consecutive years, averaging 12%–15% annual profit growth.

☑ Conceived and implemented customer-focus strategy to drive long-term product development and service delivery. Currently maintain a 97+% customer-satisfaction rating.

☑ Outpaced competition as the first in the industry to enter the Northern Canadian, Puerto Rican, and Caribbean markets. Currently project new-market revenues of more than $20 million by end of year 2.

Project Highlights Format

Places emphasis on the specific projects, their scope of responsibility, and their associated achievements.

MOLTEN METAL TECHNOLOGY (*$650 million metal products design & manufacturing company*)

PROJECT MANAGER: 1993 to Present

Travel to Molten facilities nationwide to orchestrate a series of special projects and assignments. Delivered all projects on time and within budget for 10 consecutive years. Recent projects include:

- **Recycling Facility Development & Construction** ($12.8 million). Co-led fast-track design and construction team, bringing project from concept to completion in just 16 months. ***RESULT:*** *Built an environmentally safe and regulation-compliant facility at 12% under projected cost.*

- **Capital Improvement Project** ($6.2 million). Led $50+ million in capital improvements with individual project costs at $50,000 to $750,000. ***RESULT:*** *Upgraded facilities, production lines, technical competencies, product staging, and distribution areas for a better than 22% increase in productivity.*

- **SAP Implementation Project** ($1.8 million). Led 12-person technology and support team in a massive SAP implementation project impacting virtually the entire facility and workforce. ***RESULT:*** *Created a totally integrated technology environment linking inventory, production planning, quality, cost accounting, and other core manufacturing and support functions.*

- **OSHA Compliance Project** ($500,000). Led year-long project to identify non-compliance issues and initiate appropriate remedial activity. ***RESULT:*** *Passed 2000 OSHA inspection with zero findings.*

- **Annual Shutdown & Maintenance Project** ($100,000). Planned, scheduled, and directed annual plant shutdown and maintenance programs for three facilities involving as many as 100 craftsmen. ***RESULT:*** *Restored all facilities to full operation within stringent time constraints.*

Skills-Based Format

Puts initial focus on specific skills rather than when and where they were used. Helpful in bringing less-current skill sets to the forefront and avoiding emphasis on employment gaps.

FOUNDER / GENERAL MANAGER — Law Offices of Earl W. Hadley   1995 to Present

Founded specialized legal practice providing corporate advisory services to CEOs, COOs, and other senior executives across a broad range of industries and on a broad range of business issues. Built new venture from start-up to 3 locations and 12 employees. Achieved and maintained profitability for 6 consecutive years. Excellent reputation for ethical performance and integrity.

Serve in the capacity of a **Senior Operating Executive/General Counsel** to client companies, providing hands-on leadership in:

– Strategic Planning & Vision	– Operations Management	– Human Resources
– Policies & Procedures	– Cost Control & Avoidance	– Technology
– Growth & Expansion	– Process Design & Analysis	– Capital Assets
– Market Analysis & Positioning	– Banking & Corporate Finance	– Executive Compensation
– Acquisitions & Valuations	– Asset/Stock Purchase Agreements	– A/R & Collections
– Letter of Credit & Intent	– Licensing & Leasing Agreements	– Bankruptcy/Turnaround

Clients range from start-up ventures to $200 million corporations engaged in software development, high-tech manufacturing, industrial manufacturing, consumer products, heavy equipment, transportation, automotive and marine dealerships, services, and professional trades.

Firm responsibilities include: As **General Manager,** direct all daily and long-term business planning and management functions, staffing, technology systems, and all business process/infrastructure affairs. As **Marketing & Business Development Executive,** lead client development, networking, marketing, and client relationship management. As **Principal Attorney,** manage all legal affairs and client representation.

Experience Format

Briefly emphasizes specific highlights of each position. Best used in conjunction with a detailed Career Summary.

EXPERIENCE SUMMARY

Office Manager, WEST-QUEST TECHNOLOGIES, Lewisburg, ID — 2000 to Present

- ❑ Implemented cost savings that slashed $150,000 from annual operating costs.
- ❑ Selected and directed implementation of new PC network with Ethernet technology.
- ❑ Recruited, trained, and supervised 12 administrative and office-support personnel in two operating locations.

Office Manager, Century Technologies, Ames, IA — 1997 to 2000

- ❑ Independently managed all office, administrative, and clerical functions for a small technology start-up venture in the "train-the-trainer" market.
- ❑ Designed all internal recordkeeping, reporting, accounting, project-management, and client-management systems and processes.
- ❑ Selected office equipment and technology, negotiated leases, and coordinated installation.
- ❑ Represented owners at local business and Chamber of Commerce meetings/events.

Assistant Manager, Greenwalt Architectural Systems, Ames, IA — 1994 to 1997

- ❑ Worked with owners and architects to facilitate project completion by coordinating deadlines, deliverables, and client communications.
- ❑ Implemented PC-based project-tracking and accounting systems.
- ❑ Coordinated all purchasing and inventory-management functions for office supplies and design materials.

EDUCATION, CREDENTIALS, AND CERTIFICATIONS

Your Education section should include college, certifications, credentials, licenses, registrations, and continuing education. If any are particularly notable, be sure to highlight them prominently in your Education section or bring them to the top in your Career Summary (as demonstrated by the Headline format in the previous section on writing career summaries).

Here are five sample Education sections that illustrate a variety of ways to organize and format this information.

Executive Education Format

EDUCATION	
➤ Executive Development Program	STANFORD UNIVERSITY
➤ Executive Development Program	UNIVERSITY OF CALIFORNIA AT LOS ANGELES
➤ Master of Business Administration (MBA) Degree	UNIVERSITY OF CALIFORNIA AT LOS ANGELES
➤ Bachelor of Science Degree	UNIVERSITY OF CALIFORNIA AT IRVINE

Academic Credentials Format

EDUCATION: **M.S., Management Science,** University of Colorado, 1996
B.S., Industrial Engineering, University of Nevada, 1992

Highlights of Continuing Professional Education:

▶ Organizational Management & Leadership, Colorado Leadership Association, 2001

▶ Industrial Engineering Technology in Today's Modern Manufacturing Organization, Purdue University, 2000

▶ SAP Implementation & Optimization, American Society for Quality Control, 1998

▶ Conflict Resolution & Violence Management in the Workplace, Institute for Workplace Safety, 1998

Certifications Format

Technical Certifications and Degrees

Certified Nursing Administrator (CNA), Helen Keller School of Nursing & Health Care Administration, 2001

Bachelor of Science in Nursing (BSN), Missouri State University at Columbia, 1998

Certificate in Advanced Cardiac Life Support (ACLS), State of Missouri, 1998

Certificate in Basic Cardiac Life Support (BCLS), State of Tennessee, 1996

Non-Degree Format

TRAINING & EDUCATION

UNIVERSITY OF TOLEDO, Toledo, Ohio

BS Candidate—Management & Administration (Senior class status)

UNIVERSITY OF MICHIGAN, Ann Arbor, Michigan

Dual Majors in Management & Human Resource Administration (2 years)

GRADUATE, 100+ hours of continuing professional education through the University of Illinois, University of Michigan, and University of Wisconsin.

No-College Format

PROFESSIONAL DEVELOPMENT

Management Training & Development	KELLOGG SCHOOL OF MANAGEMENT
Leadership Excellence	KELLOGG SCHOOL OF MANAGEMENT
Supervisory Training	CONNELLY COMMUNITY COLLEGE
Management Communications	PACE LEADERSHIP TRAINING

THE "EXTRAS"

The primary focus of your resume is on information (most likely, your professional experience and academic credentials) that is directly related to your career goals.

However, you also should include things that will distinguish you from other candidates and clearly demonstrate your value to a prospective employer. And, not too surprisingly, it is often the "extras" that get the interviews.

Following is a list of the other categories you might or might not include in your resume, depending on your particular experience and your current career objectives. Review the information. If it's pertinent to you, use the samples for formatting your own data. Remember, however, that if something is truly impressive, you might want to include it in your Career Summary at the beginning of your resume in order to draw even more attention to it. If this is the case, it's not necessary to repeat the information at the end of your resume.

Honors and Awards

If you have won honors and awards, you can either include them in a separate section on your resume or integrate them into the Education or Professional Experience section, whichever is most appropriate. If you choose to include them in a separate section, consider this format:

- ❖ Winner, 2001 **"Sales Leadership Award Recognition"** award from American Sales Association for outstanding contributions to sales revenues, new market penetration, and new business development.
- ❖ **"Corporate Sales Manager of the Year,"** ISP Systems, Inc., 2002
- ❖ **"Sales Manager of the Year,"** ISP Systems, 1999
- ❖ **"Sales Trainer of the Year,"** Delco Systems, 1997
- ❖ **Summa Cum Laude Graduate,** Yale University, 1989

Public Speaking

Experts are the ones who are invited to give public presentations at conferences, seminars, workshops, training programs, symposia, and other events. So if you have public-speaking experience, others must consider you an expert. Be sure to include this very complimentary information in your resume. Here's one way to present it:

- Keynote Speaker, **"Advancing Technology Innovation in the Workplace,"** 2002 National Association on Technology Excellence Conference, New York
- Panel Presenter, **"Emerging Multi-Media Technologies & Applications,"** 2002 National Association of Information Technology Executives, Dallas
- Session Leader, **"Optimizing PC Technologies,"** 2000 Data Processing Managers Association Annual Conference, Philadelphia
- Keynote Speaker, **"Technology for the Entrepreneur,"** 1999 Entrepreneur's World Conference, Chicago

Publications

If you're published, you must be an expert (or at least most people will think so). Just as with your public-speaking engagements, be sure to include your publications. They validate your knowledge, qualifications, and credibility. Publications can include books, articles, online Web site content, manuals, and other written documents. Here's an example:

> ▸ Author, *"Executive Compensation Systems,"* Society of Human Resource Management Annual Conference Proceedings, 2002
>
> ▸ Author, *"International Hiring, Employment & Retention,"* Society of Human Resource Management Journal, 2001
>
> ▸ Author, "Expatriate Employment for U.S. Corporations," IBM Corporation Employee Bulletin, March 2000
>
> ▸ Co-Author, *"Hiring For Long-Term Retention,"* American Management Association Journal, April 1999

Technology Skills and Qualifications

If you are a manager or executive in a field unrelated to technology, chances are that you'll just include a brief statement in your career summary that communicates you are PC proficient. For example:

> PC proficient with Microsoft Word, Access, Excel, and PowerPoint.

However, if you're employed in the technology industry and have unique technology qualifications, you'll want to include a separate section with this information (if it's relevant to your current career objectives). You'll also have to consider placement of this section in your resume. If the positions for which you are applying require strong technical skills, we would recommend you insert this section immediately after your Career Summary (or as a part thereof). If, on the other hand, your technical skills are a plus rather than a specific requirement, the preferred placement is after your Education section.

Here are two different samples of ways to format and present your technical qualifications:

Technology Profile	
Operating Systems:	Windows XP/98/95/3.x; Novell 3.x/4.x; NT 4.0 Workstation; MS-DOS 6.22
Manufacturing Systems:	SAP R/3, MRP, DRP, APS
Protocols/Networks:	TCP/IP, NetBEUI, IPX/SPX, Ethernet 10/100BASE-T
Hardware:	Hard drives, printers, scanners, fax/modems, CD-ROMs, Zip drives, Cat5 cables, hubs, NIC cards
Software:	Microsoft Office modules, FileMaker Pro, PC Anywhere, MS Exchange, ARCserve, Project Manager

TECHNOLOGY SKILLS SUMMARY

Windows XP/98/95/3.x	SAP	TCP/IP
Novell 5.x/6.x	MRP	Ethernet 10
NT 4.0 Workstation	DRP	IPX/SPX
Microsoft Office	MS Exchange	ARCserve
Project Manager	PC Anywhere	FileMaker Pro

Teaching and Training Experience

Many managers and executives also teach or train at colleges, universities, technical schools, and other organizations, in addition to training that they might offer "on the job." If this is applicable to you, you will want to include that experience on your resume. If someone hires you (paid or unpaid) to speak to an audience, it communicates a strong message about your skills, qualifications, knowledge, and expertise. Here's a format you might use to present that information:

- **Faculty,** Department of Finance & Economics, Morgan State University, 2000 to Present. Teach graduate-level studies in Economics, Economic Theory, Advanced Statistics, and Management Communications.

- **Adjunct Faculty,** Department of Economics, Coppin State University, 1999 to Present. Teach Micro-Economics and Macro-Economics to third- and fourth-year students.

- **Guest Lecturer,** Department of Business & Economics, Purdue University, 1997 to Present. Provide semi-annual, day-long lecture series on the integration of economic theory into the corporate workplace.

- **Lecturer,** Maryland State University, 1997 to 1999. Taught "Principles of Management" to first-year college students.

Committees and Task Forces

Many managers and executives serve on committees, task forces, and other special project teams either as part of, or in addition to, their full-time responsibilities. Again, this type of information further strengthens your credibility, qualifications, and perceived value to a prospective employer. Consider a format such as this:

- **Chairperson,** 2001–02 Corporate Planning & Reorganization Task Force

- **Member,** 2000–01 Corporate Committee on Global Market Expansion & Positioning

- **Member,** 1999–00 Study Team on "Redesigning Corporate Training Systems to Maximize Employee Productivity"

- **Chairperson,** 1997–98 Committee on "Safety & Regulatory Compliance in the Workplace"

Professional Affiliations

If you are a member of any educational, professional, or leadership associations, be sure to include that information on your resume. It communicates a message of professionalism, a desire to stay current with the industry, and a strong professional network. What's more, if you have held leadership positions within these organizations, be sure to include them. Here's an example:

AMERICAN MANAGEMENT ASSOCIATION
    Professional Member (1992 to Present)
    Professional Development Committee Member (1998 to 2000)
    Recruitment Committee Member (1996 to 1998)

AMERICAN HEALTH CARE ASSOCIATION
    Associate Member (1997 to Present)
    Professional Member (1988 to 1997)
    Technology Task Force member (1996 to 1998)

INTERNATIONAL HEALTH CARE SOCIETY
    Professional Member (2000 to Present)
    Training Committee Member (2000 to Present)

Civic Affiliations

Civic affiliations are fine to include if they

- Are with a notable organization,

- Demonstrate leadership experience, or

- Might be of interest to a prospective employer.

However, things such as treasurer of your local condo association and singer with your church choir are not generally of value in marketing your qualifications. Here's an example of what to include:

Volunteer Chairperson, United Way of America—Detroit Chapter, 1998 to Present

President, Lambert Valley Conservation District, 1997 to Present

Treasurer, Habitat for Humanity—Detroit Chapter, 1996 to 1997

Personal Information

We do not recommend that you include such personal information as birth date, marital status, number of children, and related data. However, there might be instances when personal information is appropriate. If this information will give you a competitive advantage or answer unspoken questions about your background, then by all means include it. Here's an example:

☑ Born in Argentina. U.S. Permanent Residency Status since 1987.

☑ Fluent in English, Spanish, and Portuguese.

☑ Competitive Triathlete. Top-5 finish, 1987 Midwest Triathlon and 1992 Des Moines Triathlon.

Note in the preceding example that the job seeker is multilingual. This is a particularly critical selling point and, although it might be listed under Personal Information in this example, we recommend that it is more appropriately highlighted in your Career Summary.

Consolidating the Extras

Sometimes you have so many extra categories at the end of your resume, each with only a handful of lines, that spacing becomes a problem. You certainly don't want to have to make your resume a page longer to accommodate five lines, nor do you want the "extras" to overwhelm the primary sections of your resume. Yet you believe the information is important and should be included. Or perhaps you have a few small bits of information that you think are important but don't merit an entire section. In these situations, consider consolidating the information using one of the following formats. You'll save space, avoid overemphasizing individual items, and present a professional, distinguished appearance.

PROFESSIONAL PROFILE

Technology Qualifications	IBM & HP Platforms
	Microsoft Office Suite, SAP R/3, ProjectPlanner, MRP, DRP, LAN, WAN, KPM, Lotus, Lotus Notes, Novell Networks
Affiliations	International Association of Electrical Inspectors
	American Electrical Association
	Florida Association of Electrical & Electronic Engineers
Public Speaking	Speaker, IEEE Conference, Dallas, 2000
	Presenter, AEA National Conference, San Diego, 1998
	Panelist, APICS National Conference, Miami, 1996
Foreign Languages	Fluent in English, Spanish, and German

ADDITIONAL INFORMATION

- Co-Chair, Education Committee, Detroit Technology Association.
- PC literate with MRP, DRP, SAP, and Kaizen technologies.
- Available for relocation worldwide.
- Eagle Scout ... Boy Scout Troop Leader.

Writing Tips, Techniques, and Important Lessons

At this point, you've done a lot of reading, probably taken some notes, highlighted samples that appeal to you, and are ready to plunge into writing your resume. To make this task as easy as possible, we've compiled some "insider" techniques that we've used in our professional resume-writing practices. These techniques were learned the hard way through years of experience! We know they work; they will make the writing process easier, faster, and more enjoyable for you.

GET IT DOWN—THEN POLISH AND PERFECT IT

Don't be too concerned with making your resume "perfect" the first time around. It's far better to move fairly swiftly through the process, getting the basic information organized and on paper (or on-screen), instead of agonizing about the perfect phrase or ideal formatting. Once you've completed a draft, we think you'll be surprised at how close to "final" it is, and you'll be able to edit, tighten, and improve formatting fairly quickly.

WRITE YOUR RESUME FROM THE BOTTOM UP

Here's the system:

- **Start with the easy things**—Education, Technology, Professional Affiliations, Public Speaking, Publications, and any other extras you want to include. These items require little thought and can be completed in just a few minutes.

- **Write short job descriptions for your older positions, the ones you held years ago.** Be very brief and focus on highlights such as rapid promotion, achievements, innovations, professional honors, or employment with well-respected, well-known companies.

Once you've completed this, look at how much you've written in a short period of time! Then move on to the next step:

- **Write the job descriptions for your most recent positions.** This will take a bit longer than the other sections you have written. Remember to focus on the overall scope of your responsibility, major projects and initiatives, and significant achievements. Tell your reader what you did and how well you did it. You can use any of the formats recommended earlier in this chapter, or you can create something that is unique to you and your career.

Now, see how far along you are? Your resume is 90 percent complete with only one small section left to do:

- **Write your Career Summary.** Before you start writing, remember your objective for this section. The summary should not simply rehash your previous experience. Rather, it will highlight the skills and qualifications you have that are most closely related to your current career objective(s). The summary is intended to capture the reader's attention and "sell" your expertise.

That's it. You're done. We guarantee that the process of writing your resume will be much, much easier if you follow the "bottom-up" strategy. Now, on to the next tip.

INCLUDE NOTABLE OR PROMINENT "EXTRA" STUFF IN YOUR CAREER SUMMARY

Remember the "extra-credit sections" that are normally at the bottom of your resume? If this information is particularly significant or prominent—you delivered double-digit revenue or profit growth, won a notable award, spoke at an international conference, developed a new engineering methodology, designed a new product that generated tens of millions of dollars in new revenues, or slashed 60 percent from operating costs—you might want to include it at the top in your Career Summary. Remember, the summary section is written to distinguish you from the crowd of other qualified candidates. As such, if you've accomplished anything that clearly demonstrates your knowledge, expertise, and credibility, consider moving it to your Career Summary for added attention. Refer to the sample Career Summaries earlier in this chapter for examples.

USE RESUME SAMPLES TO GET IDEAS FOR CONTENT, FORMAT, AND ORGANIZATION

This book is just one of many resources where you can review the resumes of other managers and executives to help you in formulating your strategy, writing the text, and formatting your resume. What's more, these books are published precisely for that reason. You don't have to struggle alone. Rather, use all the available resources at your disposal.

Be forewarned, however, that it's unlikely you will find a resume that fits your life and career to a "t." It's more likely that you will use "some of this sample" and "some of that sample" to create a resume that is uniquely "you."

INCLUDE DATES OR NOT?

Unless you are over age 50, we recommend that you date your work experience and your education. Without dates, your resume becomes vague and difficult for the typical hiring manager or recruiter to interpret. What's more, it often communicates the message that you are trying to hide something. Maybe you haven't worked in two years, maybe you were fired from each of your last three positions, or maybe you never graduated from college. Being vague and creating a resume that is difficult to read will, inevitably, lead to uncertainty and a quick toss into the "not-interested" pile of candidates. By including the dates of your education and your experience, you create a clean and concise picture that one can easily follow to track your career progression.

An Individual Decision

If you are over age 50, dating your early positions must be an individual decision. On the one hand, you do not want to "date" yourself out of consideration by including dates from the 1960s and early 1970s. On the other hand, it might be that those positions are worth including for any one of a number of reasons. Further, if you omit those early dates, you might feel as though you are misrepresenting yourself (or lying) to a prospective employer.

Here is a strategy to overcome those concerns while still including your early experience: Create a separate category titled "Previous Professional Experience" in which you summarize your earliest employment. You can tailor this statement to emphasize just what is most important about that experience.

If you want to focus on the reputation of your past employers, include a statement such as this:

- Previous experience includes mid- to senior-level management positions with IBM, Dell, and Xerox.

If you want to focus on the rapid progression of your career, consider this example:

> • Promoted rapidly through a series of increasingly responsible operating management and leadership positions with Zyler Form Molding, Inc.

If you want to focus on your early career achievements, include a statement such as this:

> • Earned six promotions in three years with Kodak based on outstanding performance in revenue growth, market development, and customer retention.

By including any one of the preceding paragraphs, under the heading "Previous Professional Experience," you are clearly communicating to your reader that your employment history dates further back than the dates you have indicated on your resume. In turn, you are being 100 percent above-board and not misrepresenting yourself or your career. What's more, you're focusing on the success, achievement, and prominence of your earliest assignments.

Should You Include Dates in the Education Section?

If you are over age 50, we generally do not recommend that you date your education or college degrees. Simply include the degree and the university with no date. Why exclude yourself from consideration by immediately presenting the fact that you earned your college degree in 1958, 1962, or 1966—probably about the time the hiring manager was born? Remember, the goal of your resume is to share the highlights of your career and open doors for interviews. It is *not* to give your entire life story. As such, it is not mandatory to date your college degree.

However, if you use this strategy, be aware that the reader is likely to assume there is *some* gap between when your education ended and your work experience started. Therefore, if you choose to begin your chronological work history with your first job out of college, omitting your graduation date could actually backfire, because the reader might assume you have experience that predates your first job. In this case, it's best either to *include your graduation date* or *omit dates of earliest experience*, using the summary strategy discussed previously.

ALWAYS SEND A COVER LETTER WHEN YOU FORWARD YOUR RESUME

Sending a cover letter every time you send a resume is expected and is appropriate job search etiquette. When you prepare a resume, you are writing a document that you can use for every position you apply for, assuming that the requirements for all of those positions will be similar. The cover letter, then, is the tool that allows you to customize your presentation to each company or recruiter, addressing their specific hiring requirements. It is also the appropriate place to include any specific information that has been requested, such as salary history or salary requirements (see the following section).

NEVER INCLUDE SALARY HISTORY OR SALARY REQUIREMENTS ON YOUR RESUME

Your resume is *not* the correct forum for a salary discussion. First of all, you will never provide salary information unless a company has requested that information, and then only if you choose to comply. (Studies show that if employers are interested in you, they will look at your application with or without salary information. Therefore, you might choose not to respond to this request, thereby avoiding pricing yourself out of the job or locking yourself into a lower salary than the job is worth.)

When responding to want ads, you might come across a statement like this: "Resumes without salary requirements will not be considered." In these cases, you should comply, but it's best to provide a range rather than an exact figure.

When contacting recruiters, however, we recommend that you do provide salary information, but again, only in your cover letter. With recruiters you want to "put all of your cards on the table" and help them make an appropriate placement by providing information about your current salary and salary objectives. For example, "Be advised that my current compensation is $125,000 annually and that I am interested in a management position starting at a minimum of $150,000 per year." Or, if you would prefer to be a little less specific, you might write, "My annual compensation over the past three years has averaged $75,000+."

ALWAYS REMEMBER THAT YOU ARE SELLING

As we have discussed over and over throughout this book, resume writing is sales. Understand and appreciate the value you bring to a prospective employer, and then communicate that value by focusing on your achievements. Companies don't want to hire just anyone; they want to hire "the" someone who will make a difference. Show them that you are that candidate.

CHAPTER 3

Printed, Scannable, Electronic, and Web Resumes

After you've worked so tirelessly to write a winning resume, your next challenge is the resume's design, layout, and presentation. It's not enough for it to read well; your resume must also have just the right look for the right audience. And, just as with everything else in a job search, no specific answers exist. You must make a few decisions about what your final resume presentation will look like.

The Four Types of Resumes

In today's employment market, job seekers use four types of resume presentations:

- Printed
- Scannable
- Electronic (e-mail attachments and ASCII text files)
- Web

The following sections give details on when you would need each type, as well as how to prepare these types of resumes.

THE PRINTED RESUME

We know the printed resume as the "traditional resume," the one that you mail to a recruiter, take to an interview, and forward by mail or fax in response to an advertisement. When preparing a printed resume, you want to create a sharp, professional, and visually attractive presentation. Remember, that piece of paper conveys the very first impression of you to a potential employer, and that first impression goes a long, long way. Never be fooled into thinking that just because you have the best qualifications in your industry, the visual presentation of your resume does not matter. It does, a great deal.

THE SCANNABLE RESUME

The scannable resume can be referred to as the "plain-Jane" or "plain-vanilla" resume. All of the things that you would normally do to make your printed resume look attractive—bold print, italics, multiple columns, sharp-looking type-style, and more—are stripped away in a scannable resume. You want to present a document that can be easily read and interpreted by scanning technology.

Although the technology continues to improve, and many scanning systems in fact can read a wide variety of type enhancements, it's sensible to appeal to the "lowest common denominator" when creating your scannable resume. Follow these formatting guidelines:

- Choose a commonly used, easily read font such as Arial or Times New Roman.
- Don't use bold, italic, or underlined type.
- Use a minimum of 11-point type size.
- Position your name, and nothing else, on the top line of the resume.
- Keep text left-justified, with a "ragged" right margin.
- It's okay to use common abbreviations (for instance, scanning software will recognize "B.S." as a Bachelor of Science degree). But, when in doubt, spell it out.
- Eliminate graphics, borders, and horizontal lines.
- Use plain, round bullets or asterisks.
- Avoid columns and tables, although a simple two-column listing can be read without difficulty.
- Spell out symbols such as % and &.
- If you divide words with slashes, add a space before and after the slash to be certain the scanner doesn't misread the letters.
- Print using a laser printer on smooth white paper.
- If your resume is longer than one page, be sure to print on only one side of the paper; put your name, telephone number, and e-mail address on the top of page two; and don't staple the pages together.
- For best possible results, mail your resume (don't fax it), and send it flat in a 9 × 12 envelope so that you won't have to fold it.

Of course, you can avoid scannability issues completely by sending your resume electronically, so that it will not have to pass through a scanner to enter the company's databank. Read the next section for electronic resume guidelines.

THE ELECTRONIC RESUME

Your electronic resume can take two forms: e-mail attachments and ASCII text files.

E-mail Attachments

When including your resume with an e-mail, simply attach the word-processing file of your printed resume. Because a vast majority of businesses use Microsoft Word, it is the most acceptable format and will present the fewest difficulties when attached.

However, given the tremendous variety in versions of software and operating systems, not to mention printer drivers, it's quite possible that your beautifully formatted resume will look quite different when viewed and printed at the other end. To minimize these glitches, use generous margins (at least 0.75 inch all around). Don't use unusual typefaces, and minimize fancy formatting effects.

Test your resume by e-mailing it to several friends or colleagues, and then having them view and print it on their systems. If you use WordPerfect, Microsoft Works, or another word-processing program, consider saving your resume in a more universally accepted format such as RTF or PDF. Again, try it out on friends before sending it to a potential employer.

ASCII Text Files

You'll find many uses for an ASCII text version of your resume:

- To avoid formatting problems, you can paste the text into the body of an e-mail message rather than send an attachment. Many employers actually prefer this method. Pasting text into an e-mail message lets you send your resume without the possibility of also sending a virus.

- You can readily copy and paste the text version into online job application and resume blank forms, with no worries that formatting glitches will cause confusion.

- Although it's unattractive, the text version is 100 percent scannable.

To create a text version of your resume, follow these simple steps:

1. Create a new version of your resume using the Save As feature of your word-processing program. Select "text only" or "ASCII" in the Save As option box.

2. Close the new file.

3. Reopen the file, and you'll find that your word processor has automatically reformatted your resume into Courier font, removed all formatting, and left-justified the text.

4. To promote maximum readability when sending your resume electronically, reset the margins to 2 inches left and right, so that you have a narrow column of text rather than a full-page width. (This margin setting will not be retained when you close the file, but in the meantime you can adjust the text formatting for best screen appearance. For instance, if you choose to include a horizontal line [perhaps something like this: +++++++++++++++++++++++++++] to separate sections of the resume, by working with the narrow margins you won't make the mistake of creating a line that extends past the normal screen width. Plus, you won't add hard line breaks that create odd-length lines when seen at normal screen width.)

5. Review the resume and fix any "glitches" such as odd characters that may have been inserted to take the place of "curly" quotes, dashes, accents, or other nonstandard symbols.

6. If necessary, add extra blank lines to improve readability.

7. Consider adding horizontal dividers to break the resume into sections for improved skimmability. You can use any standard typewriter symbols such as *, -, (,), =, +, ^, or #.

To illustrate what you can expect when creating these versions of your resume, on the following pages are some examples of the same resume in traditional printed format, scannable version, and electronic (text) format.

THE WEB RESUME

This newest evolution in resumes combines the visually pleasing quality of the printed resume with the technological ease of the electronic resume. You host your Web resume on your own Web site (with your own URL), to which you refer prospective employers and recruiters. Now, instead of seeing just a "plain-Jane" version of your e-mailed resume, with just one click a viewer can access, download, and print your Web resume—an attractive, nicely formatted presentation of your qualifications.

What's more, because the Web resume is such an efficient and easy-to-manage tool, you can choose to include more information than you would in a printed, scannable, or electronic resume. Consider separate pages for achievements, technology qualifications, equipment skills, honors and awards, management skills, and more, if you believe they would improve your market position. Remember, you're working to sell yourself into your next job!

Those of you in technology professions can take it one step further and create a virtual multimedia presentation that not only tells someone how talented you are, but also visually and technologically demonstrates it. Web resumes are an outstanding tool for people seeking jobs in technology-based industries.

A simplified version of the Web resume is an online version of your Microsoft Word resume. Instead of attaching a file to an e-mail to an employer, you can include a link to the online version. This format is not as graphically dynamic as a full-fledged Web resume, but it can be a very useful tool for your job search. For instance, you can offer the simplicity of text in your e-mail, plus the instant availability of a printable, formatted word-processing document for the interested recruiter or hiring manager. For a demonstration of this format, go to www.e-resume-central.com and click on "SEE A SAMPLE."

DAVID J. BLACK

113 Lowell Court
Auburn, Maine 04210

(207) 782-2222
dblack44@hotmail.com

GENERAL BUSINESS & OPERATIONS MANAGER

Experienced in Service, Production, and Project-Development Businesses
Hands-On Leader with Deep Expertise in Company Operations

"Consistently strive to optimize operations, reduce costs, and improve service quality
while strengthening bottom-line profitability."

EXPERIENCE

J.F. AITKEN FINANCIAL SERVICES (Freeport, ME)   2001–Present
(Holding company for a construction-management and real-estate-development company)
General Manager

Current Position Highlights

- Manage day-to-day operations of various business activities; meet with potential clients.
- Serve as project manager for ongoing contracts ranging from $500,000 to $5,000,000 (both residential and commercial); support and develop complementary business initiatives.
- Develop sales channels for new business activities and projects.
- Manage all financial areas (focus on profit & loss results and goals).

SOUTHERN MAINE FLOORING (Portland, ME)   1993–2001
(Retail sales and installation of carpet, linoleum, hardwood, and ceramic tile)
General Business Manager

Career Progression

Started with the company in a Sales position; advanced to Office Manager. Assisted owner in start-up of new business; organized showroom, set up price books, evaluated product lines, determined product selection and stock items, and set up all operational systems. Promoted to General Business Manager, continuing to perform the duties of Office Manager, adding supervision of support staff, and managing all administrative activities plus multiple departments—Sales, Marketing, HR, Design, and Production.

General Business Manager Highlights

- Hired staff, maintained all personnel records, administered employee benefits, and researched and administered all insurance issues including Workers' Compensation.
- Assured all safety systems were enforced in the workplace; maintained facility, showroom, and company vehicles including physical and financial documentation.
- Continually demonstrated technical proficiency by successfully researching and selecting state-of-the-art computer software and hardware; oversaw implementation of the new equipment and staff training.

ABC SUPPLY CO. (Lewiston, ME)   1989–1993
(Supplier of water, sewer, and drain materials—fire hydrants and water meters)
Inside Sales Representative / Buyer

- Handled all areas of inside sales including customer service and preparation of bids/quotes.
- Purchased goods; negotiated prices and contracts; coordinated shipments with vendors.

EDUCATION

B.S. Business Administration   University of Maine, Orono, ME, 1989
Concentration / Management and Marketing

References Available Upon Request

The print version of the resume (resume writer: Rolande LaPointe, Lewiston, ME).

DAVID J. BLACK
113 Lowell Court
Auburn, Maine 04210
(207) 782-2222
dblack44@hotmail.com

GENERAL BUSINESS & OPERATIONS MANAGER
Experienced in Service, Production, and Project-Development Businesses
Hands-On Leader with Deep Expertise in Company Operations

"Consistently strive to optimize operations, reduce costs, and improve service quality
while strengthening bottom-line profitability."

EXPERIENCE
J.F. AITKEN FINANCIAL SERVICES (Freeport, ME)   2001–Present
(Holding company for a construction-management and real-estate-development company)
General Manager

Current Position Highlights

- Manage day-to-day operations of various business activities; meet with potential clients.

- Serve as project manager for ongoing contracts ranging from $500,000 to $5,000,000 (both residential and commercial); support and develop complementary business initiatives.

- Develop sales channels for new business activities and projects.

- Manage all financial areas (focus on profit & loss results and goals).

SOUTHERN MAINE FLOORING (Portland, ME)   1993–2001
(Retail sales and installation of carpet, linoleum, hardwood, and ceramic tile)
General Business Manager

Career Progression: Started with the company in a Sales position; advanced to Office Manager. Assisted owner in start-up of new business; organized showroom, set up price books, evaluated product lines, determined product selection and stock items, and set up all operational systems. Promoted to General Business Manager, continuing to perform the duties of Office Manager, adding supervision of support staff, and managing all administrative activities plus multiple departments—Sales, Marketing, HR, Design, and Production.

General Business Manager Highlights

- Hired staff, maintained all personnel records, administered employee benefits, and researched and administered all insurance issues including Workers' Compensation.

- Assured all safety systems were enforced in the workplace; maintained facility, showroom, and company vehicles including physical and financial documentation.

- Continually demonstrated technical proficiency by successfully researching and selecting state-of-the-art computer software and hardware; oversaw implementation of the new equipment and staff training.

ABC SUPPLY CO. (Lewiston, ME)   1989–1993
(Supplier of water, sewer, and drain materials—fire hydrants and water meters)
Inside Sales Representative / Buyer

- Handled all areas of inside sales including customer service and preparation of bids/quotes.

- Purchased goods; negotiated prices and contracts; coordinated shipments with vendors.

EDUCATION
B.S. Business Administration: Concentration / Management and Marketing
University of Maine, Orono, ME, 1989

References Available Upon Request

The scannable version of the resume.

```
DAVID J. BLACK
113 Lowell Court
Auburn, Maine 04210
(207) 782-2222
dblack44@hotmail.com

======================================
GENERAL BUSINESS & OPERATIONS MANAGER
Experienced in Service, Production, and Project-Development Businesses
Hands-On Leader with Deep Expertise in Company Operations

"Consistently strive to optimize operations, reduce costs, and improve service
quality while strengthening bottom-line profitability."

======================================
EXPERIENCE
J.F. AITKEN FINANCIAL SERVICES (Freeport, ME)
2001-Present
(Holding company for a construction-management and real-estate-development
company)
== General Manager
Current Position Highlights
* Manage day-to-day operations of various business activities; meet with
potential clients.
* Serve as project manager for ongoing contracts ranging from $500,000 to
$5,000,000 (both residential and commercial); support and develop complementary
business initiatives.
* Develop sales channels for new business activities and projects.
* Manage all financial areas (focus on profit & loss results and goals).

SOUTHERN MAINE FLOORING (Portland, ME)
1993-2001
(Retail sales and installation of carpet, linoleum, hardwood, and ceramic tile)
== General Business Manager
Career Progression: Started with the company in a Sales position; advanced to
Office Manager. Assisted owner in start-up of new business; organized showroom,
set up price books, evaluated product lines, determined product selection and
stock items, and set up all operational systems. Promoted to General Business
Manager, continuing to perform the duties of Office Manager, adding supervision
of support staff, and managing all administrative activities plus multiple
departments--Sales, Marketing, HR, Design, and Production.

General Business Manager Highlights
* Hired staff, maintained all personnel records, administered employee benefits,
and researched and administered all insurance issues including Workers'
Compensation.
* Assured all safety systems were enforced in the workplace; maintained
facility, showroom, and company vehicles including physical and financial
documentation.
* Continually demonstrated technical proficiency by successfully researching and
selecting state-of-the-art computer software and hardware; oversaw
implementation of the new equipment and staff training.

ABC SUPPLY CO. (Lewiston, ME)
1989-1993
(Supplier of water, sewer, and drain materials--fire hydrants and water meters)
== Inside Sales Representative / Buyer

* Handled all areas of inside sales including customer service and preparation
of bids/quotes.
* Purchased goods; negotiated prices and contracts; coordinated shipments with
vendors.

======================================
EDUCATION

B.S. Business Administration
Concentration / Management and Marketing
University of Maine, Orono, ME, 1989

======================================
References Available Upon Request
```

The electronic/text version of the resume.

The Four Resume Types Compared

This chart quickly compares the similarities and differences between the four types of resumes we've discussed in this chapter.

	PRINTED RESUMES	**SCANNABLE RESUMES**
TYPESTYLE/ FONT	Sharp, conservative, and distinctive (see our recommendations in chapter 1).	Clean, concise, and machine-readable: Times New Roman, Arial, Helvetica.
TYPESTYLE ENHANCEMENTS	**Bold,** *italics,* and <u>underlining</u> for emphasis.	CAPITALIZATION is the only type enhancement you can be certain will transmit.
TYPE SIZE	10-, 11-, or 12-point preferred… larger type sizes (14, 18, 20, 22, and even larger, depending on typestyle) will effectively enhance your name and section headers.	11- or 12-point, or larger.
TEXT FORMAT	Use centering and indentations to optimize the visual presentation.	Type all information flush left.
PREFERRED LENGTH	1 to 2 pages; 3 if essential.	1 to 2 pages preferred, although length is not as much of a concern as with printed resumes.
PREFERRED PAPER COLOR	White, Ivory, Light Gray, Light Blue, or other conservative background.	White or very light with no prints, flecks, or other shading that might affect scannability.
WHITE SPACE	Use appropriately for best readability.	Use generously to maximize scannability.

ELECTRONIC RESUMES	WEB RESUMES
Courier.	Sharp, conservative, and distinctive... attractive onscreen and when printed from an online document.
CAPITALIZATION is the only enhancement available to you.	**Bold,** *italics,* and <u>underlining,</u> and color for emphasis.
12-point.	10-, 11-, or 12-point preferred... larger type sizes (14, 18, 20, 22, and even larger, depending on typestyle) will effectively enhance your name and section headers.
Type all information flush left.	Use centering and indentations to optimize the visual presentation.
Length is immaterial; almost definitely, converting your resume to text will make it longer.	Length is immaterial; just be sure your site is well organized so viewers can quickly find the material of greatest interest to them.
N/A.	Paper is not used, but do select your background carefully to maximize readability.
Use white space to break up dense text sections.	Use appropriately for best readability both onscreen and when printed.

Are You Ready to Write Your Resume?

To be sure that you're ready to write your resume, go through the following checklist. Each item is a critical step that you must take in the process of writing and designing your own winning resume.

❑ Clearly define "who you are" and how you want to be perceived.

❑ Document your key skills, qualifications, and knowledge.

❑ Document your notable career achievements and successes.

❑ Identify one or more specific job targets or positions.

❑ Identify one or more industries that you are targeting.

❑ Research and compile key words for your profession, industry, and specific job targets.

❑ Determine which resume format suits you and your career best.

❑ Select an attractive font.

❑ Determine whether you need a print resume, a scannable resume, an electronic resume, a Web resume, or all four.

❑ Secure a private e-mail address.

❑ Review resume samples for up-to-date ideas on resume styles, formats, organization, and language.

PART II

Sample Resumes for Managers and Executives

CHAPTER 4

Resumes for Managers and Executives in Sales, Marketing, and Retail

- Retail Manager
- Retail Executive
- Sales Representative
- Sales Executive
- Sales Manager
- Regional Manager
- Sales and Marketing Executive
- Sales Management Executive
- Business Development Executive
- Marketing Director
- Marketing Executive
- International Marketing Manager
- Senior Marketing Executive

DEBORAH CORMIER

3 Cousins Crescent ➤ Aurora, Ontario ➤ L4G 9B7 ➤ 905-841-3998

RETAIL MANAGER

PROFILE

Client-driven, quality-focused, and safety-conscious with over 20 years of progressive experience in retail operations and a **track record of top performance in a variety of challenging assignments.** Possess thorough understanding of store operations, based on actual hands-on experience, and ability to easily adapt to new and different environments. Strengths include:

- Operations Management
- High-Expectation Client Relations
- Staff Training, Scheduling, & Development
- Cash Management & Expense Control
- Advertising & Selling Techniques
- Product Receipt

- Inventory Control
- Till Set-Up & Reconciliation
- P&L Management
- Purchasing Management
- Merchandising Techniques & Colour Co-ordination

Well-developed interpersonal skills, easily able to establish and maintain favourable rapport with clients and staff from all cultures and organizational backgrounds. **Earlier professional experience includes 3 years as a Sales Associate at a local bed-and-bath boutique; assumed increasing responsibility for window treatments designed to boost customer traffic.** High level of personal and professional integrity... passionate about achieving organizational success.

PROFESSIONAL EXPERIENCE

MEGA-MART   1982–2002
2001–2002: Assistant Produce/Garden Manager — Aurora location
Promoted to oversee operations of a busy and established suburban store based on demonstrated ability to lead teams, boost employee morale, and foster client loyalty. Attractively set up merchandise in an effort to entice customers to buy product. Ensured neatness and orderliness throughout department. Revised prices and updated signage on a weekly basis to correspond with printed flyers and distribution material. Authorized to modify prices to generate additional revenues and discourage product shrinkage.

Selected Achievements:

- Created additional sales demand through effective set-up of in-store sampling demonstrations.
- Chosen to assume Produce Manager's duties in his absence. Strove to ensure smooth store operations.
- Consistently picked by Manager to brighten up store environment using seasonal themes and in-store promotional pieces.
- Assisted in apprehending two repeat offenders and dramatically reduced customer theft by introducing stringent loss-prevention measures.

1982–2001: Fast-track promotions in earlier career at Mega-Mart St. Catherines store during its start-up phase, with accountability for Cash, Produce, Health & Beauty Aids, Dairy, Bakery, Deli, Stock, and Courtesy Desk.

EDUCATION

Seneca College, Newnham Campus, Toronto
Colour Theory and Its Application Toward Effective Merchandising Techniques

Strategy: Highlight contributions and management-level activities for this grocery-store manager who wanted to change industries.

James Allen Borgen

1453 Little Fork Bridge
Tulsa, Oklahoma 74104

jamesborg@dotmail.com

918-884-3542 Residence
918-453-3484 Cellular

Professional Objective

Professional Sales/Sales Management with a progressive organization focused on quality and excellence, where partnership/consultative selling is valued.

Sales Profile

Top-producing sales professional who is driven, motivated, and self-disciplined. Relationship-builder with successful track record in developing and retaining accounts in a highly competitive marketplace.

- Effective at mentoring/coaching colleagues to build customers for life.
- Profit-driven and focused on value-added consultative selling.
- Skilled at assessing customer needs and providing win-win-win solutions.
- Cognizant of key competition, market trends, and industry changes.
- Valued by customers for consistent follow-through and caring demeanor.

Professional Sales Experience

ENGINEERED SOLUTIONS, Tulsa, Oklahoma   **1996–Present**
Tulsa-based market leader in satellite-communication systems.

Sales Consultant. Recruited by Engineered Solutions' General Manager to aggressively pursue new business throughout the state of Oklahoma. Key functions:

Sales:
- Number-one-ranked, high-performance sales professional for four consecutive years in eight branches of the organization.
- Substantially increased sales volume of existing accounts.
- Effective in reading buy-signals; possess strong closing abilities.
- Recognized as the sole sales consultant out of company's 18 consultants to achieve sales goals during most recent fiscal year.

Growth/Profitability:
- Increased sales throughout four consecutive years, consistently exceeding sales goals as outlined below, while maintaining profit margins:

2002 — 165%	2000 — 122%
2001 — 135%	1999 — 115%

- Prospected and developed an entirely new market for the organization, with majority of accounts newly recruited through personal sales efforts.
- Successful at maintaining profit margin despite strong competition.

Account/Customer Retention:
- Excel at identifying prospects and maintaining established accounts by consistent follow-through.
- Differentiate between suspects and prospects through strong consulting and interpretive skills.
- Played an integral role in developing large communications systems for major accounts. Initiated extensive infrastructure changes, working with sub-contractors, city, county, and state officials.

Education

BSBA: Marketing Major with Economics Minor   University of Tulsa, Tulsa, Oklahoma, 1996

Strategy: *Focus on strong results for this talented, aggressive sales professional.*

Rachelle Rhinehart

6260 Woolery Lane, Dayton, OH 45415
Phone: (937) 265-1581
E-mail: r_rhinehart@jitaweb.com

Retail Manager of Multiple Site Locations

Personnel Management and Training / Multi-Shift / Facility Operations
Long History of Excellent Selling and Management Skills

Business manager with an extensive history of retail operations and a track record of increasing the company's revenue base through focused marketing campaigns that included flyers, business events, and advertising programs. Handle all aspects of the business, from financial tracking and merchandise displays to inventory and stock levels and personnel / scheduling requirements. Business leader who goes "above and beyond" a job description ... history of producing added revenues through e-business and market-reach strategies, locally and nationally.

Key Abilities

Personnel —
- Labor Relations / Scheduling / Staffing
- Workflow Optimization
- Employee Management & Training

Operations —
- Store Design / Layout
- Floor Plan Optimization
- Supplier / Vendor Relations

Administration —
- Front– and Back–store Logistics
- Records Management
- Infrastructures & Processes

Business Development —
- Market Share / Revenue Growth
- Product Introduction / Displays
- Cost-Cutting Tactics

Professional Experience

MANAGER, 1986–PRESENT
Rose Dancewear, Inc., Dayton, OH
Serve as regional manager for several Dayton locations with $2 million in yearly revenues. Involved in all business start-up activities — such as demographic analysis, floor layouts, ergonomic issues, and staffing needs. Hire, train, and schedule the store's 25 employees and store leads (supervisors), shifting into cashier, floor, and inventory roles. Track and compare all financial numbers, from floor sales to gross and net revenues. Focus employee training on providing 100% customer service to ensure long-term customer loyalty and securing future sales. Monitor store stock levels, merchandising, and floor logistics to produce patron up-selling. Supervise and work with store leads to identify and address loss prevention and shrinkage issues, among a variety of other topics, such as seasonal merchandise and display windows.

- Assist with new store locations, from initial site selection and budgeting to store stock levels, staffing requirements, and grand-opening events.

- Pitched and implemented a new catalog promotional program; sent to studio owners and instructors, producing new revenues of $250,000 yearly.

- Create, edit, and run company advertising campaigns, such as "ad slicks" and flyers, participated in business networking events, and designed a coupon book program for existing patrons. Increased retail sales by 20%.

- Participated in annual dance conventions, networking with industry leaders located throughout Springfield, Cincinnati, Columbus, and Indianapolis.

Strategy: *Focus on the candidate's high-end skills and track record as the "driving force" behind her company's continuous revenue growth.*

Rhinehart, Rachelle   *Page Two*

- Authored the company's first employee handbook/guideline, covering topics such as history of company, employee benefits, dress code, and appropriate behaviors.

- Worked with website company on the design and layout of the new website, providing photographs, written copy, and catalog images.

ASSISTANT MANAGER, 1984–1986
Fashion Sense (DorothyD Corporation), Vandalia, OH
Supervised all aspects of the retail operation, from inventory control and stock levels to cash handling and customer service.

Training

Miami Valley Retail Management Training Camp, 1996

Software & Operating Systems

QuickBooks, Adobe Photoshop, MS Word, Works, Publisher, Excel,
Quicksell 2000 — POS / Manager

Willing to travel

Anthony Ranieri

93 Madison St. ▪ Cambridge, MA 02139 ▪ 781-555-5555

PROFILE

Over 20 years' experience in the convenience-store industry in positions of progressive responsibility to the position of Vice President of Operations. Proven ability to develop comprehensive sales and marketing programs that increase profitability. Strong financial-management and interpersonal skills. Background includes a position as external auditor for the World Bank and an MBA.

EXPERIENCE

KEYSTONE FUELS, Burlington, MA   2001–present
Vice President of Operations, New England Territory
Report directly to president, overseeing the operation and marketing of 22 units of gas stations/ c-stores with sales of approximately $45 million. Supervise three district managers and approve hiring of other management and staff.

- Developed policies and procedures, price book, and accounting system serving all gas-station and c-store units.
- Manage all planning, budget, and P&L for the division.
- Established marketing and merchandising programs, including D'Angelo's Sandwiches, Dunkin' Donuts, and Honeydew Donuts, which increased customer count by 25% and generated a 10% increase in sales in the first two quarters.
- Purchase all c-store equipment and supplies; negotiated savings of $10,000 in supply costs.

CAPITAL OIL CORPORATION, INC., Quincy, MA   1987–2001
Director of Operations and Marketing, Retail Division
Oversaw 30 convenience stores and gasoline stations in New England for region's largest independent gasoline distributor, with sales exceeding $50 million. Supervised four district managers and all retail personnel. Hired to establish/expand the convenience-store side of the corporation.

- Increased number of corporate c-stores from 1 to 23, and provided industry expertise to attract additional wholesale dealers and expand the wholesale division from approximately 20 to 180 units with a sales volume of over 200 million gallons.
- Developed all policies and procedures and established uniform marketing plan for all stores.
- Oversaw product/vendor selection, created price book, and promoted merchandising programs that drove a 15% increase in profits by creating a new revenue stream.
- Introduced co-branding and sold items from D'Angelo's Sandwiches, Dunkin' Donuts, and Sbarro's Pizza, which attracted higher customer traffic, generated repeat business, and increased sales 20%.
- Selected store sites based on analysis of traffic flow, income, social and economic demographics, competition, and real-estate costs; managed store design and layout; and improved appearance of original wholesale units to increase customer count and business.
- Implemented Oasis/Pinnacle systems for all c-stores to improve record-keeping process.

Strategy: *Display this executive's strong qualifications for the burgeoning convenience-store industry, in which he seeks to remain.*

Anthony Ranieri   Page 2

EXPERIENCE (continued)

STORE 24, INC., Waltham, MA   1979–1986
District Manager
Directed all business operations for 12 convenience stores in Boston area, with $15 million annual sales volume and 150+ employees. Managed all fiscal responsibilities; prepared and reviewed all budgets. Developed and implemented comprehensive sales programs. Analyzed market trends and oversaw merchandising and store layout.

- Supervised and trained 12 managers, 21 assistant managers, and 15 evening assistant managers.
- Increased territory sales by 30% in fiscal 1983, to achieve highest volume in corporation.
- Modified marketing thrust of typical convenience products toward broader merchandise base, which produced an 18% increase in customer volume.
- Added new departments, including Produce, Meats, and Deli; created a new Fast Food program, resulting in 25% sales increase.

WORLD BANK, Washington, DC   1976–1979
External Auditor
Involved in financial management and control of World Bank organizations throughout Europe, United States, South America, and Middle East. Examined accounts and financial and administrative systems; verified all financial statements, income, and expenses. Supervised activities of external auditing staff.

ARTHUR ANDERSEN AND YOUNG, New York, NY   1974–1976
Internal Auditor
Analyzed corporate accounts. Examined budget execution and prepared audit execution for field auditors. Reviewed transactions, investments, and expenses of 40 offices.

EDUCATION

MBA, Babson College, Babson Park, MA   1974

BA, Boston University, Boston, MA   1972

Continuing Education:

- Internal Control Systems — Arthur Andersen and Young, New York, NY
- Supervisor Development — National Association of Convenience Stores, Washington, DC
- Convenience Store Management — National Association of Convenience Stores, Washington, DC
- Ongoing participation in industry seminars in petroleum marketing, technology, fast-food programs, profitability, site selection, and merchandising

PROFESSIONAL AFFILIATIONS

- National Grocer's Association
- National Association of Convenience Stores
- New England Convenience Store Association
- Institute of Internal Auditors, New England Chapter

GEOFF LEWIS

1502 Woodcliff Lane • Charlotte, N.C. 28277

Mobile: (704) 483-9991

(704) 364-1414
glusa2002@aol.com

Office: (704) 347-2020

CAREER PROFILE

Dynamic, top-performing **Sports-Industry Sales Executive** with more than 15 years' experience in contracts procurement, project management, training, sports marketing, program development/implementation, and public/media relations. Expertise includes:

- Contract Negotiation
- Account Development & Retention
- Logistics Management
- Community Relations
- Relationship Management
- Staff Motivation & Mentoring
- Strategic Planning & Marketing

PROFESSIONAL EXPERIENCE

FEDERAL WRESTLING ALLIANCE/INTERNATIONAL WRESTLING ALLIANCE   2000–Present
Charlotte, N.C.
Vice President

Direct contracts administration for this international wrestling sports-entertainment organization. Scope of responsibility is diverse and includes coordinating material and equipment transportation/logistics, handling travel arrangements, recruiting, developing new talent, and procuring contracts with wrestlers. Serve as liaison between the Federal Wrestling Alliance/International Wrestling Alliance and the Pentagon to ensure contract compliance. Negotiate contract renewals. Travel worldwide. Conceive, plan, develop, and publicize all story lines, special events, promotions, advertising, and public-relations campaigns to ensure optimum TV viewership.

- Negotiated, transacted, and procured a $1 million federal contract providing professional wrestling sports entertainment to U.S. military troops and their dependents in Europe, Asia, the Balkans, the Caribbean, the Pacific Rim, Central America, and the United States. Won contract, displacing 30+ other major independent competitors. Conceived the initial procurement strategy.

- Grew company to the third-largest wrestling organization in the U.S.

- Developed concept and wrote format for BET-TV to provide syndication for the first minority-formatted pro-wrestling venue.

UNIVERSAL ENTERTAINMENT — Charlotte, N.C.   1998–2000
Chairman of Secondary Effects Study

Recruited to oversee research project, Universal Secondary Effects Study, to determine correlation between crime rates and property values in 20 local venues surrounding gentlemen's clubs.

- Organized and authored empirical study and hired all Ph.D. experts (criminologists, social psychologists, anthropologists, and urban planners) to ensure validity and authenticity of data. Worked and collaborated with Dr. David Wopak, University of Oregon; Dr. Keith Brooks, Chairman, Criminology Department, University of North Carolina at Chapel Hill; and Dr. Deborah Harrison, University of Virginia. Oversaw all aspects of study; made recommendations and implementations to ensure scientific accuracy.

Strategy: *Reflect strong sales, negotiation, and professional mentoring skills and downplay the less "respectable" elements of the candidate's career as he seeks to transition within the sports industry.*

GEOFF LEWIS

- Pioneered the development and implementation of the industry's *first* GED program for entertainers ("Operation Education"), providing the impetus for entertainers to achieve GED diplomas, while fostering self-esteem and lifetime learning skills. Taught weekly class (25 participants) and administered exams. Since implementation in March 2001, program has graduated 7 entertainers. Operation Education is certified by the State of North Carolina. Also coordinated open educational seminars (e.g., financial planning, health insurance, drug counseling, domestic violence) for entertainers.

- Orchestrated a series of aggressive marketing initiatives for the CrazyHorse Showclub that increased sales by 37% in one month. Realized growth through redesign of guest-services programs (conducting extensive interviews with entertainers and staff to identify improvement areas and empower employees), developing new marketing materials, creating theme-focused events, and building corporate relationships.

NORTHSIDE PHOTOGRAPHERS INTERNATIONAL — Nyack, N.Y.   1990–1998
President/Owner

Founded company providing photography services to the U.S. military worldwide. Directed all operations, including sales, marketing, customer service, purchasing, and human resources. Managed 35 employees.

- Grew business to $4.25 million in annual sales. Developed strategies to improve services to the military.

GANDY SPORTS MANAGEMENT — New York, N.Y.   1986–1990
Vice President

Negotiated contracts between NFL teams and individual players, serving as players' representative. Also secured major product endorsements and negotiated endorsement contracts. Solicited, scouted, and recruited top college players. Booked speaking engagements and public-relations appearances for players. Provided financial-management counseling and educational assistance to NFL players and developed pre-season training programs.

- Represented professional NFL players, including Lawrence Taylor (N.Y. Giants) and Mike Quick (Philadelphia Eagles). Reported directly to Bruce Gandy, former N.Y. Giant and Dallas Cowboy and currently CBS sports commentator.

ST. MARY'S REGIONAL HIGH SCHOOL — Montvale, N.J.   1982–1986
Physical Education & Health Sciences Teacher/Coach

Instructed classes and served as head wrestling coach and assistant varsity football coach for this parochial high school recognized for academic and athletic excellence. Assisted students with applications process and acceptance into sports programs at Yale, Harvard, and the U.S. Military Academy at West Point.

- Led wrestling and football teams to 2 state wrestling and 4 state football championships. Football team was ranked 8th nationally in 1986.

EDUCATION

M.A., Sports Fitness and Management, 1990
B.S., Physical Education/Health/Sports Management, 1982
- State University of New York (SUNY), College at Brockport

JOSEPH A. SUTTON

128 Driscoll Avenue
Atlanta, GA 30310

(404) 575-6214
Sutton128@aol.com

SENIOR SALES PROFESSIONAL

High-Tech Industry — Networking-Hardware Sales

— Pioneered wholesale networking-hardware sales & propelled company to a dominant market position —
— Grew annual revenues from $50 million to $150 million within five years —

➤ Top global-sales performer with the big-picture vision, leadership, and tenacity to successfully penetrate new markets, capture market share, and accelerate corporate revenue growth.

➤ Fifteen years of progressively responsible experience; consistently exceeded sales goals and forecasts.

➤ Extensive network of contacts with major players in the global networking-equipment market — OEMs, VARs, retail distributors, Fortune 100 / 1000 companies, and strategic partners.

➤ Dynamic sales manager skilled at developing sales teams to peak performance; training expertise in:

needs assessment / solution selling / consultative selling
market research / niche marketing / prospecting / channel & account development / pricing / forecasting
presentations / overcoming objections / closing / negotiating contracts / customer support

PROFESSIONAL EXPERIENCE

NETCONNECT, INC., Atlanta, GA
Semiconductor & networking equipment reseller with annual revenues of $250 million.

1996 to Present

Manager of Worldwide Networking Hardware Sales (1999 to 2000)

Launched the new networking-hardware division. P&L responsibility. Established product-line sales strategy. Built global relationships and made high-level presentations to customers and vendors. Hired staff. Trained, developed, and managed 100+ representatives.

- As Team Leader and individual contributor, tripled global networking sales during tenure.
- Transformed networking equipment from a small percentage of the corporate product mix to its dominant product line, accounting for 60% of the company's 2001 sales.
- Drove the product line to its current ranking as the most profitable within the company.
- Made strategic decisions about product diversification that enabled the company to dominate the market with 52% of the market space.
- Ramped up new product-line sales quickly, attaining $12 million in revenues in the first eight months.

Senior Sales Representative (1996 to 1999)

Developed and managed accounts. Negotiated contracts. Trained sales personnel in U.S., Asia, and Europe.

- Expanded into new markets. Built a broad and loyal customer base with leading networking VARs, resellers, retail distributors, and Fortune 100 companies.
- Presidents Club Winner three times.
- Personally accountable for 8% of company revenues in 1998 with $22 million in sales.
- Developed the company's first formal sales agreement incorporating volume incentives that was later adopted company-wide.

Strategy: *Ensure that sales achievements, not technical competencies, dominate the resume to prevent pigeonholing in a "dot-com" niche.*

JOSEPH A. SUTTON

PROFESSIONAL EXPERIENCE (CONTINUED)

SPAULDING, INC, Atlanta, GA   1995 to 1996
A $50 million sheet-metal manufacturer.

Senior Sales Representative

- Turned around an under-performing territory, accelerating sales to 130% of the prior year's revenues.
- Grew business to top accounts by 10%.
- Closed the most profitable order in the U.S. to date with a 45% profit margin.
- Doubled the number of accounts in the territory.

STANDARD SUPPLY COMPANY, St. Louis, MO   1988 to 1995
Construction-equipment manufacturer with $2 billion in annual revenues.

Sales Planning Manager (1993 to 1995)
Developed and implemented strategic business planning for the mechanical / electrical strategic business unit (SBU). Managed operating budgets, developed sales forecasts, established pricing guidelines, and set sales targets for all 260 divisional sales representatives and managers. Reported to the VP of Sales. Contributed to high-level decision-making.

- Developed and managed a $30 million budget.
- Successfully implemented market segmentation.

Sales Specialist, Wilmington, DE (1991 to 1993)

- Turned around downward-trending sales and increased product-line penetration by 27%.
- Established 38 new accounts, a 30+% increase over the previous year.
- Introduced a team-selling approach that was adopted by the company nationwide.
- Awarded divisional "Sales Specialist of the Month" 15 times. Achieved 200% of sales quota in 1992.

Sales Representative (1988 to 1991)

- Opened up new territory, selling to hospitals, municipalities, schools, and industry.
- Built a base of 250 accounts.

EDUCATION AND SKILLS

THE UNIVERSITY OF NORTH CAROLINA, Chapel Hill, NC
     Bachelor of Arts degree in Economics   1988
     Extensive coursework in Spanish

Languages: Working knowledge of spoken and written Spanish

Computer Software: Microsoft Word, Excel, proprietary contact-manager software

Neal Lawrence

411 W. Fulton Pkwy.
Chicago, IL 60614
773-771-1440 ▪ neallaw@yahoo.com

SENIOR SALES MANAGEMENT
Expertise in telecommunications on both regional and national levels

PROFILE

Consummate **sales executive** recognized for ability to build, guide, and sustain successful sales teams. Time and again, present proven accomplishments within the highly competitive telecommunications and wireless industries. At ease interfacing with, establishing, and maintaining excellent relationships with the world's largest organizations, including AT&T, Verizon, and BellSouth, among others. Thoroughly familiar with wireless communications, manufacturing, and distribution processes.

Areas of Expertise

- Territory / Account Development and Management
- Product Launch
- Marketing Collateral
- Trade Show Presentations
- Build-to-Suit, Co-location, and Sale/Lease-Back Agreements

- Contract Negotiations
- Public Relations
- Staff Supervision
- Team Building, Coaching, and Mentoring
- Needs Assessment
- Customer Service

CAREER HIGHLIGHTS

CALVIN INSTRUMENT COMPANY — Raleigh, NC
(Among the largest manufacturers of steel infrastructure products in the US, selling to the telecommunications industry.)
MIDWEST REGIONAL MANAGER, 1999 – present
Direct customer service, sales, purchasing, and distribution for $25 million, 10-state region, which encompasses Illinois, Indiana, Ohio, Minnesota, Wisconsin, Kansas, Arkansas, Michigan, Missouri, and Iowa. Supervise and train staff of five customer service representatives and work closely with three engineers to promote, sell, and service product line throughout region. Oversee key account relationships with SBC, BellSouth, Verizon, and Qwest, among others.

Select Accomplishments:

- Secured $10 million account to provide hardware and rack-and-stack services to SBC. Closed deal as a result of relationship building and meeting stringent conditions sought by SBC, through several quality audits.
- The Midwest region **ranked 2nd** out of five nationwide in revenue for both 2000 and 2001.

UNI GROUP — Boston, MA
(Largest non-RBOC owner of wireless towers in the US, employing 3,000 nationwide. Acquired by Towers, Inc., in 1998.)
NATIONAL SALES MANAGER, 1998 – 1999
Key player in developing relationships with national wireless carriers such as AT&T, Sprint, Ameritech, and Nextel in an effort to obtain Build-to-Suit, Co-location and Sale/Lease-Back contracts on a national level. Personally conducted assessment interviews with prospective clients to identify needs and formulate appropriate solutions.

Strategy: *Position this accomplished sales executive as an expert within the very competitive telecommunications industry.*

Neal Lawrence

Résumé – Page Two

CAREER HIGHLIGHTS

UNI GROUP *(continued…)*
Select Accomplishments:

- Attained multimillion-dollar contract with AT&T, which involved placement of 300 antennas by AT&T at 300 of Tower's sites. Contract terms specified rent of $1,200 to $3,000 monthly at each of the 300 sites for a period of 15 years. Contract was largest in UNI Group's history and instrumental in piquing Tower's interest in UNI Group.
- Developed marketing collateral and coordinated UNI Group's participation at the two largest wireless conventions.

BESTCO — Jacksonville, FL
(PCS company providing wireless services in the Southeast and Midwest US. Presently wholly owned subsidiary of Verizon.)
CORPORATE ACCOUNT MANAGER, 1996 – 1998
Targeted and sold high-revenue corporate customers in vertical markets comprising law firms, hospitals, financial institutions, and communications companies. Networked extensively throughout the business community at industry trade shows. Supervised five account coordinators that provided ongoing service to new and existing accounts.
Select Accomplishments:

- Played key role in the largest wireless commercial launch in the history of the industry, covering 11 national markets, including the state of Florida.
- Ranked in **top 10%** of all corporate account executives for 1997.

MOBILTEL *(A TeleSouth Company)* — Tampa, FL
(National provider of wireless data and paging services.)
MAJOR ACCOUNT EXECUTIVE, 1995 – 1996
SALES REPRESENTATIVE, 1994 – 1995
SALES ASSOCIATE, 1993 – 1994
Progressed rapidly in recognition of outstanding performance in sales and account management. Initially provided retail customer service and ultimately advanced to oversight of all major accounts within the state of Florida. Served as corporate liaison for training sales representatives on sales techniques, new technologies, and product launches.
Select Accomplishments:

- Placed within top **10% of 125** major account executives nationwide in 1996.
- **1st** among Jacksonville sales representatives in 1995.

EDUCATION

PROFESSIONAL DEVELOPMENT
- **STRATEGIC SELLING**
- **EAGLE SALES SYSTEM**
- Product Training on **CDMA** and **WIRELESS TECHNOLOGY**

GEORGIA SOUTHERN UNIVERSITY — Statesboro, GA
BA, MARKETING, 1993

RIVERSIDE MILITARY ACADEMY — Gainesville, GA
ACADEMIC DIPLOMA, 1989

KEVIN JOSEPH MCNEIL

500 Hero Avenue, Lake Forest, CA 92630 ■ Home: 949.555.5555 ■ Cell: 714.555.5555 ■ kjmn@hotmail.com

SENIOR SALES & MARKETING EXECUTIVE

Advertising & Publishing Industry

Strategic Sales & Marketing / Competitive Market Positioning / New Product Launch
Team Leadership / Advertising Production / Graphic Design & Layout

Twenty-year career as a member of several high-profile publishing-industry management teams. Goal-oriented individual successful in sales and marketing through expertise in business development and strategic business planning capabilities. Excellent presentation, negotiation, closing, and follow-through skills with a strong ability to build an industry presence. MBA degree.

CAREER HIGHLIGHTS

WEST COAST ADVERTISING SALES MANAGER – *Smith & Associates, Inc.,* San Francisco, CA (1999–Present)

Important member of sales management team for publishing-industry rep firm responsible for seeking and maintaining West Coast clients. Vital part of sales team that continues to grow client and revenue base year on year for national publishers. Full responsibility for West Coast advertising sales and marketing of trade show and publishing representation for various high-growth magazines.

- Directed market launch of five new publications in three years, delivering revenue growth as follows:

Publication	Advertising Increase	Monthly Revenue Increase
Washington Times	20 pages	$ 180,000
The Nation	22 pages	$ 75,000
Foreign Policy	9 pages	$ 55,000
American Prospect	4 pages	$ 16,000
Jet	4 pages	$ 7,000

- Expanded monthly revenue stream for *Washington Times* magazine to over $270,000 from $90,000 (5 pages–25 pages) through active participation in sales and business development that also included banner-ad sales and email newsletter-sponsorship sales.

WEST COAST ADVERTISING MANAGER – *The Progressive Magazine Co., Inc.,* Los Angeles, CA (1990–1998)

Established West Coast office and oversaw all advertising-sales efforts for the launch of national publication serving as a voice of national and international social justice.

- Increased annual advertising-sales volume by utilizing strong prospecting, account retention, and sales skills.
- Assisted in advertising design and layout, offering suggestions and preparing client advertisements.
- Conceived marketing strategy for an extraordinarily effective four-color advertising package and rate card.
- Generated new accounts through participation in trade shows and professional golf tournaments.

REGIONAL SALES MANAGER – *Weekly World News,* Chicago, IL (1980–1990)

In addition to focusing efforts on sales and overseeing regional sales team, responsible for all creative facets of design, layout, and production for *Weekly World News* magazine.

- Led team responsible for increasing nationwide sales by 40%–80% year over year.
- Achieved recognition as a leading agency manager for worldwide magazine.
- Spearheaded the "Taking Journalism to the Edge and Beyond" campaign that resulted in 350% increase in subscriptions nationwide.
- Obtained incisive reporting and in-depth political analyses from the most skilled, most seasoned news and editorial professionals in Washington.
- Instrumental in spearheading the redesign of *Weekly World News* with a more attractive and enhanced format and placing it first in its field.

Strategy: *The "front-and-center" chart is a compelling visual presentation of strong sales results.*

Kevin Joseph McNeil	**Page 2**	949.555.5555

EDUCATION & PROFESSIONAL DEVELOPMENT

CALIFORNIA STATE UNIVERSITY
- **MBA, International Business,** 1985
- **BS, Business Management,** 1979

PROFESSIONAL EDUCATION
- Completed more than 900 hours of Sales and Business Development courses.
- Participated in multiple Graphic Design and Editorial Layout conferences.

SPECIAL SKILLS

OPERATING SYSTEMS
- Cross-platform proficiency with PC & Mac.

SOFTWARE PROGRAMS
- Proficient with GoldMine, PageMaker, Microsoft Office, and others.

SPECIAL INTERESTS
- Skilled in Visual Arts including Photography and Design.

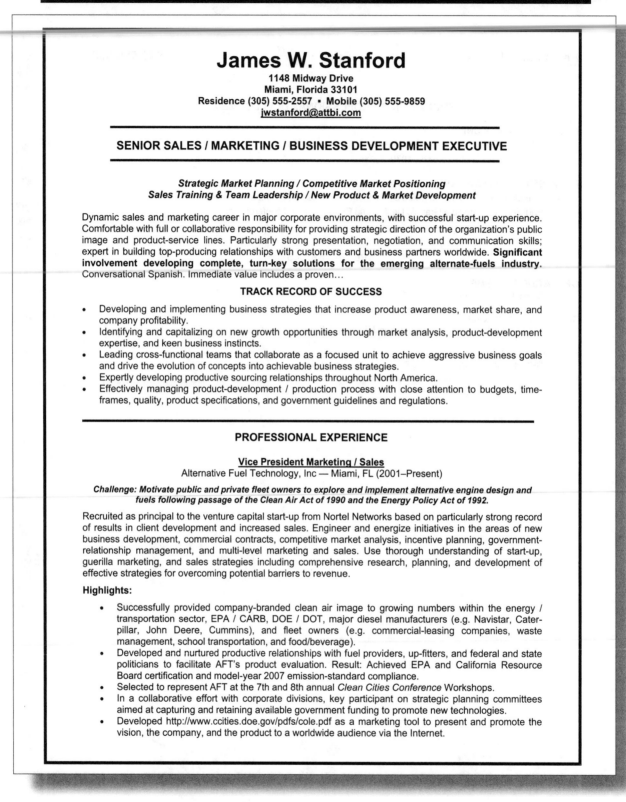

James W. Stanford

1148 Midway Drive
Miami, Florida 33101
Residence (305) 555-2557 • Mobile (305) 555-9859
jwstanford@attbi.com

SENIOR SALES / MARKETING / BUSINESS DEVELOPMENT EXECUTIVE

Strategic Market Planning / Competitive Market Positioning
Sales Training & Team Leadership / New Product & Market Development

Dynamic sales and marketing career in major corporate environments, with successful start-up experience. Comfortable with full or collaborative responsibility for providing strategic direction of the organization's public image and product-service lines. Particularly strong presentation, negotiation, and communication skills; expert in building top-producing relationships with customers and business partners worldwide. **Significant involvement developing complete, turn-key solutions for the emerging alternate-fuels industry.** Conversational Spanish. Immediate value includes a proven…

TRACK RECORD OF SUCCESS

- Developing and implementing business strategies that increase product awareness, market share, and company profitability.
- Identifying and capitalizing on new growth opportunities through market analysis, product-development expertise, and keen business instincts.
- Leading cross-functional teams that collaborate as a focused unit to achieve aggressive business goals and drive the evolution of concepts into achievable business strategies.
- Expertly developing productive sourcing relationships throughout North America.
- Effectively managing product-development / production process with close attention to budgets, time-frames, quality, product specifications, and government guidelines and regulations.

PROFESSIONAL EXPERIENCE

Vice President Marketing / Sales
Alternative Fuel Technology, Inc — Miami, FL (2001–Present)

Challenge: Motivate public and private fleet owners to explore and implement alternative engine design and fuels following passage of the Clean Air Act of 1990 and the Energy Policy Act of 1992.

Recruited as principal to the venture capital start-up from Nortel Networks based on particularly strong record of results in client development and increased sales. Engineer and energize initiatives in the areas of new business development, commercial contracts, competitive market analysis, incentive planning, government-relationship management, and multi-level marketing and sales. Use thorough understanding of start-up, guerilla marketing, and sales strategies including comprehensive research, planning, and development of effective strategies for overcoming potential barriers to revenue.

Highlights:

- Successfully provided company-branded clean air image to growing numbers within the energy / transportation sector, EPA / CARB, DOE / DOT, major diesel manufacturers (e.g. Navistar, Caterpillar, John Deere, Cummins), and fleet owners (e.g. commercial-leasing companies, waste management, school transportation, and food/beverage).
- Developed and nurtured productive relationships with fuel providers, up-fitters, and federal and state politicians to facilitate AFT's product evaluation. Result: Achieved EPA and California Resource Board certification and model-year 2007 emission-standard compliance.
- Selected to represent AFT at the 7th and 8th annual *Clean Cities Conference* Workshops.
- In a collaborative effort with corporate divisions, key participant on strategic planning committees aimed at capturing and retaining available government funding to promote new technologies.
- Developed http://www.ccities.doe.gov/pdfs/cole.pdf as a marketing tool to present and promote the vision, the company, and the product to a worldwide audience via the Internet.

Strategy: *Deemphasize age (using the Previous Career Assignments technique) and present a broad picture of qualifications across several industries.*

James W. Stanford – Page Two

National Sales Manager
Nortel Networks, Inc. — Richardson, TX (1978–2001)

Challenge: Develop and position Nortel Networks' flagship switching business solutions (voice / video / data) within the enterprise, public, and federal space.

Progressed rapidly through increasing levels of responsibility over 23-year tenure. In addition to campaign management, sales-team leadership, strategic planning, and new-market development, provided creative engineering solutions including patent design, technology white papers, pioneering standards for hi-speed terrestrial business communications, and long-term planning for NNI's product equipment.

Highlights:

- As National Sales Manager, accelerated revenue performance 400%, increased market share 30%, improved distributor revenue 350%, and increased GPM overall sales from 28% to 68%.
- Protected Nortel products against competition by leveraging new market opportunities, providing accurate market-trend analysis in emerging markets worldwide, and implementing highly effective account-management and customer-retention strategies.
- Consistently received Nortel Networks' highest customer satisfaction / loyalty survey scores.
- Conceived and closed a record-setting, ten-year service plan agreement worth in excess of $10 million with the New York City Transit Authority. Industry standard: three-year commitment.
- Designed and executed tradeshow exhibitions and assisted in the development of marketing / sales brochures, global competitive-market analysis, and sales / RFP support.
- Between 1989 and 2001, far surpassed peers by receiving four Circle of Honors Awards, four Circle of Excellence Awards, one Masters, and one President's Award for exceeding quota plus other company business objectives. In addition, recognized by executive management many times for consistently superior performance; earned honors, awards, and plaques.

PREVIOUS CAREER ASSIGNMENTS

Enroute Air Traffic Controller, Federal Aviation Agency — Albuquerque, NM
Facility Control Communications Leadman, LTV, Kentrol Hawaii, LTD. — Kwajalein, Marshall Islands
Covert Surveillance Agent, Central Intelligence Agency — Warrenton, VA

EDUCATION and PROFESSIONAL LICENSE / CERTIFICATIONS

State of Oklahoma University Systems — Norman, OK
Electrical Engineering coursework, 106 hours complete
Dean's List distinction

Diploma, Elkins Institute of Technology
Licensed Private Pilot
Diploma, Central Intelligence Agency School of Communications (Received Top Secret Security Clearance)
Radio Intelligence Certification — Army Security Agency Academy
Diploma, NEC Microwave School
Diploma, Federal Aviation Agency Academy
General Radiotelephone Operator's License (First Class Radiotelephone)
Second Class Radiotelegraph Operator's License (Ship-Shore Berthing)

CURRENT PROFESSIONAL AFFILIATIONS

Member, Institute of Electrical & Electronics Engineers
Stakeholder, Clean Cities Programs (Department of Energy)
Member, Telecommunications Consultant Programs

MILITARY SERVICE

United States Army Security Agency, Honorably Discharged

ALISON K. DAILEY

212 132nd North, Seattle, WA 98133   (206) 523-8989   akdaily@hotmail.com

MARKETING PROFESSIONAL

Driving strategic growth and product visibility in global, competitive markets.

Seventeen years' experience in marketing, public relations, and international product management. Demonstrated success record in:

- Leading business units and motivated teams.
- Guiding complex global product launches and strategic Internet technology initiatives.
- Initiating growing accounts and channel/partner relationships.
- Branding, managing, and positioning product lines.
- Creating effective multi-channel marketing campaigns.
- Providing pertinent research, content, white papers, and award-winning presentations.
- Incorporating emerging technology to achieve strategic goals. Expertise includes:
    - — Content management
    - — GUI creation, testing, CRM
    - — Deploying online services to ISPs/ASPs
    - — Personal computing operating systems
    - — Extensive list of software tools
    - — Network security/Internet file management

Industries: software, information technology, television broadcasting, and new media.

SAMPLE ACCOMPLISHMENTS

Led Executive Team and 30-person subsidiary though startup and public offering.

Increased direct-to-customer online sales by 300% as V.P. for ComputerConnect, Inc.

Secured profile of ComputerConnect CEO in The *Wall Street Journal.*

Demo God award winner, DemoMobile, 2001.

Managed corporate-identity project and successful IPO prospectus with Hornall Anderson.

PROFESSIONAL HISTORY

ComputerConnect, Inc. (formerly SCSI Software, Inc.), Redmond, WA   1999–2002

DIRECTOR OF BUSINESS DEVELOPMENT, Unit: RapidSync Technologies, Inc., Redmond, WA, 1/01–10/02

Named chief executive for new technology-licensing division, reporting to CEO. Charged with establishing business unit, developing business plan, overseeing transfer of intellectual property, creating software development kits, and securing potential licensees. Presented to potential investors. Led marketing, branding, sales, and legal research. Wrote white papers, technical data sheets, and application notes.

➤ **Managed Audio Labs partnership.** Forged licensing agreement, contract, and revenue plan.

MARKETING DIRECTOR, ComputerConnect, Inc., Redmond, WA, 5/99 to 12/00

Reported to CEO and managed a 12-person team with three director-level reports. Drove sales up 300%. Directed public relations, product marketing, marketing research, product branding, marketing communications, tradeshows and events, company web sites, advertising, direct marketing, sales team support, and business development.

Spearheaded special projects; prepared company business plan. Managed press coverage, investor relations, and strategic/tactical industry analysts contacts. Initiated the development and delivery of all sales tools for the direct customer sales teams, the corporate sales teams, and the OEM sales team.

➤ **Created highly effective retail point-of-sale, direct mail, and national radio campaigns.**

➤ **Launched technology initiative,** Internet File Management, attracting Oracle/major storage clients.

➤ **Reorganized product development process** to incorporate customer feedback.

Strategy: *Eliminate the "job-hopper" image that had come through on the candidate's prior resume by deleting some short-term jobs and using an umbrella heading to show continuity when the company name had changed. Stress significant achievements and expertise.*

RESUME 10, CONTINUED

| Alison K. Dailey | Professional History (continued) | **Page 2 of 2** |

StorageSecurity Technologies, Kirkland, WA   **1998–1999**

MARKETING MANAGER, 08/98 to 04/99

Reported to Vice President of Marketing. Hired, supervised, and evaluated a five-person team. Charged with developing partnership programs and directing customer communications, web-site sales, tradeshows and events, advertising, corporate identity, and sales-support programs. Supplemented rapid-growth phase with effective communication strategies, supporting successful IPO.

➤ **Delivered over $1,000,000 in sales per month** by creating a new web-site program.

➤ **Ran vendor-selection process for branding/IPO project,** selecting Hornall Anderson.

➤ **Produced cutting-edge event during N+I,** placing top management before key analysts and press.

➤ **Contributed to development of a first-ever firewall security service** for emerging ISP market.

MediaItalia-Presse, Milan, Italy   **1996–1998**

MANAGER, SALES AND MARKETING, North America, New York, NY, 11/96 to 07/98

Directed North American marketing communications including online/print promotions, direct mail, and VIP visits. Coordinated programs with Asian and European marketing directors. Researched North and South American information markets. Led and initiated strategic media product-development initiatives. Managed relationships/international contracts with information partners and major news organizations.

➤ **Led strategic initiative for "IntraSport" online real-time World Cup sports coverage.**
— URL reached 94% of Spanish households.
— Initiative enabled MIP to sign Spain's top five publications and Internet/portal companies worldwide.
— Garnered record revenues from sales of MIP's World Cup coverage to Spanish media firms.

Associated Press/NewsLink, New York, NY   **1994–1996**

GENERAL MANAGER, MARKETING, Associated Press, Media Unit, New York, NY, 09/94 to 11/1996

Steered development and launch of company's first Internet-based platform, NewsLink. Led NewsLink marketing, public relations, and research initiatives. Developed comprehensive profiles of publishing customers and competitors. Conducted extensive marketing research to strategically position products.

➤ **Authorized interactive database tools for measuring/monitoring new marketing initiatives.**

➤ **Positioned two industry-leading product lines** including corporate identity, new brochures, sales kits, tradeshow messages, booth design, and direct-response marketing via an interactive web site.

➤ **Developed strategic marketing relationships with international news information providers** including Agence France-Presse, Knight-Ridder/Tribune, Reuters, and UPI.

Dell Computer, Los Angeles, CA   **1992–1993**

MARKETING MANAGER, FEDERAL DIVISION, Washington, DC, 05/92 to 09/93 and 09/86 to 11/87

➤ **Managed Dell's relationship with Clinton White House** and Presidential Inaugural Committee.

➤ **Created direct-response programs, realizing 5%–8% response rates.**

➤ **Spearheaded development of cutting-edge multi-media Executive Briefing Center.**

➤ **Acted as Personal Consultant to Office of the Secretary of the Interior,** presenting first-ever interactive presentation to the United States Senate.

Other positions:
Regional Marketing Representative, Macromedia, Eastern Territory, New York, NY, 02/91 to 04/92
Assistant Interactive News Producer, NBC News, New York, NY, 03/89 to 01/01
Marketing Research Manager/Product Evangelist, GUIGuide, Inc., Washington, DC, 11/87 to 03/89

EDUCATION/PUBLICATIONS

B.S., Information Marketing, with honors. Georgetown University, Washington, DC, 1992
Co-Author: *Strategic Positioning for On-Demand New Media Technologies.*

NOEL FIORE

45 Hilgard Avenue, Los Angeles, CA 90095 ▪ noelfiore@itcom.net ▪ Cell: 310-825-0002 ▪ Work: 310-616-2020

BRANDING & CUSTOMER RETENTION EXPERT
Goal: A strategic position developing new business in a growing consumer products company.

EXECUTIVE PROFILE & SKILLS

Versatile marketeer and "green thumb" business developer with 15 years' experience in branding, product development, niche expansion, and customer marketing. Branding champion. Customer retention expert. Inspired leader and mentor.

▪ Product and brand strategy	▪ Loyalty programs	▪ Profitable corporate cultures
▪ Brand P&L management	▪ Retention marketing	▪ Winning teams
▪ Brand R&D	▪ Mature product growth	▪ Leadership development
▪ Brand acquisition	▪ Internet marketing strategy	▪ Goal-oriented management
▪ Brand launch	▪ SBU & product launch	▪ P&L management

BRANDING & BUSINESS DEVELOPMENT HIGHLIGHTS

- **Conceived and launched ancillary products for a 31-year-old business.** Simultaneously maintained existing branding and expanded marketing to attract a new segment of the niche audience.
- **Developed and launched Internet business for a health group.** Created strategy to sell web-based newsletters. Managed partners, vendors, and web experts to ensure a successful launch.
- **Turned acquisition—traditionally a loss leader—into a profitable division.** Added $13 million to the bottom line. Developed analytical and competitive-intelligence models and built a top-notch acquisition marketing team in 6 months.
- **Grew subscriber base from 0 to 30,000 in 3 months—and increased profit $6 million.** Marketed a newsletter to affluent investors; focused on increasing net wealth quickly through market timing and undervalued stocks.

CUSTOMER RETENTION & STRATEGY HIGHLIGHTS

- **Expanded readership of a mature publication from 30,000 to 100,000 in 1 year.** Increased profits 50% for a 10-year-old publication.
- **Increased lifetime value of customers and generated low-cost income stream.** Developed a new, customer-relevant, auto-shipment program and corresponding strategy, copy, and follow-up mailings.
- **Retained only 50% of an existing customer base, but increased its profitability by 20%** in just 1 year. Strategically merged the existing subscriber base into a newsletter business. Simultaneously marketed valued-added complements and maintained original branding and editorial mission.
- **Helped devise retention/add-on sales strategy for floundering product—increased profit by 15%.**

LEADERSHIP DEVELOPMENT HIGHLIGHTS

- **Turned nonprofit think-tank culture into profitable business leaders and thinkers.** Influenced profitability and value proposition as measures for "good ideas" at The Policy Institute.
- **Produced a P&L-focused, brand-aware team.** Emphasized time management and eliminated time-intensive tasks with low payoff to raise awareness/increase productivity.
- **Set a corporate standard to ensure leadership development** by retaining a team executive coach.
- **Taught teams proven database-testing/market-modeling/business-analysis methods.** Tested, evaluated, and rolled out database-marketing models and techniques to evaluate, strategize, and analyze viable business opportunities.

Strategy: *Use a functional format to show very strong accomplishments in three different areas; match functional headings with three columns of skills in the Profile.*

NOEL FIORE
Page Two

CHRONOLOGICAL EMPLOYMENT HISTORY

THE POLICY INSTITUTE — Los Angeles, CA
A public-policy research foundation promoting public-policy debate and involvement of lay people in the role of government.
General Manager & Co-Publisher, *THE PUBLIC's POLICY MAGAZINE*, 02/2000–Present

RADIO MEDIA — Los Angeles, CA
Creator, producer, and broadcaster of 1-minute direct-response radio commercials for various products.
VP, Marketing, 04/1999–01/2000

WORLDWIDE PUBLISHERS, INC. — New York, NY
$400 million publisher of quality products/services for private investors and health-conscious consumers.
VP, Customer Acquisition, Health Group, 1998–1999
VP & Group Publisher, Women's Group, 1997–1998
VP, Customer Acquisition, Newsletters Group, 1995–1997
Marketing Director & Group Publisher, Investment Group, 1990–1995
Sr. Marketing Manager, Investment Group, 1988–1990
Direct Marketing Manager, Investment Group, 1987–1988

EDUCATION & AFFILIATIONS

B.S., Marketing — UCLA (Los Angeles, CA), 1987

Leadership Development — L.A. Coaching, 1991
Leadership Coaching — Leadership Research International, 1995

Computer Skills — MS Office 2000/97, e-mail, web browsers, and Windows 2000/98/95.

Member, DMA California (Direct Mail Association) — CA, 1999–Present
Member, DMA — NY, 1990 to 1999

PUBLICATIONS & AWARDS

Publication: "Returning a Mature Newsletter to Profitability" *(Business Marketing)* — NY, 1997
Publication: "Expand Your Marketing, Expand Your Niche" *(Advertising Age)* — NY, 1999
Publication: "Branded for Life" *(Brandweek)* — NY, 2000

Award: Best Investment Magazine *(Consumer Marketing)* — NY, 1995
Award: Best Marketing Article (Adweek.com) — NY, 2000

E-mail: noelfiore@itcom.net ▪ Cell: 310-825-0002 ▪ Work: 310-616-2020

DIANE REED

803 N. 10th Street
San Jose, CA 95110

(408) 225-3421 Home   d_reed@msn.com   (408) 936-2424 Cell

International Marketing Manager

PROFESSIONAL SUMMARY

Motivational global marketing evangelist with 15 years of proven results. Strong ability to create and communicate a call to action. Proven ability to increase sales, build brand awareness, and promote a company's image. Talent for keeping both the big picture and all of its facets in mind. Strong ability to build enthusiasm around object of marketing. Ability to successfully relate to and work with diverse people, adapt to cultures, and travel extensively. Outstanding communication skills as a trainer, educator, and motivator. Unequaled professional who embraces change and thrives on challenge.

Collaborative Marketing: Established marketing relationships with big players such as Intel, Microsoft, and Sun Microsystems.

Budget Management: Managed seven-figure marketing budget. All projects delivered within or under budget.

Innovative Techniques: Successfully approached circuit-board marketing as B2C product.

International Relationship Building: Traveled worldwide, successfully developing key markets and relationships.

PROFESSIONAL EXPERIENCE

CADENCE DESIGN SYSTEMS, INC., San Jose, CA   1999–2002
Manager, Worldwide Field Marketing
Worked collaboratively to define product direction and technology enhancements to create market-driven, solution-based tools. Traveled to Europe and Pacific Rim to meet with customers and the Cadence Design Systems field organizations in a marketing evangelist role.

- Worked collaboratively to successfully launch (both externally and internally) four products in an 11-month time period.
- Successfully collaborated to enter into joint marketing relationships with Intel, Microsoft, and Sun Microsystems.

HEWLETT-PACKARD COMPANY, Palo Alto, CA   1995–1999
Corporate Director of Marketing
Managed the Hewlett-Packard products and services branding campaign by creating the most effective, visible, and consistent marketing communications of any printed circuit board company in North America. Closely collaborated with trademark attorneys to protect intellectual properties, logo, and name. Assisted in investor-relations activities, including compliance with SEC regulations and communicating to shareholders, financial media, and financial analysts. Assisted in developing prospectus when company went public in 1996.

- Instrumental in company growth from 2 to 19 divisions domestically and internationally. Revenues increased from $50 million to $240 million.
- Managed and allocated annual marketing budget, which grew from $50,000 in 1992 to $1.5 million. Met budget on every project.
- Innovator of new approach to circuit-board marketing as not only a B2B but also a B2C product.
- Developed global marketing and international collateral for Israel, Singapore, Hong Kong, Malaysia, Japan, China, Scotland, Ireland, and England. Traveled frequently to these regions and developed ongoing relationships with key influencers, including editors and publishers of trade magazines in Asia, Israel, Europe, and the United States.

Strategy: Create a strong resume to reflect the candidate's level of professionalism and highlight her relationship-building skills, record of innovation, and international expertise. Note that this individual does not have a college degree.

DIANE REED   Page Two
_____

Professional Experience, Continued

HANOVER CORPORATION (Sister Company of Hewlett-Packard), Menlo Park, CA   1994–1995
Director of Sales and Marketing

Managed sales and marketing for start-up company while on loan from Hewlett-Packard. Developed company positioning and image from start-up phase to completion. Developed collateral to launch initial product. Assisted in development of English/Hebrew user manual. Completed the mission of helping create a company and making it attractive to an outside buyer.

UNITED AIRLINES, Chicago, IL   1986–1993
On-Duty Manager, In-Flight Operations (1990–1993)

Handled all in-flight irregularities and on-board crises from a crisis-communications/damage-control standpoint. Served on various task forces to develop better ways to serve customers while saving the company money.

Corporate Sales Development and Marketing Research, UA Headquarters (1986–1990)

Researched ways to improve customer satisfaction and boost return on investment. Made recommendations on event sponsorships, product endorsements, and co-op endorsements with other companies.

EDUCATION

Working toward **B.S. in International Business/Marketing,** San Jose State University, San Jose, CA

Additional Professional Development Coursework:

High-Tech Marketing, Everest Advisory Group, 2001
Value Selling Workshop, Value Vision Associates, 2000
Value Differentiation Workshop, Value Vision Associates, 2000
Working Collaboratively, Leadership Dynamics, 2000
Fundamentals of Finance and Accounting for Non-Financial Professionals, American Management Association International, 1998
Conflict Management Skills for Women, SkillPath Seminars, 1998
Strategic Planning for High-Tech Markets, Oregon Graduate Institute, 1998
Winning Technology Leadership, Ivey Business School, Executive MBA Program, London, Ontario, Canada, 1996

PROFESSIONAL AFFILIATIONS

American Marketing Association
Women in Technology, Inc.
American Electronics Association

■ ■ ■

ROBERT S. MARTINO

198 Parkway Avenue
Chesapeake, VA 23322

(757) 626-1974
rsmartino45@earthlinnk.net

SENIOR EXECUTIVE — PRODUCT MARKETING AND MANAGEMENT

Record of defining, delivering, and marketing timely, profitable leading-edge products

High-powered senior product manager with 10 years of increasingly responsible experience driving product strategy and execution. Technology-product expertise includes networking and telecom hardware / software, enterprise-class software, brand-awareness products, and web-delivered products / services. Team builder / leader / motivator who emphasizes goal achievement.

Candidate differentiators include: a sophisticated understanding of marketing and finance that enables successful product-strategy development with a focus on profitability; ability to anticipate market trends and initiate timely product development.

HIGHLIGHTS

- Grew revenues by 250% through new- and existing-product development.
- Launched six major software product releases generating $30 million in annual revenues.
- Created a consumer-service product line that added 35% to bottom-line profits.
- Orchestrated the integration of product lines from four acquisitions, creating a unified product strategy.

PROFESSIONAL EXPERIENCE

AGILE ENTERPRISES, INC., Washington, DC
1999 to 2003
Develops and markets enterprise-software solutions to retailers, e-tailers, and publishers worldwide.

Provided strategic product and operational leadership. Defined product roadmap. Managed product-line P&L. Positioned products to customers, analysts, and sales force. Managed full product lifecycle from requirements definition through first customer ship. Directed a team of eight software engineers.

Vice President, Product Marketing and Management (2001 to 2003)

- Redesigned processes and accomplished turnaround of an underperforming function.
- Transitioned company from a focus on selling services to an out-of-the-box deployment model with higher profit margins.
- Launched six major software products generating $30 million in annual revenues.
- Built and institutionalized product-management and product-marketing functions.

Director, Product Marketing and Management (1999 to 2001)

- Drove the development of five major software releases, nine new products / services, and seven product enhancements within a $300 million business unit.
- Assessed market demand and developed service offerings for six industries.
- Added $2 million in annual revenues by identifying and delivering product enhancements with a profit margin of 80%.
- Integrated products, services, and business and financial infrastructure for four acquisitions representing a combined revenue stream of $50 million.

Strategy: *Use a "tagline" to pinpoint the key value of this candidate; use a Highlights section to emphasize four impressive achievements.*

ROBERT S. MARTINO   PAGE 2

VIDEOSOLVE CORPORATION, Alexandria, VA   1998 to 1999
Markets and manufactures voice, video, and data-communications software and equipment.

Group Product-Line Manager
Defined market and product requirements for audio-conferencing software and hardware solutions; managed product programs, facilitated new business development, and led cross-functional project teams.

- Created requirements and roadmap for entry into IP-based products.

- Defined market and product requirements for Internet-based and client-server–based conference-scheduling applications.

- Recruited and managed beta customers.

- Product champion to customers, sales force, and partners.

TECHPHONE, INC., Alexandria, VA   1997 to 1998
A venture-backed startup that markets and manufactures a small-office PBX sold directly through an on-premise call center and commerce-enabled web site.

Director, Product Marketing
Comprehensive and pivotal role that included defining the business plan for services and accessory products and developing content and e-commerce requirements for the corporate web site. Managed $1.8M budget.

- Created value-added consumer-service products contributing over 35% to the bottom line.

- Created an accessory product line. Selected products / vendors and negotiated OEM relationships, deliverables, and service agreements.

- Led e-commerce web-site project. Wrote RFQs, selected partners / vendors, and evaluated and selected commerce-related applications.

- Built and led a call-center applications team.

VIDEOTECH, INC., Washington, DC   1992 to 1997
Manufactures network equipment and software for use on circuit-switched and IP networks.

Director, Services Product Marketing
Accountable for services business development, technical-product definition, sales, customer and reseller contracts, corporate technical publications, and web site.

- Increased revenues more than 250% during tenure by identifying demand-generation opportunities and driving programs for new and existing products.

- Consistently achieved ambitious sales goals in a highly competitive market.

- Defined, positioned, branded, marketed, and sold technical service products and programs accounting for $6+ million in annual sales.

EDUCATION

ROCHESTER INSTITUTE OF TECHNOLOGY, Rochester, NY   1992
Bachelor of Technology in Computer Science

Keywords: VP of Product Marketing and Management, Senior Product Marketing Manager, requirements definition, technical specifications, beta testing, product development & release cycle, product evangelist, market requirements, product enhancements, product marketing & positioning, product strategy development, communications, networking, IP

CHAPTER 5

Resumes for Managers and Executives in Social Services, Associations and Non-Profits, Government and Military, and Law

- Counselor

- Social-Services Manager

- Social-Services Director

- Non-Profit Association Manager

- Government Contracts Manager

- Government Management Consultant

- Veterans Affairs Manager/Administrator

- Law-Enforcement Manager

- Security Director

- Prosecutor

- Trial Attorney

- Executive Director

Mary K. Trent, M.Ed., LPC

1001 Walnut Drive
McKinney, TX 75069

mkr1@cox.net

Home: 972.562.3444
Mobile: 214.794.9000

LICENSED PROFESSIONAL COUNSELOR

Over 13 years' experience as a clinician providing:

- *Crisis intervention, therapy, advocacy, and support services for victims of or witnesses to family violence, sexual assault, and other violent crimes.*
- *Therapy services to battered and abused women and their families.*
- *Therapy and support services to abused and traumatized children, adolescents, and their families.*
- *Case management and coordination and referrals for additional mental-health and social services needed by clients.*
- *Clinical services as part of multidisciplinary teams.*

Extensive training and experience in providing therapy services in both the public and private sectors. Additional areas of therapeutic expertise and experience:

- *Depression, anxiety, divorce*
- *Family relationship issues*
- *Child and adolescent issues*
- *Illness and disability issues*
- *Grief, bereavement, and loss*
- *School concerns*
- *Parenting issues*

PROFESSIONAL TRAINING AND EDUCATION

Galveston Family Institute: Individual and Family Therapy—one-year doctoral-level practicum supervised by Victor Loos, Ph.D., Clinical Psychologist

Houston Child Guidance Center: Individual and Family Therapy for Children, Adolescents and Adults—one-year training supervised by Patrick Brady, Ph.D., Clinical Psychologist

National Organization for Victim Assistance (NOVA), National Community Crisis Response Team Training—Basic and Advanced—60 hours

Numerous hours of continuing professional education including training in Family Violence, Child Abuse, Play Therapy, Sexual Abuse, Trauma, Bereavement and Loss, and Suicide Prevention

M.Ed., Counseling Psychology, University of Houston

M.A., Programs for the Deaf (Educational Administration and Supervision), California State University, Northridge

B.S., Deaf Education and Mental Retardation, Texas Tech University

LICENSURE

Texas Licensed Professional Counselor (LPC)

Strategy: *Downplay experience (most of which was in school settings) and focus on professional credentials and a strong summary to position this social-services professional who had transitioned to the health-care industry.*

Mary K. Trent, M.Ed., LPC

Page Two
mkr1@cox.net

Home: 972.562.3444
Mobile: 214.794.9000

CERTIFICATIONS

School Counselor (Texas, all-level)
Mental Retardation (Texas, all-level)
Deaf Education (Texas, all-level)

Professional Mid-Management (Texas)
Special Education Supervisor (Texas, all-level)
Educational Supervisor (Texas, all-level)

SELECTED PROFESSIONAL ACCOMPLISHMENTS

- Experienced therapist with traumatized individuals and families from multicultural backgrounds and across all income levels.

- Leader in the development and implementation of the Houston Independent School District's (HISD) North District Community Guidance Center situated in low-income and high-violence area of Houston.

- Served on multidisciplinary teams with other mental-health professionals including social workers, nurses, psychologists, speech therapists, physical therapists, and consulting physicians.

- Successful program development and implementation—assisted in writing and implementing a $1 million grant for a violence-prevention program—one of six awarded by the Department of Education.

- Designed and developed district-wide plan for the implementation of HISD's Student Assistance Programs for Safe and Drug Free Schools.

- Developed, designed, and implemented an HISD district-wide program for deaf/multi-handicapped students from 3 to 22 years.

- HISD VIPs (Volunteers in Public Schools) Outstanding Employee Award.

- Presenter at local, state, and national conferences.

EXPERIENCE

Therapist and Consultant, La Rosa—non-profit community agency serving battered women and families, Houston, TX

1998 to 2001

Counselor, North District Community Guidance Center and Alternative School, Houston Independent School District (HISD), Houston, TX

1995 to 2001

Counselor Specialist, Student Assistance Program, HISD, Houston, TX

1991 to 1995

Group Therapist, Houston International Hospital, Houston, TX

1989 to 1990

Assistant Principal, T.H. Meager School and Grady Special School—gifted and talented and deaf and multi-handicapped students; **Instructional Supervisor,** Regional Program for the Deaf; HISD, Houston, TX

1975 to 1989

MEMBERSHIPS AND VOLUNTEER ACTIVITIES

Memberships—American Counseling Association, Texas Counseling Association, AK Rice Institute, Texas Center

Volunteer activities—Family Service Center; Children's Sex Abuse Program; Casa de Esperanza, serving abused and traumatized children; and Big Brothers/Big Sisters of Houston

Mehdi Ghattas

1192 Shoreline Drive • Boca Raton, Florida 33426   561.555.5976 • mghattas@hotmail.com

Professional Profile

Highly motivated management and training professional committed to quality, documentation, and accountability to ensure the best opportunity for staff and youth success. Linear thinker whose talents lie in planning, organizing, and delivering staff-development activities that strengthen individuals, teams, and organizations. Excellent presentation and interpersonal skills. Demonstrate an ability to effectively prioritize and manage a broad range of responsibilities:

- Staff Training
- Crisis Management
- Supervision

- Curriculum Development
- Case Management
- Quality Assurance

- Behavioral Modification
- Public Relations
- Safety and Security

Skills and Experience

For over six years have supported the growth and development of innovative approaches to the treatment of high- and moderate-risk juvenile offenders.

Administration/Management

- Provide management and direction to programs and operations, ensuring the welfare and safety of staff and residents. Have provided oversight and supervision to as many as 102 students and 70 staff at various treatment facilities.
- Interface with private and government regulatory and funding agencies including the Department of Juvenile Justice, Department of Education, Home Builders Institute, OSHA, Environmental Protection Agency, and the US Department of Labor.
- Assign and instruct professional and paraprofessional employees and supervise their work performance; make recommendations for staffing assignments to gain maximum benefit from individual employee strengths.
- Serve as the rotating Duty Officer, on 24-hour call for emergencies; use appropriate crisis-intervention and behavioral-management techniques to maintain control.

Quality Assurance

- Plan and administer quality-assurance and health-and-safety programs to ensure standards, goals, and objectives are being met.
- Conduct ongoing internal audits to ensure the highest standards of contract compliance are met, in accordance with government regulations and all federal, state, and local laws.
- Direct the establishment and maintenance of financial records, student demographic and treatment records, operational policies and procedures, EPA/OSHA compliance documentation, and personnel files.
- Prepare clear, sound, accurate, and informative written reports, containing findings, conclusions, and recommendations concerning the status and improvement of the quality-assurance and risk-management programs.
- Identified and addressed a weakness in the documentation system at one facility by better defining requirements and assuming position as "point person" for the review and evaluation of all paperwork.

Strategy: *Use a skills-based format to convey highly transferable skills; combine education and work history to minimize several short-term positions.*

Mehdi Ghattas
561.453.5976
Page 2

Training and Staff Development

- Design and conduct numerous staff development programs using a wide variety of teaching aids, motivational techniques, and implementation strategies to engage participants in active learning.
- Have trained hundreds of youth-development professionals using a combination of commercial and custom-designed curriculum materials. Training expertise includes:

  - Adolescent Development
  - Stress Management
  - Defensive Tactics
  - Child Abuse and Neglect
  - Behavioral Modification
  - Suicide Prevention
  - Cultural Diversity
  - Gang Awareness
  - Leadership Skills

- Prepare and maintain reports and records of staff training activities to ensure ongoing certification requirements, using Access, Excel, and Word.
- Develop personal rapport with staff, nurturing their individual strengths while helping them overcome employment challenges.
- Address staff retention issues by integrating career planning and personal goal setting into the staff orientation program.

Education and Professional Training

BA Organizational Management, Warner Southern College, Lake Wales, FL

Certified Crisis Intervention Techniques Instructor

Certified Use-of-Force Instructor
   Florida Department of Law Enforcement, Miami-Dade Community College

Certified Peer Reviewer, Florida State Department of Quality Assurance

CPR and First Aid Certified

Employment History

Florida Youth Academy, Boca Raton, FL   Nov 1999 to Present
Hired as a Group Home Manager; promoted to Community Manager within the first month and assigned responsibility for staff training and quality assurance.

Youth Services International (a wholly owned subsidiary of Correctional Services Corporation)
Employed in various capacities at facilities in MD, DE, FL   Sep 1994 to May 1995 and
                                                                   Jul 1996 to Nov 1999

   Senior Youth Counselor, Youth Academy, Sabillasville, MD
   Team Leader, Program Director and Assistant Director, Youth Academy, Florida City, FL
   Training Manager, Juvenile Detention School, Baltimore, MD
   Training Manager, Youth Center, Wilmington, DE
   Program Director and Assistant Program Director, Bartow, FL

KEITH A. GARDNER, LCSW

2551 Barton Avenue, Rotterdam, New York 12306 • Tel: 518-355-5600 • Email: kagdirect@mindspring.com

ADMINISTRATIVE DIRECTOR

BUSINESS DEVELOPMENT — STAFF DEVELOPMENT — TRAINING/COACHING/MENTORING

RESIDENTIAL TREATMENT • HOSPITAL • FOSTER CARE • WILDERNESS PROGRAMS
Early Intervention and Group Treatment for Adolescent Sex Offenders

DYNAMIC, GOAL-ORIENTED LICENSED CLINICAL SOCIAL WORKER combining broad-spectrum life experiences with 18 years' extensive hands-on experience directing and working in all facets of 24/7 residential treatment. Solid track record of launching successful programs to enhance development and rehabilitation of youth. Strong interpersonal skills and innate ability to relate to diverse personalities with emphasis on team leadership and development. Demonstrated leadership skill to drive ground-breaking concepts to revolutionize change initiatives that affect social work industry-wide while expanding operational revenues. Will relocate and travel.

❑ **STRATEGIC AND CREATIVE THINKER** with solid background of delivering decisive, action-driven administrative leadership. Demonstrated insight and proficiency in developing and streamlining early-intervention programs.

❑ **RESULTS-ORIENTED,** with proven capacity to accelerate growth and deliver substantial profits. Catalyst for success with powerful capacity to build and create from concept.

❑ **PERFORMANCE-DRIVEN TEAM LEADER** with excellent interpersonal skills, optimally utilizing all channels of communication to develop team momentum, enthusiasm, and pride. Promote group harmony.

CORE LEADERSHIP QUALIFICATIONS

- Strategic Business Planning & Development
- Change Management
- New Business Development
- Project Management
- Problem Identification/Resolution
- Case Management/Support Services

- New Venture & Program Start-up/Launch
- General Operating Management
- Process Reengineering
- Tactical Planning/Leadership
- Strategic Marketing & Sales
- Cross-Functional Team Leadership

"DRIVING CHANGE TO IMPROVE LIVES"

SELECTED ACCOMPLISHMENTS

❑ **SARATOGA RANCH:** Conceived, developed, and launched from ground up an early-intervention, work-ethics program for state-custody adolescent males 13–17. Delivered innovative strategies and concepts to enhance the lives of over 500 youth that **resulted in only 10% recidivism** after three years.

❑ **MAPLE GROVE BOYS RANCH:** Developed concept and format of program for 18-bed facility housing state-custody adolescent male sex offenders age 13–18. **First program of its kind in New York State.**

❑ **JUVENILES NETWORK ON OFFENDING SEXUALLY (JNOOS):** Co-Founder and Charter Member. Developed and created initial standards and protocols. New York State, State University of New York at Albany, and the Juvenile Justice endorse organization, with current membership of about 100.

❑ **APPLE RIDGE RANCH SCHOOL:** Spearheaded development from conception to successful launch of accredited school delivering curriculum to 25 students and resulting in **dramatic increase in individual test scores.** Wrote proposals to receive funding of $240,000 annually through Youth in Custody grants.

❑ **BUILD A BETTER YOU:** Co-founder of 12-bed program for teenage girls age 12–17.

Strategy: *Highlight specific, significant programs in the Selected Accomplishments section, which follows a comprehensive summary outlining key qualifications. Emphasize successful outcomes throughout the resume.*

KEITH A. GARDNER, LCSW

PROFESSIONAL CAREER HISTORY

Highland Ridge Youth Services, Schenectady, NY   1984–present
Private agency providing foster care and support services for adolescents in state custody.

CLINICAL DIRECTOR (1991–present)
MEDICAID ENHANCEMENT SERVICES COORDINATOR (1993–present, concurrent with above)

Manage and oversee residential care for three group homes providing sex-offender-specific program, residential group home care, clinical services, proctors, and tracking. Coordinate intake screenings, clinical treatment, and all oversight for seven licensed clinicians. Scope of responsibility includes Quality Assurance and Medicaid enhancement as well as training and staff development.

- Introduced Saratoga Ranch, which **increased revenues by 40%** ($700,000 annual budget) based on fixed contract as well as **consistent 90% occupancy rate.**
- Delivered **100% Quality Assurance rating,** with no sanctions.
- Oversee and direct Apple Ridge Ranch, 15-bed facility for non-sex-offending males and self-contained accredited school.
- Administer and manage Build A Better You Ranch, 12-bed group home for teenaged girls, as well as Maple Grove Aftercare Program.

CLINICIAN (1991–1993)
Facilitated sex-offender-specific program for clients in custody of Division of Youth Corrections and Division of Child and Family Services.

PROGRAM COORDINATOR — Maple Grove Boys Ranch (1987–1993)
Assisted in the development and launch of program for 18-bed inpatient treatment program for adolescent male sex offenders. Directed and oversaw all aspects of operation including supervision and coordination of staff. Provided clinical oversight for residents in program.

SUPERVISED RESTITUTION COORDINATOR (1984–1987)
Coordinated daily progress notes, monthly and court reports, summaries, intakes, and screening of adolescent youth for program.

EDUCATION & PROFESSIONAL DEVELOPMENT

Licensed Clinical Social Worker (LCSW), 1993
Master of Social Work Program, 1991
Bachelor of Science — Sociology, Criminology Certificate, 1987
STATE UNIVERSITY OF NEW YORK, ALBANY, NEW YORK

Primary Children's Child Protection Team, 1990
TREATMENT OF SEXUALLY REACTIVE CHILDREN AND VICTIMS OF SEXUAL ABUSE

Certificate: Treatment of Juvenile Sex Offender, 1988
SYMPOSIUM SPONSORED BY STATE UNIVERSITY OF NEW YORK
STATE UNIVERSITY OF NEW YORK / COMMISSION ON CRIMINAL AND JUVENILE JUSTICE

Certified Addictions Counselor, 1987
O'HENRY HOUSE ADOLESCENT UNIT — INTERNSHIP

PROFESSIONAL AFFILIATIONS

National Affiliation of Social Workers — NASW, 1998–present
Private Psychology Network, Member 1994–2002
Juveniles Network On Offending Sexually (JNOOS), Charter Member 1990–present

Diana M. Drexel

21 Towbridge Court, Lawrenceville, NJ 08648
(609) 883-5555 Home ▪ dmdrexel5555@hotmail.com

Director / Program Administrator / Development Coordinator
Not-for-Profit Service Agencies ▪ Professional & Trade Associations

Committed, experienced non-profit administrator of federally funded human-services program, with additional leadership experience in diverse non-profit activities. Successful in revenue raising and volunteer recruitment and retention, as well as corporate development, community outreach, and media relations. Expertise in:

✓ Special Events Management	✓ Volunteer Recruitment & Training	✓ Grant Writing
✓ Marketing Communications	✓ Financial / Budgetary Management	✓ Fundraising
✓ Educational Programming	✓ Public / Private Partnerships	✓ Public Relations

Effective organizational skills, proactive team involvement, and independent decision-making have yielded dramatic results for development and program expansion. Proven talent for writing, interpersonal relations, and communications. Computer literate: Windows NT/2000, MS Office 2000, Word, Excel, MS Outlook, Internet.

PROFESSIONAL EXPERIENCE

Seniors in Service to America (SSA), Princeton, NJ   1999–present
United Way of Central New Jersey program serving seniors age 55 and older in member-driven organization. Provides volunteer opportunities for work or mentoring in non-profit agencies throughout Mercer County, as well as member development, education, and services.

Director
Recruited to oversee revitalization of established federal program. Collaborated with Advisory Council in strategic planning, policy development, and mission planning. Administered 3 key programs concurrently, including daily operations, public and media relations, and marketing. Budget allocation ($200K) kept on target.

- **Organizational Leadership.** Directed and supervised 800-member volunteer activities at 80 local agencies, as well as the Breast Screening Awareness Program and Food Direct Program (providing homeless shelters with food). Served as liaison with United Way senior management, agency directors, site managers, corporate sponsors, community groups, and government officials.

- **Volunteer Recruitment.** Acquired 175 new volunteers through persuasive public speaking at targeted community / senior centers and corporations. Kept member-retention figures stable in challenging times.

- **Member Services & Training.** Promoted realistic expectations for volunteer services, ensuring proper volunteer training at site agencies, as well as staff development and training for site managers. Expanded member communications (including quarterly newsletter) and updated marketing collaterals.

- **Program Expansion.** Grew Breast Screening Awareness program from 3 to 8 sites, recruiting 12 new leaders. Quadrupled grant awards for Food Direct Program and secured high-profile community ties.

- **Grant Writing & Fundraising.** Wrote successful grant proposal for renewed federal and United Way funding. Won state funding for Breast Screening Awareness Program by showing program's viability.

- **Sponsorship Procurement.** Gained corporate sponsorship from CommunityOne (Princeton nursing home) for the Food Direct Program, contributing to increased revenues and improved community visibility.

- **Event Planning.** Spearheaded and directed all aspects of annual Recognition Brunch for 800+ participants including volunteers, public officials, sponsors, and site managers. Doubled revenues from previous year.

Continued

Strategy: "Interrupt" reverse-chronological work history with a category for Volunteer Activities because they are more directly related to the candidate's present career focus than are her previous jobs.

RESUME 17, CONTINUED

Diana M. Drexel

(609) 883-5555 Home ▪ dmdrexel5555@hotmail.com

Page 2

VOLUNTEER / NON-PROFIT EXPERIENCE

Community Ties, Inc., Princeton, NJ   1997–2002
Steering Committee / Publicity Chairperson

- Created and implemented a comprehensive public-relations and advertising program for the annual Gourmet Tour Dinner fundraising event, benefiting local hunger-relief programs. Increased revenues year-over-year at this event attended by 600 people. Grew revenues by 50% in 5 years to $90,000 in 2002.

South Brunswick High School, South Brunswick, NJ   1994

- Won highest level of corporate giving from local and national companies (such as Kraft Foods), including $17K in contributions and $21K in gifts-in-kind, as Chairperson of one-day post-prom event for 750 seniors. Directed and integrated activities of 8 committees providing food, entertainment, and prizes.

Rotary Club of Central New Jersey, Trenton, NJ   1992

- Pioneered concept of restaurant and gourmet gift shop for annual Community House Tour event, which raised $25K in revenues within 3 weeks of operation for this non-profit fundraiser.

- Coordinated year-long project management, supervised staff of 10, and assisted in planning successful advertising campaign, including increasing advertising from corporate sponsors in program book.

OTHER RELATED EXPERIENCE

Account Consultant, Psychometric Consulting, Inc., Woodbridge, NJ   1998

- Advised and consulted with Fortune 500 and other companies on psychological assessment results for this international human-resources consulting firm. Analyzed test results and wrote 5-8 in-depth individual reports daily, clearly and concisely communicating complex psychological constructs and impact of results.

Freelance Writer and Consultant   1987–1997

- Wrote general-interest and investigative feature articles published in local newspapers and national trade publications including *The Princeton Packet, The Trenton Times, Holistic Living* magazine, *ACT/Advertising Communications Times,* KYW News Radio, AARP's *Modern Maturity* magazine, and *Philadelphia NOW.*

Instructor — Journalism Department, Rutgers State University, New Brunswick, PA   1985–1987

- Taught introductory journalism courses (including Introduction to Mass Media) to undergraduate students.

Feature Writer & Investigative Staff Reporter, *The Trenton Times,* Trenton, NJ   1983–1985

- Published revealing feature article on teenage drug abuse that proved instrumental in the award of a $100K federal grant for a methadone maintenance clinic, enabling the clinic to remain in operation.

EDUCATION & TRAINING

Bachelor of Science — Communications, Rutgers State University, New Brunswick, NJ

Ongoing Professional Development:
Grant Writing Skills Seminar, Rutgers University, New Brunswick, NJ (2002)
Leadership and Team Excellence Workshop, United Way of America, Washington, DC (2001)
Community Service in Action Training Conference (2000)

AFFILIATIONS

Association of Fundraising Professionals (AFP) ▪ Communications and Marketing Association (CAMA)

LISA DAVIDSON

1668 West King Street, Honolulu, Hawaii 96734 • (808) 555-0127 • yogarose@coconut.org

*Seeking **Management** position in a*
NON-PROFIT ORGANIZATION

QUALIFIED TO PERFORM

- *Mission Planning and Implementation*
- *Organizational Development*
- *Leadership Training*
- *Marketing Communications*
- *Media Relations*
- *Public Relations*
- *Corporate Relations*
- *Fundraising*
- *Grassroots Campaigns*
- *Community Outreach*
- *Educational Programming*
- *Member Development and Retention*
- *Member Communications*
- *Volunteer Recruitment*
- *Volunteer Training*
- *Special Events Management*

EDUCATION

Columbia College, Columbia University—
New York, NY
B.S., English Literature
(Journalism/Ancient Religions concentration)
- Editor of campus weekly magazine
- Awarded Cornell Woolrich Fellowship

PROFILE

18+ years' experience in dynamic organizational settings, including past 8 years in positions of bottom-line accountability. Background includes history of creating and building various small businesses. Effective communicator highly skilled in multiple environments— public speaking, groups, and one-on-one. *Core skills include:*

Organizational Leadership	Project Management
Persuasive Communications	Problem Resolution
Staff Management	Training and Development
Presentations	Workshops
Customer Service	Cross-Cultural Awareness
Research	Written Communications

PROFESSIONAL HISTORY

Career and Life Coach 1995–Present
Honolulu, HI; Seattle, WA; Florence, Italy; London, England

Consult with and advise—in-person and by telephone—clients of a variety of personal backgrounds and professional levels. Select clients include: lawyers, child services professionals, non-profit board members, non-profit fundraisers, artists, and cultural diversity trainers. Work closely with one assistant on scheduling matters.
- Successfully partner with clients, assisting them through major life transitions.
- Conceptualize, plan, and write all marketing materials for life and career-development workshops.
- Communicate with media regarding workshop promotional plans. Consistently attract 5 to 20 participants.
- Mentor other professional teachers and workshop presenters on planning, implementation, and problem resolution.
- Publish quarterly client newsletter with circulation of 150.
- Have designed and led weekly workshops on subjects ranging from stress management to decision making.

Certified Yoga Instructor 1999–Present
Honolulu, HI; London, England

Currently perform private therapeutic sessions. Have taught daily classes of up to 40 students, including new-student orientations. Handled all administrative functions.
- Employ various levels of persuasive communication according to individual student's level, expectations, and goals.
- Have assisted hundreds of people in recovering from injuries, addiction, and stress, helping them develop positive mind and body attitudes.

PROFESSIONAL HISTORY Continued on Page 2 →

Strategy: *Focus on highly transferable skills from the candidate's diverse career experience as a business owner, instructor, and office administrator. Use distinctive left-column format for eye-catching list of qualifications.*

LISA DAVIDSON
Page 2 of 2

Founder/Manager/Sales Representative   **1997–1999**
Handworks, Inc.—Seattle, WA

Accountable for bottom-line success of this on-site chair massage service at natural-food supermarket franchises. Contracted out and supervised 11 massage therapists. Acted as liaison between customers, employees, and corporate management.
- Spearheaded comprehensive public relations campaign to educate public about services.
- Successfully planned and built business from scratch. Sold it after only two years.

Jin Shin Jyutsu Practitioner   **1994–1999**
Private Practice—Seattle, WA

Built thriving private practice providing Japanese *Jin Shin Jyutsu* style of bodywork.

Founder/Manager/Sales Representative   **1994–1995**
Davidson Delicacies—Seattle, WA

Managed all aspects—production, sales, distribution—of this wholesale natural-food venture, including materials procurement, kitchen operations, order fulfillment, and account maintenance. Negotiated terms for 20+ accounts throughout Seattle area.
- Launched and grew profitable business, starting with no knowledge of business world or industry.
- Positioned company for success by implementing unique marketing message. Attracted attention of national buyers (including a national food distributor).
- Created *Climbing Cookie* and other unique concept products. Customers still ask for them at area stores.

Administrative Assistant   **1992–1993**
The Family Schools—Seattle, WA

Oversaw all front- and back-office operations for experimental alternative school program of the Seattle public school system. Program focused on community development of elementary school programs.

Program Assistant   **1990–1992**
Neighborhood Initiative Programs—Seattle, WA

Accountable for program and event planning for this government-funded program providing leadership training and education for low-income and minority communities. Wrote grant proposals, press releases, business communications, and marketing materials. Assisted in design of Community Leadership Training Program.

Communications Assistant   **1989–1990**
Williams & Stevenson—Baltimore, MD

Collaborated to compose marketing proposals and newsletter pieces. Managed administrative functions in communications department of this international law firm.

Communications Assistant   **1984–1988**
Pratt, Gregg, & Nakamoto—Baltimore, MD

Charged with authority to assess prospective client case potential. Generated press releases and marketing materials for this entertainment law firm. Researched and wrote one partner's weekly column for New York newspaper.

~ References Furnished on Request ~

JOHN N. FINE

8321 Tree Branch Road
Columbia, MD 21045

301.884.0321
jnf@aol.com

CAREER FOCUS

ACQUISITIONS MANAGEMENT
Contract Administration · Proposals · Purchasing · Logistics · Inventory · Supply Chain

EXECUTIVE PROFILE

Optimize investments with effective acquisition solutions—building high profits in relation to cost. Skilled business analyst, process planner, and technical expert. Conduct advanced and complex systematic reviews to formulate and execute business strategies, reducing risk and enhancing customer satisfaction. Business Advisor—provide functional guidance on multifaceted projects. Operations Executive and Senior Logistician with emphasis in the following:

▪ Department of Defense Contracts	▪ Equipment & Services	▪ Create Teaching Tools
▪ Medical Supply	▪ Quality Assurance	▪ Author Guidebooks & SOPs
▪ 'Customer Relations First' Philosophy	▪ Commercial Contracts	▪ Design Web Sites

- Twenty years' in-depth acquisition experience including detailed knowledge of FAR, DFAR, and AFAR. Combined expertise in logistics, information management, proposals development, contract administration, organizational requirements, supply, personnel needs, financials, and executive-level leadership.
- Department of Defense (DoD)/Federal, State, and Local Government Contract Technical Expert.
- Contract Knowledge: Firm Fixed Price (FFP), Information Management & Information Technology, Facilities, Time & Material, Blanket Purchase Agreements, Competitive, IDIQ and Requirements, Sole Source, Performance Based, Labor Hour, and Incentive Contracts. Follow acquisitions through complete lifecycles.
- Manage proposal and solicitation preparation, develop cost/price analyses, write contracts, conduct negotiations, and oversee contract administration, awards, termination and audits, and systematic reviews. Formulate contract polices, procedures, methods, and performance standards.
- Assemble and motivate cohesive working teams. Build consensus and mobilize resources.
- Microsoft Office Suite, Procurement Desktop (PD2), Standard Army Contracting System, dBASE.

PROFESSIONAL EXPERIENCE

Certified Professional Contract Manager (CPCM) / Top Secret Clearance

Director/Acquisition Business Advisor, Contracting Office Center—North America
The Pentagon, U.S. Air Force (*Contracting Warrant: Unlimited*)   1997–Present
- Plan, direct, and oversee major contracting activities for various elements, maintaining high quality, responsive contracting support covering 40 states. Develop and implement operating policy and procedures for supplies, services, and equipment.
- Direct the contracting and purchasing activities of a 70-person staff responsible for $200 million in procurement and contract actions annually. Manage a $7.1 million operating budget. Provide technical advice to senior management, staff, and supported activities. Translate problems into practical solutions.
- Utilize Action Reform Techniques including commercial purchases, performance-based statements of work, and award term contracts.
- Supervised contract administration personnel for a health insurance contract worth $3.7 billion.
- Awarded 27,000 contract actions valued at $90 million in a four-year period.

Strategy: *Condense a 20-year military career into a compelling two-page resume for this military acquisitions and procurement manager transitioning to the government or corporate sector.*

John N. Fine, Page 2

Accomplishments Continued
- Implemented initiatives to provide excellent customer support: designed and authored handbooks and web-site content including organizational links to assist customers in processing requests. Developed web-based on-line credit-card customer training, now the standard within the organization.
- Met or exceeded metric goals for competition, small business, credit card, and women-owned businesses.

Acquisition Resident, Directorate of Contracting, U.S. Air Force, Washington, DC   **1995–1997**
- Completed the federally mandated Defense Acquisition Course to attain certification as a contracting professional. Warranted contracting officer for contract actions up to $25 million.
- Contract Specialist: Procured, coordinated, and administered contracts/actions including medical equipment and architectural-engineering/construction contracts. Served as Program Manager, Contracting Interface, and Financial Manager for acquisitions worth $40 million in programs worldwide.

Distribution Program Manager, Directorate of Materiel, VA   **1993–1995**
- Directed major distribution program functions including excess, samples, depot balance reports, ready-for-issue stocks, and government-furnished materials.
- Coordinated with six DoD distribution centers and one Defense Depot Headquarters. Conducted assistance visits, reviewed processes, performed inventories, tracked progress and implementation of programs, and determined the adequacy and effectiveness of operations.
- Educated the depots regarding their role in various programs. Made recommendations for improvements of the depot/distribution system—including interim solutions allowing the depots to receive commercial materials without impacting their systems or workload. Conducted training to units on supply automation.
- Combined inventory-management practices and automation skills to design a "down-load" for the depots that interfaced directly into their automated systems—allowing the program to be expanded system-wide, resulting in an inventory reduction of $81 million.
- Established and headed a Joint Committee, with representatives from various DoD agencies, to make recommendations on interfaces and working procedures required between private industry and DoD.

Chief, Logistics Division, Materiel Management Command, Europe   **1990–1993**
- Directed logistical administration for a $175,000 supply contract, a $145,000 housekeeping contract, and $81,000 in linen; managed a $4.5 million property book account, monitored biomedical maintenance operations, and supervised the equipment-acquisition programs for a $35 million major construction project. Coordinated directly with engineers for facility support.
- Developed a responsive Logistics Customer Assistance Program and a Logistics Quality Assurance Program, significantly improving logistical indicators. Instituted a division-wide training program.

Chief, Materiel Branch; Accountable Officer, Services Branch, Logistics Division, AF Base, FL   **1986–1990**
Supply Officer/Administrative Manager, Fort Bragg, NC   **1984-1986**

EDUCATION & PROFESSIONAL DEVELOPMENT

Master of Science, Procurement and Contract Management, University of Maryland, 1989
Bachelor of Science, Management Science, Virginia State University, 1985

Acquisition Logistics Management · Configuration Management · Executive Contracting
· Defense Acquisition Internship, Directorate of Contracting
(Level III Certified in Contracting, Level III Trained and Level II Certified in Acquisitions Logistics)

· National Association of Contract Managers, member

PROFILE

- Senior management/administrative skills combined with a lifetime of service in the public sector.
- Conceptual talent for seeing "the big picture," pinpointing an organizational objective, and setting goals and priorities to achieve it.
- Expertise in strategic planning, program development and management, budget development and administration, human resource management, daily operations, team building, and staff development.
- Dedicated to implementation of EEO principles and practices, including special emphasis programs. Excellent trainer, speaker, motivator.
- Advanced knowledge of public administration, law, police, and security issues. In-depth understanding of U.S. Federal Law Enforcement and Customs Aviation/Marine Programs.
- Background includes extensive cross-cultural experience, with worldwide contacts in government and law enforcement.
- Consistently commended for professionalism and outstanding performance—two investigations remain among the biggest in Customs history.
- Basic comprehension of Spanish language.
- Licensed private pilot and open-water SCUBA diver.

Devon W. White

777 West Georgia Avenue
Billings, WA 98080
(330) 334-8800

Management Consultant—
Top Secret Security Clearance

*"...implemented a management philosophy
which is founded in honesty, integrity,
and responsibility...
one of the finest managers the USCS
employs."*
LGB, Acting Branch Chief

"When leaders are responsive, their people will be enabled, will accomplish program goals, and will implement the organizational vision." D.W. White

Awards and Recognition

Special Achievement Awards, United States Customs, Office of Investigations and Office of Aviation Operations
Letter of Commendation, United States Department of Justice
Letter of Commendation, United States Attorney General, San Diego, California
Department of Treasury Certificates of Award
United States Customs Service Employee Recognition Awards

Association Membership

International Association of Chiefs of Police
Retired Federal Investigators
Association of Border RATS

Education

Law Enforcement / Management—U.S. Government
Administration of Justice—Michigan State
Pre-Med—Michigan State

Strategy: *Clearly identify the job target ("management consultant") and support it with a strong profile, awards, and recognition before detailing experience on page 2.*

EXPERIENCE VITA   DEVON W. WHITE

U.S. BUREAU OF CUSTOMS, Washington, DC   1969–2000
Criminal Investigations

- Participated in management/administrative capacity through growth of Aviation Program, its maturation, expansion into the foreign arena, and current state of fiscal constraint and downsizing. Provided executive leadership for Aviation Program; interfaced with high levels of administration and Congress; directed staff of 760 and C3I operations for nine branch locations. Oversaw $260 million annual budget and over a billion dollars in aircraft and watercraft. Testified before Congress and presented information, justification, and persuasion in support of programs and activities. Developed, implemented, and integrated the Command Control Communication and Intelligence activities. Supervised, planned, and directed the work of others.

- Developed, implemented, monitored, and coordinated regional and national policy, guidelines, and programs concerning all aspects of Air Division and Patrol operations throughout U.S. Conducted complex organizational and procedural studies to include both operational and administrative activities. Identified problems and effected remedial action. Coordinated intensified enforcement activities with other elements of Customs and federal, state, and local agencies.

- Coordinated intensified enforcement activities with other elements of Customs as well as federal, state, and local agencies. Acted as Regional Patrol Director when designated, assuming direct-line authority over regional contingent of Air Support personnel.

- Conducted, coordinated, and supervised complex Congressional, special-inquiry, and full-field investigations that required thorough knowledge of all policies, regulations, and laws concerning Customs Service. Made arrests, took sworn statements, prepared extensive criminal and non-criminal case reports, submitted affidavits in support of arrest and search warrants, testified in courts of law. Developed criminal and public sources of information.

- Enforced all laws and regulations under jurisdiction of Drug Enforcement Administration. Developed confidential sources of information and directed activities. Coordinated and supervised development of complex criminal-conspiracy investigations. Wrote complex criminal case reports, submitted support affidavits, made arrests, and testified in courts of law. Made calm, sound judgments based on experience and initiated appropriate enforcement actions.

Director, Customs Aviation and Marine Programs, San Diego, CA, 12/96–6/00
Deputy Director, Customs Aviation Operations Center West/DAICC, Riverside, CA, 1987–1996
Operations Branch Chief/Customs Aviation Operations Division, Washington, DC, 1984–1987
Group Supervisor, Houston Aviation Operations Branch, Spring, TX, 1983–1984
Director of Aviation Operations, Southwest Region, Houston, TX, 1982–1983
Air Division Staff, Customs, Washington, DC, 11/80–3/82
Assistant Regional Patrol Director, Regional Customs Facility, Long Beach, CA, 1978–1980
Special Agent / Criminal Investigator, Internal Affairs, Long Beach, CA, 1973–1978
Criminal Investigator, Drug Enforcement Administration (DEA), San Diego, CA, 7/73–12/73
Criminal Investigator, Customs, Office of Investigations, San Ysidro, CA, 4/70–6/73

ESCONDIDO POLICE DEPARTMENT, Escondido, CA, 1965–1970
Detective, Narcotics, 1967–1970
Conceived and implemented office narcotics program.
Patrol Officer, Escondido Police Department, 1965–1967

Walter E. Cook, Jr.

4218 Springfield Drive
Knoxville, TN 37075

waltcook@comcast.net

Home (865) 826-3908
Office (865) 736-8300

SENIOR-LEVEL MANAGER / ADMINISTRATOR

Veterans Affairs / Disability Claims / VA Health-Care Eligibility / VA Law

- More than 20 years of successful performance in the diverse and complex arena of Veterans Affairs, including 15 years of management experience as a National Service Officer for Disabled American Veterans.

- Sound leadership and business-management abilities complemented by professional, hands-on, administrative style that inspires a goal-oriented work environment and ultimately enhances the quality of care for veterans.

- Consistently achieve budget- and grant-funding goals. Ten-year history of successfully preparing annual grant proposals for DAV Colorado Trust and DAV Charitable Trust.

- Solid business insight, with the ability to ascertain and analyze needs, forecast goals, streamline operations, and implement new program concepts. Proven skill at reorganization and successful turnaround of nonproductive, inefficient operations.

- Strong strategic vision coupled with overall business sense and attention to detail.

- Extensive knowledge of anatomy, medical terminology, and physiology; VA claims processing (from initial application, to rating decision, through appellate process); VA Nursing Program; Aid to States for Care of Veterans in State Homes; and VA Benefit Delivery Network (BDN).

- Accredited to practice before US Department of Veterans Affairs. Have testified before US Congress and state legislatures of Maryland and Montana.

Professional Experience

DISABLED AMERICAN VETERANS — US Department of Veterans Affairs   1978–Present

Supervisor, National Service Officer, 1983–Present, Knoxville, TN & Fort Hamilton, MT
Associate National Service Officer, 1978–1983, Washington, DC

Operations Management
- Oversee and direct all daily operations, functions, and decisions of state nonprofit veterans' organization that represents veterans in dealing with VA health-care eligibility and processing disability claims.
- Ensure effective representation of DAV clients through application of laws and regulations administered by US Department of Veterans Affairs.

Budget Development / Grant Writing
- Develop budgets and write grant proposals to ensure sufficient funding for Field Service Office program. Secure funding from DAV Colorado Trust and DAV Charitable Trust.
- Create budgets for six field offices, including salary, training, travel, and supplies.

Human Resources Management
- Supervise four National Service Officers, six Field Service Officers, and two secretaries, as well as volunteer support staff throughout the state.
- Created state program to define and develop job descriptions, employment policies, and employee manuals for state field offices.
- Have trained and supervised professional, accredited Service Officers to practice before US Department of Veterans Affairs.

Strategy: *Emphasize Veterans-industry expertise plus general administrative skills for this federal government administrator seeking to transition into a management role for the VA at the state level.*

Walter E. Cook, Jr. _____ Page 2

Professional Experience (continued)

Persuasive Communication
- Develop and nurture effective dialogue and cooperation between DAV state office and directors of each VA Medical Center and Regional Office Center in Tennessee.
- Extensive interaction with elected officials at federal, state, and local levels; nonprofit veterans' organizations; volunteer agencies; and oversight committees.

Educational Background

MANAGEMENT AND LEADERSHIP PROGRAM — 1996 — University of Colorado at Denver

DAV STRUCTURED AND CONTINUING TRAINING PROGRAM, PHASES I, II, & III

BACHELOR OF SCIENCE — University of Baltimore

Military Service / Veteran Status

US Army Military Police, 1969–1972
Served in Republic of Vietnam from 1970–1972. Service-connected, compensably disabled veteran.

Presentations / Public Speaking

- **Instructor, DAV Training Academy,** University of Colorado at Denver, October 2000

  Led two-week course on proper application of Parts III and IV of 38 Code of Federal Regulations. Developed detailed lesson plan and created practical models to clearly demonstrate specific rating concepts. Also developed comprehensive final examination to fully evaluate each trainee's knowledge and understanding of principles of rating disabilities.

- **Keynote speaker** before delegates of state DAV conventions; federal, state, and local conferences; and panels with leading veterans' organizations regarding veteran-related issues. Spoke to Johns Hopkins School of Law to argue legal defense of post-traumatic stress.

- **Conducted seminars** on readjustment problems of Vietnam veterans. **Made numerous presentations** to mental health professionals and medical schools, up to 2,000 audience members.

- **Testified** before Maryland State Assembly, Montana State Assembly, and Veterans Affairs Subcommittee in Washington, DC. **Submitted written briefs** before US Department of Veterans Affairs supporting specific arguments.

Professional Affiliations

Disabled American Veterans' Guild of Attorneys-in-Fact
Life Member, Knoxville Chapter, Disabled American Veterans

CHARLES WILSON

2158 Hampton Lane, Cincinnati, OH 45219
513.426.9568
cwilson@ci.cincinnati.oh.us

CAREER PROFILE

A results-oriented, high-energy LAW ENFORCEMENT LIEUTENANT with 20+ years of progressively responsible experience in the Public Service area. Highly developed administrative and analytical skills as evidenced by the ability to continuously improve division operations. Qualified by:

Investigative Techniques	DEA Certification	Evidence Collection
Police Media Relations	Supervision & Training	Emergency Response
Conflict Resolution	Search & Seizure	Technical Surveillance
Protection Programs	Defense Management	Professional Development

PROFESSIONAL EXPERIENCE

CINCINNATI POLICE DEPARTMENT, Cincinnati, OH   1984–Present

Lieutenant of Detective Division, 1997–Present
Lieutenant of Patrol Division, 1996–1997
Sergeant of Patrol Division, 1994–1996
Detective Division—Forensics, 1992–1994
Field Training Officer, 1989–1992
Patrol Officer, 1984–1989
Prior police experience in various security positions, 1981–1984

KEY ACCOMPLISHMENTS

- Supervise 7 investigators assigned 330+ cases per year, gathering and analyzing sufficient evidence in major crime cases to achieve an average solvability rate of 40%.

- Supervised three-year investigation of a major drug enterprise leading to the seizure of 200 kilos of cocaine and the indictment of 40+ individuals on state and federal charges.

- Increased charge rate 10% due to advanced investigative techniques and technology training.

- Redesigned police department schedules to allow for 100 hours per year of in-service training for all officers in the department.

- Modernized Detective Division's infrastructure by purchasing new computers and reconfiguring office space to allow for increased communications.

- Equipped cruisers with laptop computers and CAD-RMS (Computer-Aided Dispatch—Records Management System) software, increasing report-writing efficiency and reducing paperwork 80% for Patrol Division officers.

- Led Patrol Division with 50 drunk-driving arrests, accounting for 10% of total arrests.

- Updated forensic lab equipment and coordinated training for all officers, leading to increased evidence-collection capabilities for the police department.

- Police "Officer of the Month" presented by the Cincinnati Police Department—October 1993.

Strategy: *Place the most important information on page 1; then enhance page-2 listings with the logos of highly sought-after accomplishments in law enforcement.*

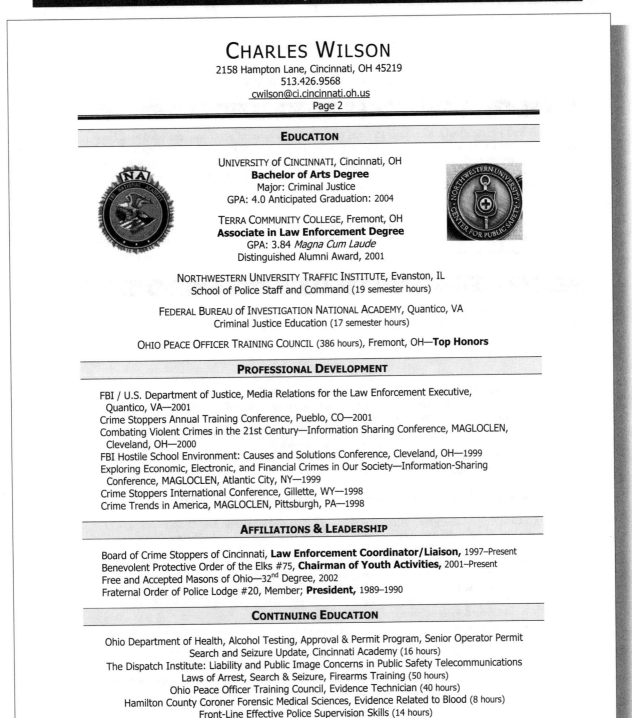

CHARLES WILSON
2158 Hampton Lane, Cincinnati, OH 45219
513.426.9568
cwilson@ci.cincinnati.oh.us
Page 2

EDUCATION

UNIVERSITY of CINCINNATI, Cincinnati, OH
Bachelor of Arts Degree
Major: Criminal Justice
GPA: 4.0 Anticipated Graduation: 2004

TERRA COMMUNITY COLLEGE, Fremont, OH
Associate in Law Enforcement Degree
GPA: 3.84 *Magna Cum Laude*
Distinguished Alumni Award, 2001

NORTHWESTERN UNIVERSITY TRAFFIC INSTITUTE, Evanston, IL
School of Police Staff and Command (19 semester hours)

FEDERAL BUREAU of INVESTIGATION NATIONAL ACADEMY, Quantico, VA
Criminal Justice Education (17 semester hours)

OHIO PEACE OFFICER TRAINING COUNCIL (386 hours), Fremont, OH—**Top Honors**

PROFESSIONAL DEVELOPMENT

FBI / U.S. Department of Justice, Media Relations for the Law Enforcement Executive,
  Quantico, VA—2001
Crime Stoppers Annual Training Conference, Pueblo, CO—2001
Combating Violent Crimes in the 21st Century—Information Sharing Conference, MAGLOCLEN,
  Cleveland, OH—2000
FBI Hostile School Environment: Causes and Solutions Conference, Cleveland, OH—1999
Exploring Economic, Electronic, and Financial Crimes in Our Society—Information-Sharing
  Conference, MAGLOCLEN, Atlantic City, NY—1999
Crime Stoppers International Conference, Gillette, WY—1998
Crime Trends in America, MAGLOCLEN, Pittsburgh, PA—1998

AFFILIATIONS & LEADERSHIP

Board of Crime Stoppers of Cincinnati, **Law Enforcement Coordinator/Liaison,** 1997–Present
Benevolent Protective Order of the Elks #75, **Chairman of Youth Activities,** 2001–Present
Free and Accepted Masons of Ohio—32nd Degree, 2002
Fraternal Order of Police Lodge #20, Member; **President,** 1989–1990

CONTINUING EDUCATION

Ohio Department of Health, Alcohol Testing, Approval & Permit Program, Senior Operator Permit
Search and Seizure Update, Cincinnati Academy (16 hours)
The Dispatch Institute: Liability and Public Image Concerns in Public Safety Telecommunications
Laws of Arrest, Search & Seizure, Firearms Training (50 hours)
Ohio Peace Officer Training Council, Evidence Technician (40 hours)
Hamilton County Coroner Forensic Medical Sciences, Evidence Related to Blood (8 hours)
Front-Line Effective Police Supervision Skills (14 hours)
Defensive Tactics Training (16 hours); Public Safety Training, Saving Our Own Lives (16 hours)
FBI / U.S. Department of Justice / DEA, Basic Narcotics and Dangerous Drug Law Enforcement (80 hours)

PAUL ANDERSEN

4733 Mockingbird Lane, Fairfax, VA 22033
(571) 631-8595   pandersen@email.com

QUALIFICATIONS SUMMARY

Results-oriented individual with more than 15 years of security-management experience preceded by a law-enforcement career with the Dade County (Florida) Police Department. Skilled at collaborating with law enforcement officials to develop and promote crime-prevention initiatives. Adept at implementing procedures to reduce theft and increase employee awareness. Accustomed to working with individuals at all levels of responsibility within corporate, retail, and governmental organizations.

AREAS OF STRENGTH:

- Physical Security
- Multi-Site Management
- Investigative Activities

- Law Enforcement
- Theft Prevention
- Project Administration

- Employee Training
- Community Partnerships
- Corrective Actions

PROFESSIONAL EXPERIENCE

AMERICAN CAR RENTAL COMPANY, INC.   1988–2001
Promoted through increasingly responsible security-supervision positions with this leading car-rental company.

Director of Security, Orlando, FL (1999–2001)

Selected to investigate criminal activity and human-resource issues, under the Executive Vice President's direction, at more than 200 locations throughout the United States and Canada.
- Investigated complaints of sexual harassment, discrimination, and workplace violence and recommended corrective actions to upper management.
- Promoted the prevention of internal and external theft, employee drug use, and credit-card fraud, serving as a liaison to law-enforcement agencies.
- Participated in internal mediation and provided testimony in the event of employee litigation.
- Instituted employee training on credit-card fraud and employee awareness.

Regional Security Manager, Combined East Coast/Florida Regions, Orlando, FL (1994–1999)

Maintained responsibility for a 20,000-car fleet and 2,000 employees at all East Coast locations in 13 states from Maine to Florida. Administered a "hands-on" approach to improve the area's status as number two on the list of cities with the most car thefts.
- Collaborated with security officials throughout the City of Orlando to establish a rapid-response communication system between the police department and hotels and car-rental agencies.
  - Achieved zero car thefts from American's Orlando facilities for more than three years.
- Instituted physical security measures, increased employee awareness, and installed theft-deterrent devices on commonly stolen vehicles.
- Established a cooperative program with Miami's Police Department and Airport Authority that achieved the following results:
  - Reduced Miami's rate of car thefts by 50% from approximately 12,000 to 6,000 annually, with 50% decreases occurring in subsequent years.
  - Implemented cooperative programs throughout Florida based on the success in Miami.
  - Achieved the car-rental industry's lowest rate of car theft.
  - Achieved zero car thefts from American's Miami facilities for more than 13 months.
  - Received two awards from the City of Miami Police Department and the Miami Airport Authority for "outstanding contributions to law enforcement efforts."

Continued

Strategy: *Develop a strong executive resume, loaded with achievements, for a well-qualified law-enforcement and security professional.*

RESUME 23, CONTINUED

Paul Andersen   **Page 2**

Regional Security Manager, Florida Region, Orlando, FL (1993–1994)

Supervised a 12,000-car fleet at 11 Florida locations, reporting to the Regional Vice President.
- Coordinated an annual security seminar for up to 300 participants from Florida law-enforcement agencies, the automobile and hotel industries, county officials, and American's employees.

City Security Manager, Washington, DC (1988–1993)

Selected to define a newly created position for preventing and investigating internal and external theft.
- Maintained responsibility for a fleet of 5,000 automobiles, reporting to the City Manager.
- Monitored the activities of more than 200 employees, serving as a liaison to law-enforcement agencies in investigating criminal activities including credit-card fraud and stolen automobiles.

CALLOWAY CORPORATION, Washington, DC   1984–1988

Security Manager

Supervised a staff of 23 people to prevent and investigate internal and external theft for one of the country's largest-volume discount retailers.
- Monitored the activities of approximately 200 employees to detect and prevent internal theft.
- Guided staff in apprehending more than 1,000 shoplifters during a 13-month period.
- Completed a comprehensive, five-week classroom and on-the-job training program addressing auditing and retail industry practices.
- Administered responsibilities in various departments including shipping and receiving, the front office, and hardware and software.

DADE COUNTY POLICE DEPARTMENT, Orlando, FL   1969–1984
Retired from the Force as a Detective, Grade 1, following a distinguished law enforcement career, having received outstanding performance awards from the Chief of Police and numerous letters of commendation from citizens.

Narcotics Investigator (1971–1984)
- Advised and assisted undercover officers among the county's seven districts.
- Administered the county's centralized handling of narcotics investigations.
- Initiated investigations of narcotics trafficking throughout the county.
- Served as a law-enforcement expert providing testimony in federal and local courts.
- Lectured and trained officers in conducting undercover investigations.
- Prepared cases for successful prosecution in court.

Uniform Beat Officer (1969–1971)

EDUCATION

Police Administration Certification, University of Florida, Orlando, FL
Economics/Business Courses (13 semester hours), Dade County Community College, Orlando, FL

COMPUTER SKILLS

Proficient with database software, MS Word, e-mail, and Internet applications.

RESUME 24: ARNOLD BOLDT, CPRW, JCTC; ROCHESTER, NY

PETER H. DESMOND, ESQ.

123 Garden Street
Hackensack, New Jersey 07602
(201) 321-9376 (Days) / (201) 209-6204 (Evenings)
desmondph@netscape.net

Admitted to the Bar — State of New Jersey

SUMMARY

Accomplished felony prosecutor with 10-year track record that encompasses successfully trying rapes, robberies, armed assaults, and firearms crimes in New Jersey Superior Court, County Court, and municipal courts.

- **Demonstrated capacity to cooperate effectively with a broad array of law-enforcement agencies and prosecuting attorneys at federal, state, and local levels.**
- **Extensive experience researching, analyzing, and interpreting case law relating to both criminal and civil issues.**
- **Direct experience prosecuting firearm felonies as part of "Project Exile" task force.**
- **Highly organized, with excellent time-management skills and ability to balance demands of heavy caseload.**

LEGAL EXPERIENCE

BERGEN COUNTY DISTRICT ATTORNEY'S OFFICE; Hackensack, New Jersey (1992–Present)
Assistant District Attorney
Ten years' experience prosecuting a broad range of misdemeanor and felony cases at various levels and in various courts within the jurisdiction.

Major Felony Bureau   June 2002–Present
Accountable for prosecuting violent felonies, including assaults with firearms and weapons, robberies, rapes, and burglaries.

- Confer with police investigators to review case evidence.
- Appear in court and before Grand Juries to seek arraignments and indictments.
- Interview witnesses and prepare them for trial.
- Meet with defendants and defense counsel to negotiate plea agreements.
- Develop cases for trial and handle all aspects of trying cases in court, as appropriate.

Gun Interdiction Unit / Project Exile   June 2000–June 2002
Served as member of this cross-jurisdictional task force charged with curtailing illegal firearms trafficking and illegal use of firearms in commission of other felonies.

- Collaborated with FBI, US Attorney, BATF, and state/local police agencies to further program goals.
- Conferred with representatives of other agencies to assess appropriate venue for prosecuting cases.
- Developed and managed confidential informants in conjunction with other agencies.
- Attended regular meetings to maintain rapport and enhance cooperation between agencies.

City Court — Non-Violent Felonies & Property Crimes   Feb. 1999–June 2000
Felony DWI / Fatal Traffic Accident Bureau   Dec. 1997–Feb. 1999
City Court — Misdemeanors   Sept. 1995–Dec. 1997

Municipal Courts   1992–1995
In addition to criminal prosecutions, participated in Drug Diversion Court over an eight-month period. This program offered alternatives to incarceration for non-violent drug offenders with no significant criminal records.

Strategy: *Highlight cross-jurisdictional experience for this individual seeking a position with the Department of Justice, where interagency cooperation is highly valued.*

Peter H. Desmond, Esq.   Résumé — Page Two

LEGAL EXPERIENCE (continued)

LEGAL ASSISTANCE OF NORTHERN NEW JERSEY; Hackensack, New Jersey
Legal Aid Attorney   **1991**
Assisted economically disadvantaged clients with landlord/tenant issues and other routine legal matters.

US DISTRICT COURT — NORTHERN DISTRICT OF NEW JERSEY; Hackensack, New Jersey
Judicial Intern to Hon. Warren G. Nestor   **Sept. 1988 – May 1989**
Researched legal issues and drafted Memoranda Decisions and Orders for habeas corpus petitions, civil rights actions, and social security actions. Discussed case decisions and rulings on motions with judge to gain further understanding of trial law and procedures.

STATE OF NEW JERSEY DEPARTMENT OF TAXATION & FINANCE; Trenton, New Jersey
Law Clerk — Litigation Division   **May 1988 – Aug. 1989**
Researched laws pertaining to real property transfer and corporate transfer taxes. Analyzed statutory and regulatory issues and prepared memoranda based on interpretations. Developed case strategies and drafted briefs and motions.

US ATTORNEY'S OFFICE — DISTRICT OF COLUMBIA, SUPERIOR COURT DIVISION; Washington, DC
Undergraduate Legal Internship   **Sept. 1986 – Dec. 1986**
Reviewed evidence, interviewed witnesses, and conducted legal research in support of attorneys preparing misdemeanor cases for trial.

EDUCATION

Juris Doctor   **June 1990**
College of Law, Syracuse University; Syracuse, New York

Bachelor of Science, Criminal Justice   **May 1987**
Syracuse University; Syracuse, New York
Graduate With Honors / GPA: 3.68
Published article on Entrapment Defense in undergraduate law review.

PROFESSIONAL DEVELOPMENT

Trial Advocacy II, National Advocacy Center; Columbia, South Carolina   **Aug. 2002**
Intensive week-long program focusing on DNA, Trace, Firearm, and Psychiatric Evidence; Forensic Pathology; and Examination of Expert Witnesses. Program culminated with practical experience conducting direct and cross-examinations of experts and delivering closing arguments.

References Provided on Request

Angela Ferguson, Esq.

142 Concord Avenue
Hollywood, FL 33021
(954) 585.7445 • AngieFerg2@aol.com

PROFESSIONAL PROFILE

- Effective *Trial Lawyer* routinely handling caseload of 100+ cases.

- Resolve legal matters quickly and effectively yet persistently pursue the most effective and appropriate course of action.

- Strengths include witness interviewing and preparation, case theory development, presentation of facts, and persuasive argument abilities.

BAR MEMBERSHIPS

Florida Bar, admitted March 2000.

Georgia Bar, admitted July 2000.

LEGAL EXPERIENCE

Florida County District Attorney's Office (Miami, FL) **Trial Division** **ASSISTANT DISTRICT ATTORNEY**	**09/99 to** **Present**

Individually handle all phases of criminal prosecutions from pre-trial practice through trial, post-trial motions, and sentencing. Responsibilities include extensive legal research, drafting pleadings, motions, discovery, witness interviewing and preparation, drafting pre-sentencing memoranda, and routinely and effectively negotiating plea bargains with opposing counsel.

Extensive courtroom experience includes arraignments, calendar appearances, hearings, arguing motions to suppress evidence and motions in limine, conducting voir dire, and all other aspects of trial and arguing post-trial motions. Consistently establish credibility and trust with juries through a combination of effective presentation of facts and persuasive argument skills.

Manage rotating caseload of 100+ felony and misdemeanor cases, involving:

- **Felonies:** domestic violence assault, stalking, burglary, robbery, grand larceny, A-1 drug possession and sale, and identity theft.

- **Misdemeanors:** assault, petit larceny, trademark counterfeiting, and aggravated harassment.

Selected achievements and accomplishments:

- Within 2 years, successfully tried and won convictions in 2 bench and 5 jury trials.

- Convicted defendant for Criminal Sale of a Controlled Substance on or Near School Grounds. **Result:** Despite minimal evidence (one rock of crack cocaine), successfully argued that defendant receive 4 ½-to-9-year prison sentence.

United States District Court, D.F.L. (Tallahassee, FL) **Federal Judicial Clerkship** **STUDENT INTERN for Honorable Ken Stern**	**8/98 to 5/99**

Conducted extensive research and writing. Prepared federal habeas corpus opinions and orders. Obtained exposure to court procedures through attendance at trials, arraignments, and hearings.

Selected achievements and accomplishments:

- Drafted extensive opinion denying habeas corpus relief to defendant convicted of aggravated sexual assault, sexual assault, and endangering the welfare of a child, based on defendant's erroneous claim of *inter alia*, a violation of his Sixth Amendment rights.

Strategy: Redesign resume for an experienced attorney seeking to transition from a role as prosecutor to a general litigation position with a law firm. Emphasize transferable skills as well as education and experience.

Angela Ferguson, Esq.

Page 2

LEGAL EXPERIENCE (continued)	**United States Attorney's Office (Boston, MA)** **Criminal Division, Narcotics Unit** **SUMMER INTERN**	**5/98 to 8/98**

Conducted research and writing. Observed judicial process and courtroom procedure including pleas, verdicts, summations, and sentencings. Met with cooperating informants, interviewed witnesses, and prepared warrants.

Family Court of Boston (Boston, MA)   **5/97 to 8/97**
SUMMER LAW CLERK for Honorable Judith Steiner

Managed juvenile delinquent and dependency case files. Conducted legal research and wrote opinions and appeals.

EDUCATION

JD, University of Florida, Gainesville, FL   **1999**
Dean's Honor List, Fall 1998 and Spring 1999

Awards

- C.A.L.I. Award for Excellence in Advanced Trial Advocacy
- Victor A. Jaczun Award for Excellence in Trial Advocacy

National / Regional Trial Team Competitor and Champion

- National Champion, NACDL Student Trial Competition (1997)
- National Champion, ATLA Student Trial Competition (1998)
- Eastern-Regional Champion, ATLA Student Trial Competition (1998)
- Finalist, NACDL Student Trial Competition (1998)
- Best Advocate (Semifinal Round), NACDL Student Trial Competition (1998)
- Semifinalist, National ATLA Student Trial Competition (1999)
- Eastern-Regional Champion, ATLA Student Trial Competition (1999)

Achieved Distinguished Class Performance in the following courses:

Civil Procedure I; Contracts II; Evidence; Criminal Procedure I; and Advanced Trial Advocacy

BA ENGLISH, Florida State University, Tallahassee, FL   **1994**
Dean's List, Spring 1991 and Spring 1993.

PROFESSIONAL DEVELOPMENT

Regularly participate in CLE seminars. To date, have completed 53+ hours of continuing education courses spanning areas including Criminal, Family, Real Estate, Landlord/Tenant, Small Business, Civil, Administrative, Professional Responsibility and Wills/Trusts.

PROFESSIONAL ASSOCIATIONS

- American Bar Association
- Florida State Bar Association
- Association of Trial Lawyers of America
- National Black Prosecutor's Association

COMPUTER SKILLS

Proficient in Westlaw, Lexis-Nexis, Microsoft Office Suite, Internet, and e-mail applications.

BUFFY A. CARLTON

1037 Grand Vista Drive • Irving, TX 75039
Home: (972) 831-2435 • Cell: (972) 820-4243 • E-mail: buffycarlton@mailbox.com

EXECUTIVE DIRECTOR

Senior non-profit and educational development specialist with a unique education-industry background, having served effectively in senior management, supervisory, and foundation-administration positions. Demonstrated history of success in creating and implementing comprehensive non-profit funding programs. Adept at developing multimillion-dollar partnerships with corporations and in securing foundation grants.

PROFESSIONAL EXPERIENCE

EDUCATION INNOVATIONS, Dallas, TX   2001–Present
Executive Director for Strategic Alliances

Develop partnerships with non-profit and for-profit organizations that deliver technology-based instruction for this Internet-based, customized network of online learning communities.
  Key Achievements:
  • Developed a three-year, $2 million financial-literacy program for students through corporate sponsorship.
  • Secured a three-year, $1.5 million online homework-assistance program with Mega Corporation.
  • Fostered successful partnerships with national newspapers, the Smithsonian Institution, major book publishers, and the U.S. Department of Education.

TEXAS ART GROUP, Dallas, TX   1999–2001
Executive Director

Developed and directed a philanthropic donation program and created innovative national sales events for this internationally renowned, culturally diverse group of more than 100 U.S. and European artists and craftspeople.
  Key Achievements:
  • Collaborated with non-profit organizations on revenue-producing promotional events at national venues.
  • Penetrated new markets through creative approaches in reaching non-traditional markets for art sales.
  • Coordinated special gallery events, including a four-day international art sale extravaganza.

NATIONAL ORGANIZATION OF SCHOOL PRINCIPALS (NOSP), Washington, DC   1989–1999
Associate Executive Director

Managed a $15 million annual budget and supervised a staff of 40, among five departments, for this 46,000-member school leadership organization that provides professional development programs to assist students and administrators in the U.S. and abroad.
  Key Achievements:
  • Generated more than $14 million in corporate contributions within six years.
  • Reengineered the $3.3 million travel budget, reducing annual costs by $150,000.
  • Launched an NOSP foundation that generated more than $110,000 within six months.
  • Recruited corporate partners and jointly designed programs with international organizations.

DISTRICT OF COLUMBIA PUBLIC SCHOOLS, Washington, DC   1970–1989
Principal, Presidential High School (1985–1989)

Promoted through increasingly responsible positions with one of the largest high-school districts in the U.S., serving more than 35,000 students. (Prior positions include the following: Assistant Principal, Guidance Counselor, Vocational Design/Development Specialist, and Teacher.)

EDUCATION

M.Ed., Administration • **B.S., Vocational Education,** Georgetown University, Washington, DC

Strategy: *Develop a one-page "calling-card" resume for a highly experienced executive targeting a specific non-profit educational organization.*

CHAPTER 6

Resumes for Managers and Executives in Human Resources, Organizational Development, and Education

- Human Resources Executive
- Human Resources Manager
- Program Director
- University Instructor
- Teacher
- Elementary Principal (Educational Administrator)

Allen J. Campbell

1850 McCormick Street
Kalamazoo, Michigan 49001

616-555-9833
ajbell@network.com

Executive Profile

Human Resources . . . Organizational Development . . . Project Management

✓ Accomplished management career in banking industry in progressively responsible capacities.

✓ Impressive record of streamlining operations, developing and implementing organizational solutions, and applying overall human resources expertise.

✓ Consistently successful in improving efficiency, increasing revenue, and reducing costs.

✓ Strong employee management and team development skills.

✓ Keen ability to understand and interpret broad multidisciplinary perspectives and relate them to individual components.

✓ Communication skills include ability to knowledgeably interact with technical and non-technical staff.

✓ Regularly tapped to lead challenging projects to analyze, assess, and implement resolution.

✓ Keen ability to focus on direction and organizational planning.

Professional Experience

Practical Consulting Services (PCS) • Kalamazoo, Michigan   2000–Present
Principal/Partner/Co-Founder
> Provide businesses with consulting services, specializing in human resources, organizational performance, and strategic planning.
> *Challenge:* Develop market niche capitalizing on principals' areas of expertise.
> *Action:* Research topics for training programs likely to be in demand by organizations. Conduct strategic planning for two banks.
> *Result*: Ongoing. Develop strategic planning processes and self-directed teller training programs.

Nations Bank • Detroit, Michigan   1971–2001
The fifth largest banking institution in the United States with 68,000+ employees
> Navigated three transitions of corporate ownership (original employer Home Town Bank purchased by First Federal in 1985; merged with Twin City Federal in 1995; acquired by Nations Bank in 1998).

Project Manager — Mortgage Services (1999–2001)
> Recruited by and reported to Senior Vice President and National Sales Manager for 6-month project relating to mortgage servicing across the United States.
> *Challenge:* Identify and resolve intra- and inter-telecommunications problems involving 18 toll-free number and 14 voice-response units and causing 32% call-abandonment rate.
> *Action:* Evaluated existing system to identify specific trouble spots. Maintained communication with on-site staff (assigned to project with limited availability). Researched, developed, and implemented solutions that systematized work flows and procedures and fully exploited telecommunications processing capacity.
> *Result:* Raised organization's annual mortgage-processing capacity by $64 million and improved overall customer satisfaction rating.

Strategy: *Emphasize human resources aspects of the candidate's experience, whether in HR or in broader management positions. Use the Challenge, Action, and Results format (see page 25) to showcase his problem-solving abilities.*

Allen J. Campbell   616-555-9833

Professional Experience

- continued -

Project Manager — Corporate Consumer Loans (1998–1999)

Acted as Team Leader on project that involved consolidating all legacy consumer loan systems to a common system.

Challenge: Identify and address issues and products directly affecting branches and customers.

Action: Represented technical and other employees as liaison with other facets of project team, including Andersen Consulting representatives. Coordinated issue resolution for system testing.

Result: Identified and confirmed viability of all branch and customer-contact product issues (such as coupon books, statements, credit reports, and compatibility of six central information files) prior to project's successful implementation.

Manager — Mid-Michigan Support (1996–1998)

Directed all training, regional marketing, communications, quality, branch operations, and financial analysis for the Mid-Michigan Division. Successfully coordinated distribution of cash bonuses and stock awards for 1,400 officers throughout the state.

Challenge: Centralize activities of 12 independently operated regions within division.

Action: Participated in the development and introduction of *Cooperative Market Management* initiative to 164 branch offices. Ensured consistency with corporate procedures and between branches.

Result: Controlled marketing expenditures. Increased profitability by 20%. Achieved ranking as most profitable retail division for Twin City Federal.

Director of Compensation and Health Cost Management (1993–1996)

Managed compensation programs, executive benefit programs, and health-care cost containment.

Challenge: Investigate and develop methods to maximize corporate expense of compensation-related programs.

Action: Collected, analyzed, and prepared compensation recommendations for presentation to Board of Directors Compensation Committee. Researched health-care packages.

Result: Coordinated development of and introduced new job-evaluation system that survived two subsequent corporate mergers. Developed consistent methodology and reporting for over 140 incentive and compensation programs. Reduced organization's annual health-care costs by $1.2 million by standardizing HMO plan design.

Earlier positions:

Lansing Human Resources Manager (1991–1993)   **Commercial Loan Officer** (1975–1976)
Personnel Director (1981–1991)   **Credit Analyst** (1974–1975)
Credit Manager (1980–1981)   **Assistant Branch Manager** and
Bookkeeping Manager (1976–1980)   **Management Trainee** (1971–1974)

Education

Northwestern University   University of Illinois
Master of Business Administration   **Bachelor of Arts** — Industrial Administration

Community Affiliations

✓ Trustee, The Children's Health Center
✓ Past Board of Directors, Kalamazoo Urban Coalition
✓ Past President, Kalamazoo Chapter American Institute of Banking

✓ Past President, Kent County/UI Alumni Association

RESUME 28: RIC LANHAM, MDIV, MA, MRE, CCM, CECC; INDIANAPOLIS, IN

Matthew D. Thoma

109 West Lindenview Drive
Bloomington, Indiana 41331

388-650-0483
mdthoma@comcast.net

Human Resources Management · Strategic Planning · Organizational Design

Professional career reflects over 20 years' experience in administrative leadership, human resources management, resource utilization, and organizational development in highly competitive and diligently structured institutions. Leadership abilities have been utilized in re-organization of programs, services, and resources for leading academic institution. Entrepreneurial skills were developed in the start-up of retail specialty operation from concept to implementation.

Selected Accomplishments

- Established strategic business plan from concept to implementation to start two retail specialty shops that grew in size, market share, and customer base, with revenues in excess of $350K per year.

- Held supervisory responsibility for all aspects of student life, capital facilities, program management and event planning, to position Franklin as one of the top 7 American Higher Education "best buys."

- Took strategic steps to enhance interaction between professional staff, board members, and students to create a world-class environment for success and leadership development.

- Held multi-functional management responsibilities, including vendor/distributor contracts for supplies, lease negotiations, purchasing, payroll, marketing, promotions, training and development, policy development, and fund utilization.

- Served as key facilitator between student groups and administration in event planning, leadership development, public relations, pre-construction facility design, and administration of services.

- Supervised campus-life event-planning projects and established student-life policies for university campus with 300 diverse organizations and an enrollment in excess of 33,000.

- Developed and demonstrated excellent oral/written communication skills in extensive interface with public relations and news media from New York City, Kansas City, St. Louis, Denver, Louisville, Indianapolis, and Detroit.

Career History

Owner/President	Pictures Incorporated	1990–present
Director of Student Affairs	Franklin University	1987–1990
Human Resources Associate	Michigan State University	1980–1987
Administrator of Leadership Programs	Purdue University	1975–1980

Academic Credentials

MA Student Personnel Services in Higher Education, Michigan State University
BS Business Administration—Human Resource Management focus, Purdue University

Strategy: *Use the functional style to focus attention on relevant achievements within academic HR/student services rather than a recent entrepreneurial venture.*

KAREN L. HOLLMANN

822 SW Dosch Road
Portland, OR 97239

(503) 224-5201 Residence · k_hollmann@hotmail.com · (503) 235-1198 Business

Workforce Development Program Director

PROFESSIONAL SUMMARY

Creative, visionary human-services manager with over 20 years' experience in the employment and training field in both public and private sectors. Over 10 years' experience directing regional workforce-development programs and managing a continuous-improvement organization. Strong skills in facilitating team building and an open work environment. Sound ability to successfully work with the ebb and flow of funding sources, including innovating fee-for-service programs. Excellent skills in assessing organizational challenges and creating solutions. Strategic thinker, passionate, true leader.

Personnel Management: Led staff of workforce-development professionals to consistently exceed goals for participant numbers and expense control on all contracts.

Fiscal Management: By leveraging $750,000+ in extra funding, staff was able to serve twice as many needy clients as in the previous year.

Organizational Development: Facilitated innovation and change in multiple companies, both as director and as consultant.

PROFESSIONAL EXPERIENCE

PORTLAND COMMUNITY COLLEGE, Portland, OR   1990–Present
Director, Employment Programs (1992–Present)
Manager of Operations and Programs (1990–1992)

Oversee the planning and operation of various federal, state, and private employment, training, and management contracts averaging over $5 million annually. Manage three local offices in two counties. Coordinate and direct all administrative and program activities for staff of 40+. Establish and manage program plans, goals, budgets, contracts, and performance standards. Act as national strategic partner for Profiles International, an employment assessment system. Fiscal Agent and One-Stop Operator to regional Workforce Investment Board.

- Leveraged over $750,000 in extra funding beyond allocated job-training contracts for the region in 2001, nearly four times the leveraged funding of the previous year.
- Empowered staff to innovate several fee-for-service programs, including a coffee cart run by program participants, fiber-optics training to assist clients from the fishing industry change careers, and private contract-management and employment seminars. Fee-for-service programs accounted for nearly $70K in company revenues in 2001.
- Sought out to serve at the national, state, and local levels on One-Stop program initiatives, helping to influence legislation and program regulations.
- Consistently receive outstanding financial and program audits, including Department of Labor, State of Oregon, The Oregon Consortium, and independent audits.
- Worked closely with local elected officials, private-sector members, and workforce partners to operate the Region #2 Workforce Investment Board, implement the state-approved five-year workforce plan for the region, and enforce a Memo of Understanding among partners.
- Active in One-Stop System development in partnership with regional, state, and employer partners, resulting in delivery of seamless, high-quality services.

Strategy: *Use a professional summary to highlight strong skills in managing people and dollars and in organizational development; enhance these facts with strong personal descriptors.*

RESUME 29, CONTINUED

KAREN L. HOLLMANN   Page Two

Professional Experience, Continued

MT. HOOD COMMUNITY COLLEGE, Gresham, OR   2001–Present
Instructor

Instructor for cohort-based community-college 39-credit credential in Workforce Development. Developed curriculum; designed and marketed Career Development Specialist certificate program.

◆ Developed curriculum/program from the ground up in three-month period for one of the few Workforce Development programs in the U.S.

J.E.C. CONSULTING, Portland, OR   1988–1990
Co-Owner/Consultant

Provided contracted services to businesses for on-site assessment of employee needs and system/procedural challenges. Designed and implemented programs and trainings for staff development and system reorganization/organizational development.

EMPLOYMENT, TRAINING, AND BUSINESS SERVICES, Marylhurst, OR   1986–1990
Trainer/Account Representative/Competency Specialist

Trained youth in employment and job-search techniques. Developed training activity competencies. Completed participant enrollments and program modifications and terminations as required. Collaborated with colleagues to develop employability plans for program enrollees. Wrote curriculum, competency systems, and assessment tools. Facilitated agency-wide retreats and training sessions for 100+ employees.

STATE OF OREGON EMPLOYMENT DEPARTMENT, Oregon City, OR   1985–1986
Job Service Representative/Liaison

Contacted employers within the community and solicited job orders. Matched job orders with qualified job seekers. Instructed job seekers in job-search techniques through workshops and one-to-one counseling sessions. Acted as liaison between Employment Department and Employment, Training, and Business Services.

EDUCATION

Ed.M. in Organizational Development, Portland State University, Portland, OR, 2001

B.A. in Speech Communications, University of Oregon, Eugene, OR

Additional Professional Development Coursework:

Profiles Executive Advanced Training Certification, Dallas, TX, 2001

PROFESSIONAL AWARDS

National Advancement of the Workforce Profession Customer Service Award, 2002
Oregon Governor's Workforce Award, 2000
Job Corps Community Supporter of the Year Award, 1999
Certificate of Leadership, Oregon Career Network, 1997–1998
Commitment in Action Award for Passion, Innovation, and Energy, Oregon Employment and Training Association, 1996

KAREN L. HOLLMANN   Page Three

HIGHLIGHTS OF PRESENTATIONS

"Profiles—Job Match Assessments," OETA The Rendezvous 2001, Bend, OR, 2001
"Overcoming Barriers to Employability," NAWDP Annual Conference, Reno, NV, 2000
"Fee for Service," Washington State Workforce Development Providers' Conference, Seattle, WA, 1998
"The Instructions Are Inside the Box," NAWDP Annual Conference, Miami Beach, FL, 1998
"Beyond JTPA: Becoming a Community Service Provider," National Association of Counties Workforce
Development Conference, Tulsa County, OK, 1997
"Integration: What Does It Really Mean?" Georgia Workforce Development Conference, Atlanta, GA, 1996

PROFESSIONAL AFFILIATIONS

National Department of Labor Appointments

National Summit on the Future of the Workforce Development Profession, Washington, DC, 2002
Labor Force Measures Workgroup, 1998–1999
Performance Measures and Applications Technical Workgroup, 1998–1999
JTPA SPIR Revision Technical Workgroup, 1998–1999
Performance Standards Workgroup, 1997–1999
Workforce Development Performance Measures Initiative: Efficiency Workgroup, 1997–1998
Technical Assistance Group for Performance Standards, 1990–1991

Boards

Board Member, Region #2 Regional Workforce Investment Board, 1999–Present
Executive Board Officer, National Association of Workforce Development Professionals and Partnership
Education Fund, 1995–2001
Board Member, Oregon Career Information System, 1999–2000
Chairperson, The Oregon Consortium Program Directors, 1997–1999
Board Member, Oregon Employment and Training Association, 1987–1990, 1999
Board Member, Rotary Club International, 1997

Working Committees

National Certification Team, Workforce Development Professional Certification, National Association of
Workforce Development Professionals, 1999–Present
Co-Chair, Oregon Governor's State Workforce Investment Act Performance Accountability Task Force, 1999
Executive Officer, North Coast Workforce Quality Committee, 1994–1999
State Committee Member, Governor's Student Retention Initiative, Paroled and Incarcerated Youth, 1988–1989

Professional Association Memberships

National Association of Workforce Development Professionals, 1994–Present
Oregon Workforce Partnership, Oregon Directors of Workforce Development Programs, 1992–Present
Oregon Employment and Training Association, 1987–Present
Rotary Club International, 1993–1999; Paul Harris Fellow, 1999

SUSAN B. ALMANN

589 Brighton View
Croton, NY 10520

(914) 271-5567   Sbalm345@aol.com

CAREER PROFILE

Strategic **Human Resources Executive** and proactive business partner to senior management to guide in the development of performance-driven, customer-driven, and market-driven organizations. Proven effectiveness in providing vision and counsel in steering organizations through periods of accelerated growth and economic downturn. Diverse background includes multinational organizations in the medical-equipment and manufacturing industries.

Expertise in all generalist HR initiatives:

Recruitment & Employment Management … Leadership Training & Development … Benefits & Compensation Design … Reorganization & Culture Change … Merger & Acquisition Integration … Union & Non-Union Employee Relations … Succession Planning … Expatriate Programs … Long-Range Business Planning … HR Policies & Procedures.

PROFESSIONAL EXPERIENCE

MARCON MANUFACTURING COMPANY, Peekskill, NY
Vice President, Human Resources (1996–Present)

Challenge: Recruited to create HR infrastructure to support business growth at a $30 million global manufacturing company with underachieving sales, exceedingly high turnover and lack of cohesive management processes among business entities in U.S. and Asia.

Action: Partnered with President and Board of Directors to reorganize company, reduce overhead expenses, rebuild sales, and institute solid management infrastructure.

Results: ◆ Established HR with staff of 5, including development of policies and procedures; renegotiated cost-effective benefit programs that saved $1.5 million annually.
   ◆ Reorganized operations and facilitated seamless integration within parent company of 150 employees from two recent acquisitions.
   ◆ Reduced sales-force turnover to nearly nonexistent and upgraded quality of candidates hired by implementing interview-skills training and management-development programs. Results led to measurable improvements in sales performance.
   ◆ Recruited all management personnel, developed HR policies, and fostered team culture at new Malaysian plant with 125 employees.
   ◆ Initiated business reorganization plan, resulting in consolidation of New York and Virginia operations for $6.5 million in cost reductions.

BINGHAMTON COMPANY, New York, NY
Director, Human Resources & Administration (1993–1996)

Challenge: Lead HR and Administration functions and staff that support 1,600 employees at $500 million medical equipment manufacturer. Contribute to company's turnaround efforts, business unit consolidations, and transition to focus on consumer products.

Action: Established cross-functional teams from each site and provided training in team building to coordinate product development efforts, implement new manufacturing processes, and speed products to market. Identified cost reduction opportunities; instrumental in reorganization initiatives that included closing union plant in Texas and building new plant in North Carolina.

Strategy: *Use the Challenge, Action, and Results format (see page 25) to emphasize extensive experience in key areas that impact an organization's business performance well beyond HR.*

SUSAN B. ALMANN • PAGE 2

Director, Human Resources & Administration, continued...

Results:
- Instituted worldwide cross-functional team culture that provided foundation for successful new product launches and recapture of company's leading edge despite intense market competition.
- Spearheaded flawless integration of two operations into single, cohesive European business unit, resulting in profitable turnaround.
- Restructured and positioned HR organization in the German business unit as customer-focused partner to support European sales and marketing units.
- Initiated major benefit cost reductions of $3 million in first year and $1 million annually while gaining employee acceptance through concerted education and communications efforts.

ARCADIA CORPORATION, New York, NY
Director, Human Resources (1989–1993)
Assistant Director of Human Resources (1987–1989)

Challenge: HR support to corporate office and field units of an $800 million organization with 150 global operations employing 4,500 people.

Action: Promoted to lead staff of 10 in all HR and labor relations activities. Established separate international recruitment function and designed staffing plan to accommodate rapid business growth. Negotiated cost-effective benefits contracts for union and non-union employees.

Results:
- Oversaw successful UAW, Teamsters, and labor contract negotiations.
- Established and staffed HR function for multimillion-dollar contract with U.S. government agency.
- Introduced incentive plans for field unit managers and an expatriate program that attracted both internal and external candidates for international assignments in the Middle East.
- Resolved HR issues associated with two business acquisitions while accomplishing a smooth transition and retention of all key personnel.
- Restructured HR function with no service disruption to the business while saving $1.5 million annually.

EDUCATION

M.B.A., Cornell University, New York, NY
B.A., Business Administration, Amherst College, Amherst, MA

AFFILIATIONS

Society for Human Resource Management
Human Resource Council of Albany

Gretchen L. Van Garten
Genesis Park ♦ Oakton, VA 22124 ♦ 703.716.5735
Email: glvangarten@earthlink.net

PROFESSIONAL GOAL & PROFILE	**University Teaching Position** — All levels of Ballet and/or Kinesiology, Choreography, Arts Administration, Theatrical Dance, and Dance Pedagogy. Possess broad scope of instructional ballet including pointe, men's technique, variations teaching choreography, kinesiology, arts management, theatrical dance and dance pedagogy. Innovative and versatile with a commitment to excellence in all endeavors. Exceptional record of professionalism, creativity, productivity improvement, and motivational teaching with a *true passion for the art of ballet*.
EDUCATIONAL ACHIEVEMENTS	**MFA, Dance Education** University of California, Irvine, CA **Activities:** Choreographer, Master of Fine Arts Performances (2); Dance Hall Girl, Billy the Kid; Lighting Technician, Master of Fine Arts Performance **BA, Kinesiotherapy and Stage Movement** California State University, Stanislaus ACTF Award for Excellence, *The Diviners* (Theatrical Properties); *Anything Goes* (Choreographer); Choreographer, *Bye Bye, Verdi* and *5,6,7,8* (Choreography Showcase)
EXPERIENCE	CENTRAL BALLET COMPANY — Riverside, VA **FOUNDING ARTISTIC DIRECTOR** (1987 to Present) Founded this pre-professional, non-profit ballet company. Extensive involvement in training and coaching dancers, hiring guest choreographers and dancers, and managing the design, marketing, and public relations of all performances. Hold budget authority, develop policies and procedures, and direct grant-writing and fund-raising from federal, state, and municipal governments as well as business, foundation, and private resources. Supervise staff of five and volunteer pool of 100; design all printed materials and press releases; coordinate rehearsal and production activities. Maintained high productivity level during continuous growth and expansion. **Achievements** ➤ **Steered company into a nationally recognized organization** *(one of 35 companies designated Regional Honor Company in the organization Regional Dance America).* ➤ **Realized significant budget growth** (3rd largest in State of Virginia) and consistently increased sales during tenure through delivery of exceptional productions and innovative marketing. ➤ **Introduced "Arts in Education" educational outreach program** to sustain enthusiasm, maximize ticket sales, and fuel company growth. ➤ **Maintained cost-effective operation and high-quality productions** while orchestrating three major productions annually on just $264K per year. ➤ **Secured necessary production funds** by implementing innovative participant program that breaks down production needs/contribution vs. blanket donations (ex: Terminix underwrote cost of spider webs in *Sleeping Beauty*).

Strategy: *Balance presentation of professional skills with strong business contributions, such as growth of revenues and students and innovative funding ideas, for this accomplished dance teacher.*

Gretchen L. Van Garten   Resume, Page Two

Continued...   Meshpiel School of Dance & Ballet — Modesto, CA
                      ASSOCIATE DIRECTOR, PART OWNER (1980 to 2001)

Charged with instructing all levels of ballet, men's technique, pointe, and variations. Provided day-to-day operational administration for 650 students and 23 staff managers with primary focus on the Pre-Professional Training Program.

Achievements

➤ **Spearheaded activities** related to association with Central California Summer Dance Conservatory.
➤ Instrumental in **guiding students to successful professional dance careers** in performance, teaching, and choreography.
➤ Pivotal role in **boosting student levels from 80 to over 600** during tenure by evaluating overall training quality, improving programs, and cultivating relationship with Dance Conservatory.
➤ Facilitated teacher training to **ensure the ongoing cohesion of teaching styles.**

University of Rochester — Rochester, CA
ADJUNCT PROFESSOR (1987 to 2001, intermittently)

Developed dance curriculum for Theatre Majors class; taught, supervised, and evaluated student progress; choreographed variety of musicals.

➤ **Created innovative syllabus** and course materials to improve student performance and understanding of dance theories.
➤ Teamed with show director on appropriate choreography, rehearsals, and expectations to **deliver triumphant, well-received productions.**

Exceptional Letters of Recommendation upon Request

KITTY WOLFSON

kwolfson@ca.k12.ca.us

1553 Orange Lane
Imperial, California 92251

Residence: (760) 355-4175
Cellular: (760) 427-6209

CONSULTING and LEAD EDUCATOR / PEER COACH
Pedagogy Management / Retaining Teachers in the Profession

Innovative, resourceful, tenacious yet personable, multitasked Administrator and Teacher with 25 years' experience in union issues. Participating member of Peer Assistance and Review Program, as well as Associated Calexico Teachers negotiating team. Quick, flexible/adaptable learner.

Training and Development Professional with extensive experience in the design, delivery, evaluation, and enhancement of effective hands-on instructional programs that improve efficiency, increase productivity, enhance quality, and strengthen financial results.

Combination of strong analysis, planning, organization, and consensus-building abilities with effective problem resolution, negotiation, and relationship-management skills. Proven expertise in computer software: Proficient in Print Shop Premier, Microsoft Office 2000 (Word, PowerPoint, Publisher, Outlook); currently enrolled in online training for Excel and Access.

Organized, take-charge professional with exceptional follow-through abilities and detail orientation; able to oversee projects from concept to successful conclusion. Efficiently and effectively prioritize a broad range of responsibilities to consistently meet tight deadlines. Demonstrated success in surpassing productivity and performance objectives.

Highly articulate and effective communicator. Excellent team-building and interpersonal skills; work well with individuals on all levels. Recognized as resource person, problem solver, and creative leader.

Administrative Strengths

< Aggressively negotiate contracts using traditional and interest-based bargaining techniques.
< Consistently safeguard contract integrity using grievance process.
< Demonstrate strong organization and advocacy skills.
< Direct daily operations of a service business entailing public relations, promotions, financial record-keeping, hiring, training, supervision, and termination.

Teaching Strengths

< Skilled in building positive rapport with students and colleagues. Proficient in developing effective and innovative curriculum and authentic assessment models. Demonstrated leadership ability with capacity to align groups in whole system change. Natural leader and team builder with practical administrative-level experience. Positive motivator, combining creativity with strong verbal, written, and presentation skills. Extensive work in multicultural environments; **fully bilingual (English/Spanish).**
< Expertise in development and implementation of school improvement and curriculum programs that impact accomplishment of district-wide strategic planning goals. Ability to apply creative thinking skills toward short- and long-range goals.
< 53% of my 2000 9th-grade students in an underperforming school passed the High School Exit Exam.

Strategy: *Emphasize both teaching and peer-coaching qualifications to show strong qualifications for a coaching role in a school setting.*

KITTY WOLFSON   Page 2

Accomplishments

< Prepared initial contract language for Peer Assistance and Review article of 1998–2000 contract.

< Negotiated contract (as participating team member) resulting in **8.4% increase in salary and benefits** for 1998–2000.

< Edited first association newsletter, which prompted **200% increase in attendance** at local monthly meetings.

< Served as site grievance rep for five years, resulting in **75% resolution at informal level.**

< Trained/presented Teachers and the Law at local conference on legal and contract issues.

< Currently organize, implement, and train district administrators and staff on Peer Assistance and Review Program.

CAREER HIGHLIGHTS

CONSULTING / LEAD TEACHER — PEER ASSISTANCE AND REVIEW PROGRAM   2001–Present
Associated Redlands Teachers, Redlands, CA

Participated in negotiations of new article in local ACT contract from state-enacted legislation in 1999. One of 5-member team to write Peer Assistance and Review article to add to contract.

Established new department in District from the ground up with $156,000 budget. Sourced and negotiated with vendors for all computer and office supplies. Developed forms to match panel procedures and PowerPoint presentation for teacher clarification on article eligibility.

VICE PRESIDENT, ACT, Membership   (concurrently)   2001–Present
TEACHER, Grades 7–9, English and Social Science, Redlands Unified School District   1987–2001
TEACHER, Grades 3–5, Wm. S. Hart Union School District   1977–1987

CTA TRAINING AND UNION POSITIONS

Workshops and training:	Summer Leadership Institute	1998
	Region IV Spring Leadership Conference	1997
	Region IV Fall Leadership Conference	1996
	Region IV Spring Leadership Conference	1996

Positions held at local level:	Presenter at Redlands Teachers Conference	1999
	Newsletter Editor, Associated Redlands Teachers	1998–2000
	Negotiation Team Member, Associated Redlands Teachers	1997–2000
	Building Representative, Associated Redlands Teachers	1995–1997
	President, Wm. S. Hart Union Teachers Association	1982–1984
	Negotiation Chairperson, Wm. S. Hart Union Teachers Assn.	1980–1982
	Secretary, Wm. S. Hart Union Teachers Association	1977–1979

CALIFORNIA TEACHING CREDENTIALS

K–12 Multiple Subject, Life
Social Studies, Single Subject, Clear
English, Single Subject, Clear

EDUCATION

Candidate, Master of Arts, Education Administration, San Jose State University
Expected graduation: May 2004
80 Post-Graduate Units, San Jose State University, Multiple Topics
Bachelor of Arts, Multiple Subjects/Social Science, San Jose State University
Associate of Arts, Death Valley College

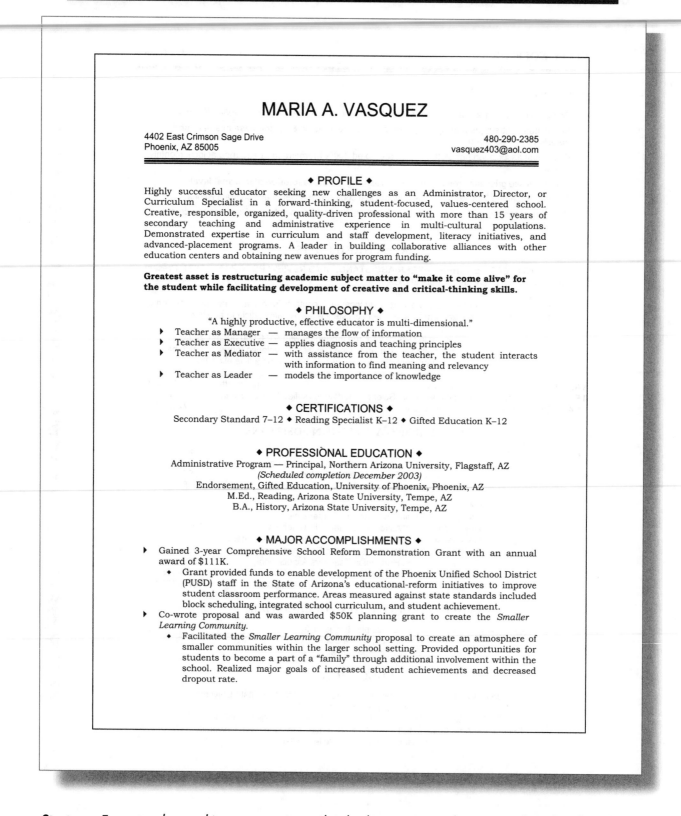

MARIA A. VASQUEZ

4402 East Crimson Sage Drive
Phoenix, AZ 85005

480-290-2385
vasquez403@aol.com

◆ PROFILE ◆

Highly successful educator seeking new challenges as an Administrator, Director, or Curriculum Specialist in a forward-thinking, student-focused, values-centered school. Creative, responsible, organized, quality-driven professional with more than 15 years of secondary teaching and administrative experience in multi-cultural populations. Demonstrated expertise in curriculum and staff development, literacy initiatives, and advanced-placement programs. A leader in building collaborative alliances with other education centers and obtaining new avenues for program funding.

Greatest asset is restructuring academic subject matter to "make it come alive" for the student while facilitating development of creative and critical-thinking skills.

◆ PHILOSOPHY ◆

"A highly productive, effective educator is multi-dimensional."

▸ Teacher as Manager — manages the flow of information
▸ Teacher as Executive — applies diagnosis and teaching principles
▸ Teacher as Mediator — with assistance from the teacher, the student interacts with information to find meaning and relevancy
▸ Teacher as Leader — models the importance of knowledge

◆ CERTIFICATIONS ◆

Secondary Standard 7–12 ◆ Reading Specialist K–12 ◆ Gifted Education K–12

◆ PROFESSIONAL EDUCATION ◆

Administrative Program — Principal, Northern Arizona University, Flagstaff, AZ
(Scheduled completion December 2003)
Endorsement, Gifted Education, University of Phoenix, Phoenix, AZ
M.Ed., Reading, Arizona State University, Tempe, AZ
B.A., History, Arizona State University, Tempe, AZ

◆ MAJOR ACCOMPLISHMENTS ◆

▸ Gained 3-year Comprehensive School Reform Demonstration Grant with an annual award of $111K.
  ◆ Grant provided funds to enable development of the Phoenix Unified School District (PUSD) staff in the State of Arizona's educational-reform initiatives to improve student classroom performance. Areas measured against state standards included block scheduling, integrated school curriculum, and student achievement.
▸ Co-wrote proposal and was awarded $50K planning grant to create the *Smaller Learning Community.*
  ◆ Facilitated the *Smaller Learning Community* proposal to create an atmosphere of smaller communities within the larger school setting. Provided opportunities for students to become a part of a "family" through additional involvement within the school. Realized major goals of increased student achievements and decreased dropout rate.

Strategy: *For a teacher seeking to move into school administration, show strengths related to obtaining grants, designing programs, and improving and developing relevant, workable curricula.*

MARIA A. VASQUEZ
Page 2

▸ Proven track record in designing, coordinating, and implementing innovative programs, methods, and instructions.

- As Department Chair, introduced and provided staff development in Thematic Instruction for the Social Studies curriculum. Connected World History and American History with World Literature and American Literature.
- Wrote and developed the Visual & Performing Arts, Science, and Technology portion of Phoenix High Magnet School's (PHMS) proposal for a Magnet Grant.
- Assigned to collaborate with the Assistant Principal for Curriculum and Instruction with primary responsibilities as the Department Chair for Counselors, Curriculum Lead Teacher, and Staff Development.
- Developed and upgraded sophomore integrated curriculum blocks for Fine Arts, Social Studies, English, Science, and Technology.
- Facilitated the implementation of AP classes in Pre-AP American Literature, European History, Environmental Science, Studio Art, Art History, and Music Theory to increase the PHMS course offerings from 8 to 14.
- Developed and wrote proposals to the PUSD Professional Development Office that enabled teachers to obtain Professional Continuing Education Credits.
- Pioneered program that provided teachers with summer curriculum development and new teaching strategies that addressed increasing student achievement.
- Worked closely with administration in planning and implementing community-outreach programs. Organized open houses, school visitations, parent tours, curriculum presentations, and the Camp MAST program.

◆ PROFESSIONAL EXPERIENCE ◆

PHOENIX MAGNET HIGH SCHOOL, Phoenix, AZ

Curriculum Lead Teacher	2001–Present
Magnet Lead Teacher for Visual & Performing Arts	1996–2001
Fine Arts Department Chair	1996–2000
Social Studies Department Chair	1995–1997
Advanced Placement/GATE Coordinator	1993–2001
Staff and Curriculum Development Team	1993–2001
Literacy and School-wide Portfolio Coordinator	1993–1998
Classroom Teacher; 9th–10th–11th grades; Sophomore GATE	1987–1995

GLENDALE MIDDLE SCHOOL, Glendale, AZ
Classroom Teacher — 1981–1987

MOUNTIAN VIEW MIDDLE SCHOOL, Tempe, AZ
Classroom Teacher — 1977–1981

◆ ADDITIONAL ACTIVITIES ◆

◆ MSA Spring Conference Entertainment Chair, 2000 ◆ Yearbook Advisor, 4 years
◆ PHMS Leadership Team Instructional Council, 6 years ◆ Student Council Advisor, 6 years
◆ Grants Writer and Facilitator, 3 years ◆ Magnet School Lead Teacher and Recruiter, 5 years

◆ PROFESSIONAL AFFILIATIONS ◆

◆ Arizona School Administrators ◆ National Association of Secondary School Principals
◆ Association for Supervision and Curriculum Development
◆ International Network of Performing & Visual Arts

GORDON CHAPMAN
Email: GChapman@aol.com

1433 Meadowlark Lane
Madison, Wisconsin 53405

Work: (608) 255-6710
Residence: (608) 873-2398

PROFILE

An enthusiastic and dynamic education professional with 17 years of successful elementary-level teaching experience seeking a position as **Elementary Principal/Administrator.** Innovative and creative with a positive, can-do attitude and genuine compassion for others. Expertise working with Special Education populations/processes and a core belief that all children can have a successful educational experience. Excellent interpersonal, group presentation, and written communication skills. A well-respected and active community leader with documented, positive results from participation in school and civic projects. Demonstrated core competencies include:

- Strategic & Tactical Planning
- Visionary Leadership
- Continuous Process Improvement
- School/Community Relations
- Special Programs & Events Planning
- Textbook Review
- Instructional Resource Selection

- High Standards Curriculum, Instruction, & Administration
- Team-Based Culture
- Training & Development
- Crisis Planning & Emergency Preparedness
- Classroom Technology Initiatives

PROFESSIONAL EXPERIENCE

MADISON PUBLIC SCHOOL DISTRICT—Madison, Wisconsin   1985 to Present

Summer School Assistant Principal—Practicum (January 2002 to Present)
- Practicum administered under direction of John Fliss, Summer School Coordinator and Elementary Principal, Lincoln School.
- Pre-program accountabilities include timeline development, program scheduling, and staff selection.
- Accountabilities during program (7 weeks) include daily program monitoring, parent/staff communications, busing coordination, and behavior/discipline issues.

Third-Grade Classroom Teacher—Forest Elementary (1999 to Present)
Third-Grade Classroom Teacher— Linden Avenue Elementary (1993 to 1999)
- Serve as Principal-In-Charge (Forest) with full accountability for building supervision, parental communications, staff/classroom scheduling, and student behavior/discipline.
- Selected as Grade-Level Team Leader (Linden Avenue); served 2 years.
- Serve on District Science Committee accountable for new curriculum selection and adoption.
- Initiated and organized biannual Science Day (Forest & Linden Avenue) a hands-on, interactive learning activity involving students, volunteers, and staff. Coordinate annual Science Fair (Forest).
- Implementing Professional Learning Community Initiative (Forest) through team collaboration, shared decision making, and sound leadership.
- Implemented Student Council (Forest); teach problem-solving skills and assist students with service projects such as food/clothing drives and fundraisers.
- Serve on Planning Committee (Forest) charged with initiating programs to develop a distinct identity for school.
- Serve on Technology Committee (Forest & Linden Avenue) challenged to assess classroom hardware/software needs and determine staff training requirements.

I believe that Gordon Chapman has the special qualities of understanding, compassion, discipline, and the exceptional work ethic that would make him an excellent elementary school principal.

He has the support of his fellow workers, which would be of extreme importance in the position for which he is applying. His experience … and his many job descriptions give him the knowledge which would be very beneficial to the school community.

Shelly Hughes Former Madison Schools Staff Member

Strategy: *Embed strong recommendations into the left column of the resume so that these powerful sales tools won't be overlooked.*

Gordon Chapman	Work: (608) 255-6710	Residence: (608) 873-2398	Page 2 of 2
RÉSUMÉ			

PROFESSIONAL EXPERIENCE (continued)

HAMILTON-SUSSEX SCHOOL DISTRICT (continued)

Primary LD Teacher—Linden Avenue Elementary (1985 to 1993)
- Implemented mainstreaming with team teaching and other inclusionary efforts.

Assistant Varsity Football Coach—Madison High School (1987 to 2001)
- Led team to 11 consecutive Division II Playoff appearances; State Runner-Up in 2000.

CAREER ACHIEVEMENTS

- Received the Wisconsin Elementary and Middle School Teachers (WEMST) Distinguished Teacher Award for efforts to promote science education within the state.
- Received the Madison Education Foundation "A Class Act" Award in 2000 for excellence in the classroom.
- Awarded Madison Foundation Grant in 1998 for LEGOs in the Classroom initiative. Grant supplied simple machine kits to all district schools, currently used in third-grade classrooms. Designed and presented teacher in-service on classroom implementation.
- Recognized by the Madison School District's Board of Education with Certificates of Appreciation in 1993, 1994, 1996, and 1998 for excellence in teaching.

EDUCATION

MA in Educational Leadership—Marquette University, Milwaukee, Wisconsin, 2002
BA in Education—Appleton College, Appleton, Wisconsin, 1985

Professional Development
Professional Learning Community Training—Lincolnshire, Illinois, 2001

LICENSURE & CERTIFICATIONS

Certified Principal (PK–12), State of Wisconsin 51, 2002
Certified Elementary Teacher (K–8), State of Wisconsin 108, 1985
Certified Learning Disabilities (K–8), State of Wisconsin 811, 1985

PROFESSIONAL AFFILIATIONS

Director-at-Large for Wisconsin Elementary and Middle School Teachers (WEMST)
- Lead strategic planning efforts to promote science initiatives statewide.

Lead Teacher for Academy of Staff Development Initiative (ASDI)

Presenter at District In-Services, Workshops, and WEAC Conference

CIVIC ACTIVITIES

Co-Chair, Facilities Advisory Committee—Monona Public School District, 1998
- Assessed district facility requirements, prioritized needs, and presented Board of Education with options to address current and future expansion plans, community utilization of facilities, safety issues, and community growth projections.

CHAPTER 7

Resumes for Managers and Executives in Real Estate and Construction

- Property Management Executive
- Facilities and Property Manager
- Facilities Engineer
- Project Superintendent
- Transit Planner
- Construction Industry Executive
- Construction Manager

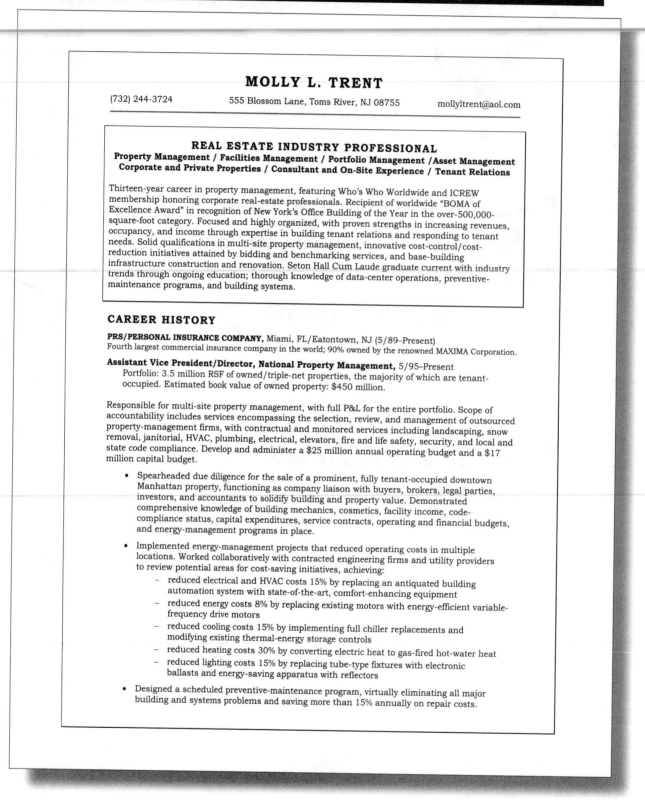

MOLLY L. TRENT

(732) 244-3724   555 Blossom Lane, Toms River, NJ 08755   mollyltrent@aol.com

REAL ESTATE INDUSTRY PROFESSIONAL
**Property Management / Facilities Management / Portfolio Management /Asset Management
Corporate and Private Properties / Consultant and On-Site Experience / Tenant Relations**

Thirteen-year career in property management, featuring Who's Who Worldwide and ICREW membership honoring corporate real-estate professionals. Recipient of worldwide "BOMA of Excellence Award" in recognition of New York's Office Building of the Year in the over-500,000-square-foot category. Focused and highly organized, with proven strengths in increasing revenues, occupancy, and income through expertise in building tenant relations and responding to tenant needs. Solid qualifications in multi-site property management, innovative cost-control/cost-reduction initiatives attained by bidding and benchmarking services, and base-building infrastructure construction and renovation. Seton Hall Cum Laude graduate current with industry trends through ongoing education; thorough knowledge of data-center operations, preventive-maintenance programs, and building systems.

CAREER HISTORY

PRS/PERSONAL INSURANCE COMPANY, Miami, FL/Eatontown, NJ (5/89–Present)
Fourth largest commercial insurance company in the world; 90% owned by the renowned MAXIMA Corporation.

Assistant Vice President/Director, National Property Management, 5/95–Present
   Portfolio: 3.5 million RSF of owned/triple-net properties, the majority of which are tenant-occupied. Estimated book value of owned property: $450 million.

Responsible for multi-site property management, with full P&L for the entire portfolio. Scope of accountability includes services encompassing the selection, review, and management of outsourced property-management firms, with contractual and monitored services including landscaping, snow removal, janitorial, HVAC, plumbing, electrical, elevators, fire and life safety, security, and local and state code compliance. Develop and administer a $25 million annual operating budget and a $17 million capital budget.

- Spearheaded due diligence for the sale of a prominent, fully tenant-occupied downtown Manhattan property, functioning as company liaison with buyers, brokers, legal parties, investors, and accountants to solidify building and property value. Demonstrated comprehensive knowledge of building mechanics, cosmetics, facility income, code-compliance status, capital expenditures, service contracts, operating and financial budgets, and energy-management programs in place.

- Implemented energy-management projects that reduced operating costs in multiple locations. Worked collaboratively with contracted engineering firms and utility providers to review potential areas for cost-saving initiatives, achieving:
  - reduced electrical and HVAC costs 15% by replacing an antiquated building automation system with state-of-the-art, comfort-enhancing equipment
  - reduced energy costs 8% by replacing existing motors with energy-efficient variable-frequency drive motors
  - reduced cooling costs 15% by implementing full chiller replacements and modifying existing thermal-energy storage controls
  - reduced heating costs 30% by converting electric heat to gas-fired hot-water heat
  - reduced lighting costs 15% by replacing tube-type fixtures with electronic ballasts and energy-saving apparatus with reflectors

- Designed a scheduled preventive-maintenance program, virtually eliminating all major building and systems problems and saving more than 15% annually on repair costs.

Strategy: *Showcase strong industry expertise by highlighting verifiable accomplishments, credentials, and awards.*

MOLLY L. TRENT
Page Two

PRS/PERSONAL INSURANCE COMPANY (Continued)

- Coordinated and led an Indoor Air Quality Program in conjunction with risk management that aided in the reduction of workers' compensation claims.

- Managed tenant relations, improving tenant retention by 15% over previous year. Interacted with brokers to select potential tenants, reviewed financial analysis and space selection, and responded to Requests for Proposals.

Senior Facilities Manager, 2/94–5/95
Achieved fast-track promotion with the efficient management of the physical operation of two facilities totaling 550,000 RSF.

- Directed the building engineering staff in both preventive and general maintenance programs; functioned as liaison between vendors, contractors, utilities, and local authorities; and administered both operating and capital budgets.

- Selected and coordinated the activities of vendors, obtained building permits, led competitive bidding, and scheduled and budgeted projects.

- Implemented energy-conservation practices, executed cost-avoidance programs, secured rebates, and ensured building code compliance with OSHA, NFPA, ASHRAE, ADA, and state and local mandates.

- Coordinated and led monthly tenant meetings.

Facilities Manager/Consultant, 5/89–2/94
Managed the operation and maintenance of three buildings totaling 350,000 RSF.

- Gained skills and demonstrated strengths in lease negotiation, infrastructure construction/renovation, and multi-faceted project design and development.

FDG SERVICES, Livingston, NJ (9/87–5/89)

Director of Operations
Directed on-site operations for this management company providing managerial, janitorial, and engineering services, with responsibility for supervising commercial, multiple-tenant, institutional, and industrial projects totaling 6 million RSF.

- Negotiated contractual terms with clients and analyzed cost of labor and materials to develop competitive bids.

- Procured new equipment that both reduced expenses and improved operational efficiency.

EDUCATION

BS, Political Science — Public Administration, Seton Hall University, South Orange, NJ
- Graduated May 1987, Cum Laude

PROFESSIONAL TRAINING

- Real Property Administrator, Safety and Loss Control Management, Tenant Relations, Leasing, Safety Awareness, Terror in the Workplace, Contract Outsourcing Versus In-House Employees

PROFESSIONAL AFFILIATIONS

- Who's Who Worldwide
- Building Owners and Managers Association of New Jersey (BOMA)
- International Facility Management Association (IFMA)
- Industrial/Commercial Real Estate Women (ICREW), NJ Chapter of NNCREW
- CORENET Global — Corporate Real Estate Network

RESUME 36: FREDDIE CHEEK, M.S.ED., CPRW, CWDP, CRW; AMHERST, NY

SARAH STONE

245 Lower Fountain Street
(509) 555-7653

Spokane, Washington 99202
sstone245@aol.com

FACILITIES AND PROPERTY MANAGER
Lease Management / Facility Planning / Purchasing

Professional Profile:

Creative facilities planner and manager with over 20 years' experience planning, organizing, and coordinating facility expansion, renovation, relocation, and construction. Coordinate spatial planning with expertise in combining function and aesthetics in business, medical, and warehouse environments. Work with design consultants in developing schematic designs for new and existing facilities. Utilize superior organizational skills to ensure that the total facility, down to the smallest detail, meets user needs while upholding corporate standards.

Core Skills: Cost Savings ... Space Planning ... Vendor Sourcing / Selection ... Contract Negotiation ... JIT Purchasing / Delivery ... Microsoft Office ... Lotus 1-2-3 ... Strategic Planning ... Team Building ... OSHA Compliance ... Inventory Reduction ... Interior Design ... Staff Supervision ... Ergonomics

Experience:

<u>Mount Mercy Healthcare</u>, Spokane, Washington   1980–Present
Senior Manager of Purchasing and Facility Support
Assist senior management with strategic facility planning for 13 corporate, warehouse, and medical facilities, totaling 480,000 square feet. Supervise nine-member staff. Procure capital equipment for all facilities. Coordinate ergonomics program for work stations and office space. Oversee the production of space-planning drawings, color presentation boards, and signage. Develop and maintain standards program for interior-design elements, including color and finish, for furniture, upholstery fabrics, and floor coverings. Select and acquire accessories, artwork, wall coverings, carpeting, plants, and furnishings.

Conduct quarterly assessment of facilities for appropriateness of design, ensuring maintenance of corporate standards. Negotiate bids and purchase a diversity of commodities, including medical supplies, printed materials, and office supplies. Coordinate delivery and installation of equipment and furniture for all facilities. Administer and maintain space-planning guidelines. Maintain fixed asset register and prepare monthly depreciation reports. Serve on Supply Cost Reduction and Value Analysis Teams. Ensure compliance with OSHA regulations. Maintain facility management database.

Accomplishments:

➤ *Served on Corporate Facilities Team responsible for relocating 732 employees from two locations (62,000 square feet) to new corporate headquarters (145,000 square feet) in 2001.*

➤ *Implemented "Just in Time" purchasing and delivery program for medical, office, and computer supplies, resulting in $1 million savings in inventory costs.*

➤ *Negotiated new office supply contract, achieving $275,000 savings over four years.*

➤ *Managed renovation project for two medical centers and saved $125,000 by eliminating need for outsourcing of all construction work.*

➤ *Reduced leasing costs by relocating In-Home Services Department from leased office space to corporate office.*

➤ *Received peer-voted Employee Recognition Award for outstanding and dedicated service.*

➤ *Coordinated interior design of Archway Physical Therapy facility, winning Washington 2000 design award for healthcare construction.*

Strategy: *Highlight exceptional work experience; amplify Professional Development section to compensate for lack of a degree; include strong Core Skills list that encompasses several diverse job targets.*

Sarah Stone   **Page Two**

Education:

Washington State Real Estate Licensing Course   1992

Spokane University, Spokane, Washington
Courses in Business Administration   1980–1985

<u>Professional Development</u>:
SkillPath's Conference on Women and Communication, 2001
National Association of Purchasing Management Seminar on Purchasing and the Law, 2000
Symposium on Healthcare Design, 2000
Seminars on Team Building, Corrective Actions, and How to Avoid Discrimination, 1997–1999

Affiliations:

International Facilities Management Association (IFMA)
National Administrative Services Purchasing Council (NASPURC)
Institute for Supply Management (ISM)

References:

Furnished upon request.

Daniel E. Guzman

9838 Bowling Green Avenue
Chicago Heights, Illinois 60690

deguzman@aol.com
(773) 779-9908

CHIEF ENGINEER

Facilities Planning / Construction Management / Building Operations

Highly motivated quality-engineering professional with over 15 years' experience in project management, construction management, building systems, grounds maintenance, special-event coordination, and safety management. Exceptional organizational, problem-solving, team-building, leadership, budget-management, and negotiation skills. Effective interpersonal, communications, and conflict-management abilities. Computer literate.

Core Competencies:

◆ Maintenance Engineering	◆ Preventive Maintenance	◆ Safety Management
◆ Facilities Engineering	◆ HVAC/R Systems	◆ Training & Development
◆ Plant Operations	◆ Grounds Maintenance	◆ Supervision
◆ Operations & Maintenance	◆ Building Trades	◆ Purchasing Management
◆ Project Management & Planning	◆ OSHA Recording	◆ Relationship Management

PROFESSIONAL EXPERIENCE

WRIGHT COLLEGE, Chicago Heights, Illinois   1983 to Present
Chief Engineer
Spearhead maintenance-engineering day-to-day activities, including budget management, purchasing, salaries, contracts, and contracted work. Charged with facility maintenance for the City Colleges of Chicago. Schedule preventive maintenance of HVAC/R and fire-protection systems, including landscaping and housekeeping equipment. Utilize MS Windows, Word, and Excel for reporting/documentation processes.

Supervise 25 housekeeping and 8 engineering staff; implement and prioritize work orders, purchasing, and various contracts with trade-related companies to meet fluctuating and tight deadlines. Cultivate relationships with building owners and administrators; attend meetings to provide reports and technical assistance. Oversee construction-management affairs and all building trades during construction projects.

Key Accomplishments / Values Offered:

❑ Delivered departmental efficiency through advanced engineering , technical support, and documentation procedures.

❑ Analyzed efficiency and energy savings potential, resulting in 30% reduction in utility-consumption costs.

❑ Noted for exercising good judgment in hiring work crews, technical competence, work ethic, staff training and development, and take-charge-teamwork attitude.

❑ Appointed as representative for the college on all capital improvement projects from project conception, specifications, and pre-bid to construction management.

❑ Outsourced vendors, negotiated contracts, coordinated competitive bidding, and monitored quality of services and products.

…Continued…

Strategy: *Equally emphasize three areas of expertise: facilities planning, construction management, and building management. Show relevant accomplishments and values.*

Daniel E. Guzman Page Two

Professional Experience, Continued

FINE ARTS CENTER MUSEUM, Decatur, Illinois 2001 to Present
Construction Consultant
Concurrently assist as consultant for new construction of $8.1 million museum addition. Advise on security concerns and administer contract work. Train building engineer and housekeeping staff. Develop work schedules for all shifts. Research equipment specifications and construction prints to establish infrastructure development.

Additional **5+ years prior experience** working at Peoples Energy Corporation.

LICENSES AND CERTIFICATIONS

License: City of Chicago Stationary Engineer
Certification: Universal Proper Refrigerant Practices

EDUCATION AND TRAINING

University of Illinois, Chicago, Illinois
Illinois Institute of Technology
Concentration: **Mechanical Engineering**

Technical: HVAC/R Technician, Coyne American Institute, Chicago Heights, Illinois
Pneumatic Controls, Building Engineers Institute, Chicago Heights, Illinois

Professional Development

OSHA Recording, Padget Thompson	(02/01)
Industrial Electricity II, Performance Training Associates	(04/00)
Building Electrical Systems I & II	(04/00)
Direct Digital Controls, Refrigeration Service Engineers Society	(02/00)
Deregulation, ComEd	(11/99)
Basic Supervision, American Management Association	(11/99)
LCN Door Closer Installation and Maintenance, Ingersol Rand Corp.	(09/99)
BEST Door Hardware Maintenance, Best Access Systems	(04/99)
Von Duprin Panic Hardware Installation and Maintenance	(01/99)
Conflict Resolution, American Management Association	(07/98)
Hydronic Systems Service and Maintenance, ITT Fluid Handling Div.	(02/98)
CVHE/CVHF Chiller Operation, Chicago Trane University	(01/98)
Direct Digital Controls, Andover Controls Corporation	(07/94)
Proper Refrigerant Usage, Refrigeration Service Engineers Society	(04/93)

PUBLICATIONS

Maintenance Technology, Building Systems Solutions, Buildings, The News-HVAC
Building Design and Construction, Refrigeration Service Engineers Society Journal, Engineered Systems

MEMBERSHIPS

Refrigeration Service Engineers Society, #0039324

TED A. HOFFMAN
Route 9, Box 2255
Martinsburg, WV 25411
304-555-7640 ▪ 304-555-0703 (cell)

Project Manager ▪ Site Superintendent ▪ Field Superintendent with comprehensive construction experience, from initial clearing and sediment/erosion control to final punch-out. Seasoned builder of commercial, industrial, and residential sites, including bridge, tunnel, and highway construction.

- Outstanding safety record; committed to quality improvement and environmental compliance.
- Motivated by mastering the challenges of complex projects or learning new skills; have earned numerous professional certifications.
- Effective crew leader who promotes continuous learning and advancement through on-the-job training; demonstrate a natural teaching ability.
- Well organized; implement a system of thorough documentation through maintenance of daily activity logs.

Broad-based responsibilities in the following areas:

- materials purchasing management	- arbitration & conflict resolution
- vendor/supplier negotiations	- quality assurance & inspection
- contract negotiation & review	- heavy equipment troubleshooting &
- reading & scaling blueprints	maintenance
- coordinating subcontractors	

EMPLOYMENT HISTORY

Grading Superintendent, SW BUILDERS, Leesburg, VA   2000–Present
- Recruited based on professional reputation and expertise in the field.
- Currently involved in a 168-acre site development for a shopping mall in Dulles, VA. This $14M project is slated for completion in June 2003.

General Superintendent, EAST COAST DEVELOPMENT, Fredericksburg, VA   1998–2000
- Simultaneously managed four job sites in Maryland (Frederick, Gaithersburg, Silver Spring, and Lexington Park).
- Responsible for site equipment and movement; managing all personnel; coordinating with the project manager; and meeting one-on-one with city, county, and state inspectors.
  Key Project: Completed, on-time and under budget, a $1M housing development (single-family and townhouses).

Field Superintendent, ARNOLD CORPORATION, Rockville, MD   1995–1999
- Effectively managed numerous simultaneous projects, including work for the Army Corps of Engineers.
  Key Project: Built the Major League Stadium. Coordinated 109 pieces of machinery and a crew of 139 personnel. This $16.5M, two-year project was completed in 17 months.

Project Manager/Site Superintendent, REESE EXCAVATION, INC., Mt. Airy, MD   1992–1995
- Managed site development for four new schools and expansion of two existing businesses in Frederick County, MD.
- Demonstrated a proven track record in passing inspection on first as-built.
  Key Projects: Damascus Middle School, $1.5M; Clarksburg Middle School, $1.3M; Urbana High School and football stadium, $1.3M; COMSTAT, $1M; Solarex, $1M.

Strategy: *Match resume style with the individual: right to the point, shooting for immediate results with high impact. Citing size, value, and outcome for each position is an effective way to communicate his expertise and diverse experience.*

TED A. HOFFMAN
304-555-7640
PAGE 2

EMPLOYMENT HISTORY (continued)

Site Superintendent, CITY CONSTRUCTION COMPANY, New York — 1990–1992
- Completed major site development for a 200-acre, $3M housing development off Martin Luther King Boulevard in Washington, DC.

Site Superintendent, LMS, INC., Frederick, MD — 1983–1990
- Built a 7.5-mile stretch of major highway, coordinating with both state and county inspectors. This $14.6M project involved four bridges and three major Class A stream crossings.

Shift Superintendent, WESTERN HEIGHTS CORPORATION, Colorado — 1981–1983
- Sunk two tunnels under the Anacostia River for the Washington Subway System. This two-year, $10M project presented the additional challenge of working under air pressure, 110 feet underground.

Five years' prior experience: BUFFALO COAL COMPANY, Bayard, WV
  Responsible for all above- and below-ground blasting.

PROFESSIONAL TRAINING AND CERTIFICATION

Mining Enforcement & Safety	US Department of the Interior
Explosive Engineer	Allegheny Community College
Health & Safety Underground Mining	Garrett Community College
Diesel Mechanics Certification	Diesel Institute of America
Seismology	Vibra Tech
Medic First Aid	State of Virginia

Certificates of Competency from the State of Maryland:

Confined Space	**Traffic Control**
First Responder & First Aid	**Sediment & Erosion Control**

FORMAL EDUCATION

Frostburg State University, Reality Therapy & GPI
Certificate program designed to teach skills in personnel management, effective communication, crisis intervention, and anger management.

University of Maryland, Teaching/Environmental Engineering
Completed two years of bachelor's degree program.

Jane C. Erickson

9112 8th Avenue N.
Seattle, Washington 98117   erickJ@msn.com   (206) 789-1234 home
(206) 527-9999 work

SENIOR TRANSIT PLANNER

Team & Project Leadership ▪ Public/Private Partnerships ▪ TDM Strategies ▪ Multi-Modal Development

PROFILE

- **Transportation projects manager with 15-year success record** as a leader/ supervisor, public/private liaison, troubleshooter/bridge builder, grants/projects manager, and strategic relationships point person. Strong analytical, budgeting, and financial skills: former banking professional. Award-winning program developer, leading innovative and motivated teams.

- **Strength: creating profitable win-win situations and mediating conflicts** between internal departments, union labor and management, private industry and government, other government agencies, and team members. Multi-task easily. Work at all levels, forging harmony, common goals, and cooperation between widely disparate players. Proven problem solver and negotiator. Skilled listener and supervisor: hiring, training, and evaluating. Excellent written and verbal communicator.

- **Sound knowledge of transportation operations, federal/local funding, and TDM marketing.** Propel transit and multi-modal commuting via contracted/grant-funded programs with private-sector developers and major employers. Create new products, i.e., transportation pass and commuter incentive programs. Work with elected officials, senior managers, and front-line decision makers, incorporating transit/bike/carpool/vanpool-friendly parking and transportation demand management (TDM) strategies into cities' urban plans, new development design, and employee benefit programs.

- **Excel at all stages of program and product design.** Steer concept and product development; grant, budget, and resource development; demonstration projects and testing; community outreach and partnership development; project implementation; and program maintenance and evaluation.

EDUCATION

M.S., Management, Seattle University, Seattle, Washington   **GPA 3.8**

B.S., Liberal Studies, Regents College, Albany, New York

Management Training Program, First Tennessee Bank, Memphis, Tennessee

PROFESSIONAL HISTORY

Puget Sound Transit, Lynnwood, WA   **1987–present**

Transit Planner, Market Development Section, 1994–present
Acting Supervisor, Market Development Section, May–September 2001
Lead 9 planners in design and implementation of employer programs and products that encourage non-drive-alone commuting. Oversee cost-benefits analysis, sales material, pricing, operational policy, and contract terms development. Facilitate regional transportation initiatives. Represent section at all levels.

Notable Projects

FlexPass: Program and product manager for a customized multi-modal pass program generating $1.5 million revenues, FY 2001. Lead a 5-person pass-design/contract-proposal team, working with 1,300+ employers.

Lynnwood Village FlexPass: Addressed retail commuting and parking overflows, upping bus use 300%.

Commuter Bonus/Commuter Bonus Plus: Project lead for a voucher/alternative-commute incentive program that currently enjoys more than 900 employer participants.

Regional Smart Card Pass Development Project: Member, technical development team.

Research Study: Federal Tax Implications to Employers Providing Commuting Benefits. Co-author.

Notable Relationships:

Microsoft, Bank of America, Unico Properties, University of Washington, Wright Runstead, WSDOT, City of Redmond, City of Bellevue, City of Seattle, Pierce Transit, Sound Transit, King County Metro

Strategy: *Create a strong profile that encapsulates the candidate's extensive, broad experience within the transportation industry. Identify key projects and relationships under her current high-profile position.*

JANE C. ERICKSON   Page 2 of 2

PROFESSIONAL HISTORY (continued)

Puget Sound Transit (continued)

Management Analyst, Transit Operations Division, 1987–1994
  Monitored and maintained $98 million annual budget. Managed special projects. Research, analyzed and monitored special issues for division.

First Tennessee Bank, Memphis, TN   **1984–1987**
Marketing Services Representative
  Supported corporate and division marketing and public relations projects for financial institution.

U.S. Department of Defense, Catania, Sicily (ITALY)   **1982–1984**
Training Coordinator
  Curriculum developer and presenter, delivering 40-hour educational programs to overseas military personnel. Studied Italian, developing fluency.

University of California, San Diego, CA   **1980–1982**
Career Needs Assessment Program Coordinator ▪ Office Manager

AWARDS & NOMINATIONS

2001
Special Recognition: Association for Commuter Transportation (ACT)
Awarded for co-chairing planning and implementation of 2001 International Conference

2000
Washington State Commuter Choice Governor's Award for Excellence — Team lead
Harvard University John F. Kennedy School of Government Innovations Award — Team member

1999
U.S. Environmental Protection Agency (EPA) and Renew America "Way to Go" Award
Awarded for Lynnwood Village FlexPass Project — Project Lead

1997
Washington State Wall of Fame, Nominee — Team member
Washington State Wall of Fame, Awarded individually for driving project success
Association for Commuter Transportation (ACT), Nominee, Joint Service Award — Team member

PROFESSIONAL ACTIVITIES

Boards, Conferences & Task Forces
Excellence in Commuting (employer recognition program) — Chairman of the Board — 2002
Women's Transportation Seminar (WTS) — Board member for 5 years — 1993–present
ACT International Conference, Spokesperson/Moderator Multiple Sessions — 2001
National Academy of Sciences Transportation Research Board (TRB) — Presenter — 2001
National Task Force, Federal Reauthorization (TEA-3) — 1998

Memberships
Transportation Research Board (TRB) — 1998–present
Association for Commuter Transportation (ACT) — 1999–present
Regional Representative, National Public Policy Committee — 1999–present
Washington State Rideshare Organization (WSRO) — 1999–present

RESUME 40: DEBRA O'REILLY, CPRW, JCTC, CEIP; BRISTOL, CT

Robert Saminger, P.E.

4443 Old Sawmill Road
Farmington, CT 06032

860-212-0113 (mobile)
860-675-5555 (home)
Rsaminger17@hotmail.com

Construction Industry Executive
Business Development / Pre-Construction Services / Project Development
Start-up, turnaround, and high-growth experience

Twenty-plus years of experience in construction, engineering, and business management; expertise in healthcare facility and multi-state retail rollout construction. Stable and profitable presence in the "repetitive build" industry. Registered Engineer.

Strengths in general management, business / project development, design-build process management, P&L management, consultative client relations, and team leadership. Recognized for enhancing bottom-line profitability through cost control, cultivating high-margin opportunities, and improving business processes. Noteworthy integrity; highly ethical.

Highlights of accomplishments:
- Provided strategic leadership in turnaround / corporate growth, earning corporate recognition as one of *Business Journal*'s "Top 50 Fastest-Growing Private Companies" for three consecutive years.
- Key player in 250% corporate growth, from $9 million to $23 million.
- Managed nationwide retail expansion, opening 89 stores in a single year.
- Successfully negotiated $28 million product contract with major U.S. retailer.

PROFESSIONAL HISTORY

The Command Group   *$50 million construction / specialty construction group*   1995–Present
(including Command Healthcare Group, Inc. and Command Construction Group, Inc.)
Service in capacities including:
– **President,** Command Healthcare Group, Inc. (1996–2002)
– **Vice President,** Command Construction Group, Inc. (2000–Present)
– **President** and **Chief Operating Officer,** The Command Group (1997–1999)

Steered Command companies through tumultuous growth and major organizational changes.
Originally recruited to lead the growth of Command Healthcare Group, Inc., a newly formed construction corporation. Elected to presidency in early 1996. Increased market visibility, expanded existing customer accounts, and procured new design-build negotiated contracts. Instituted financial forecasting; stabilized divisional accounting procedures; established a pay-when-paid system to control cash flow. Recruited well-qualified project managers and superintendents experienced in the healthcare industry and in multi-state construction. Implemented unique subcontract invoicing methodology to enhance efficiency and control billing accuracy. Automated field administration and initiated employee computer-literacy program.

Delegated to apply successful Command Healthcare principles to the Command Group in 1997. Succeeded in turning around and re-energizing forward momentum of the company. In 2002, assisted in merging of Healthcare Group functions with Command Construction.

Accomplishments:
- Completed 40+ freestanding projects, valued at over $70 million, in 11 states and more than 50 renovations / additions in 9 states. Contracted both publicly and privately funded assisted-living facilities, medical specialty units, skilled nursing facilities, and hospital renovations as well as funeral homes and retirement communities.

Strategy: *To downplay a change in title following a restructuring, present job titles in rank order rather than chronological order and combine job responsibilities into one section instead of repeating them for each job held.*

Robert Saminger, P.E. Page 2

Accomplishments (continued):

- Using digital technology, developed unique and cost-saving "Book of Do's & Don'ts," a supplemental management tool to disseminate field-learned knowledge among project managers and superintendents.
- Maintained strong national client / consulting relationships with leading healthcare companies.
- Continued to win lucrative, multimillion-dollar contracts despite corporate upheaval—e.g., in early 2002, launched a retail / restaurant competitive-bid program, procuring 18 projects totaling over $10 million.
- Led highly successful redesign of a national chain's prototype restaurant, from concept and design to build, to reduce the chain's capital expenditures. Restructured vital systems without sacrificing square footage or trademark appearance, reducing cost by 25%. As a result, Command has won three more contracts.

Corporate Engineering Manager, MLJ Computer Corporation　　1989–1995

Originally recruited to direct massive $15 million expansion of retail-store chain. Negotiated contracts; directed store design / construction, including fixtures, equipment, and supplies. Developed / implemented store security policies, escalation procedures, and more.

Accomplishments:

- Opened 89 stores in first year and 124 stores in 38 states overall.
- After expansion was completed, was internally recruited to Point-of-Sale (POS) division to market the first-ever computer-based cash-register systems to leading national retail clients. Directed marketing / sales, installation, help-desk functions, and product engineering.
- Developed business plan and marketed healthy POS division even as MLJ Computer's PC business plummeted. Division was acquired by a Fortune 500 company and maintains profitability today.
- Successfully negotiated $28 million contract for POS systems with a leading retailer: Initiated sale prior to acquisition; maintained positive client relationship and closed sale six months after acquisition.

Project Engineer, Connecticut Contractors, Inc.　　1983–1989

Managed four major projects totaling $30 million. Retail Plaza development: A three-building complex with a 15-story glass curtain-wall building, a nine-story pre-cast clad building, a five-story EIFS building, and a two-story underground parking structure. Also completed interior finish-out of 15 floors. Other projects included educational and commercial additions, renovations, and finish-outs.

Research Engineer, Connecticut State University　　1981–1983

Managed nine research projects targeting highway maintenance, rehabilitation, and design. Completed 17 hours toward Ph.D. in Engineering.

Engineering Assistant, Department of Highways and Public Transportation　　1979–1981

EDUCATION / LICENSURE

Professional Engineer	1987
Connecticut State University: Doctoral Studies, **Engineering**	1981–1983
Fairfield State University:	
Master of Engineering	1979
Bachelor of Science, Civil Engineering	Graduated **cum laude,** 1977

        Honors:
            Member, Engineering Honor Society
            Member, Civil Engineering Honor Society
            Member, University Honor Society

CHARLES "CHUCK" TIMPER

2335 Boulevard • Colonial Heights, VA 23834 • Tel: 804-504-6600 • Mobile: 804-504-0002

COMMERCIAL CONSTRUCTION SUPERINTENDENT

Site Management / Construction Supervision / Negotiation / Bidding / Contractor Relations

Accomplished Superintendent with over 20 years' broad-spectrum experience in all phases of commercial construction, directing projects valued to $36 million. Skill includes concrete tilt-ups, steel erection, ceramic tile, and carpentry. Trade proficiency includes mechanical, electrical, and framing. Strong capacity to provide team leadership and training; supervised staff of up to 120 with 50 direct reports. Goal oriented and results driven with strong ability to combine cutting-edge technologies with expert problem identification and resolution. Outstanding communication skills with capacity to interface with inspectors, auditors, engineers, architects, and other team members associated with a project.

Core competencies include:

- Purchasing / Estimating
- Vendor Relations / Customer Service
- Project Planning & Management
- Building & Site Layout

- Logistics & Strategic Planning
- Team Building & Leadership
- Plan & Spec Reading
- Problem Identification & Resolution

> **HIGH PERFORMANCE LEADER** who goes above and beyond to exceed expectations.
> *"I give it everything I've got."* —Chuck Timper

SELECTED PROJECTS

- **Colonial Heights County Hospital**—$6 million addition/remodel   Colonial Heights, VA
- **Richmond Museum & Library**—$7.5 million   Richmond, VA
- **State of Virginia Youth Authority Prison/School**—$7 million   Chesterfield, VA
- **Colonial Heights Retirement Center**—$5 million   Colonial Heights, VA
- **United States Post Offices**—combined value over $36 million   VA, MD, NC & SC

Additional projects and details available upon request.

CAREER HISTORY

Oversaw, managed, and directed all aspects of commercial construction and development strategy including supervision of all direct-hire and subcontractors to coordinate all facets of construction. Ensured streamlining of operations to produce cost savings; increased productivity and business capacity to generate profitability.

Bowers-Fontaine Company, Richmond, VA **PROJECT SUPERINTENDENT**	1987–1991 / 1993–2002
Arch Oakland, Richmond, VA (concurrent with above) **PROJECT SUPERINTENDENT**	1994–1995
T. Clark Jones, Baltimore, MD **PROJECT SUPERINTENDENT**	1992–1993
Otis & Goodman Construction, Scranton, PA **ASSISTANT SUPERINTENDENT**	1986–1987

EARLY HISTORY

Between 1978–1986, worked on a variety of projects encompassing remodeling, carpentry, steel buildings, and storage systems as both business owner and employed professional. These formative years constructed the backbone of my expertise and skill, which I utilize as a Superintendent today. Details of prior experience available upon request.

Strategy: *Create a trim, one-page presentation that emphasizes skills and selected projects while listing the candidate's career history with minimal details.*

CHAPTER 8

Resumes for Managers and Executives in Food and Beverage, Hotels, and Travel and Tourism

- Restaurant Manager
- Hotel General Manager
- Hospitality Executive
- Travel and Tourism Executive
- Bar and Grill Manager

RESUME 42: ANITA RADOSEVICH, CPRW, IJCTC, CEIP; LODI, CA

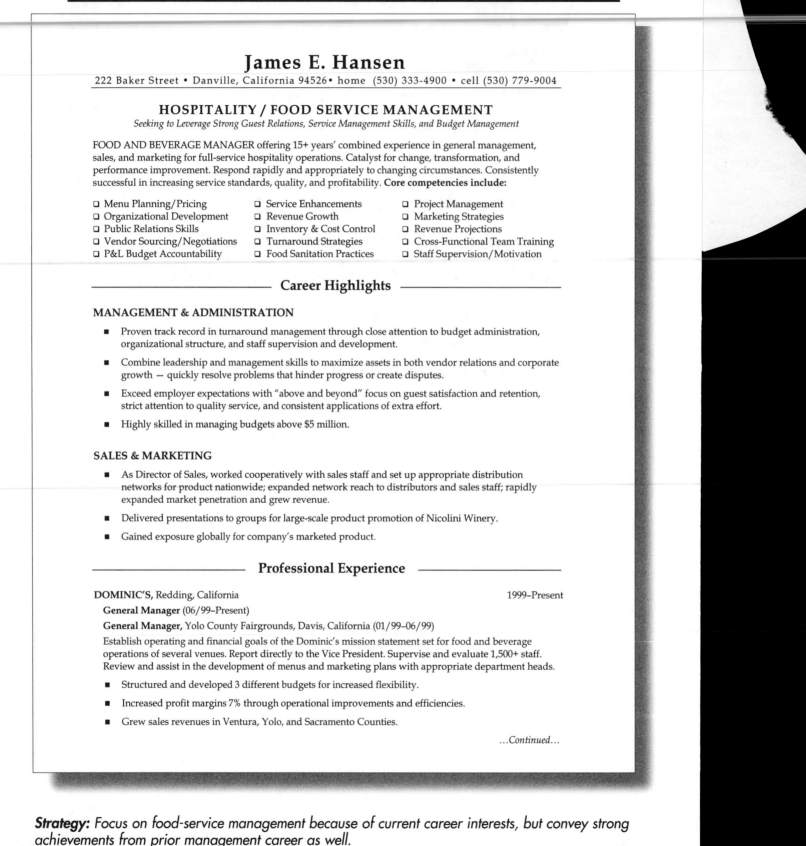

James E. Hansen

222 Baker Street • Danville, California 94526• home (530) 333-4900 • cell (530) 779-9004

HOSPITALITY / FOOD SERVICE MANAGEMENT

Seeking to Leverage Strong Guest Relations, Service Management Skills, and Budget Management

FOOD AND BEVERAGE MANAGER offering 15+ years' combined experience in general management, sales, and marketing for full-service hospitality operations. Catalyst for change, transformation, and performance improvement. Respond rapidly and appropriately to changing circumstances. Consistently successful in increasing service standards, quality, and profitability. **Core competencies include:**

❑ Menu Planning/Pricing	❑ Service Enhancements	❑ Project Management
❑ Organizational Development	❑ Revenue Growth	❑ Marketing Strategies
❑ Public Relations Skills	❑ Inventory & Cost Control	❑ Revenue Projections
❑ Vendor Sourcing/Negotiations	❑ Turnaround Strategies	❑ Cross-Functional Team Training
❑ P&L Budget Accountability	❑ Food Sanitation Practices	❑ Staff Supervision/Motivation

——————————————— **Career Highlights** ———————————————

MANAGEMENT & ADMINISTRATION

- Proven track record in turnaround management through close attention to budget administration, organizational structure, and staff supervision and development.

- Combine leadership and management skills to maximize assets in both vendor relations and corporate growth — quickly resolve problems that hinder progress or create disputes.

- Exceed employer expectations with "above and beyond" focus on guest satisfaction and retention, strict attention to quality service, and consistent applications of extra effort.

- Highly skilled in managing budgets above $5 million.

SALES & MARKETING

- As Director of Sales, worked cooperatively with sales staff and set up appropriate distribution networks for product nationwide; expanded network reach to distributors and sales staff; rapidly expanded market penetration and grew revenue.

- Delivered presentations to groups for large-scale product promotion of Nicolini Winery.

- Gained exposure globally for company's marketed product.

——————————————— **Professional Experience** ———————————————

DOMINIC'S, Redding, California   1999–Present

General Manager (06/99–Present)

General Manager, Yolo County Fairgrounds, Davis, California (01/99–06/99)

Establish operating and financial goals of the Dominic's mission statement set for food and beverage operations of several venues. Report directly to the Vice President. Supervise and evaluate 1,500+ staff. Review and assist in the development of menus and marketing plans with appropriate department heads.

- Structured and developed 3 different budgets for increased flexibility.

- Increased profit margins 7% through operational improvements and efficiencies.

- Grew sales revenues in Ventura, Yolo, and Sacramento Counties.

...Continued...

Strategy: *Focus on food-service management because of current career interests, but convey strong achievements from prior management career as well.*

James E. Hansen   Page Two

Professional Experience, Continued

MARINA RESORT, Sacramento, California   1995–1999

Director of Food and Beverage

Charged with budget management for nightclub/restaurant. Streamlined catering, concerts, and special events. Recruited, supervised, trained, and scheduled staff. Oversaw scheduling, inventory management, and menu development. Maintained daily and annual sales records.

CATERINA'S SPAGHETTI HOUSE, Davis, California   1994–1995

Bartender / Customer Service

Acted as Event and Entertainment Coordinator during holidays, weekends, and special events.

MARINA RESORT, Sacramento, California   1991–1994

Club Manager

Oversaw event planning and coordination.

WAREHOUSE CONCERT SERIES, Davis, California   1993

Special Event Coordinator

Coordinated and supervised concert beer sales for the Fish Market and Petra's Restaurants at the Warehouse Concert during popular rock-band performances.

NICOLINI WINERY, Napa, California   1981–1988

Director of Sales and R & D

Brought on board as the driving force to spearhead rapid, profitable growth. Vigorously pursued strategic partnerships to build visibility and support product. Developed progressive marketing and negotiated exclusive contracts with 176 distributorships.

Professional Development

Seminars: General Management, Dale Carnegie — Leadership and Presentation Training

Computer Skills: PC skills, Internet, and proprietary applications

Marketing Development Expertise: New Client Development, Territory Management, Key Account Management, New Product Introduction, and Sales Presentations

Certification: California Food Certification

Military: United States Marine Corps, Honorable Discharge
Leadership Training, Noncommissioned Officers' School

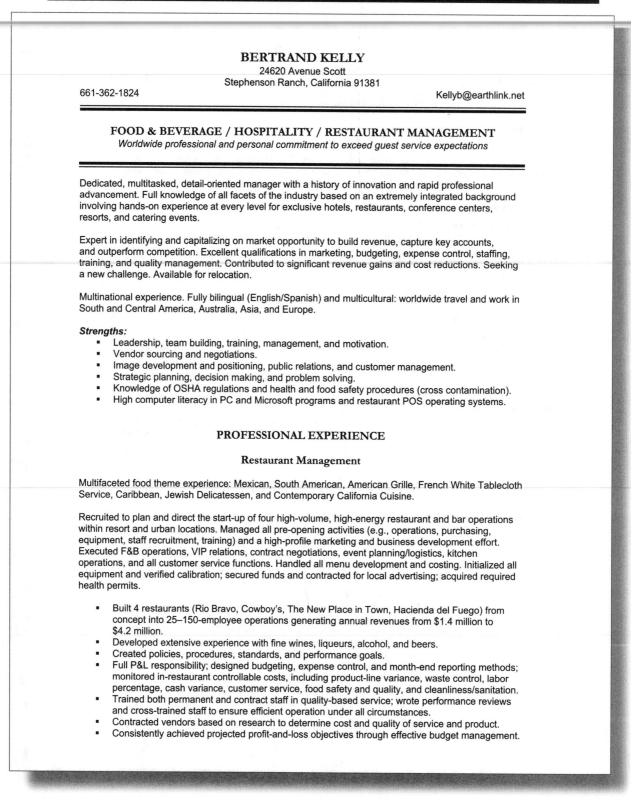

BERTRAND KELLY
24620 Avenue Scott
Stephenson Ranch, California 91381

661-362-1824   Kellyb@earthlink.net

FOOD & BEVERAGE / HOSPITALITY / RESTAURANT MANAGEMENT
Worldwide professional and personal commitment to exceed guest service expectations

Dedicated, multitasked, detail-oriented manager with a history of innovation and rapid professional advancement. Full knowledge of all facets of the industry based on an extremely integrated background involving hands-on experience at every level for exclusive hotels, restaurants, conference centers, resorts, and catering events.

Expert in identifying and capitalizing on market opportunity to build revenue, capture key accounts, and outperform competition. Excellent qualifications in marketing, budgeting, expense control, staffing, training, and quality management. Contributed to significant revenue gains and cost reductions. Seeking a new challenge. Available for relocation.

Multinational experience. Fully bilingual (English/Spanish) and multicultural: worldwide travel and work in South and Central America, Australia, Asia, and Europe.

Strengths:
- Leadership, team building, training, management, and motivation.
- Vendor sourcing and negotiations.
- Image development and positioning, public relations, and customer management.
- Strategic planning, decision making, and problem solving.
- Knowledge of OSHA regulations and health and food safety procedures (cross contamination).
- High computer literacy in PC and Microsoft programs and restaurant POS operating systems.

PROFESSIONAL EXPERIENCE

Restaurant Management

Multifaceted food theme experience: Mexican, South American, American Grille, French White Tablecloth Service, Caribbean, Jewish Delicatessen, and Contemporary California Cuisine.

Recruited to plan and direct the start-up of four high-volume, high-energy restaurant and bar operations within resort and urban locations. Managed all pre-opening activities (e.g., operations, purchasing, equipment, staff recruitment, training) and a high-profile marketing and business development effort. Executed F&B operations, VIP relations, contract negotiations, event planning/logistics, kitchen operations, and all customer service functions. Handled all menu development and costing. Initialized all equipment and verified calibration; secured funds and contracted for local advertising; acquired required health permits.

- Built 4 restaurants (Rio Bravo, Cowboy's, The New Place in Town, Hacienda del Fuego) from concept into 25–150-employee operations generating annual revenues from $1.4 million to $4.2 million.
- Developed extensive experience with fine wines, liqueurs, alcohol, and beers.
- Created policies, procedures, standards, and performance goals.
- Full P&L responsibility; designed budgeting, expense control, and month-end reporting methods; monitored in-restaurant controllable costs, including product-line variance, waste control, labor percentage, cash variance, customer service, food safety and quality, and cleanliness/sanitation.
- Trained both permanent and contract staff in quality-based service; wrote performance reviews and cross-trained staff to ensure efficient operation under all circumstances.
- Contracted vendors based on research to determine cost and quality of service and product.
- Consistently achieved projected profit-and-loss objectives through effective budget management.

Strategy: *Use a functional format to tie together the diverse activities and achievements of a career spent traveling from one resort to the next as both a ski instructor and food-and-beverage manager. Highlight restaurant experience because of goal to continue in this field.*

BERTRAND KELLY — Page 2

Management

Operations Manager leading Gunnison Ski & Golf Company's Ski and Snowboard Schools' $1.6 million division through tremendous growth. Held full P&L responsibility; all strategic and business planning functions, finance and budgeting, operating management, marketing, human resources, MIS, and administrative affairs.

Financial Achievements:
- Increased revenues from 50% to 70% of department's net.
- Launched an aggressive reengineering of existing operations to reduce costs, improve service, and accelerate profit gains. Reduced operating costs by more than 20%.
- Consistently exceeded budget in projected revenues and profit margins.

Operating Achievements:
- Developed dynamic organizational infrastructure responsive to constantly changing market and financial and customer demands.
- Created high-profile marketing, advertising, service, and employee-incentive programs critical to the company's sustained growth cycle.
- Spearheaded development, training, and implementation of a fully computerized system for all department products.

AWARDS / HONORS

Company Manager of the Year	Gunnison Ski & Golf Company	1999
12-time nominee for Employee of the Month	Gunnison Ski & Golf Company	1994–2000
Top 5 Revenue Producer (out of staff of 500)	Ski Schools of Aspen	1991–1994
Board of Directors — 2 terms	Professional Ski Instructors of America	1989–1994

EMPLOYMENT HISTORY

Restaurant/Food & Beverage Management

General Manager	Rio Bravo Cantina, Simi Valley, CA	2001
Manager	Maria's Delicatessen, Sedona, AZ	1994
Manager	Kansas City Banquet, Kansas City, MO	1993
Assistant Manager	The Cantina, Kansas City, MO	1992
Floor Manager	Cowboy's Grille, Telluride, CO	1991–1992
Manager	The New Place in Town, Silverstar Hotel, Aspen, CO	1990
General Manager	The Mine Company Restaurant, Vale, CO	1989–1990
Assistant F&B Director	The Great Lakes Country Club, Aspen, CO	1987–1989
Captain Dining Room	Le Soleil French Restaurant, Reno, NV	1985
Bar Manager	Hacienda del Fuego, Reno, NV	1980–1981

National & International Group Sales and Management

Guest Relations Docent	Gunnison Historical Museum, Gunnison, CO	2001
Supervisor, Group Sales	Gunnison Ski & Golf Company, Gunnison, CO	1994–2000
Asst. Ski School Director	Sal Si Puede Ski Resort, Sal Si Puede, Chile	1983–1985
Senior Instructor	Falls Creek Ski Resort, Falls Creek, Australia	1981–1983

EDUCATION

Master of Arts, Psychology, San Diego State University, San Diego, CA
Bachelor of Arts, Psychology and Business Administration, University of Arizona, Tucson, AZ

RESUME 44: ROBERTA GAMZA, JCTC, CEIP, CJST; LOUISVILLE, CO

Cliff Stanton

HOTEL DIRECTOR
OPERATIONS / ROOMS / FOOD AND BEVERAGE
CONTROLLER / SALES

REVERSING UNDERPERFORMING PROPERTIES AND OPERATIONS
TRANSFORMING ORDINARY PROPERTIES INTO EXTRAORDINARY PROPERTIES

STRENGTHS
- Improving guest relations and enhancing the overall guest experience.
- Controlling costs and tenaciously demanding quality service.
- Strengthening financial performance — reducing expenses, recovering write-offs, up-selling services.
- Reducing employee turnover by developing "team-spirited" organizations and employees.
- Gaining market position and market share in highly competitive locations.
- Mentoring/training employees for promotion to management.

CERTIFICATIONS AND TRAINING
- Blood-Borne Pathogens Certification (2000)
- POS Certification (Micros 8700)
- Property Automation Training Certification (1999)
- Hotel Management and REVPAR Training (1998)
- Management Certification (1998)
- Restaurant Management Training (1996)

TECHNICAL EXPERTISE AND KNOWLEDGE
- PMS (Micros 3500, Innsure, Innstar)
- UMS (accounting software)
- PBX System
- POS (Microns 8700, Aloha)
- Vincard Vision 3.1
- Harmony Database System

PROFESSIONAL HISTORY

General Manager, Imperial Hotel, Denver, CO   **2001–Present**
(A full-service hotel with 198 guest rooms, restaurant, lounge, pool, exercise room, and 6,800 sq. ft. of meeting rooms and banquet facilities.)

Recruited as Assistant General Manager and promoted to General Manager within 4 months. Challenged to turn around declining property—formulate new development plans and budgets, tackle staffing problems, and address customer-satisfaction issues.

- ✓ Actively engaged in marketing activities resulting in increased occupancy.
- ✓ Won multiple contracts with breakthrough accounts: airlines and major trucking company.
- ✓ Developed operational and remodeling budgets for changeover to an assisted living facility.
- ✓ Recognized by customers for outstanding customer service.

Rooms Division Manager/Controller, Sturbridge House Historic Inn, Sturbridge, MA   **1999–2001**
(An award-winning historic-register hotel dating back to the Revolutionary War, comprising 126 rooms, 3 restaurants, and 11 banquet rooms across 4 locations on 120 acres.)

Managed all aspects of the rooms division. Appointed by Area VP to replace outgoing controller. Requested to manage and assist major functions for the dining/banquet areas on holidays and special events.

- ✓ Simplified pricing structure resulting in $159K increase in revenue and significant improvements to ADR.
- ✓ Reduced renovation costs by $39K through contract negotiations and close supervision of work.
- ✓ Reduced guest complaints by 89% by training employees on proactive customer service and raising cleaning standards.
- ✓ Improved management/labor relations through wage compensation and incentive programs saving over $53K in annual labor expenses. Reduced employee turnover rate by 75%. Achieved highest Sturbridge Group employee-satisfaction ranking.
- ✓ Developed operating budgets for Sturbridge Group, five separate units with total sales of $10M.
- ✓ Recovered 76% ($430K) of over-120-days receivables from previously abandoned accounts.

P.O. Box 15342 · Denver, CO 80239 · Home (303) 555-5210 · Mobile/Pager (303) 555-1823 · cliffs@yahoo.net

Strategy: *To meet the candidate's goal of a management position with a top hotel chain, emphasize his solid track record of turning around faltering properties.*

Cliff Stanton
Page 2

Hotel General Manager, Quality Inn, Amarillo, TX   1998–1999

Recruited to turn around faltering 121-room hotel. Analyzed operations/business processes; recommended and implemented corrective actions to restore profitability, increase employee morale, and raise customer satisfaction.

- ✓ Transformed hotel into a lucrative $1M operation through innovative marketing/business strategies, enthusiastic guest relations, and improved operations.
- ✓ Increased revenue by $110K ($89K of controllable profit).
- ✓ Recognized as the first manager to maintain costs at optimal levels to show yearly profitability.
- ✓ Consistently ranked #1 of 15 in area for the most improved occupancy.
- ✓ Increased motel's quality score from 52 to 90 (out of 100).

Food and Beverage Director, Lafitte Town House, New Orleans, LA   1995–1998

Managed all food-and-beverage operations of an upscale private club, generating over $1.5M annually. Directed human resources, marketing, purchasing, financial reporting, inventory control, regulatory compliance, and guest relations. Led a staff of 20+ in an 8,000-sq.-ft., three-story building.

- ✓ Revitalized languishing food operation by introducing new menus and offering functions, meetings, and catering based on guest preferences and seasonal considerations.
- ✓ Increased revenues 167% over three years by increasing member base and check average.
- ✓ Reduced annual labor expenses by $50K by changing staffing mix, improving guest/staff ratio, and employing part-time help.

Banquet Manager, Holiday Inn, Lafayette, LA   1993–1995

Coordinated and directed all aspects of the banquet operations in a 3-star, 300-room hotel with over 7,500 sq. ft. of meeting and banquet facilities.

- ✓ Generated $1.2M in food and beverage sales.
- ✓ Trained largely inexperienced staff to implement the highest standards of customer service and productivity.
- ✓ Achieved 45% controllable profit through strategic marketing planning (up-selling most functions by 15%), creative labor engineering (less than 50% turnover), cost controls, and high service standards.
- ✓ Recognized for strong leadership and customer focus, earning a series of promotions to increasingly more responsible positions.

PROFESSIONAL AFFILIATIONS

Board Member, Worcester County Convention & Visitor Bureau (WCCVB)
Member, Sturbridge Economic Development Association (SEDA)
Board of Directors, Massachusetts Hotel Association

EDUCATION

Auburn University, Microbiology Major — completed 3½ years of Bachelor of Science Degree, 1991–1993
University of Southwestern Louisiana, Associate of Applied Science, Business Management, 1990

MILITARY SPECIAL HONORS

United States Army, Operation Sergeant/Squad Leader
- ✓ Chosen "Honor Graduate" out of the 250 enrolled in the Primary Leadership Development Course.
- ✓ Awarded three Army Achievement and two Good Conduct Medals for outstanding performance.

P.O. Box 15342 · Denver, CO 80239 · Home (303) 555-5210 · Mobile/Pager (303) 555-1823 · cliffs@yahoo.net

RESUME 45: GAYLE HOWARD, CPRW, CRW, CCM; MELBOURNE, AUSTRALIA

ANGUS O'SULLIVAN

Apartment 2, 5 Foelsche Street
San Francisco, CA 94101
Email: angsul@yahoo.com

Residence: (918) 942-1211
Business: (918) 981-2323
Mobile: (918) 999-3178

SENIOR MANAGER – HOSPITALITY
General Management • Venue Management • Operations

Participative management professional; results focused, entrepreneurial, and practical. 12+ years' progressive leadership experiences have created a passion for surpassing financial and service objectives via a combination of world-class service delivery, lean operating methods, renewed marketing directions, and incentive-driven rewards for team achievement. Acknowledged for capacity to observe, calculate, and react swiftly to avert conflict and restore workplace harmony. Derive genuine pleasure from transforming high-potential staff into outstanding leaders demonstrating the creativity critical to financial and operational success. Flourish in turnaround situations, restoring profits and instituting the essential infrastructure crucial to sustained prosperity.

Professional strengths include:

- ✓ Profit Maximization
- ✓ Multimillion-Dollar Budgets
- ✓ Team Building & Motivation
- ✓ Staff Training & Development
- ✓ Retail Operations Management

- ✓ Profit & Loss Accountability
- ✓ Marketing & Promotions
- ✓ First-Class Customer Service
- ✓ Venue Management
- ✓ Stock & Inventory Control

- ✓ Supplier Negotiations
- ✓ Risk Management & Minimization
- ✓ Upgrade/Refurbishment Projects

Technology—Microsoft Word, Excel, Access, PowerPoint; Email; Internet; Visypay

EDUCATION

Bachelor of Science, Business Administration (Marketing)
University of Southern California

Bachelor of Engineering (Mining)
University of New South Wales, Australia

Hundreds of hours devoted to ongoing professional development throughout career including workshops, conferences, information sessions, and formal short courses. Includes Train Small Groups—Certificate IV (California Chamber of Commerce and Industry).

BENCHMARKS & MILESTONES

✓ **Relocated to Australia and revitalized hotel with worn reputation and steady financial losses into a dynamic, economically buoyant award winner,** recognized for excellence by the prestigious Australian Hospitality Association. Won Best Hotel for the Northern Territory 2001; awarded Best Northern Territory Bottle Shop two years consecutively and Best Bar Presentation 1999.

✓ **Transformed nightclub with steeply declining profits into a money-spinner** that quadrupled revenue returns to $45,000 in just 16 months. Executed plan to refocus entertainment offerings towards patrons with high disposable incomes; introduced daily "theme nights" featuring R&B music and styles from the '70s, '80s, and '90s, attracting older patrons with new style and inherent capacity to spend.

✓ **Increased bottle-shop gross profits to 27%.** Overhauled pricing levels through minimal discounting on traditionally slow trade nights and vigorously promoted slow-moving stock. Renewed customer patronage prompted additional "on sales" that increased average bottle shop GP by 4%.

Angus O'Sullivan   Page 1   Confidential

Strategy: *Convey vibrant and current image through striking design and upbeat language while not losing "management" feel of the resume.*

CAREER CHRONOLOGY

CROSSMODE GROUP OF COMPANIES   1999–Present

General Manager/Licensee, Hi-UP Hotel, Darwin, Australia

<u>Report to</u>: Director, Hotels Crossmode

Hi-UP Hotel, Darwin, boasts up to 100 staff in peak periods and revenues of $9.5 million per annum generated from 5 bars, a bottle shop, 40-room accommodations, and function rooms.

Handpicked to turn around hotel in Australia, combating declining profits and aggressive market competition. Established a 12-point strategic blueprint aimed at delivering across-the-board improvements in staff numbers, availability, entertainment, security, and departmental operations through intensive cost assessment and market analysis. With scant attention paid to marketing, the necessity of establishing an image as an innovator was critical, as was the need to revitalize grounds, revamp sluggish and costly processes, and instill a sense of pride and achievement throughout a largely dispirited staff.

Hotel complex has realized remarkable turnaround, becoming a venue of choice for the local customer base and generating $3 million in healthy and sustainable profits over 3 years.

Actions & Contributions:

✓ Consolidated entertainment decision-making by appointing an entertainment professional, savvy to local band pricing, and a seasoned negotiator on contract benefits.

✓ Improved tracking systems for staff rosters and payroll, monitoring labor costs and more effectively assessing the need for senior personnel.

✓ Reduced headcount and recovered funds earmarked for revenue generation by removing costly in-house accountant from the payroll.

✓ Tripled revenues and cut costs 90% by transforming the poorly attended five-star restaurant into a conference room open to bookings for personal and corporate celebrations.

✓ Managed major refurbishment project—a combined hotel and motel upgrade, from concept through implementation without incident.

✓ Divided year into "wet" and "dry" segments that responded to the peaks and troughs of seasonal patronage and allowed a "floating" dollar emphasis to be placed in areas most needed.

✓ Transitioned focus from tourist operation to local trade base capitalizing on the 8 months of the year Darwin is outside tourism season. Completed extensive SWOT analysis providing the foundation to respond to patrons' requests for live entertainment, pub food, good atmosphere, and good service.

✓ Established in-house training program. Investing in a core group of high-performance team members, won outstanding loyalty and unparalleled staff retention.

✓ Established series of "signature" events attracting up to 7000 people per night to maintain interest and momentum. Includes the Beer Festival (7000 pax), Miss Swim Suit (4000 pax), Wine Festival (4000 pax), October Fest (6000 pax), Greek Night (1000 pax), R & B Night (2000 pax).

✓ Defended noise complaint vigorously and successfully, winning case and establishing reputation as a responsible licensee with solid business practices and community affinity.

Results:

✓ Improved bottom line by over $3m in 3 years.

✓ Doubled 2001/2002 projections in budget.

✓ Transitioned hotel from breakeven to 17% ROI.

PRIOR EMPLOYMENT

HOLIDAY TODAY CHAIN, San Francisco, CA, **Food & Beverage Manager**   1995–1999

RFT CATERING, San Francisco, CA, **Restaurant Staff**   1990–1994

DENISE CHAN

denisechan@email.com

125 Morrison Avenue
San Francisco, California 94132

Residence: (415) 555-3344
Mobile: (408) 555-2222

TRAVEL & TOURISM INDUSTRY EXECUTIVE

Extensive Knowledge of Tour and Cruise Industry
Innovator in Packaging Cruise Programs and Tours

- Well-respected Industry Executive with 20+ years professional and managerial experience leading tour companies from start-up through fast-track growth and market expansion.
- Consistently successful in identifying and capitalizing upon market opportunities to drive revenue growth and expand market penetration.
- Pioneer in strategic alliances and business partnerships to grow business.
- Strong leadership and team-building skills with a participatory management style.

Sales & Marketing / Key Account Management / P&L Management / Information Technology
Team Building / Public Relations & Promotions / Strategic Business Partnerships

---

PROFESSIONAL EXPERIENCE

President • 1995 to Present
INTERNATIONAL SPECIALTY TOURS, LTD., San Francisco, CA

Recruited by Chairman to spearhead growth of mass-market tour company with programs to Europe, Britain, and the Mediterranean. Charged with full responsibility for US operations including P&L accountability, business and market planning, sales training and management, information technology, and administrative affairs. Negotiate and manage strategic partnerships with travel agencies, airlines, and cruise lines.

- Delivered consistent increases in sales performance, building revenues from $12 million to $32 million within 2 years. During the same period, reduced expenses by 15% and improved bottom line by more than $1 million.
- Evaluated market trends and implemented strategies to reposition company as a niche operator.
- Developed key strategic partnership with leading international cruise line.
- Secured sole representation for major airline vacation packages.
- Introduced improved computerized technologies including online connection to Apollo Leisure Shopper. Additionally, working on additional tour systems and electronic distribution methods.
- Improved brand recognition through focus on improved product and service.
- Awarded "Office of the Year" in 1999 and "Executive of the Year" in 2000.

Sr. Vice President Sales & Marketing • 1994 to 1995
WORLDTRAVELER TOURS, Tampa, FL

Charged with all sales and marketing functions for $150 million Caribbean tour operator. Hired, trained, and managed sales team. Developed and implemented marketing budget. Created sales/marketing strategies including development of collateral materials and seminar presentations.

- Repositioned regional company as a national competitor.
- Increasing revenues by 30% within 1 year.
- Brought a "Sales and Reservations" approach to focus on top producers, which increased revenues and reduced selling cost.

Strategy: Use bold and italic text to promote the candidate's expertise as an innovator as well as some key market strengths. Throughout, demonstrate bottom-line results contributed throughout her career.

DENISE CHAN   Resume (Page 2)

PROFESSIONAL EXPERIENCE, continued

Vice President Sales and Marketing (1985 to 1994)
BARKELEY TOURS, INC., New York, NY

Recruited for newly formed company to package and market tours of Europe and Eastern Mediterranean with full autonomy for establishing marketing plans and building a competitive presence. Established initial marketing infrastructure and developed long-term strategic and short-term tactical marketing plans.

- Drove revenues from start-up to $120 million, positioning company as the mass-market leader to Europe.
- Obtained exclusive contracts with airlines, including vacation tour program to Europe with major airline.
- Created innovative, distinctive, and successful direct-mail, advertising, promotion, and business-development campaigns.
- Built national sales and marketing network, negotiating strategic partnerships and alliances.
- Awarded "Salesman of the Year," 1987, 1988, 1990, 1994.

EDUCATION

OXFORD POLYTECHNIC, Sheffield, UK
Degree in Hotel Management and Tourism

Management Training: Suisse Hotels and Restaurants, Switzerland; Hotel Geneve, Geneva, Switzerland.

Continuing Education / Professional Development: Stephen Covey seminar: *7 Habits of Highly Effective People;* Tom Peters *WOW Seminars;* Harvard Business School training.

Certified Travel Counselor Course, 1981

FOREIGN LANGUAGE SKILLS

Fluent in French; working knowledge of Spanish

PROFESSIONAL AFFILIATIONS

Member—USTOA (United States Tour Operators Association)
Member—ASTA (American Society of Travel Agents)
Member—New York Athletic Club
Member—SKAL

ADDITIONAL SKILLS

Accomplished and articulate public speaker, frequently selected to deliver presentations to industry gatherings of 250 to 1500 people.

—Available for Domestic/International Travel and/or Relocation—

RESUME 47: ART FRANK, MBA; OLDSMAR, FL

Debra Winters

155 Greendale St. ♦ Tampa, FL 34688 ♦ (823) 552-6711 ♦ debrawinters@aol.com

QUICK PROFILE

Eight years' experience managing a popular pub-style community bar & grill. General management expertise includes growth and revenue enhancement, costing, sales and profit analyses, personnel management, supplier and distributor negotiations, and kitchen operations. Detailed knowledge of food and beverage brands, purchasing, and inventory control.

RELEVANT EXPERIENCE

1995–Present   **Airport Lounge & Grill,** Tampa, FL
                 General Manager / Partner

♦ Airport Lounge & Grill is a 2200sf combination neighborhood bar / restaurant with a seating capacity of 299 that has attained a reputation as a warm, pub-style "eatery." Strong interpersonal skills combined with a commitment to customer service paved the way for driving annual sales revenues from approximately $300,000 to $750,000. The latest growth figures show increments of around $75,000 per year, a good percentage of which is derived from repeat trade. Always set examples for staff by being a leader in guest courtesy and *Total Customer Satisfaction.*

♦ Supervise a staff of 15 consisting of 8 bartenders and waitresses, 4 barbacks, and 3 to 4 cooks.

♦ Oversee all food preparation, cash transactions, cleanliness protocols, and general facility upkeep; includes adherence to state health and sanitation regulations and fire codes, preparation of work schedules as well as payroll, payables, sales-tax preparation, theft control, and building security.

♦ Oversee all hiring, scheduling, terminations, training, and miscellaneous personnel issues.

♦ Established strong relationships with beer distributors, i.e. J.J.Taylor and Pepin Distributors, and sold all leading imported and domestic beer brands.

♦ Created a positive public image via community outreach, club sponsorships, radio promos, co-op advertising, and fundraisers.

♦ Voted *"Best Bar in the Bay"* by the *Weekly Planet,* 2000.

2001–2002   **World Party News,** Tampa, FL (Concurrent with above)
                 Publisher/Editor

♦ Created a travel magazine targeting the young-adult market. Traveled to "hot party" resort destinations (Cancun, Bahamas, New Orleans, Lake Havasu) to obtain suitable stories and graphics.

♦ Obtained film footage, still pictures, and videos; interviewed attendees for news content at various club venues.

1994–1995   **Beef O'Brady's,** Bloomingdale, FL
                 Bartender / Waitress

♦ Performed standard restaurant duties in a heavy-volume national chain establishment.

1991–1994   Ford Motor Credit Co., Ft. Lauderdale, FL
                 Cashier
                 Lease Administrator

EDUCATION / CERTIFICATIONS

♦ University of South Florida, Tampa, FL: 2 Years ♦ AA Curriculum
♦ Certified Food Handler, State of Florida

MISCELLANEOUS

Enjoy reading, scuba diving, boating, and other water activities.

TRANSFERABLE SKILLS & ATTRIBUTES

Profit Conscious	Persistent, Quick Learner	Flexible	Troubleshooter	Caring Nature

Strategy: *Focus the bulk of the resume on the candidate's most recent experience as manager of a popular pub-style restaurant. Use eye-catching graphics and a concise one-page format to keep the reader's attention riveted on key accomplishments and attributes.*

CHAPTER 9

Resumes for Managers and Executives in Health Care

- Legal Nurse Consultant
- Home-Care Executive
- Public-Health Administrator
- Retirement-Community Administrator
- Long-Term-Care Facility Administrator
- Fitness-Facility Executive
- Health-Care Executive
- Health-Care Administrator

Danielle Winker R.N.

15 Boynton Beach Court
Deerfield Beach, FL 33441
(H) 954.567.6196   (Fax) 954.567.6197
Email: daniellewinker@aol.com

LEGAL NURSE CONSULTANT / NURSE PARALEGAL
Registered Nurse / Case Management & Assessment / Chart Review

Accomplished nursing professional with 15+ years' clinical experience as Staff Nurse and Charge Nurse. Recent graduate of *Legal Nurse Consulting / Paralegal Studies program*. Studied all aspects of legal process with emphasis on tort law, legal research, litigation skills and support, and principles and concepts of legal nurse consulting. **Key strengths include:**

- Registered Nurse, States of New York and New Jersey; Certified Childbirth Educator; Certified Inpatient Obstetrics Nurse.
- BA in English. Superior writing skills and ability to draft concise, effective legal documents with meticulous attention to detail.
- Strong interpersonal skills with proven ability to establish rapport with difficult clients, patients, and other medical personnel.
- Highly organized, with demonstrated ability to set priorities and manage multiple projects.
- Results-driven. Work well under pressure and against deadlines.
- Experienced Office Manager with strengths in accounts payable and receivable, vendor negotiations, payroll, billing, insurance, and fee collection.

PROFESSIONAL TRAINING AND EDUCATION

DIPLOMA, LEGAL NURSE CONSULTING / PARALEGAL STUDIES
FAU College, Boca Raton, FL 2002 **(GPA: 4.0)**
Honors Graduate
Delta Epsilon Tau International Honor Society

Legal Coursework Included: *Principles and Concepts of Legal Nurse Consulting; Tort Law; Civil Litigation; Criminal Law Process; Contracts; Insurance Law; Wills/Trusts/Estate Planning; Interviewing and Investigation; Business Organizations; Legal Research Specialty; Legal Ethics; Litigation Assistantship Specialty; Administrative Law; and Risk Management.*

AAS NURSING, Grady Hospital School of Nursing, Atlanta, GA
Recipient, Mary Frances Betar Scholarship Award for Scholastic Excellence

BA ENGLISH LITERATURE, City College of Boca Raton, Boca Raton, FL

RELEVANT SKILLS AND EXPERIENCE

Legal Core Competencies
- Analyze and summarize medical records.
- Perform personal injury case analysis for plaintiffs and defendants.
- Assist attorneys in screening medical malpractice cases and determining "case worthiness."
- Prepare fact and expert witnesses for deposition and trial.
- Assist attorneys in preparation of various discovery requests, demand letters, and other correspondence.
- Assist in locating and evaluating qualified medical experts.

Strategy: *Show strong qualifications for new niche of Legal Nurse Consultant, combining legal and health-care expertise; place education up front because it is recent and required; show core skills and related achievements under three functional headings.*

Danielle Winker R.N.

Obstetrical Nursing

- Implemented high quality of care for low and high-risk patients (premature labor, multiple births, and critical-care situations) throughout entire labor and delivery process at large, tertiary-care centers.
- Proficient in fetal monitor strip interpretation.
- Monitored and assessed patients at risk for pre-term labor, wrote weekly reports for physicians, and provided post-partum summary of patients' care and outcome.
- Designed and delivered highly informative childbirth education classes for audiences of 8 to 10 couples for over 10 years. Frequently recognized and recommended by doctors as "preferred" childbirth educator.
- Assisted with "rape kit" evidence collection while on staff at large inner-city hospital.
- Specially chosen for 3-month rotation in Recovery Room at Mt. Sinai to care for critically ill patients.
- Coordinated all aspects of patient care for large infertility practice, requiring ability to synchronize multiple events to increase probability of successful outcome.

Leadership / Office Management / Administration

- As Staff Nurse for medical corporation, chosen to relocate to Miami to lead and establish new branch office. Responsible for space planning, ordering supplies and equipment, and organizing all office-management procedures.
- As Charge Nurse, assisted in establishing start-up labor and delivery unit. Designed and wrote policies and procedures manual, directed scheduling, managed staff, and coordinated patient care in delivery room.
- Managed all aspects of multi-physician GYN office including bookkeeping, billing, accounts payable and receivable, and vendor negotiations.
- Implemented highly efficient accounting and payroll structure for OB/GYN office by creating filing system and organizing payables and receivables.
- Managed entire labor and delivery units in absence of supervisor.

WORK HISTORY

Treasurer, Medical Associates of Metropolitan Atlanta, Atlanta, GA (1997 to 2000)

Staff Nurse, Grady Medical Center, Atlanta, GA (1988 to 1992)

Staff Nurse, Tokos Medical Corporation, Boca Raton, FL (1986 to 1988)

Staff Nurse, Memorial Hospital, Hollywood, FL (1985 to 1987)

Charge Nurse, NW Regional Hospital, Miramar, FL (1984 to 1985)

Childbirth Educator, Boca Raton Community Hospital, Boca Raton, FL (1981 to 1983)

Assistant Office Manager, Kaufman, Bernard & Gross M.D., P.C., Deerfield Beach, FL (1981 to 1982)

Staff Nurse, Jackson Medical Center, Miami, FL (1980 to 1983)

PROFESSIONAL ASSOCIATIONS

- American Association of Legal Nurse Consultants (Member)
- International Association of Forensic Nurses (Member)
- Delta Epsilon Tau International Honor Society (Member)

COMPUTER SKILLS

PC proficient: Lexis-Nexis (familiar), Windows, MS Word, Internet, and electronic-mail applications.

NICKOLE ANDREWS PENN

113 N.E. 21st Street	nickole@yahoo.com	Home (503) 894-2646
Portland, Oregon 97201		Cell (503) 226-7315

HOME-CARE EXECUTIVE AND LEGISLATIVE ADVOCATE

► **Prominent home-care leader driving advancement of personal-care industry through federal, state, and local legislative activities.**

► **Top-flight administrator dedicated to promoting the highest standards of care in the industry.**

► **Recognized speaker/presenter at workshops throughout the United States.**

► **Business owner/entrepreneur in home-care industry.**

► **Published author, teacher, trainer.**

PROFESSIONAL ACHIEVEMENTS

HOMECARE   Portland, OR
Founder • VP, Human Resources • VP, Quality, Regulatory Affairs, Training   1999–2002

Co-founded company to provide quality home-care services for elderly and disabled. Grew from start-up to $45 million in three years by launching key initiatives associated with company's strategic goals: Set industry standard for quality, training, innovation, and professionalism; streamlined and standardized operating processes and procedures to improve quality, consistency, and overall client care; integrated new acquisitions into company; incorporated back-office functions into centralized delivery systems; developed team of customer-focused management and staff.

Staff Leadership & Training
- Led managers and inter-departmental teams new to home care.
- Structured and delivered new-hire orientation and ongoing training/customer-service programs for new managers, caregivers, and staff.

Operations & Financial Performance
- Managed annual budget of $2,250,000. Supervised department of seven with four direct reports: HR, Administration, Training, and Risk Management.
- Designed and successfully implemented company-standard policies, procedures, and processes.
- Fostered development of business rules, training materials, and integration process for home-care-specific software.
- Increased efficiency and reduced cost by $83,560 annually as result of recommended change in background-check vendor.
- Restructured Risk Management Department, reducing Workers' Comp Experience Modification Rating from 123 to 75 in two years for savings of $250,000 annually.

Technology Leadership
- Successfully completed software conversion of 18 locations in six months, with support staff of two, achieving company's strategic goal of centralizing back-office functions.
- Managed complex HR, operations, and systems integration with newly acquired companies.
- Provided functional home-care expertise to development team tasked with designing proprietary IVR (Interactive Voice Response) system.

Industry & Regulatory Leadership
- Advocated legislatively at national, state, and local levels for protection of state and federal home-care exemptions. Gained national reputation for driving opposition to Department of Labor's attempt to eliminate patient exemptions.
- Designed and executed company-wide customer-satisfaction survey used to develop quality improvement objectives and positive client outcomes.

Strategy: *Highlight accomplishments in teaching, training, legislative activities, and management within the industry to position this experienced individual for her target positions: training newcomers to the field or serving as an industry lobbyist.*

Nickole Andrews Penn
nickole@yahoo.com

Home (503) 894-2646
Cell (503) 226-7315

PROFESSIONAL ACHIEVEMENTS, continued

HEALTH CARE FOR HANDICAPPED
Owner/Executive Director

Seattle, WA
1992–2002

Grew, from start-up, successful business providing in-home personal-care services to elderly and disabled. Directed all aspects of business start-up and growth including operations, strategic planning, business development, budgeting, hiring, and training. Established and implemented quality standards specific to home-care organizations.

- Tripled revenue in 18 months and grew from start-up to $6,000,000 in six years.
- Leading advocate in home-care legislative concerns, attending national policy conferences and developing relationships with and lobbying local, state, and federal legislators.
- Credited with being one of Washington's first health-care companies to implement industry-specific scheduling/billing/payroll software.
- Pioneer in IVR (Interactive Voice Response) technology in home-care industry.
- Launched use of satisfaction surveys and QI process in home-care industry.

SEATTLE UNION SCHOOL DISTRICT
Special Needs Teacher

Seattle, WA
1988–1999

- Engaged in many district-wide committees for development of programs, processes, and curriculum for special-needs children ages three to five.
- Significant contributor to grant-writing projects resulting in $3 million for Special Education programs.

NORTHWEST WASHINGTON BOARD OF COOPERATIVE EDUCATIONAL SERVICES
Special Needs Teacher

Seattle, WA
1981–1988

- Served as Program Specialist coordinating speech/language services for nine rural districts.
- Member of nine-district team selected to write and implement $90,000 grant proposal to develop innovative programs for special-needs students; served as consultant to district administrators/teaching professionals during implementation phase.
- Provided speech/language services to three school districts, preschool through twelfth grade. Instrumental in integrating speech/language services into the classroom.

PORTLAND SCHOOL DISTRICT
Speech/Language Specialist

Portland, OR
1986–1988

Created program for six mainstreamed, hearing-impaired students. Provided speech/language services to children in kindergarten through second grade.

OREGON DEPARTMENT OF HEALTH
Consultant/Parent Trainer

Salem, OR
1982–1988

Empowered parents of hearing-impaired infants by providing skills related to auditory training, communications, language development, and hearing-aid maintenance.

EDUCATION

M.A. Speech Pathology
Arizona State University, Flagstaff, Arizona

1984

B.S. Speech Pathology/Audiology
Oklahoma State University, Stillwater, Oklahoma

1975

David T. Evans, M.D., M.P.H.

5110 Creekbranch Drive
Chapel Hill, NC 27512
919-942-8888
davidevansmd@earthlink.net

HIGHLIGHTS OF QUALIFICATIONS

Public Health Administrator with directorial and clinical experience at the federal, state, and county government levels. Proven ability to identify problems and implement practical solutions. Develop innovative programs from a long-range perspective. Able to work effectively with people of various cultural backgrounds, ages, and socioeconomic statuses.

Core competencies include:

- Program management
- Data collection and analysis
- Budgetary management
- Public health education
- Community-based healthcare interventions

- Grant writing
- Public health monitoring
- Legislative involvement in public health
- Staff training and supervision
- Media relations

PROFESSIONAL EXPERIENCE

Director of Preventive Medicine/Assistant Professor   2000–present
University of North Carolina, Chapel Hill, NC

- Led a faculty team in developing a community-based preventive-medicine program that was suitable for a rural population and cost only 30% of the projected curriculum expense.
- Created and tested the region's first community-health survey instrument in 20 years.
- Served as a public-health advocate before the governor and state legislature.
- Recruited by the governor to institute a hypertension-reduction program for a 4-county area where the prevalence of hypertension is 3 times greater than the national average.
- Obtained funding to address the special medical needs of the local population.

Associate Chief of Staff for Preventive Medicine   1997–2000
Veterans Administration Medical Center, Winston-Salem, NC

- Fostered the increased utilization of primary-care clinics. This reduced the use of emergency rooms for primary care.
- Developed and implemented a preventive care program consisting of age-specific physical exams, screening tests, and medical services.
- Instituted a daycare program for homeless veterans that included treatment of mental illness.
- Hired, trained, and managed a medical staff of 230.
- Established policies that promoted high-quality patient care. Analyzed clinical problems such as violations of patients' rights or breaches in protocol.

Strategy: *Emphasize strong contributions within the public-health field, using a traditional chronological format and a keyword-dense summary.*

David T. Evans, M.D., M.P.H.   **Page 2**

Medical Director   1990–1996
Fayette County Department of Public Health, Lexington, KY

- Recommended and instituted a high-school health program that resulted in a 12% decrease in teenage pregnancy and STDs among inner-city adolescents.
- Obtained federal funding to launch a county health-care program for individuals who did not qualify for Medicaid, yet were unable to afford primary care. This program utilized local health departments and decreased emergency-room visits for primary care.
- Actively lobbied for 12 health-care bills that concerned indigents. Nine of the bills were passed.
- Participated on a team that proposed and implemented the purchase of public-health clinics by the University of Kentucky College of Medicine. This pilot program provided effective medical care for many of the area's uninsured or underinsured residents.

Clinical Director   1988–1990
South Bend Federal Detention Center, South Bend, IN

- Established protocols that emphasized preventive care and decreased poly-pharmacy.
- Reduced clinical expenses 28% by bringing all services in-house except for surgery.
- Ensured that all medical staff members were licensed and certified. Implemented a CME program for staff.
- Trained and supervised a multidisciplinary staff of 20.

EDUCATION

Master's in Public Health   1998
University of North Carolina, Greensboro, NC

Doctor of Medicine   1982
Temple University School of Medicine, Philadelphia, PA

Donald F. Clarkson

105 West End Avenue, Apt. 2G
New York, NY 10026

dfclarkson@verizon.net

Phone: (212) 489-7409
Fax: (212) 489-7410

Qualifications

EXECUTIVE ADMINISTRATOR qualified for senior-level management opportunities within an assisted-living or retirement-community organization. Strengths include planning, development, and visionary leadership.

- *Market-driven executive* with 25 years' experience in residential care/health care including areas of building and grounds management, facility restoration, budget preparation and control, personnel/employee relations, recruiting, foodservice management, and customer service.

- *Independent problem solver* with ability to assist and resolve specific client concerns to everyone's satisfaction.

- *Skilled communicator* who consistently motivates staff to provide total quality service to clients.

Professional Experience

ADMINISTRATOR, MOUNT VERNON CENTER SOUTH
Franklin Institute of Aging, Yonkers, NY   2001–present
Skilled nursing facility with $5.5 million in annual revenue. Manage $4 million annual budget, 200+ member staff, overall resident care, all business functions, facility management, and Department of Health compliance.

- Increased annual resident revenue through additional admissions by securing Medicare certification for entire facility.
- Spearheaded large collection effort on delinquent accounts; reduced average outstanding receivables from 80 to 62 days.
- Reduced monthly nursing temporary-help expenses from $80K to $20K through intensive recruiting efforts and by providing in-house training for certified nursing assistant candidates.
- Led first facility remodeling project in 25 years by allocating $25K in funds towards refurbishing and improving residential areas.

EXECUTIVE DIRECTOR, GOTHAM PLACE
Ulysses Retirement Home, Inc., Stamford, CT   1989–1999
Retirement community with over $5 million in annual revenue. Managed all organizational operations; facility and service marketing efforts; financial management; strategic planning; and major restoration project supervision.

- Managed $3 million renovation of upscale facility, ensuring state and local building code compliance.
- Coordinated architectural efforts, doubling facility's resident capacity.
- Doubled home's revenue stream while holding expense increases to 25% through careful financial planning and operations management.
- Developed and implemented private-pay revenue system by replacing facility's long-time contract with more financially sound monthly rental system.

ADMINISTRATOR, LONG VALLEY COMMUNITY HOSPITAL AND HEALTH SYSTEM
Northern Region Community Healthcare, Inc., Los Angeles, CA   1985–1988
Hospital and health system with over $5 million in annual revenue. Managed acute-care hospital, MD/DO office practice, and home health-care service; recruited physicians; and bolstered publicity efforts for Pain Treatment program throughout Southern California area.

- Rejuvenated operations to salvage hospital and health system from bankruptcy.
- Increased outpatient revenue by approximately 80% through establishment of Pain Management program servicing patients in Southern California.
- Resolved serious cash-flow problem by leading three-month employee wage-reduction program, restoring lost wages at end following establishment of permanent solutions.
- Improved marketing efforts in Southern California region, increasing visibility of facility and services.

Strategy: *Extract and summarize major accomplishments to paint a picture of career-long achievement.*

Donald F. Clarkson   Page 2

Professional Experience   continued

VICE PRESIDENT/ADMINISTRATOR, ANDREWS MEDICAL CENTER   1984–1985
Phoenix Baptist Hospital, Phoenix, AZ

ASSISTANT ADMINISTRATOR   1977–1984
Community General Hospital, Cleveland, OH

Education

MBA, Hospital and Health Services Administration — Boston College, Boston, MA   1978
BS, Business Administration — University of Notre Dame, South Bend, IN   1974

Certification, Licenses

Nursing Home Administrator's License

Affiliations

Member, New York State Chamber of Commerce   2001–present
Member, New York Extended Care Federation   1999–present
Member, New York Association of Services for the Aging   1989–1999
Member, American College of Hospital Administrators   1979–1989
Member, Beta Gamma Sigma (Business School Honor Society)   1975–present

DEBBIE A. MYERS

1210 Meadow Lane ▪ Odenton, MD 21113
443.273.9280 ▪ debbiea@hotmail.com

CAREER FOCUS

EXECUTIVE MANAGEMENT ▪ TEACHING & TRAINING ▪ OPERATIONS
Medical-Supply Industry ▪ Health-Care Industry ▪ Professional Services

EXECUTIVE PROFILE

· Long-Term-Care Facility Mgmt.	· Creative Problem Solving	· State Regulations
· Sales Cycle	· Negotiations & Contracts	· Presentations & Proposals
· Customer Relations	· Supply Chain Management	· Pharmaceutical Services
· Account Management	· Excellent Oral & Written Skills	· Medical Supplies
· Staff Recruiting & Motivation	· Budgets & Financials / P&L	· Strategic Alliances

- Health-Care Facility Administrator with a broad range of technical expertise, consistently successful at furnishing complete hi-tech, training, financial, or contract/negotiations/acquisitions solutions through the definition of customer requirements.

- Listen intently and accurately to assess service needs and design, deliver, evaluate, and administer customized programs/requirements to meet needs, increase overall services, and boost revenue.

- Accomplished professional with refined interpersonal and communications skills. Poised presenter and teacher. Provide guidance to other health-care organizations with complex program questions and implementation requirements. Write technical manuals and policies. Use Microsoft Office Suite.

- Skilled facilitator, able to bring together diverse working groups and project teams—fostering a genuine sense of motivation.

- Often invited to tour, review, and evaluate geriatric facilities for such renowned organizations as Johns Hopkins Hospital. Engage in round–table discussions and serve as a state-regulations authority for long-term-care facilities and geriatrics management.

PROFESSIONAL EXPERIENCE

Senior Health Systems, Baltimore, MD   **1990–Present**
Fast track of promotions to senior management, serving in a variety of critical positions culminating as COO with oversight accountability for performance and financial requirements in all nursing centers with six administrators and 1,200 employees. Manage administration, staffing, multimillion-dollar budgets, and medical-supply contracts.

COO/Director of Long Term Care Operations, 2000–Present
- Promoted to COO to correct a major financial downturn. Took charge and turned the company around from losing $7.2M in 1999 to profitability in 2001. Provided strong leadership, rebuilt customer relationships, heightened team morale, revamped operations, implemented appropriate business practices and accountability-tracking systems, developed new management teams, implemented budgets, properly trained administrators and staff, and heightened profits.
- Successfully guided a decertified facility back into compliance and reorganized management of the facility, achieving profitability.

Accomplishments, continued…

Strategy: *Highlight business as well as clinical expertise for this accomplished, senior-level administrator who is seeking new challenges in the areas of teaching or medical/pharmaceutical sales.*

Debbie A. Myers, Page 2

Accomplishments, continued…

- Maintained extensive medical-supply vendor lists and personally negotiated, contracted, and procured medical supplies and services for all nursing centers. Negotiated unique supply and delivery contracts including terms and delivery, attaining the best product at the lowest price and receiving cash-back bonuses. Collaborated with the CEO to procure pharmaceutical services.

- Created a training process for the administrators to teach financial-management and budgeting practices in their facilities, resulting in consistent cost reductions during the past two years.

- Directed the company's financial transition to the Medicare PPS program in an environment of increased regulations and surveys by the Office of Health Care Quality.

- Coordinated and led a team that developed a model for five new assisted-living communities.

- Hired a contractor to manage a project to identify, inventory, catalog, and database over 2,000 pieces of expensive medical and operational equipment within the company's six regional facilities. Implemented processes to track equipment where none previously existed.

- The project reduced monthly rentals of ventilators and concentrators from more than $5,000 to zero by locating and using company-owned equipment; saved the company over $17,000 in the first 45 days of initiating the project.

Administrator, Senior Health Systems Nursing and Rehabilitation Center, 1997–2000
- Completed the Administrator in Training Program, resulting in promotion to Administrator.
- Guided the transition of the facility into a new Medicare PPS reimbursement program, increasing income from $200K to $1.2M in two years.

Clinical Director, Senior Health Systems, 1995–1997
- Directed and coordinated clinical services for 720 long-term-care residents and 238 assisted-living clients including Laboratory, X-ray, Pharmacy, Rehabilitation, Respiratory Therapy, and Medical Records. Provided clinical guidance to each facility.
- Served on a number of committees to organize in-house nursing, ancillary services, and assisted-living services, saving contractor costs.

Director of Nursing, Senior Health Systems Nursing & Rehabilitation Center, 1990–1995
- Directed nursing operations for a 361-bed long-term-care facility—the largest for-profit nursing home in the state. Participated in transitioning the facility to a new Medicaid-reimbursement system. The facility consistently ranked high in survey status and cost effectiveness.
- Opened the first ventilator program in a long-term-care facility in the state as a joint venture. Soon after, the company took over the program and operated a sub-acute program. Participated in writing state regulations for the Special Respiratory Care units.

EDUCATION & LICENSURE

- Bachelor of Science in Nursing, University of Maryland, 1990
- Long Term Care Facility Administrator & Licensed Nursing Home Administrator, 1998
- RN, Maryland (1990) and Virginia (1992) & Nurse Certification in Geriatrics, 1994

PRESENTER

- University of Maryland, "Process of Aging and Geriatrics in the Nursing Program," Guest Lecturer
- Virginia Pharmacists State Convention, "Role of Consultant Pharmacist"
- Pharmacy Seminar — Sub Acute Care Facility, "How to Make It Work"
- Local Fire and Police Departments, "Geriatric Assessment" (Seminar videotaped for continual use)

DAVID A. WILLIAMS

215 James Place
Ladera Ranch, CA 92694

(714) 336-8998
dwilliams@mailnet.net

COO / VICE PRESIDENT / EXECUTIVE DIRECTOR
Expertise in Multi-Facility Health and Fitness Organizations

PROFILE

Operations and Sales Executive with a track record of increasing sales and profits, turning around under-performing locations / regions, and leading expansion for multi-unit operations with up to $10 million in annual revenues (both profit-driven and non-profit). Consistently exceeded goals, sales plans, and turnaround objectives for each employer.

Expert in analyzing existing operations and implementing the necessary strategies and formal business practices to improve profit performance, grow membership sales, and increase retention rates. Proven financial and business acumen combined with practical experience and formal training in health and fitness. Strong educational foundation with MA and BBA degrees. Areas of strength include:

- **Multi-Unit Operations Management**
- **Budgeting / Expense Control**
- **Sales Management / Sales Training**
- **Marketing / Sales Promotions**

- **Business Development**
- **Fitness Program Development**
- **New Facility Design / Opening**
- **Staff Leadership / Motivation**

PROFESSIONAL EXPERIENCE

ORANGE COUNTY COMMUNITY HEALTH AND FITNESS ORGANIZATION — Tustin, CA   2000 to Present
(Non-profit organization offering sports, aquatics, and fitness programs for member families)

Vice President, Health and Fitness

Hired to orchestrate an aggressive turnaround for the region from a $1.2 million loss to sustainable net gains within 2 years. Hold full responsibility for the planning, staffing, and operating performance of 6 locations with 200+ employees, 18,000+ members, and $5.5 million in annual revenues.

Broad scope of accountability includes day-to-day operations, revenue performance, membership sales, staff training, program development / implementation, and customer service. Supervise 6 facility directors and 18 program managers. Develop and manage a $5.5 million program budget. Provide leadership to capital campaign and facility design phase for 2 new locations with a $20 million budget.

- **Turned region around from a $1.2 million loss to a projected positive net in 2 years.**
- **Grew new membership sales from 3,500 in 2000 to over 7,000 in 2001.**
- **Increased revenue from personal training programs more than 100% within one year.**
- **Strengthened member-retention rate to 70% across all locations through improved customer-service training and procedures.**
- **Improved lead generation 15% by designing a prospect-management / tracking system.**

T.S. FITNESS / EMERALD GYM – locations in TX and SC   1994 to 1999
(Operator of fitness clubs in 2 states)

Chief Operating Officer

Senior operations manager with full responsibility for day-to-day facility operations, sales, accounting, human resources, and fitness programs for a newly established company with 3 facilities, 60–80 full- and part-time staff, and $2.5 million in annual sales.

Strategy: *Create an executive presentation to position the candidate as viable in an industry where very few senior-level positions exist.*

David A. Williams ▪ Page 2 ▪ (714) 336-8998

T.S. FITNESS / EMERALD GYM *(continued)*

Established formal business practices and standardized sales and operations processes across all locations to support continued growth and expansion.

- **Grew profits more than 20% each year.**
- **Developed and implemented formal sales procedures that resulted in a 20%–30% increase in new memberships each year.**
- **Increased personal-fitness and group-fitness revenues more than 50% per year.**
- **Developed new business by establishing relationships / alliances with corporate and allied health providers.**

MEGA FITNESS / MEGA GYM — Houston, San Antonio, and Dallas, TX   1991 to 1994
(Operator of fitness clubs with $10 million in annual revenues)

Vice President, Sales and Operations

Led operations, sales, staff training, and fitness programs for 12 Mega Gyms with nearly 100,000 members and up to $10 million in combined annual sales. Provided leadership and direction for 250+ sales and fitness staff, 12 general managers, and 4 regional managers in a rapidly growing organization. Worked closely with general managers of each location, providing guidance in maximizing sales and increasing member-retention rate while reducing expenses.

- **Delivered double-digit sales growth each year.**
- **Maintained member retention rate at more than 70%.**
- **Established and launched a comprehensive fitness and nutrition program, which included over 200 personal trainers.**
- **Contributed to design and pre-sale phases for 5 new facilities.**

FORT BEND GENERAL HOSPITAL — Needville, TX   1989 to 1991
(A 150-bed community hospital)

Director, Business Development

Directed business-development activities to revitalize an older hospital in an industrial suburb of Houston. Developed and coordinated promotions, community-relations activities, and special programs for physician recruitment.

- **Established a local Preferred Provider Organization (PPO) from scratch with over 10,000 participants. Model was duplicated at other Houston-area hospitals.**

EDUCATION

SOUTHWEST TEXAS STATE UNIVERSITY — New Braunfels, TX
- **Master of Arts, Kinesiology,** GPA 4.0 (1989)
- **Bachelor of Business Administration,** Cum Laude (1987)

Available to travel and/or relocate

LAWRENCE A. MAKRIS

44 West Greene Street • Coral Springs, FL 32405 • Cell: (407) 555-4994 • Home: (407) 555-8889
lmakris@aol.com

QUALIFICATIONS PROFILE

Motivated and dedicated senior-level professional with extensive healthcare experience and proven track record of success in hands-on leadership, organizational management, acquisitions, and strategic planning. Accomplished in team development and empowerment, instilling sense of pride and autonomy in staff. Highly skilled in ROI analysis and capital-expenditure budget administration. Recognized for ability to identify key markets, customers, and vendors, leading to increased revenue.

PROFESSIONAL BACKGROUND

MEDICAL SOLUTIONS, INC., Miami, FL   1/1995–Present
President & Founder

Established three distinct entities of corporation to meet diagnostic technology needs of various healthcare facilities and communities. Positioned company for long-term sustainable growth and profitability. Responsible for hiring staff, building effective teams, financial planning, budgeting, corporate acquisition, and operations management for five locations with a staff of 25. Created and led strategic initiatives. Developed and established policies and procedures. Oversaw P&L for all locations.

- Grew business from one to six locations within five-year period with gross revenue of $2.4 million by end of 2000.

- Significantly expanded market through development of three distinct company entities and establishment of internal referral system.

- Increased client base from zero to several thousand, including 250 facility-based clients.

- Developed and implemented strategic plans to target both facilities and patients, significantly increasing revenue and efficiency.

- Originated and implemented budget-analysis system to track operational expenses, marketing, billing, and inventory for each facility on a quarterly basis, consistently meeting or exceeding goals.

- Established centralized computer networking system, enabling facilities to interface with each other, monitor inventory, and track client base.

- Managed private and third-party billing and collections in-house.

MEDICAL DEVICE SALE & LEASING (1995–Present)

- Provided per-diem leasing of diagnostic devices to rehabilitation facilities and hospitals.

- Successfully negotiated leases directly with manufacturers, sub-leasing to clients and avoiding need to maintain huge inventory of product.

- Expanded market into durable medical equipment (DME) company within six months, significantly increasing revenue through patient referral system.

- Acquired Southern Medical Equipment Company and all assets, establishing Medical Solutions, Inc., as competitive DME provider.

- Led company from zero revenue to $340,000 within the first year and $750,000 within two years.

- Managed and directed six sales representatives for entire region between Florida and Texas.

Continued

Strategy: *Paint a picture of an accomplished industry leader with strong business achievements to help this individual transition from a self-owned business to a larger corporation.*

LAWRENCE A. MAKRIS   PAGE TWO

DIAGNOSTIC TESTING (1996–Present)

- Initiated polysomnogram testing (sleep studies) to patients and provided patients with DME for treatment for conditions.
- Established in-house diagnostic center and eliminated single-vendor outsourcing systems previously utilized at VA Hospital in Tampa.
- Streamlined purchasing through alliance with Acme Buying Group.
- Established contracts with six facilities, providing technical and clinical component.

DIAGNOSTIC IMAGERY (1998–Present)

- Streamlined organization through addition of Diagnostic Imagery to list of services available to existing clients.
- Expanded market into Texas through alliance with Southwestern Medical Center in Dallas, which led to contracts with West Texas Rehabilitation Center and Timothy J. Harner Burn Centers.

EDUCATION

HARVARD UNIVERSITY, Cambridge, MA
Master of Business Administration, 1994

FLORIDA STATE UNIVERSITY, Tallahassee, FL
Bachelor of Business Administration with emphasis in Financial Analysis, 1990
Alpha Lambda Delta National Scholastic Honor Society, 1989
Outstanding College Students of America, 1988

PROFESSIONAL ASSOCIATIONS

National Association of Medical Equipment Suppliers
Miami Kiwanis

Keywords: Vice President of Business Development, VP of Acquisitions, Corporate Officer

RAYMOND J. CASEY

1445 Tinker Court, Brandon, FL 33650
(813) 555-1212 • raycasey@aol.com

OBJECTIVE	**Healthcare Administration**
EXPERIENCE	U.S. Navy, 08/81–11/02

Regional Medical Administrator, Tampa, FL   **May 95–Present**
Director of a 5-office, 30-member medical department.
- Coordinate routine and occupational health programs for over 800 employees throughout the Southeast.
- Advise CEO on all organizational issues involving employee health and safety.
- Manage Workers' Compensation, Back-to-Work Program, and medical claims.
- Monitor the installation of new medical information systems software. Implement employee training.
- Schedule and coordinate medical support and supplies for over 25 national and international operations.
- Authorize contracts and medical supplies and equipment purchases through vendors.
- Negotiate bids for building renovations. Saved over $125K, acquiring 3 portable classrooms for free.
- Awarded Commendation medal for orchestrating large-scale medical exercise involving 150 personnel.

Administrative Director, Atlanta, GA   **May 92–May 95**
Directed 20 staff in administrative services for employee outpatient clinic providing health-care services to over 100,000 members, averaging 20,000 visits annually.
- Assisted Chief Operating Officer in developing, implementing, and monitoring strategic plans.
- Administered $2.4M budget to include forecasting, planning, accounting, and purchasing.
- Negotiated fees and contracts with specialty physician group practices.
- Saved $150K in annual budget and increased man-hours by 20,000 through strategic analysis.
- Managed $5M warehouse inventory. Reduced inventory, saving $35K annually.

Safety Manager, New York, NY   **Dec 88–May 92**
Supervised 5 employees of a large industrial-maintenance facility employing over 300.
- Managed occupational health programs, medical records, and mishap reports.
- Monitored hearing, sight, respiratory, and asbestos medical-surveillance programs.
- Inspected machinery, equipment, and working conditions to ensure compliance with OSHA regulations.
- Disseminated information regarding toxic substances, hazards, carcinogens, and risk management.
- Awarded 2 Achievement medals for superior service. Designated Employee of the Year.

EDUCATION & TRAINING	Bachelor of Science in Health Care Leadership National-Louis University, Wheaton, IL	1998
	Claims Management & Legal Issues in Risk Management	1999
	Medical Staff Planning	1997
	Total Quality management/Team Facilitator Instructor	1996
	Health Resources Management	1996
	Government Contracting	1995
	Adult Education Instructor	1994
PROFESSIONAL MEMBERSHIPS	Associate, American College of Healthcare Executives Member, American Society for Healthcare Risk Management	

Strategy: Use a concise chronological format to detail strong health-care-administration experience gained over more than a decade in the U.S. Navy.

CHAPTER 10

Resumes for Managers and Executives in Science, Engineering, and Technology

- Laboratory Manager
- Industrial Chemist
- Engineer
- Engineering Executive
- Technology Program Manager
- Project Manager
- HRIS Director
- Computer Systems Manager
- Information Technology Executive
- Software Development Executive
- IT Executive
- Aviation Maintenance Manager

Shelley E. Croft

43 Maxine Road • Bristol, CT 06010-3781
860-920-2929 • secroft@aol.com

Dynamic Research-Science Laboratory-Management Professional

Areas of Expertise

- LABORATORY MANAGEMENT
- FORMULATIONS
- PRODUCTION OVERSIGHT

- RESEARCH
- TESTING
- METHODS DEVELOPMENT

- DATA COLLECTION/ANALYSIS
- PILOT & SCALE-UP PROCESSES
- DATA EVALUATION

Technically proficient, detail oriented, and accurate. Analytical troubleshooter with demonstrated ability to identify problems and implement solutions. Proven expertise in assembling and organizing data. Excellent interpersonal and communication skills. Well-organized and adept at multitasking. Team player/team builder. Extensive background working with cross-functional scientific and research teams. Familiar with good manufacturing/laboratory practices including ISO and SPC. Computer skills include **Microsoft Word, Access, Excel,** and **PowerPoint; Internet** savvy.

Highlights of Achievements

- ❖ *Developed complete set of laboratory analytical methods, operational procedures and other documentation to meet ISO requirements.*
- ❖ *Pioneered use of chlorine dioxide for oxidation of toxic chemicals, increasing annual revenues by 77%.*
- ❖ *Developed polymer synthesis process, enabling company to obtain better price (20% reduction) from suppliers.*
- ❖ *Determined optimum process for product activation, resulting in competitive advantage and increasing sales by 10%.*
- ❖ *Developed new process, reducing number of manufacturing steps by one third. Resulted in 50% increase in output.*

Employment History

1989 to 2003   RAFFIN CHEMICALS   Hartford, CT
Laboratory Manager

Oversaw all facets of laboratory operations for 175-employee chemical company.

- Designed, equipped, and created new water-analysis and process laboratory to support wastewater and pure-water business.
- Conducted process studies to develop wastewater recycle processes. Technologies evaluated included jar studies, ion exchange, micro, ultra, nano-filtration, and reverse osmosis.
- Acted as company-wide consultant on chemical treatment of water.
- Created computer spreadsheets, enabling application engineers to calculate chemical additions for customer applications.
- Coordinated laboratory efforts within operating budget. Prepared capital laboratory appropriation requests.
- Oversaw activities and efforts of a chemist, laboratory technician, and microbiologist. Wrote and conducted performance appraisals.
- Screened and evaluated resumes of potential employees. Interviewed candidates. Made hiring recommendations.

U.S. Patents — Raffin Chemicals

| #6,127,549 | April 2, 1999 | METHOD FOR INHIBITING SCALE USING CALCIUM HYPOCHLORITE COMPOSITIONS |
| #5,112,001 | May 12, 1996 | CALCIUM HYPOCHLORITE COMPOSITION CONTAINING PHOSPHONOBUTANE POLYCARBOXYLIC ACID SALTS |

Education

UNIVERSITY OF CONNECTICUT, Storrs, CT
Master of Science in Chemistry

Strategy: *Attract readers' interest in the top third of the resume by immediately conveying areas of expertise and marketable soft skills. These are followed by impressive, quantified achievements.*

Mina Hartshorne, Ph.D.

78 Lilac Lane
Cincinnati, Ohio 45220

513-555-2760
hartsmina@hotmail.com

INDUSTRIAL CHEMIST & SENIOR PROJECT MANAGER

Senior Scientist with advanced degrees, exceptional technical skills, practical experience and comprehensive understanding of the unlimited commercial potential and humanistic value of chemical research and development activities. Experienced in planning, conducting, managing and documenting full-scale project lifecycles. Successful in achieving technical, financial, productivity and quality goals. Extremely analytical, innovative and resourceful. Strong team-building and leadership skills.

R&D Strategy & Management	**Project Design & Management**
Product Development & Redesign	**Process Development & Improvement**
Statistical & Comparative Analysis	**Process Flow Diagramming & Reengineering**
Industrial Compound Preparation	**GLC, QA & Safety Programs/Controls**

PROFESSIONAL EXPERIENCE

US Environmental Protection Agency — EPA, Washington, D.C.   1999 to Present

SENIOR CHEMIST & PROJECT MANAGER

Manage the conduct of scientific R&D projects with specialization in synthetic organic chemistry and biocatalysis related to industrially important compounds, products, materials, processes and applications. Supervise the preparation of a wide range of industrial compounds (e.g., benzhydryl ethers, oximes, cyanuric acid and its trialkyl derivatives, herbicides, carbamates, carbonates) utilizing traditional and green chemistry methodologies.

Provide technical and managerial oversight to complete project cycles — developing concepts and strategies; defining scope, procedures and objectives; procuring and coordinating resources; procuring supplies; implementing safety plans; setting up equipment and lab; conducting, observing and documenting experiments; interpreting and documenting results; and presenting and defending published research. Supervise teams of up to 10 scientists working on as many as five concurrently running projects. Report to the Principal Investigator and serve as key contact to quality and regulatory officials.

Project Highlights:

- Nafion-H catalyzed preparation of benzhydryl ethers
- Microwave-assisted preparation of cyanuric acid and its alkylated derivatives
- Preparation of 2,4 Dichlorophenoxy acetic acid (2,4-D) ester herbicides
- Biodesulfurization of crude oils in supercritical fluids
- Aggregation of squaraine-cholesterol in Langmuir-Blodgett (LB) films
- Investigation of behavior of a new class of gelators (Squaraines) and the aggregation properties of their gels
- Methyl esters of sunflower oil by enzymatic transesterification and acyl exchange of trilinolein in supercritical fluids

EDUCATION

Ph.D. – Organic Chemistry, 1999
MS – Physical Chemistry, 1996
GEORGE WASHINGTON UNIVERSITY, Washington, D.C.

TECHNICAL SKILLS

Areas of Specialization

Organic Synthetic Chemistry	Applied & Basic Research	Biocatalysis
Physical Organic Chemistry	Photochemical Reaction	Conventional & High Pressure Synthesis
Organic Chemistry Technology	Specialty Chemicals	Reactions in Emulsions

Applications & Materials

Solid Supported Reagent	Crude Oils & Petroleum Products	Emulsion & Microemulsion
Desulfurization	Supercritical Fluids	Aromatic Intermediates
Surfactants & Reverse Micelles	Squaraines & Azobenzenes	Ultrasound, Aggregation, LB Films

Instrumentation

UV-VIS	NMR, DSC, HPLC	GC & GC/MS
Radial Chromatography	Karl Fisher Titration	Fluorescence Spectroscopy

Strategy: *Keywords and project highlights drive the strategy of this resume. The experience section is presented up front, before technical skills, to draw attention to tenure at a large, well-known organization.*

ROBERT H. RATNICT

33 Plum Road
Florida, NY 10990

(201) 818-6200x12 (W)
(845) 922-9154 (H)
ratnict@optonline.net

PROJECT ENGINEER

PROFILE: Highly skilled and motivated project and design engineer with extensive experience using Solid Works to engineer and design industrial equipment. Strong background in project work for the printing industry. Excellent leadership, management, communication, customer service, and problem-solving skills.

Expertise: Product and Equipment Design, Project Management, Electrical Controls, Power Control, Temperature Control, PLCs, Test Equipment, and Measuring Devices

Computer Skills: Industry Software: AutoCAD R14, Solid Works (3D Design/Modeling)
General Software: Microsoft Word, Excel, & Outlook; Adobe Illustrator & Acrobat

PROFESSIONAL EXPERIENCE

COMPUTER SERVICES, INC.
➤ **Project Engineer**

Ramsey, NJ
1997–Present

Engineering and Development Contract Services company. Report to President. Manage all phases of projects, including conception, engineering/design, testing, evaluation, production, and assembly. Meet with engineers to review designs and implement design changes as needed. Document designs and maintain engineering documentation. Initiate and complete various designs using AutoCAD and Solid Works. Design controls and electrical schematics to operate equipment. Interact with clients to provide support, assess needs, develop specifications, and prepare competitive bids. Oversee major day-to-day activities such as meetings, problem-solving, and training. Manage staff of 3.

Major Accomplishments

- *Challenge:* Integrate proprietary printing equipment with client's existing manufacturing process to reduce costs and increase efficiency.
  Action: Conducted on-site measurements, performed CAD work, and developed design for assembly, manufacturing, shipping, implementation, and training of new numbering system for finishing process.
  Results: Saved $150,000 in annual manufacturing costs by streamlining finishing process and eliminating secondary operation. Company ordered second machine at $200,000.

- *Challenge:* Integrate our Mark VI MICR encoder for in-line installation with OEM's web press.
  Action: Worked with OEM web-press manufacturer to retrofit our equipment to their web press by introducing such items as mechanical drives, custom clutches, and a numbering synchronization process.
  Results: Reduced production costs 50% and increased turnaround time 25% by enabling the process to produce laser checks in one pass.

- *Challenge:* Largest manufacturer of fluted coffee filters needed a reproduction of their release-applicator machine.
  Action: Went on-site to observe process, take measurements, produce drawings, and create new specifications by reverse-engineering from a sample machine.
  Results: A custom-designed release applicator with reduced roller weight, improved release material-carrying capability of the applicator roller, and improved controls and corrosion resistance of the applicator mechanism. Reproduction completed and 3 units installed in under 120 days.

Strategy: *Use the "CAR" (Challenge, Action, and Results) approach (see page 25) to highlight accomplishments and quantifiable results.*

ROBERT H. RATNICT   Page 2

PROFESSIONAL EXPERIENCE

Major Accomplishments (continued)

- *Challenge:* Design a sheeter with a quick-change feature for converting one cut-off size to another.
  Action: Designed and implemented a prototype with an AC follower drive system for use in-line with other pieces of equipment.
  Results: Reduced labor costs by 30% by increasing efficiency and eliminating a major operation.

- *Challenge:* Increase production rates of manufacturing process for Moore Business Forms and Systems.
  Action: Went on-site to observe process, identify bottlenecks, and make recommendations.
  Results: Increased productivity 10% by recommending upgrading old stepper-drive package to current technology components. Trained operators on correct set-up procedures.

- *Challenge:* Assist distributor in Australia to develop market for Autographic Numbering Systems.
  Action: Made 5 trips to Australia over 5 years to provide technical expertise for closing clients on sales calls.
  Results: Increased sales $500,000 over 5-year period.

- *Challenge:* Engineer a control for short-wave infrared drying systems that was easy to assemble, durable, and easy to operate.
  Action: Incorporated a PLC with color HMI for graphical operator interface with additional I/O for switching loads.
  Results: A high-power drying system that was easy to assemble and operate.

➤ **Designer**   1987–97
Designed equipment to customer specification. Interfaced with clients to develop custom specifications. Worked with subcontractors utilizing computer software and hardware.
- Designed computer-controlled numbering-initialization system that reduced set-up time by 15%.

➤ **Draftsman**   1984–87
Created design layouts from sketches, completed detail drawings, and created product drawings. Revised product drawings in accordance with engineering change orders and/or marked prints.
- Worked under project engineer on system for numbering and bar-coding Federal Express form for shipping labels.

ERIKA, INC.   Rockleigh, NJ
➤ **Draftsman**   1981–84
Created design layouts from sketches, completed detail drawings of medical devices from sketches, and created product drawings for medical components/devices.
- Member of team that designed a proportioning pump.

EDUCATION

- **Engineering Science,** coursework completed at Rockland Community College, Airmont, NY
- **Technical Drawing,** coursework completed at State University of NY, Agricultural and Technical College, Delhi, NY

John Anderson

950 S. Wynn Blvd., Portland, OR 97292 • (503) 555-2434 • janderson@app.net

---

DIRECTOR/VP ENGINEERING

Design Automation, Software Programming, Infrastructure

In-depth expertise in Engineering and IT Management, strategic business-planning and development, process and product improvement, R & D, and operations. Highly experienced in engineering architecture, design automation, communication protocols, electrical engineering, process flow, and computing infrastructure. Foster an environment of high productivity and team orientation.

CAREER HIGHLIGHTS

➤ Created shorter time-to-market and higher quality process for Finity's first functional silicon chip.

➤ Saved company $3 million by effective hardware and software vendor negotiations.

➤ Led substantial engineering Y2K project, completed smoothly one month ahead of schedule.

➤ Saved $2 million by effective hardware and software contract negotiations at Mondel Technology.

➤ Increased systems uptime from 75% to 99% and realized $3 million in savings at Elkon Electronics.

➤ Founder of successful software-development firm and innovative product sold to Rayden Corporation.

PROFESSIONAL EXPERIENCE

Finity, Inc., Portland, OR   1999–2003
Department Manager

Key leadership role that contributed value-added expertise, significant cost reductions, and growth to this manufacturer of programmable integrated circuits and memory products. Designed three-year engineering process improvement plan for President and VP of Engineering. Managed 10 vendor engineers and 2 direct reports.

➤ Introduced design-automation tools and methodology, resulting in company producing first functional silicon chip and accelerating product's time-to-market.

➤ Saved company more than $3 million in hardware and software contract negotiations.

➤ Reduced time to generate product information from one day to <10 minutes.

➤ Restructured engineering computing environment, improving throughput by 100% and ensuring no downtime during production.

➤ Engineering Manager for Y2K program, completed smoothly and a month ahead of schedule.

Mondel Technology, Inc., Seattle, WA   1997–1999
Manager

Managed software engineers/layout designers for this supplier of semiconductor interconnect services. Designed and installed UNIX & Windows systems, engineering file servers, networks, and security.

➤ Developed and successfully implemented design automation plan for ASIC flow.

➤ Saved the company $2 million by negotiating with major hardware and software vendors.

➤ Designed process flow and verification methodology, introduced automation tools, and managed programs.

➤ Reduced process time for CMP from hours to minutes by creating software-program capabilities.

Strategy: *Position this individual for a director or VP position by emphasizing leadership roles with his prior companies and previous experience as founder of a successful software-design automation company.*

John Anderson   Page Two

P.A.C.E. Corporation, Portland, OR   1989–1997
Founder/President
Managed development and commercialization of Windows-based design-automation tools and data-management systems. Full P&L responsibility.

➢ Hired and managed 50 employees, managers, software engineers, and sales professionals.

➢ Created business plan and raised capital for development and marketing.

➢ Sold product to Rayden Corporation.

Fortune 50 Company, Eugene, OR   1987–1989
Senior Staff Member
Division developed and manufactured Integrated Circuits for automotive industry and airplane sub-systems for DoD.

➢ Developed and presented strategic plan for next-generation design-automation tools.

➢ Evaluated automation tools and defined methodology for next-generation computer systems.

➢ Increased productivity by standardizing System Operating Systems/Data Management Systems.

Start-up, Portland, OR   1986–1987
Founder

➢ Created a business plan and raised $5 million to start a workstation/server company.

Elkon Electronics, Los Angeles, CA   1981–1986
Project Leader/Engineer
Managed 10 software designers/engineers involved in the development, SQA, documentation, and implementation of design-automation tools.

➢ Increased systems uptime from 75% to 99% by developing software uniformity throughout company.

➢ Obtained production-worthy status for internal design system, providing major tool for all divisions.

➢ Saved more than $3 million through hardware vendor negotiations.

EDUCATION

M.S. Engineering, Massachusetts Institute of Technology (M.I.T.)
M.S. Electrical Engineering, Worcester Polytechnic Institute (W.P.I.)
B.S. Electrical Engineering, Merrimack College

Member, Eta Kappa Nu Association

TECHNICAL EXPERTISE

Hardware/OS: Microsoft Windows 95, 98, Me, NT; Sun Solaris; Oracle; SQL; TCP/IP; Frame Relay
Software: C/C++, Java, PL1, Pascal, Fortran, BASIC

CARLTON HEMINGWAY

1322 Mission Way
Glenridge, NJ 07028

hemway@enj.rr.com

Home: (973) 555-1212
Cellular: (973) 444-1212

PROGRAM / PROJECT MANAGEMENT ~ TECHNOLOGY OPERATIONS

*Cited for "unparalleled technical expertise in information technology (IT)
… commitment to quality … dedication to managing resources responsibly."*

Talented Technology Manager with experience directing multimillion-dollar technology programs. Excel in planning, implementation and leveraging emerging technologies to achieve innovative yet cost-effective product and service solutions. Possess a Top Secret Clearance.

Information Technology
- IT Acquisition
- Communications Security
- Intranets, LANs & WANs
- Workstations
- Software Upgrades

- Multilevel Security Systems
- Trouble Desk Management
- Troubleshooting
- End User Support & Training
- System Administration

- Life Cycle Management
- Web Services / HTML
- Windows NT Servers
- System Upgrades
- Technology Transfer

Management
- Multi-Site Operations
- Budget Administration

- Training & Development
- Resource Allocation

- Policy & Procedure
- Customer Relations

EDUCATION

MBA with emphasis in Information Technology — Webster University
BS in Computer Information Studies — State University of New York at Stony Brook

PROFESSIONAL EXPERIENCE

Held notable positions in the US Air Force including:
Technology Director (Web Services & Information Systems Security) • IT Manager

TECHNOLOGY DIRECTOR — 1999–2003
Directed system administration of 140 servers and 1,850 multi-platform (UNIX and Windows NT 4.0), multi-security workstations, robotic hierarchical storage management backup system and six intrusion-detection systems (information security, firewalls and virus control) valued at over $35 million in support of 350,000 users. Supervised a staff of 35.

- **Web Services:** Managed development team and centers responsible for web services and production.

  - Provided technical lead for groundbreaking project using metadata to revolutionize data retrieval.
  - Directed web mirroring project to replicate web server on three domains with real-time access.

- **System Administration:** Managed five work centers responsible for networking and security.

  - Implemented Internet LAN with flawless execution of two Windows NT software upgrades.
  - Integrated NT Exchange Server e-mail, allowing users to seamlessly exchange mail across platforms.

- **Systems / Information Security:** Maintained network integrity during numerous exploitation alerts.

  - Researched intrusion-detection system for feasibility of host-based IDS vs. network-based.
  - Validated over two million lines of code to mitigate attacks on web pages.
  - Authored contingency plans and revised security policies.

- **Technical Support:** Ensured 24/7 expert resolution of trouble calls for over 5,000 personnel.

continued

Strategy: *Adapt military titles and duties with a stronger emphasis on technologies served for the civilian market.*

CARLTON HEMINGWAY   Resume, Page Two

PROFESSIONAL EXPERIENCE continued

INFORMATION TECHNOLOGY MANAGER — 1996–1999
Provided executive oversight of information technology acquisition and lifecycle management program.

- *Technology Transfer:* Served as company focal point to lead 13 geographically distributed, technologically diverse sites through consolidation of data for time-critical assessment and conversion.

  - Energized teams at sites throughout five countries to address conversion issues and execute plans.
  - Rapidly executed delivery of $2.5 million of IT infrastructure to remote sites to comply with standards.

- *Technical Support:* Played crucial role in setup and implementation of new trouble desk reporting procedures that increased customer response time by over 36%.

- *Database Development:* Developed and implemented database program in Oracle that resulted in error-free accounting for over $2 million in computer equipment.

INFORMATION SYSTEMS SECURITY MANAGER —1992–1996
Controlled all IS security issues to ensure integrity and reliability of classified LANs, mainframe computer and numerous stand-alone PCs.

- *Information Systems Security:* Maintained internal and external security controls, issued passwords, created accounts and ensured users adhered to policies.

  - Devised procedures for implementation of secure voice and data dial-in access for over 13 site locations.
  - Revised outdated security plan to institute policies and controls including risk management / assessment.
  - Ensured timely support of operational security requirements for multi-media devices.
  - Formulated procedures for the detection, isolation, eradication and reporting of PC viruses.

- *System Modification / Upgrade:* Developed transition plan to support a site relocation, implementing technology equipment to provide continuity of operations throughout transition.

- *Database Administration:* Managed security database comprised of over 5,000 user accounts.

- *End-User Support:* Supervised a team of four technical support staff in providing timely telephone and on-line virtual end-user support for software, e-mail, system administration and application.

ADDITIONAL TECHNICAL KNOWLEDGE

- **Software, Languages & Platforms:** Windows New Technology (NT) 4.0, NT Exchange Server; UNIX; HyperText Markup Language (HTML); JavaScript; MS Office and MS Project.

Nicholas J. Watkins, PMP

10122 South Shore Drive
Pacifica, CA 94044
650-555-9028
watkinsassociates@aol.com

SENIOR PROJECT MANAGER

Expert in the Planning and Management of Complex Projects that Increase Efficiency, Productivity, and Profitability.

Project Management Professional with more than 15 years of experience across diverse markets and industries. Strong track record of matrix-managing cross-functional teams that collaborate as a focused unit to achieve aggressive business goals. Particularly effective directing the evolution of technical and non-technical solutions from concept through implementation, constantly managing the needs of the customer, the team, and the project. Core competencies include:

- Strategic Planning & Leadership
- Productivity & Efficiency Improvement
- Team Management/Team Building
- New Product / Service Development
- Cost Reduction & Avoidance
- Facilitation / JAD

PROFESSIONAL EXPERIENCE

Watkins & Associates — Pacifica, CA   2000–Present
Independent Project Management Consultant hired to plan and conduct consulting engagements to meet client needs. Verifiable track record of success providing project / process leadership to a varied group of companies including start-ups, financial institutions, and software providers. Contributions include development of business requirements, management and direction of system design and development, rollout and installation supervision, data mapping and conversion, acceptance testing, end-user training, and documentation.

<u>Legato Systems</u> (4/01–current)
- Recruited to lead a team of 10 employees and consultants in the implementation of Oracle 11i Contracts for Service module. Converted several thousand existing contracts from multiple legacy systems into Oracle.
- Managed the upgrade from Clarify v6.0 to v10.1. Converted several thousand open and closed cases into Clarify v10.1.
- Spearheaded and directed data clean-up efforts, ultimately leading to the successful conversion of tens of thousands of installed base records.
- Managed project staff of 8 in the development of an innovative web-based quoting tool to increase efficiency and provide forecasting opportunities not previously available. Decreased quote creation time by 80% and quote modification turnaround by 95%, thereby increasing monthly output to more than 2,000 quotes.
- Created Introduction to Project Management materials for the Corporate Services Group. Introduced the group to the principles of project management outlined in the Project Management Body of Knowledge (PMBOK).

<u>Gap, Inc.</u> (11/00–2/01)
- Successfully served as PM on five projects involving infrastructure development for the MIS Technical Services Group. Managed the schedule and ensured on-time deliverables.

<u>iMotors.com</u> (6/00–10/00)
- Successfully installed five releases with over 50 enhancements. Created business requirements; managed development, testing, and creation of end-user documentation. Provided live-day support and training.
- Managed the revision of the vehicle tracking process on the intranet site. The project provided more detailed information to the sales and support personnel, resulting in improved inventory management and a more informed customer service experience.

Strategy: *Present multi-industry experience while maintaining a clear focus on the goal of senior IT project/program manager.*

Nicholas J. Watkins, PMP   Confidential Résumé, Page Two

PROFESSIONAL EXPERIENCE (Continued ...)

Synchrony Communications — Cincinnati, Ohio   2000
Project Manager for the Internet start-up provider of customer relationship management (CRM) systems. Managed customer installations including requirements documentation, implementation management, end user training, and live-day support.
- Managed key customer implementations in locations throughout the U.S.
- Developed the project management processes used by all project managers in the Professional Services organization.

Visa International — Foster City, CA   1998–1999
Project Manager for the International Division. Assigned to the IT Group managing projects on a continuing, and sometimes concurrent, basis.
- Managed project designed to improve customer service by providing member profile reports to be used by support personnel and member banks.
- Also selected to manage project designed to identify at-risk member setups. In a collaborative effort with other regions, delivered the program responsible for a significant reduction in at-risk and fraudulent setups.

Bank of America — San Francisco, CA   1980–1997
Project Manager. Progressed through positions of increasing responsibility during tenure. Recognized for superior performance and the ability to direct large, complex projects.

Fraud
- Led team of 8–10 employees in the development and implementation of a program to monitor customer check-writing patterns, identifying activity falling outside usual parameters, and allowing the bank to reduce fraud losses.
- Served as project lead for multi-functional task force of 20 employees chartered to reduce losses due to check processing fraud. Result: reduced the rate of loss by $25 million.

Payment Services
- Managed the purchase and installation of statement processing equipment in the Los Angeles and Oregon processing centers. Total project budget: $1 million. Directed vendors, contractors, employee training, and project schedule. Result: increased statement-processing throughput by 10%.
- Managed the successful effort (20 team members) to centralize NSF check processing from over 1000 BofA branches throughout California into two data centers.

Mergers & Rollouts
- Managed equipment deployment to hundreds of BofA branches located throughout California and Hawaii. Supervised testing efforts and managed end-user training and live-day support.
- During the merger with Security Pacific, coordinated activities of four other Project Managers, directing equipment deployment to former SP branches and managing live-day efforts.
- Selected to provide on-site management for rollout of online system in Hawaii.

EDUCATION AND PROFESSIONAL TRAINING

George Washington University — Washington, DC
Master of Science, Project Management
Projected date of completion, 2003
(Currently pursuing coursework)

University of Phoenix — San Jose, CA
Bachelor of Science, Business Administration

Project Management Institute — Newton Square, PA
Project Management Professional (PMP)

Doris Healy, SPHR

CONFIDENTIAL RÉSUMÉ

4 Dutton Road, Royal Oak, MI 48067
dorishealy@earthlink.net

home (248) 422-4219
mobile (248) 985-5539

Director of HRIS

- Unique combination of technical and HR functional skills with 15 years' management experience.
- Project-management and team-leadership capabilities have contributed to the successful completion of many full life-cycle projects within aggressive timeframes.
- Track record of developing integrated systems for Human Resources, Payroll, Base Benefits, Benefits Administration, Training, Position Management, and Payroll.
- 4 years' PeopleSoft experience—customizations, implementations, and conversions—with diverse organizations in support of business objectives.
- Broad-based technical knowledge to maximize effectiveness of current data processing techniques.
- Additional competencies in: Vendor Relationship Management, Client Focus, Communication, Analytical Thinking, Decision Making, Strategic Planning, and Troubleshooting.

Information Systems Experience

Senior Technical Consultant
WBH & Associates, Inc., Detroit, MI

1998 to Present

HRIS Consulting firm with $25 million annual revenue and 75 employees.

Plan and implement PeopleSoft for HR, Benefits, and Payroll and support current client systems. Develop customized add-on applications using PeopleCode. Teach PeopleSoft to end-users and database administrators. Consult on best practices in HR, Benefits, Payroll and coding with PeopleTools and SQR (for conversion, reports, interfaces, etc.). **Select Achievements:**

Kroger's
- Developed customized leave set-up tables and leave-accrual SQRs that processed 25 different leave plans, increased accuracy of the number of vacation and sick hours to which each employee was entitled, and minimized issues with upgrades.

Bank of America
- Turned around a project to rollout a consolidated HR, Payroll, Benefits Administration, and Position Management system that was one year behind and $15 million over budget. Redeveloped plan and went live on budget and on time.
- Awarded project to manage data conversion for legacy system including the conversion of history.

Merrill Lynch
- Reduced payroll errors 90% by creating audit reports to identify issues with the Cobols that calculate pay. These reports were adopted by WBH for all clients using PeopleSoft.
- Led redesign of sluggish Retroactive Benefit Deductions programs. Programs now run in several minutes with expected results and are part of the core PeopleSoft application.

HR Database Administrator
Spectrum Resource, Detroit, MI

1998

Charged with PeopleSoft production support for HR and Base Benefits (with ADP payroll interface) and implementing a risk management system with Informix back-end.
- Amended employee data reporting errors that corrected 401(k) deductions.
- Launched risk-management system on time by efficiently analyzing the new system and writing programs to convert from legacy system.

- Continued -

Strategy: *Use a qualifications summary to position this individual for her career target of Director of HRIS; focus on transferable skills and achievements to make the most of her experience, which is primarily in consulting.*

Doris Healy, SPHR   PAGE TWO

                                                           1996 to 1997
Consultant
User-Centric Consulting, Rochester, MI

Directed this computer programming firm. Gained experience working with a variety of companies to address needs with Web pages, and Access and SQL Server databases.

                                                           1993 to 1996
Director of Managed Care Services
Radiology Corporation, Grand Rapids, MI

Designed and implemented a physician-networking tracking application in Access with customized reports.

Management Experience

                                                           1983 to 1993
Assistant Administrator
St. Theresa Hospital, Rochester, MI

Managed 88-bed JCAHO-accredited facility. Oversaw Admissions, Human Resources, Facilities Management, and Business Office to provide operational efficiency and quality health care.

Technical Skills

Operating Systems:	UNIX, Windows NT
HRIS Software:	PeopleSoft through Version 8, PeopleTools, PeopleCode
Programming Languages:	SQR, C, Visual Basic, HTML, JavaScript
Databases:	Oracle, Informix, DB2

Education

Master of Arts & Bachelor of Music Education
Wayne State University, Wayne, MI

Certifications/Training:
Senior Professional in Human Resources (SPHR)
PeopleSoft Version 8 Certification
PeopleTools
HRMS

Memberships

Society for Human Resource Management

International Oracle Users Group

Sierra Club (15 years)
- Former Chair of Detroit-Area Chapter
- Won Earl Burnum Conservation Award

DAVID NELSON KENT

1234 Kalanianaole Hwy.   •   Honolulu, Hawaii 96816   •   808.555.6789   •   dnkent@oahuweb.com

COMPUTER AND INFORMATION SYSTEMS MANAGER

PUBLIC WEB SITES • ADMINISTRATIVE INTRANETS • SOFTWARE ENGINEERING

- Seven years of experience in Web Site Planning, Development, and Administration.
- Keen foresight of Web Development and Internet industry trends in technology.
- Thorough knowledge and effective execution of state-of-the-art Internet and Intranet systems technology.
- Develop and manage Web sites for large single and multi-institutional organizations, including academia.
- Superb communication and presentation skills, easily introducing technical information to project participants and to the public.

RELEVANT EXPERIENCE

RESEARCH CORPORATION OF THE UNIVERSITY OF HAWAII, Honolulu, HI   1998–Present

Computer and Information Systems Manager, Marine Bioproducts Engineering Center (MarBEC)
January 2000–Present

Supervise Information and Reporting System (IRS) software-development team of 8 (2 faculty and 6 students). Establish IRS content-management and administrative procedures. Handle quality assurance/control, ensuring integrity of Web-site content. Administer Web and database servers. Recommend and purchase all hardware and software. Obtain and disseminate information regarding IRS, student internship program, NSF site visits, annual reporting, and annual Engineering Research Center (ERC) meetings.

Database/Web Development Specialist, MarBEC
July 1999–January 2000

Coordinated planning, development, and implementation of Relational Database Management System (RDMS), including time frame for deliverables. Maintained and estimated budgets for subcontracted work and personal assistant. Created Internet and intranet content and applications in support of MarBEC's internal and external activities. Trained users at multiple sites and developed related standards, policies, and procedures.

Computer Specialist III, NOAA National Marine Fisheries Service (NMFS) Honolulu Laboratory
June 1998–June 1999

Coordinated the NMFS Honolulu Laboratory, PIAO, WPACFIN, and Coast Watch Web sites to comply with NOAA standards. Collaborated to develop and implement standards for these and other sub-webs. Established and chaired Laboratory's Web Committee. Established the Laboratory's Web presence. Identified, obtained, and published Web-site material.

CHESAPEAKE BAY RESEARCH CONSORTIUM, Annapolis, MD   1995–1998

Environmental Management Fellow, EPA Chesapeake Bay Program (CBP) Office

Worked closely and in coordination with CBP management-committee members and other federal, state, and university staff to provide means of publishing and maintaining CBP Web-site material. Provided suggestions to non-technical staff on the options for adding and maintaining content.

Strategy: *Position this self-taught webmaster for the same position at a new organization. Detail depth of his expertise in position descriptions; then use concrete accomplishments to provide evidence of his skill sets.*

DAVID NELSON KENT

Page 2

REPRESENTATIVE ACCOMPLISHMENTS

- Designed and developed proprietary IRS software, securing $500,000 in additional funding for MarBEC. System expected to save National Science Foundation $2.2 million on ERC expenditures annually.

- Delivered beta version of Annual Report Volume II reporting system for MarBEC 8 weeks ahead of schedule. Delivered full system version 1.01 on schedule and within budget.

- Presented several successful Web-development and software-engineering multi-media seminars for MarBEC: PowerPoint site visit presentations, 1999/2000; ERC annual meeting IRS demonstrations, 1999/2000; IRS demo to University Information and Computing Sciences Department (ICS), 2000.

- Ensured prominent Web presence by orchestrating 3-phase development of MarBEC's database and Web site.

- Designed and developed NMFS Honolulu Laboratory intranet and Internet Web sites in six months, 10 weeks ahead of schedule. Conceptualized and built from scratch NOAA R/V *Townsend Cromwell* student connection outreach Web site.

- Established a noticeable Web presence through coding, designing, and administering Chesapeake Bay Program's intranet and Internet World Wide Web sites. Co-authored Chesapeake Bay Program *Web Document Guidance*.

TECHNICAL KNOWLEDGE

HARDWARE—Intel Based Systems • Macintosh • UNIX • Digital Imaging Devices • Telecommunications • Local Area Networks

SOFTWARE—Operating Systems • HTML • Database/Spreadsheet • Microsoft Project 2000 • Graphics Packages • File Manipulations • E-Mail Editors • GIS • FTP • Word Processors • Directory Manipulations • Multimedia Digital Imaging

PROGRAMMING AND CODING—HTML • XHTML • CSS • JavaScript • Dynamic HTML • SQL • CGI Scripting • Visual Basic • DOM • COM • FORTRAN • Cold Fusion Markup Language • DTDs • XML • XSL • XSLT

ADDITIONAL TRAINING

XML Certification • Web Process and Project Management • Web Site Development and Design • Brochure, Catalog, Ad, Newsletter, and Report Design • Graphics and Animation Creation • Data and Information Presentation • Windows-Based Environment Programming

EDUCATION

B.S., Oceanography, Mathematics Emphasis, 1992
Humboldt State University, Arcata, CA

• • •

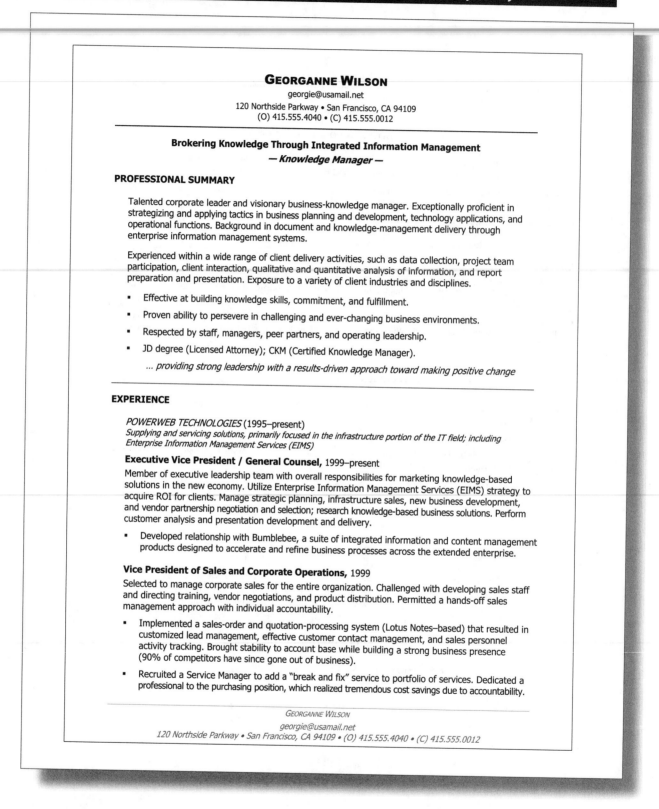

GEORGANNE WILSON

georgie@usamail.net

120 Northside Parkway • San Francisco, CA 94109
(O) 415.555.4040 • (C) 415.555.0012

Brokering Knowledge Through Integrated Information Management
— *Knowledge Manager* —

PROFESSIONAL SUMMARY

Talented corporate leader and visionary business-knowledge manager. Exceptionally proficient in strategizing and applying tactics in business planning and development, technology applications, and operational functions. Background in document and knowledge-management delivery through enterprise information management systems.

Experienced within a wide range of client delivery activities, such as data collection, project team participation, client interaction, qualitative and quantitative analysis of information, and report preparation and presentation. Exposure to a variety of client industries and disciplines.

- Effective at building knowledge skills, commitment, and fulfillment.

- Proven ability to persevere in challenging and ever-changing business environments.

- Respected by staff, managers, peer partners, and operating leadership.

- JD degree (Licensed Attorney); CKM (Certified Knowledge Manager).

   … providing strong leadership with a results-driven approach toward making positive change

EXPERIENCE

POWERWEB TECHNOLOGIES (1995–present)
Supplying and servicing solutions, primarily focused in the infrastructure portion of the IT field; including Enterprise Information Management Services (EIMS)

Executive Vice President / General Counsel, 1999–present
Member of executive leadership team with overall responsibilities for marketing knowledge-based solutions in the new economy. Utilize Enterprise Information Management Services (EIMS) strategy to acquire ROI for clients. Manage strategic planning, infrastructure sales, new business development, and vendor partnership negotiation and selection; research knowledge-based business solutions. Perform customer analysis and presentation development and delivery.

- Developed relationship with Bumblebee, a suite of integrated information and content management products designed to accelerate and refine business processes across the extended enterprise.

Vice President of Sales and Corporate Operations, 1999
Selected to manage corporate sales for the entire organization. Challenged with developing sales staff and directing training, vendor negotiations, and product distribution. Permitted a hands-off sales management approach with individual accountability.

- Implemented a sales-order and quotation-processing system (Lotus Notes–based) that resulted in customized lead management, effective customer contact management, and sales personnel activity tracking. Brought stability to account base while building a strong business presence (90% of competitors have since gone out of business).

- Recruited a Service Manager to add a "break and fix" service to portfolio of services. Dedicated a professional to the purchasing position, which realized tremendous cost savings due to accountability.

GEORGANNE WILSON
georgie@usamail.net
120 Northside Parkway • San Francisco, CA 94109 • (O) 415.555.4040 • (C) 415.555.0012

Strategy: *Equally emphasize technology and legal expertise required for a Knowledge Management role in a technology company.*

Vice President of Sales, 1997–98

Appointed to lead direct-sales activities, develop new client associations, advance existing customer activity, and manage the sales staff.

- Developed client relationships and won a major pharmaceutical company account.

- Positioned the company in a growth mode in a down economy.

- Increased the sales staff retention rate to five years.

Vice President of Marketing and Finance, 1996–97

Commissioned with accounting/finance responsibilities in addition to existing marketing activities. Directed strategic planning for budgets, personnel, and operating procedures for both business units.

- System efficiencies increased through structured auditing processes for general ledger, balance sheet, cash flow, and tax filing. Created audit accountability.

Vice President of Marketing, 1994–96

Managed marketing business directed at prospecting and acquiring new accounts. Developed innovative marketing material including newsletters and targeted customer contact messaging. Interacted with internal groups to create a consistent corporate marketing message.

- Successfully certified DCC through Small Business 8A program to create inroads with the federal government and penetrate vendor opportunities. Enabled company to acquire substantial account base with the Department of Defense prime contractors.

TOYOTA CORPORATION

Staff Attorney, 1993–94

EDUCATION / CERTIFICATION

Juris Doctor degree, 1992 — *CALIFORNIA PACIFIC SCHOOL OF LAW;* Bakersfield, CA

Bachelor of Arts degree in Political Science, 1989 — *UNIVERSITY OF OHIO;* Columbus, OH

Certified Knowledge Manager (CKM) — *One of only 85 certified KM professionals worldwide.* Certified through IMII/eKnowledgeCenter; offering the only certification training to pass the ISO/IEC–based GKEC Certification Test, based on the internationally recognized ISO/IEC Certification Standards.

Member — State Bar of California, 1992

ROBERT D. JONES

Home: (360) 260-0238   rdjones@aol.com   Cell: (360) 750-3901

VP OPERATIONS • VP SOFTWARE DEVELOPMENT

IT professional with 9 years' management and hands-on experience providing technology solutions to support strategic business objectives:

- Achieved multimillion-dollar cost savings while producing double-digit efficiency increase.
- Proven change agent, gaining cross-functional cooperation and collaboration during three corporate mergers involving innovative leaders such as Occasions.com, Network Services, BlueDolphin.com, and MicroNet.

Technology expertise includes:

- System and application integration. Programming (C, Perl, Java, and C++) in transactional and distributed environments with emphasis on Web / database transaction.
- Maintenance and performance tuning of operating systems: Linux, Solaris, FreeBSD, Win32.
- Storage systems with multiple RDBMS applications: Oracle, Informix, DB2, MySq1, Sqlserver.

HIGHLIGHT OF ACHIEVEMENTS

- **Problem Solving:** Increased revenue capability 50–70% through software and operational architecture redesign allowing e-commerce applications. Project completed on time while maintaining 100% operational capacity. (Occasions.com)

- **Financial Analysis / Cost Control:** Uncovered $3 million in cost savings over 2-year period while increasing efficiency 20%. (Occasions.com)

- **Database Administration / Development:** Saved more than $100K annually through development of new, user-friendly billing system that eliminated yearly consulting fees. (Northwest Telenet)

- **Adaptability / Flexibility:** Maintained momentum of multimillion-dollar project when strategic focus shifted from customer retention to revenue generation. Project completed on time and within budget. (ARWA.com)

- **Programming:** Improved Web operational efficiency 20% through development of searching and parsing algorithm that became the basis of code for the entire Web rewrite project. (Occasions.com)

PROFESSIONAL EXPERIENCE

Occasions.com   **VP Web Operations**   1999 – Present
Formerly ARWA.com   Beaverton, OR
Formerly BlueDolphin.com

Leading online greeting card company ranking in the top 15 most popular US Web sites. Maintain site reliability and performance to support traffic load of 1.1 gigabytes and more than 12.5 million monthly visitors generating $45 million in annual revenue. Direct and lead cross-functional team of 20 including department heads over QA, Systems Administration, and Networking in San Diego, San Francisco, and Cleveland. Manage annual operating budget of $13 million. Direct strategic planning, development, implementation, and maintenance of data-processing operations across multiple hardware and software platforms.

- Led project to rebuild application allowing additional $6 million annual revenue while saving $500K in outside consulting fees. New application led to partnerships with major online retailers MarthaStewart.com, SharperImage.com, 1800flowers.com, and AT&T.

- Saved $600K annually while improving production efficiency 20% through leadership and implementation of card-customization project.

Continued

1906 McGilvary Street • Vancouver, WA 98683

Strategy: *For this upward-climbing manager, focus on management rather than technical skills; create a strong first page that appropriately highlights management accomplishments, transferable skills, and executive-level experience.*

ROBERT D. JONES

Home: (360) 260-0238   rdjones@aol.com   Cell: (360) 750-3901
Page 2

Northwest Telenet	**Manager, Systems Development**	1999
Network Services		Camas, WA
Formerly MicroNet		

Regional Internet hosting firm. Developed architectural hosting solutions for corporate clients such as Disney, MP3.com, and Sony. Provided hosting support and system administration as well as spec design for product requirements.

- Generated team cohesiveness and cooperation during acquisition, which led to creation of new, faster, and more reliable products.
- Created new revenue stream through research and development of shared database service.
- Transitioned group of system administrators into the data center / managed hosting market to provide Tier 3 and 4 support and consulting services for fully managed hosting solutions.

Pacific Supercomputer Center	**Programmer / Analyst**	1997 – 1999
		Portland, OR

Scientific research facility (one of two national computing laboratories). Provided all system administration, programming, database administration, and database development. Supplied all in-house technical support and training for 150 personnel. Maintained research database for 9 scientists for projects funded at up to $7 million.

- Created $100K annual cost savings by rewriting outdated, costly accounting system. New user-friendly system (Oracle) was 25% faster while allowing greater data accuracy.
- Helped scientists secure additional funding by designing Web solutions that allowed online publication of research projects.
- Contributed to the retention of high-level scientists through facilitating cooperation and positive communication throughout scientific staff.

Alaska Scientific	**Research Assistant / Application Developer**	1995 – 1997
		Fairbanks, AK

Research facility supporting the scientific community. Wrote interferometry applications as well as applications to automate the mosaicing of satellite image data.

- Helped secure two years' funding through Herculean effort to complete project in less than 48 hours that included designing 3D-animated flight of satellite images for presentation to the Science & Technology Committee of the US House of Representatives. Worked 36 hours straight to complete ahead of schedule.

EDUCATION

University of Alaska	**M.Ed., Education**	1996
Fairbanks, AK		
University of California	**B.A., Physical Sciences**	1993
Berkeley, CA		

1906 McGilvary Street • Vancouver, WA 98683

STEPHEN C. PEARSON

133 Dresden Road, Baltimore, Maryland 21218
410-555-0584 • spearson@app.net

Senior Executive • Information Technology

IT Planning & Development / Systems Design & Implementation / Technology Team Leadership

Profit & Loss Management / Project Management / Process Re-engineering / e-Enabling Initiatives

Results-oriented MBA Executive with 20 years of experience combining leading-edge technologies with sound business leadership. Specific expertise in e-Business, Enterprise Information and Decision Support Systems, product development and implementation, operations and strategic/tactical business planning.

CAREER HIGHLIGHTS

- Achieved Best-In-Class performance and cost savings at multiple management levels.
- Saved over $10 million by producing new Enterprise Information System/DSS.
- Captured $4 million in savings by re-engineering and e-Enabling Network Services.
- Created highly profitable OEM division, generating $28 million in first 3 years of operation.
- Earned *Data* Magazine's "Product of the Year" Award.
- Rated #1 Product Manager in Computer Systems Division.

PROFESSIONAL EXPERIENCE

Network Datacom, Baltimore, Maryland   1982–present

Director, Networks, Operations & Program Management (2000–present)

Direct all corporate technology for the Net program. Manage a team of 8 direct reports/120 indirect reports.

✓ Salvaged and enhanced program resulting in $128 million in additional revenue in 2001, $5 million in access cost savings, and 117% of planned portfolio growth.

✓ Produced a 60% productivity improvement and $4 million in cost savings by initiating and directing a re-engineering of the organization's entire portfolio of processes and generating an e-Enabling program.

✓ Reduced data defects and rework over 95% by consolidating and e-Enabling organization's databases.

Director, Y2K Program Management (1997–2000)

Orchestrated global program management and systems compliance for 33 of the company's 36 business units. Managed a team of 7 direct reports and over 300 indirect reports; administered a $130 million budget encompassing over 1,800 software applications, 60,000 network elements, and over 1,500 external interfaces.

✓ Achieved best-in-class cost and performance levels.

✓ Successfully passed Y2K with no incidents. Outperformed all other colleagues despite a significantly larger unit responsibility.

Division Manager, New Business Development (1996)

Secured technology critical to the launch of new services such as Interglobal Net and Fast World Wide Web. Coordinated corporate acquisition, divestiture, software licensing and co-branding with emerging vendors such as Netscape and Veritz Corporation. Supervised 2 direct reports and over 80 staff members.

✓ Boosted overall productivity 200% by initiating the design and development of an automated GroupWare system utilized by board-level executives in tracking and analyzing new business-development deals.

Division Manager, IVR Development (1995)

Selected to ignite profitability and lead the IVR product-development organization charged with designing and building custom interactive voice-response applications and related platforms.

✓ Increased "on-time" delivery to 98%, enhanced customer satisfaction ratings to 95% from 40%, improved morale and substantially reduced employee turnover, all within 8 months and ahead of plan.

Strategy: *Reduce this candidate's original four-page resume to two concise pages, emphasizing accomplishments and including an attention-getting Career Highlights section on page 1.*

Stephen C. Pearson

District Manager, Enterprise Systems (1994–1995)

Designed and directed development of a leading-edge enterprise information and decision support system, the first of its kind to use a single interface to enable decision makers to view all facets of the business: financial, operational, marketing, sales, customer satisfaction, human resources, and competition.

✓ Brought project to completion in just 10 weeks and 50% under budget.

✓ Saved over $10 million and improved productivity and efficiency by consolidating over 20 "mini-enterprise systems" and creating one new system, utilizing sophisticated data warehousing and OLAP technologies.

District Manager, Strategic Planning, Communication Services (1992–1993)

Responsible for the entire division's strategic planning process, mission, forecasting and business planning.

✓ Initiated development of strategic research and market plans in support of the globalization of CS services.

✓ Developed a comprehensive business plan and set of interlocking strategic initiatives that served as the baseline for the evolution of new services portfolio.

Product Marketing Manager, Hospitality Infrastructure Service (1991–1992)

Brought in to revitalize sales and restore profitability to Hospitality Infrastructure Service. Managed 6 reports.

✓ Increased revenues to $12 million during the first 6 months, doubling revenues earned in all of 1991.

✓ Streamlined and intensified marketing efforts and devised more competitive sales compensation plans, strengthening sales force commitment and increasing customer acquisition.

Senior Product Manager, Network Software (1988–1991)

Recruited to oversee market introduction of 25+ network software products for Computer Systems Division. Managed product architecture and development, competitive pricing, production and packaging, marketing/sales, operations, and end-user customer training and support. Led team of 60 employees.

✓ Generated $28 million the first 3 years of operation by creating a highly profitable OEM division for implementation of UNIX Net Manager.

✓ Boosted revenues 400% over a 3-year period, producing sales of over $25 million without any advertising budget. Earned recognition company-wide for spearheading the development and launch of one of Computer Systems' most profitable product lines.

✓ Captured a $3 million savings by negotiating license agreements with major software vendors, including Microsoft and Apple Computer, enabling company to take advantage of significantly discounted royalty fees.

✓ Earned *Data* Magazine's "1991 Product of the Year" award and *Systems* Magazine's "1991 Finalist" award for the UNIX Net Manager product.

✓ Led transition team challenged with merging two companies' networking software products.

EDUCATION

M.B.A., Finance, Western Michigan University
B.S., Industrial Psychology, Loyola University of Chicago

TECHNICAL EXPERTISE

Needs Assessment • Systems / Applications Integration • Global Systems Support • Emerging Technologies • Cross-Functional Technology Team Leadership • Vendor Partnerships • Client / Server Architecture • Disaster Planning and Recovery • Benchmarking • Application Service Providers (ASPs) • Data Networks • Data Warehousing • GroupWare Systems • Interactive Voice Response (IVR) Systems • LAN / WAN Design and Implementation • Servers and Mid-Range Computers • Software Engineering and Development • Network Operating Systems • Programming Languages • Technology Licensing • Telecommunications Technology • Web Authoring Languages and Tools

James J. Olsen

3616 S. MacDill Ave.
Brandon, FL, 33615

(813) 668-6688
jjolsen@aol.com

OBJECTIVE

Avionics / Aerospace Management

EXPERIENCE

Aviation Maintenance Manager, U.S. Air Force, 1991–2003

Management / Supervision

- Supervise shop of 15 avionics technicians responsible for maintaining 12 aircraft.
- Create duty schedules and prioritize shop tasks and qualifications schedules.
- Monitor, counsel, and rate subordinates. Write performance reports.
- Identify and plot career progression for subordinate career development.
- Forecast, schedule, and directly supervise implementation and control of assigned aircraft avionics systems upgrades and modifications.
- Primary on-the-job trainer for Avionics Technician qualifications and upgrades.
- Perform supervisory-level quality-assurance inspections of accomplished work and aircraft documentation.
- Create, maintain, and track training documents for each avionics technician.
- Collect, analyze, and present performance data to superiors for their review.
- Designed and utilized a qualifications tracking system, reducing upgrade time by 20%.

Technical

- Perform on- and off-equipment inspections and repairs of avionics systems including:

Fuel Quantity Indication	Pilot-Static	Engine Indication
Flight Management	Inertial Navigation	Color Weather Radar
Flight Control Augmentation	Flight Director	Digital Autopilot
Digital Interphone	Global Positioning	Traffic Collision Avoidance
Flight Data Recorder	Magnetic Compass	Turbine Engine Management

- Utilize wiring diagrams, schematics, handbooks, and technical data to perform in-depth trouble-shooting, fault isolation, and maintenance on electrical and avionics systems.
- Perform rewire and modification of aircraft electrical and avionics systems.
- Selected to head up team to correct elusive recurring system malfunctions.
- Hand-picked as unit's #1 avionics technician.

EDUCATION / TRAINING

MS, Aeronautical Science Specializing in Management; GPA: 4.0	Embry-Riddle Aeronautical University	2000
BS, Professional Aeronautics GPA: 3.73	Embry-Riddle Aeronautical University	1998
AAS, Avionics Technology	Community College of the Air Force	1997

Equal Opportunity and Treatment	2000	Flight Management System	1999
Operational Risk Management	1999	Inertial Navigation	1995
Avionics Guidance and Control Supervisor	1999	Compass Calibration	1994
Aircraft Maintenance Trainer / Supervisor	1997	High Reliability Soldering	1994
Airman Leadership School	1996	Micro-Miniature Soldering	1994
Total Quality Management	1995	ASQ-141 Flight Director	1993

Strategy: *The functional style groups key areas of expertise in two key categories; the technical section includes a keyword-dense list of systems expertise. Extensive relevant training is listed at the bottom.*

CHAPTER 11

Resumes for Managers and Executives in Accounting, Corporate Finance, Banking, and Financial/Investment Management

- Accounting Manager
- Chief Financial Officer
- Corporate Finance Executive
- Tax Executive
- Equipment Leasing and Finance Executive
- Financial Consultant
- Finance and General Management Executive
- Portfolio Manager
- Financial Services Manager
- Investments Executive
- International Financial Executive
- Investment-Services Executive
- Risk Management Professional

DAVID L. PRINCE

P.O. Box 802 ▪ San Diego, CA 92001 ▪ 609.555.4560 ▪ dlprince@hotmail.com

SUMMARY

Accounting Professional / Payroll Administrator combining cross-functional competencies in all phases of accounting, information systems, and staff supervision and management. Proficient in managing and developing financial reports and controls using staffing and technology efficiencies. Ability to contribute as a team player and interface with professionals on all levels. Expertise includes:

- Payroll Administration
- Automated Accounting Information Systems
- Inventory Control & Purchasing
- Financial Reporting

- Quarterly & Year-End Reporting
- Corporate Tax Compliance
- Corporate Accounting
- Job Costing

PROFESSIONAL EXPERIENCE

Platinum Choice, Los Angeles, CA   1998–Present
    CONTROLLER (2001–Present)
    ACCOUNTANT (2000–2001)
    OUTSOURCED ACCOUNTANT (1998–2000)

Plan, manage, and provide leadership for accounting department including payroll, budgeting, cost accounting, managerial accounting, financial reporting, financial analysis, and purchasing. Scope of responsibility spans both the corporate and divisional level including two out-of-state subsidiary business units. Provide financial expertise to outside firms, including banks, auditors, and government authorities.

- Managed $4 million in annual operating budgets allocated for personnel, facilities, and administrative expenses.
- Established improved accounts receivable and collection policies that reduced outstanding receivables by 25% during the first quarter.
- Implemented automated cost accounting systems to analyze profit improvement opportunities.
- Worked in cooperation with management teams to restructure corporate pricing on all major product lines, resulting in a 14% profit improvement.
- Oversaw implementation and development of MRP system; ensuring the integration of all reporting processes.
- Successfully guided the company through annual outside audits.
- Complete timely federal and multi-state sales, payroll, and property tax return filings.

Smith, Jones, & Heath, CPAs, Lake Forest, CA   1995–1998
    ACCOUNTING CONSULTANT

Recruited to provide diverse finance, accounting, payroll, and tax-preparation functions for one of the largest independent Orange County CPA firms.

- Responsible for preparation of financial statements: payroll, sales and property tax returns, and federal, state, and local income tax returns.
- Streamlined accounting processes to reduce workpaper and document requirements.
- Worked closely with clients in structuring general ledgers and evaluating their software needs.

Strategy: *Align resume with career goals by emphasizing payroll expertise in the summary, position descriptions, achievement statements, and computer-skills section.*

DAVID L. PRINCE   609.555.4560   PAGE TWO

PROFESSIONAL EXPERIENCE (CONTINUED)

1985–1994

Taylor Baking Company; Chicago, IL
  DIVISIONAL SALES MANAGER (1990–1994)
  ROUTE SALES SUPERVISOR (1988–1990)
  SALES ROUTE DRIVER (1985–1988)
Total responsibility for all sales and operations in the Northern Illinois and Southern Wisconsin territory. Hired, trained, and directed the development of approximately 20 employees.

- Managed high-profile territory, generating new business and maximizing existing account sales for over 400 accounts.
- Sales talent to cultivate relationships, expand customer base, and maximize account sales.
- Managed the route sales force and supervised all inside operational personnel at various locations.

EDUCATION

San Diego State University
  DEGREE: **BUSINESS MANAGEMENT** (1984)

COMPUTER SKILLS

- Experienced with the following software for payroll preparation: QuickBooks/QuickBooks Pro, Peachtree, PenSoft Payroll, Class, and CFS Payroll Systems.
- Skilled in most accounting software programs including Impact Encore, Peachtree 6, QuickBooks, QuickBooks Pro 5, Accountants ATB, T-value, Depreciation Solutions, Class, WS-2, Preform Plus, ProSystems, and Quicken.
- Proficient in Excel, Word, Access, Lotus 1-2-3, WordPerfect, Goldmine, and Pacs.

RESUME 69: MICHELE HAFFNER, CPRW, JCTC; GLENDALE, WI

JULIA JACKSON, CPA, CMA
Email: jjackson@mail.com

204 East 5th Avenue
New York, New York 10011

Office: (718) 567-8904
Residence: (914) 764-0967

DIVISIONAL CONTROLLER/CHIEF FINANCIAL OFFICER

Senior accounting professional with 14 years of experience in financial reporting, analysis, forecasting, budgeting, cash management, auditing, and controls for multi-site manufacturing and industrial organizations. Solid interpersonal skills and cross-functional team interactions (Sales, Production, Information Systems, Human Resources) coupled with effective leadership abilities. Core competencies include:

- A/R, A/P & G/L Account Analysis
- Financial Statements & Management Reporting
- Operating & Capital Budget Preparation
- Tax Reporting & Preparation
- Credit Reviews & Approvals
- Job Costing & Variance Analysis
- Banking & Insurance Management

- Accounting Policies/Procedures Development & Establishment
- Inventory Management & Reconciliation
- Staff Training & Development
- HR, Benefits & Risk Management
- Automated Financial System & Business Software (PC & Mainframe)
- Regulatory Compliance

PROFESSIONAL EXPERIENCE

NORTHEAST FORGING INDUSTRIES, INC. — New York, New York   2000 to 2003
A division of Regulation Corporation, with 2 locations and combined annual revenues of $85 million. Company supplies carbon, alloy, and stainless forgings primarily to heavy truck, construction, automotive, aircraft, and oil industries.

DIVISION CONTROLLER
Challenged to hire/train professional staff, strengthen divisional accounting functions, and implement/maintain financial controls. Position (subsequently downsized) managed a staff of 4 responsible for A/R, A/P, Payroll/Benefits, and Cost Accounting. Position reported directly to site General Managers with dotted line to Corporate Controller.

Key Accountabilities & Accomplishments
- Managed month-end/year-end close and financial statement preparation. Analyzed balance sheets, P&L, cash flows, and budget variances. Assisted operational management to resolve variances.
- Supported corporate and divisional strategic planning efforts through forecasting and operational/capital budget development activities.
- Managed physical inventory ($12 million combined value) and reviewed for obsolescence, movement, and valuation.
- Established and maintained credit/collection policies; reviewed and managed divisional banking and lending relationships. Supervised and audited daily bank account reconciliations for 3 cash accounts.
- Monitored self-funded insurance account and prepared monthly forecasts.
- Traveled monthly to Wisconsin location for staff training and supervision. Developed strong relationships with operational managers.
- Oversaw external audit process and provided all necessary worksheets/data to minimize billable hours.

Strategy: *For this individual seeking a divisional controller position with a manufacturing corporation, stress hands-on corporate accounting experience over public accounting background.*

JULIA JACKSON RÉSUMÉ   O: (718) 567-8904 / R: (914) 764-0967   jjackson@mail.com   Page 2 of 2

PROFESSIONAL EXPERIENCE (continued)

CHEYENNE, INCORPORATED — Milwaukee, Wisconsin   1995 to 2000
A $40 million, wholly owned subsidiary of Point Footwear, Incorporated (acquired in 1996). A manufacturer and global distributor of industrial footwear and protective clothing.

CONTROLLER
Recruited to manage a professional staff of 5 responsible for credit management, A/R, A/P, cost accounting, and MIS. Challenged to hire and train staff in key management positions (accounting, credit, MIS) vacated shortly after merger. Additionally, challenged to match reporting/procedures to parent corporation. Position reported to Cheyenne COO with dotted line to corporate CFO (Point Footwear).

- Oversaw financials; performed divisional reporting, analysis, forecasting, and budgeting.
- Tracked operational improvements versus targets; assisted operational management in cost-savings initiatives and working-capital optimization.
- Oversaw MIS department; worked closely with IT staff to integrate parent requirements with existing automated financial systems.

CONLEY, MC DONALD & COMPANY — Milwaukee, Wisconsin   1994 to 1995
Local public accounting firm serving clients statewide.

AUDIT SENIOR
Performed auditing procedures, prepared monthly/quarterly statements and entries, and monitored performance of various clients including banking institutions and non-profits.

PRICEWATERHOUSE — Milwaukee, Wisconsin   1993 to 1994
Big 6 public accounting firm with 50+ offices nationwide.

AUDIT SENIOR
Performed external audits for manufacturing/industrial firms and informed senior managers of performance and findings.

CLIFTON GUNDERSON, LLP — Madison, Wisconsin   1988 to 1993
13th largest public accounting firm in U.S. with offices in 13 states.

AUDIT SUPERVISOR (1991 to 1993)
STAFF ACCOUNTANT/IN CHARGE (1988 to 1991)
Performed public accounting activities for client base of manufacturing and construction firms.

EDUCATION, CERTIFICATIONS & PROFESSIONAL AFFILIATIONS

Accounting Coursework (21 Credits) — Marquette University — Milwaukee, Wisconsin
BS (Finance) — University of Wisconsin — Madison, Wisconsin

Certified Management Accountant, 1995
Certified Public Accountant, 1988

American Institute of Certified Public Accountants (AICPS)
Wisconsin Institute of Certified Public Accountants (WICPA)
Financial Executives Institute (FEI)

ROBERT T. DANILOFF

402–835–8941
rtd@email.com
34223 Wind Mill Drive, Omaha, NE 68046

FINANCIAL MANAGEMENT EXECUTIVE
Expert in cost control, team building, and financial analysis

Results–oriented senior management professional with the reputation of a goal-oriented visionary and effective communicator. Effective in reorganizing, streamlining, and strengthening financial operations to maximize performance and profitability. Respond to operational and financial challenges with confidence, determination, and focus.

Strategic & Business Planning	Information Systems Management
Internal Financial Controls & Budgeting	Cash Management
Turnarounds, Acquisitions & Mergers	Regulatory Compliance

PROFESSIONAL EXPERIENCE

NATIONAL INVESTMENT, LTD., Omaha, Nebraska
(A four-broker dealer holding company with more than $350 million in annual revenues)

Chief Financial Officer — 2000 to 2001
Selected to lead the organization's financial operations post-acquisition. Member of the executive management team reporting to the CEO. Directed financial analysis; internal and regulatory reporting; cash management; G/L, A/P, and A/R; tax reporting; budgeting; forecasting; internal and external auditing; and payroll processing activities that led to long-term improvements in cost savings, profitability, and productivity. Full P&L responsibility for a $60 million operating and $2.5 million finance budget.

- *Reduced monthly reporting processing time by 20 man hours, delivered reports in half the time, and significantly improved reporting accuracy* by centralizing and consolidating GL closing procedures.

- *Championed key performance metrics* in soundness, profitability, growth, and productivity for broker-dealers, *profitably impacting goal attainment and performance.*

INVESTMENT & HOLDINGS CORP., Arlington, Virginia
($100 million holding company acquired by American National Bank)

Chief Administrative Officer — 1999 to 2000
Selected to turn around numerous leadership challenges and restore operational stability. Managed a $30 million operating budget and a $1.5 million finance budget. Directed a 110–person staff in finance, brokerage operations, technology, and project management.

- Implemented cost controls, reporting requirements, and training to control escalating expense run rates. *Within two months, reduced expenses by 10%, generating a cost savings of $3 million annually.*

- Change-managed failing customer service initiatives. *Deployed new training, hiring practices, incentive programs, and processes, increasing customer satisfaction ratings by 22% and improving employee morale within the first year of implementation.*

- Negotiated and structured the clearing agreement that achieved a $500,000 savings over three years and resulted in significantly improved and personalized service.

Strategy: *Turn a responsibility-based resume into an accomplishment-oriented "sales" document, positioning this individual as a senior-level executive.*

ROBERT T. DANILOFF   Page 2   402-835-8941

Chief Financial Officer — 1997 to 1999
Promoted following acquisition to manage all accounting and finance functions for this newly acquired holding company. Conducted due diligence that precipitated a $9 million acquisition. Oversaw regulatory relations and compliance.

- Pioneered the corporate data warehouse to improve information management. Collaborated with outside consultants to consolidate disparate reporting and tracking processes. *Within first 100 days of implementation, reduced vendor billing cycle times by 30 days, facilitated production of monthly reports to the third business day, and improved revenue-forecasting accuracy from 85% to 95%.*

- Turned around 2.5 years of unprofitability by implementing expense controls and a contract approval and negotiation process. *Reduced monthly operating expenses by $200,000 within 30 days, achieved immediate profitability, and sustained profitability for 38 consecutive months.*

- Established employee training and support programs to turn around low morale, reduce excessive overtime, and improve financial management. Executed mentoring and relationship-building programs, implemented standards and values, and supported training programs. *Reduced overtime by 75% and slashed turnover by more than half.*

FIRST AMERICAN NATIONAL BANK (n/k/a AMSOUTH), Birmingham, Alabama
(Providing financial services to individuals, small and mid-sized businesses, and large corporations)

Hired as a Deposit Operations Manager and fast-tracked through a series of increasingly responsible management positions over a 10-year period. **Developed CSR and Teller Certification Programs** as Branch Operations Manager and **established the organization's first-ever budget processing and controls** as Marketing Retail Program Manager.

Senior Vice President / Strategic Project Director, Nashville, Tennessee — 1996 to 1997
Managed strategic and business planning, directed budgeting activities, and championed non-traditional revenue-generating initiatives. Reported directly to the Vice Chairman.

Brokerage and Trust Division Controller, Nashville, Tennessee — 1994 to 1996
Marketing Retail Program Manager, Nashville, Tennessee — 1992 to 1994

CREDENTIALS / LICENSES

Passed **Certified Public Accountant** exam on first try — 2001
NASD Series 7, 24, 27 and 65

EDUCATION

Bachelor of Science in Accounting
Graduate coursework in Computer Hardware, Marketing, Economics, and Management
University of Tennessee, Knoxville, Tennessee

Continuing education courses in Financial Analysis, Regulatory Financial Operations and Reporting, and Banking

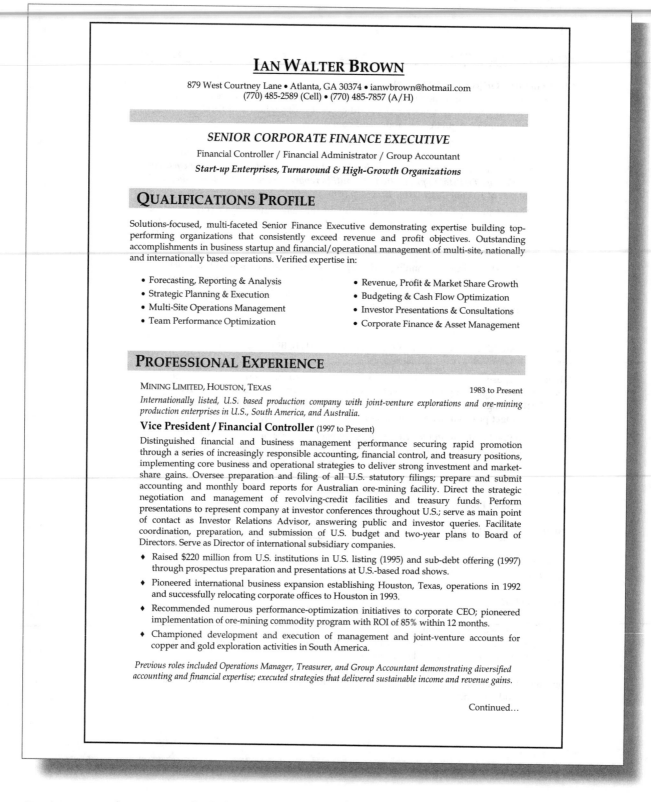

IAN WALTER BROWN

879 West Courtney Lane • Atlanta, GA 30374 • ianwbrown@hotmail.com
(770) 485-2589 (Cell) • (770) 485-7857 (A/H)

SENIOR CORPORATE FINANCE EXECUTIVE

Financial Controller / Financial Administrator / Group Accountant
Start-up Enterprises, Turnaround & High-Growth Organizations

QUALIFICATIONS PROFILE

Solutions-focused, multi-faceted Senior Finance Executive demonstrating expertise building top-performing organizations that consistently exceed revenue and profit objectives. Outstanding accomplishments in business startup and financial/operational management of multi-site, nationally and internationally based operations. Verified expertise in:

- Forecasting, Reporting & Analysis
- Strategic Planning & Execution
- Multi-Site Operations Management
- Team Performance Optimization

- Revenue, Profit & Market Share Growth
- Budgeting & Cash Flow Optimization
- Investor Presentations & Consultations
- Corporate Finance & Asset Management

PROFESSIONAL EXPERIENCE

MINING LIMITED, HOUSTON, TEXAS   1983 to Present

Internationally listed, U.S. based production company with joint-venture explorations and ore-mining production enterprises in U.S., South America, and Australia.

Vice President / Financial Controller (1997 to Present)

Distinguished financial and business management performance securing rapid promotion through a series of increasingly responsible accounting, financial control, and treasury positions, implementing core business and operational strategies to deliver strong investment and market-share gains. Oversee preparation and filing of all U.S. statutory filings; prepare and submit accounting and monthly board reports for Australian ore-mining facility. Direct the strategic negotiation and management of revolving-credit facilities and treasury funds. Perform presentations to represent company at investor conferences throughout U.S.; serve as main point of contact as Investor Relations Advisor, answering public and investor queries. Facilitate coordination, preparation, and submission of U.S. budget and two-year plans to Board of Directors. Serve as Director of international subsidiary companies.

- Raised $220 million from U.S. institutions in U.S. listing (1995) and sub-debt offering (1997) through prospectus preparation and presentations at U.S.-based road shows.
- Pioneered international business expansion establishing Houston, Texas, operations in 1992 and successfully relocating corporate offices to Houston in 1993.
- Recommended numerous performance-optimization initiatives to corporate CEO; pioneered implementation of ore-mining commodity program with ROI of 85% within 12 months.
- Championed development and execution of management and joint-venture accounts for copper and gold exploration activities in South America.

Previous roles included Operations Manager, Treasurer, and Group Accountant demonstrating diversified accounting and financial expertise; executed strategies that delivered sustainable income and revenue gains.

Continued…

Strategy: *Avoid repetition of job functions by presenting them as key competencies in the Qualifications Profile; create a summarizing paragraph for the most recent experience to identify progression through the company.*

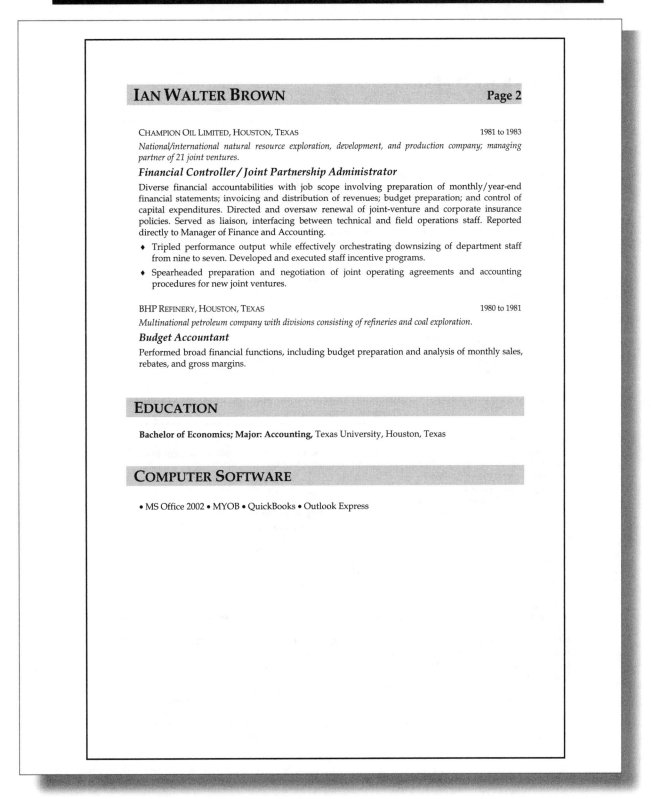

IAN WALTER BROWN   Page 2

CHAMPION OIL LIMITED, HOUSTON, TEXAS   1981 to 1983

National/international natural resource exploration, development, and production company; managing partner of 21 joint ventures.

Financial Controller / Joint Partnership Administrator

Diverse financial accountabilities with job scope involving preparation of monthly/year-end financial statements; invoicing and distribution of revenues; budget preparation; and control of capital expenditures. Directed and oversaw renewal of joint-venture and corporate insurance policies. Served as liaison, interfacing between technical and field operations staff. Reported directly to Manager of Finance and Accounting.

♦ Tripled performance output while effectively orchestrating downsizing of department staff from nine to seven. Developed and executed staff incentive programs.

♦ Spearheaded preparation and negotiation of joint operating agreements and accounting procedures for new joint ventures.

BHP REFINERY, HOUSTON, TEXAS   1980 to 1981

Multinational petroleum company with divisions consisting of refineries and coal exploration.

Budget Accountant

Performed broad financial functions, including budget preparation and analysis of monthly sales, rebates, and gross margins.

EDUCATION

Bachelor of Economics; Major: Accounting, Texas University, Houston, Texas

COMPUTER SOFTWARE

• MS Office 2002 • MYOB • QuickBooks • Outlook Express

James A. Hastings

1803 Harmon Boulevard
Shaker Heights, OH 44122
216-881-1928
william.hastings@att.net

SENIOR TAX EXECUTIVE
Expert in International and Domestic Taxation Issues

Resourceful and intuitive tax executive respected for expertise on international and domestic taxation. Regularly invited to speak before forums on international taxation, and personally argued private letter ruling before the IRS in Washington, DC with regard to favorable tax treatment theory formulated on behalf of a multimillion-dollar acquisition. Successfully integrated legal background into a career as a tax expert, providing clients with sound guidance in tax planning and management processes. Regarded as a hands-on manager who is capable of building strong team environments and fosters a sense of pride and integrity among the staff.

Areas of Expertise:

- Organizational Restructuring
- Business Development
- Account Management
- Staff Building, Coaching, and Mentoring
- Foreign tax credit: source of income; allocation and apportionment; deemed paid credit; and excess limitation/excess credit
- Subpart F: contract manufacturing; and branch rule

- Partnerships and Check-the-Box
- Foreign Currency
- Foreign Taxation: permanent establishment; VAT; GST; withholding taxes; employment taxes; tax treaties; and choice of entity
- Recordkeeping, Reporting, and Disclosure
- Transfer Pricing
- ProFX Tax Preparation Software: BNA Planning Software: CCH, BNA, and RIA online and CD Tax Research Tools

CAREER HIGHLIGHTS

JENSEN & PLATTE, LLP — Cleveland, OH
(Major public accounting firm providing broad business advisory and traditional compliance services to middle-market businesses. Employs 1,300 employees at 12 offices throughout Ohio and Michigan.)
PARTNER, June 2000 to present
Selected to oversee integration of Cleveland office following firm's acquisition of Clifton Gunderson's Cleveland office. Identified key objectives and goals and oriented both staff and clients on new services while continuing to oversee ongoing projects. ***Key Accomplishments:***
- Successfully transitioned staff and clients into new corporate culture.
- Established productivity goals related to chargeable hours, business growth, and service delivery.
- Retained 100% of client base in 16-month period following acquisition.
- Identified new opportunities that melded with new organization and secured new client financial institution and SEC relationships, while increasing personal billings 15%.
- Provided hands-on leadership for successful IT conversions.

GARDNER CLIFTON, LLC — Cleveland, OH
(Among the largest independent public accounting firms in the United States, with 45 offices in 12 states, serving a wide array of publicly and closely held companies.)
MANAGING PARTNER, CLEVELAND / FIRM-WIDE INTERNATIONAL TAX COORDINATOR, 1999 – 2000
PARTNER / FIRM-WIDE INTERNATIONAL TAX COORDINATOR, 1995 – 1999
TAX MANAGER / FIRM-WIDE INTERNATIONAL TAX COORDINATOR, 1991 – 1995
INTERNATIONAL TAX SPECIALIST, 1989 – 1991
Progressed through organization, culminating in oversight of Cleveland office and firm-wide international tax operations. Accountable for recruitment, hiring, supervision, staff performance and evaluation, fiscal planning, and administration of 15-person regional office. Additionally, provided direct oversight of partners and staff on all matters relating to international tax planning and compliance. Enacted directives on technology and expertise syndication.

Strategy: *Avoid the "dryness" of a complex tax background by incorporating multiple business contributions as well as areas of professional expertise.*

James A. Hastings

Résumé - Page Two

CAREER HIGHLIGHTS

GARDNER CLIFTON, LLC *(continued...)*
Key Accomplishments:

- Forged relationship with major commercial clients, contributing significantly to growth of Cleveland-office revenue from $887,000 to $1,281,000 and personal book of business from $140,000 to over $500,000 within four years.
- Coordinated $50 million leveraged acquisition of US-based multinational group with subsidiaries in Belgium, Denmark, France, the United Kingdom, and Hong Kong.
- Collaborated with institutional lenders, domestic and foreign law firms, and foreign-chartered accountants to carry out above deal. Provided complex structural planning models and solved "deal-busting" EU corporate-directive problems.
- Invited on numerous occasions to speak on US tax matters affecting international business both domestically and abroad.
- As member of international tax committee, traveled extensively overseas, provided multinational tax consulting services, and developed and instituted international tax training programs.

Prior Professional Experience
TAX STAFF, Meaden & Moore, Inc. — Cleveland, OH, 1987 – 1989
TAX STAFF, Packer Thomas & Co. — Warren, OH, 1985 – 1986
ATTORNEY-AT-LAW — Cleveland, OH, 1982 – 1985

EDUCATION

FRANKLIN THOMAS BACKUS SCHOOL OF LAW,
CASE WESTERN UNIVERSITY — Cleveland, OH
JURIS DOCTOR, 1981

UNIVERSITY OF WISCONSIN — Milwaukee, WI
BBA, ACCOUNTING, 1978

PROFESSIONAL DEVELOPMENT

- American Bar Association, **TAX SECTION MEETINGS,** twice annually, since 1990
- Internal Revenue Service Institute on **CURRENT ISSUES IN INTERNATIONAL TAXATION,** George Washington University, Washington, DC, 1989, 1990, 1998
- Florida Bar and Florida CPAs Joint **INTERNATIONAL TAX INSTITUTE,** Miami, FL, 1991, 1992, 1996
- **CITE INTERNATIONAL TAX SEMINARS,** Toronto, ON and Los Angeles, CA, 1995, 1997
- Harvard University, Tufts University, and MIT Joint Program on **NEGOTIATION FOR SENIOR EXECUTIVES,** Cambridge, MA, 1999

PUBLISHING CREDITS / CONFERENCES / AFFILIATIONS

- "S-Corp Shareholder Salaries: Source Questions," International Taxation, 8 Mar. 2002, p. 1,500
- Ohio Export Launch, State of Ohio, June 2001
- 10th Immigration and Naturalization Law Seminar, Federal Bar Association, December 1998
- American Institute of Certified Public Accountants (AICPA)
- American Bar Association (ABA); 10-year Member Tax Section, Foreign Activities of US Taxpayers Committee
- International Fiscal Association (IFA)
- Ohio Bar
- Ohio Society of Certified Public Accountants
- Board of Directors Cleveland Engineering Society, 1998 – 2000
- Board of Directors, Cleveland School of the Arts, 1999 – 2000

MICHAEL D. KARAS

3245 Shadow Trail — Old Hickory, Tennessee 37138

Home (615) 758-4467 — mikekaras@mindspring.com

EQUIPMENT LEASING & FINANCE EXECUTIVE

Top-producing equipment leasing and finance specialist with ten years of experience in originating, negotiating, structuring, and closing profitable deals. Cultivate and maintain strong, established network of contacts with bank officers, lease brokers and dealers, and equipment vendors. Expert knowledge of lease financing terms, lease structures, documentation procedures, and current tax and depreciation laws, including Tax Relief Act of 2001.

An articulate communicator able to convey complex information in meaningful terms. Adapt quickly to new circumstances and environments. Outstanding organizational skills and attention to detail. Professional and personable manner.

Computer expertise in both PC and Macintosh environments. Experienced with MS Office (Excel, Word), MS Publisher, WordPerfect, Lotus 1-2-3, AmiPro, Publish It, Pagemaker, InfoLease, InfoAnalysis, SuperTrump, LeasePak, Internet navigation and research, and email. Confident in learning and using new business applications.

Experience Summary

▸ Manage all facets of leasing operations, including sales and marketing, structuring, documentation, and accounting.

▸ Follow through with a high degree of customer service to ensure repeat business from all sources.

▸ Proactively solicit new business prospects through direct contact, cold calling, networking, and referrals.

▸ Establish and maintain positive relationships with key equipment vendors to ensure profitable disposition of used equipment. Assist in the collection of delinquent accounts.

▸ Provide individual and group sales training to commercial and corporate bank officers, with a focus on how to recognize a qualified prospect.

Career History

VICE PRESIDENT 1997-Present
Volunteer Leasing Corporation / Volunteer Bank — Nashville, Tennessee

▸ Challenged to lead start-up operations for Volunteer Leasing's entry into the East Tennessee market, from Athens to the Tri-Cities area, including sales, documentation, and accounting. Presently manage a five-state territory comprised of MO, KS, KY, TN, and AR. Report to Group Vice President and Sales Manager.

▸ Target middle-market and large-ticket transactions, such as hi-tech, tractor-trailer, manufacturing, and energy management. Currently on track to generate $40 million in lease transactions for 2003.

▸ After Volunteer's merger with Northstar Bank in 2000, was selected as part of team to determine pricing and accounting systems for new, consolidated leasing department.

ASSISTANT VICE PRESIDENT 1995-1997
First National Bank — Knoxville, Tennessee

▸ Established new sales territory in East Tennessee, from Chattanooga to the Tri-Cities area. Reported to Group Vice President of Leasing.

▸ Closed $6 million in sales the first year; increased sales 66% the second year to $10 million.

Strategy: *Use a combination format to avoid overlap of job duties; create an expansive Experience Summary to include these areas of expertise right up front.*

MICHAEL D. KARAS

Page Two

Career History (continued)

BANK OFFICER 1993-1995
National Exchange Bank — Memphis, Tennessee

▸ Collaborated with bank lending officers, lease brokers, and equipment vendors to provide small-ticket leasing services. Sales territory included entire southeastern US except Florida. Reported to First Vice President.
▸ Generated $5 million in annual transactions.

ASSISTANT SALES MANAGER 1992-1993
US Lease Plans, Inc. — Hendersonville, Tennessee

▸ Networked with customers, developed sales leads, and strengthened relationships with other leasing companies and funding sources.
▸ Prepared documentation for equipment lease transactions, including UCC filings, resolutions, master lease documents, and other supporting documentation.

Education

BACHELOR OF ARTS — Marketing — Minor in German — 1992
Vanderbilt University — Nashville, Tennessee

Affiliations

▸ Tennessee Trucking Association
▸ National Association of Equipment Lessors
▸ Equipment Lessors Association

MARK WHITE

103 Watson Street
San Diego, CA 92101

Email: mark.e.white@tedra.com

Mobile: 619-663-0101
Residence: 619-421-1900

FINANCE DIRECTOR • CFO • GENERAL MANAGER FINANCE • GROUP FINANCIAL CONTROLLER

Commercially focused senior finance executive poised to deliver responsible growth and genuine results. Rich mix of technical accounting, operations, and leadership talents complement advanced finance studies. A change agent; acknowledged for balanced judgment, stability, and capacity to steer consensus among core business disciplines with diverse agendas and visions.

Professional strengths include:

- Management & Financial Reporting
- Business Opportunity Assessments
- Cross-Functional Team Leadership
- Feasibility Analysis
- Strategic Planning & Recommendations

- Productivity/Efficiency Improvements
- Cross-Cultural Work Environments
- Process Reengineering
- Risk Management
- Cost-Avoidance & Reduction
- Legislative Compliance

- Policy Development
- Relationship Building
- Technology Implementations
- Global Market Modeling
- Statutory Accounts Preparation
- Budget Management

Computer: SAP, Excel, PowerPoint, Oracle Financial Analyzer, Word.

Chartered Accountant

EXECUTIVE PERFORMANCE - OVERVIEW

Definitive leader bringing divergent interests into consensus. Despite a period of significant business upheaval stemming from a new planning process and computer integration project, as GM Sales & Operations Planning, analyzed each department's ad-hoc functions and produced standardized business model after negotiating an agreed structure.

Catalyst for driving superior staff multi-tasking and efficiency initiatives. Management approach has promoted flexibility, accountability, and accuracy in a deadline-dependent environment. As Group Management Accountant, reduced reporting days by 50% without changing underlying financial systems.

Quantifiable successes in devising innovative systems and processes. Conceived and added new strategic KPIs to traditional finance mix after identifying system lacked key performance indicators linked to strategy. Recommendations were accepted by management and remain a critical analytical tool for management decision-making.

EDUCATION

Master's in Applied Finance, University of California

Bachelor of Economics, University of Sydney, Australia
Majors: Accounting & Economics

CAREER CHRONOLOGY

SOBAIN GLOBAL, **Management Consultant**	Sep 01–Present
SOUTHERN WINES	1994–2001
General Manager, Sales & Operations Planning .... (2000–2001)	
Group Financial Controller .... (1999–2000)	
Group Management Accountant .... (1997–1999)	
Management Accountant .... (1994–1996)	
BGT GROUP PLC, London, **Financial Accountant**	1993
TAYLOR BROWN AGB PLC, London, **Financial Accountant**	1993
DON FLIGHT SERVICES LTD, London, **Management Accountant**	1991–1992
BOON & JOHNSON, London, Toronto & Sydney, **Manager General Practice**	1986–1991

Mark White   Page 1   Confidential

Strategy: *Create a quick-view "snapshot" of the candidate's entire career (which includes valuable international and accounting experience) on page 1; then focus on milestones and achievements on page 2.*

ACHIEVEMENTS IN-DEPTH: REVENUES • GROWTH • OPERATIONS

SOBAIN GLOBAL   Sep 01–Present
International business consultancy strategically positioning multinationals and major industry leaders for long-term revenue growth.

Management Consultant

Assigned to project team consulting to an FMCG client tasked with identifying value drivers in the business and industry best practice, and with developing a value-creation model to maximize ROI and economic profit. Analyzed financial results, reviewed economic profit calculations, and evaluated the potential of different value-creation models to understand the revenue-generating potential of the existing business. Presentation by Sobain incorporated all key recommendations to the client's Board of Directors.

SOUTHERN WINES   1994–2001
Leading premium wine company with worldwide presence, boasting revenues of $1.1+ billion and 2,400 employees.

General Manager, Sales & Operations Planning (2000–2001)

Budget: $500,000. Member, Executive Team. Reported to Managing Director. Staff: 15.

Ad-hoc systems and processes developed over a 6-month period without management direction, saw sales and operations departments fragment and form individual structures, despite an earlier agreement to adopt a standardized model. Pending company merger and restructure, together with new system implementation delayed by flaws in planning, and dramatic SAP issues needing serious review, presented difficult and diverse challenges to the newly designed role of GM, Sales & Operations Planning. **Action & Results:**

- Identified core similarities between systems, and negotiated successfully for a new standardized approach across regions that would eliminate duplicated tasks and restore cost efficiencies. Prepared and gained acceptance for new model by management team, returning a period of business turmoil to a more cooperative mindset.

- Created a global marketing model overcoming previous failed attempts. Model provided the definitive comparison that identified gaps where plans were misaligned with total market view, and offered greater marketing department involvement in the planning process.

- Executed deadline-dependent team project to resolve critical SAP system fault in stock control and customer service, apparent only after implementation, and negatively impacting service delivery levels with customers facing lengthy delays in ordering. Team rapidly identified and corrected issues, reduced product allocations by 95%, and vastly improved systems and procedures.

Group Financial Controller (1999–2000)

Challenged initially by newly promoted and recruited staff, a lack of quality and accuracy in statutory account preparation, a financial accountant struggling with unresolved long-term problems, and undocumented procedures. Recruited, trained and developed staff, emphasized the importance of deadline-dependent environments, and settled long-term processing issues. Standardized procedures and recorded step-by-step tasks for future years, reversing a chaotic consolidation process to one of accuracy and quality. **Actions & Results:**

- Prepared and delivered Wine Group budget of $900 million. Planned budget cycle across the organization, formulated and analyzed results, and conducted presentation to senior executives.

- Identified savings of $300,000 in finance area through system and staff changes and expenditure fine-tuning. Coordinated centralization project transferring A/P function from New South Wales to South Australia.

- Reduced level of risk and restructured poorly managed processes that potentially breached policy limits to the Board for forward cover. Instituted new system, improved communications, and assured levels of forward cover were aligned with sales forecasts.

- Represented Finance and Planning areas on $22 million SAP project rollout. Documented existing systems and procedures, reviewed proposed solution, and monitored rollout across the business. Quickly became primary contact point for questions from technical personnel, department heads, and management.

Group Management Accountant (1997–1999)

Managed monthly reporting, budgeting, strategic plan financials and EVA analysis. Selected to join management team to review performance of product category globally. Co-produced and presented assessment of initiatives designed to save $1.6 million annually and slash inventory levels by $10 million. **Actions & Results:**

- Identified deficiencies in KPIs with no indicators tied to strategy. Initiatives presented to management were successfully embraced and still remain in force.

- Dramatically reduced reporting days from 12 to 6 without changes in fundamental financial systems.

* References provided upon request *

Mark White   Page 2   Confidential

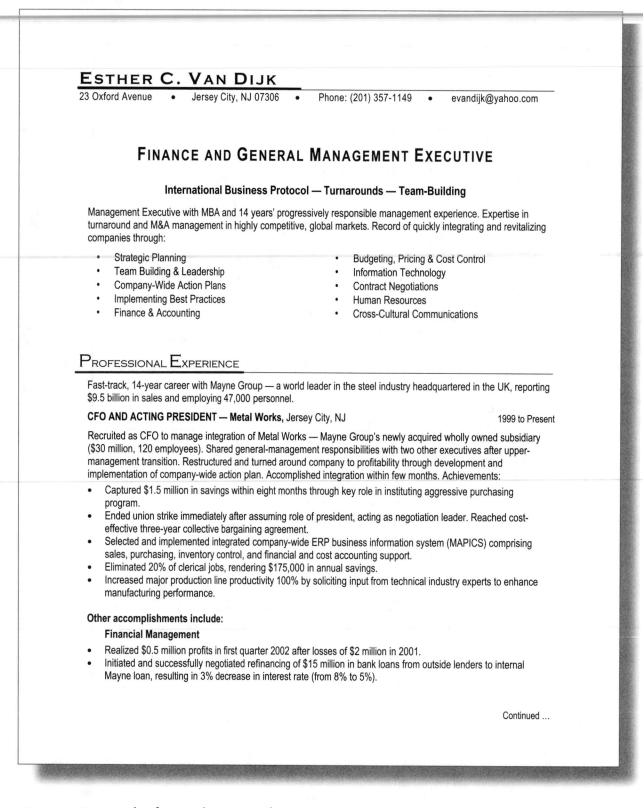

ESTHER C. VAN DIJK

23 Oxford Avenue • Jersey City, NJ 07306 • Phone: (201) 357-1149 • evandijk@yahoo.com

FINANCE AND GENERAL MANAGEMENT EXECUTIVE

International Business Protocol — Turnarounds — Team-Building

Management Executive with MBA and 14 years' progressively responsible management experience. Expertise in turnaround and M&A management in highly competitive, global markets. Record of quickly integrating and revitalizing companies through:

- Strategic Planning
- Team Building & Leadership
- Company-Wide Action Plans
- Implementing Best Practices
- Finance & Accounting

- Budgeting, Pricing & Cost Control
- Information Technology
- Contract Negotiations
- Human Resources
- Cross-Cultural Communications

PROFESSIONAL EXPERIENCE

Fast-track, 14-year career with Mayne Group — a world leader in the steel industry headquartered in the UK, reporting $9.5 billion in sales and employing 47,000 personnel.

CFO AND ACTING PRESIDENT — Metal Works, Jersey City, NJ   1999 to Present

Recruited as CFO to manage integration of Metal Works — Mayne Group's newly acquired wholly owned subsidiary ($30 million, 120 employees). Shared general-management responsibilities with two other executives after upper-management transition. Restructured and turned around company to profitability through development and implementation of company-wide action plan. Accomplished integration within few months. Achievements:

- Captured $1.5 million in savings within eight months through key role in instituting aggressive purchasing program.
- Ended union strike immediately after assuming role of president, acting as negotiation leader. Reached cost-effective three-year collective bargaining agreement.
- Selected and implemented integrated company-wide ERP business information system (MAPICS) comprising sales, purchasing, inventory control, and financial and cost accounting support.
- Eliminated 20% of clerical jobs, rendering $175,000 in annual savings.
- Increased major production line productivity 100% by soliciting input from technical industry experts to enhance manufacturing performance.

Other accomplishments include:

Financial Management

- Realized $0.5 million profits in first quarter 2002 after losses of $2 million in 2001.
- Initiated and successfully negotiated refinancing of $15 million in bank loans from outside lenders to internal Mayne loan, resulting in 3% decrease in interest rate (from 8% to 5%).

Continued ...

Strategy: *Position this financial executive for a general-management role by emphasizing her skills and achievements in both areas.*

ESTHER C. VAN DIJK

Page 2 of 2

General Management/Human Resources

- Spearheaded cultural change through input from office and factory employees, instituting employee suggestion system and open-door policy.
- Thwarted lawsuit using mediation skills to reach agreement and settle out of court.
- Developed objectives-based performance measurement system as tool to create strong, cohesive teams, focused on common goals.
- Realized union relationship improvements through diplomatic negotiations.

FINANCE CONTROLLER — Lyon Steel Company, Lyon, France   1996 to 1999

Appointed Finance Controller for Lyon Steel Company, a $75 million French global market leader of plated steel for the battery industry, employing 500 employees; 50% subsidiary of Mayne Group at time of hire. Member of management team; supervised staff of 25. Integrated Lyon Steel Company with Mayne Group and benchmarked with sister company in the United States. Achievements:

- Facilitated 100% acquisition by Mayne Group in1997.
- Played key role in successful turnaround from losses to profitability within one year by developing and implementing company-wide restructuring program.
- Authored business plan and developed and implemented system of key-performer indicators.
- Assumed project leadership for seamless Y2K preparation and Euro implementation transitions.
- Eliminated 15% of workforce while maintaining operability, focusing on high performers.

PLANT CONTROLLER — Mayne Group — Various sites, The Netherlands   1988 to 1996

Selected by senior management for prestigious position of Plant Controller in 1994 after proven abilities in increasingly responsible positions. Handled $1.5 billion Flat Products Division after various controlling assignments for 15,000-employee production site (1988 to 1992) and for $500 million Steel Processing & Trading Division (1992 to 1994). Directed 30 employees at largest of five product groups, consisting of three major plants with 2,200 employees. Key accomplishments in various positions included:

- Facilitated $200 million cost cut by compiling categorized data of cost-reduction options.
- Reduced staff 10% for entire product group by initiating proactive and creative cost-reduction program following thorough financial and functional analysis.
- Handled communication with technical personnel: able to "translate" lingo and reach core issues.
- Joined international team that led $200 million joint venture initiative with an Italian steel manufacturer.
- Interfaced extensively with trade, production, and distribution companies.

EDUCATION, TRAINING, AND AFFILIATION

POST-MASTER'S CONTROLLERS PROGRAM (1993)
(Equivalent of American Ph.D. Program)
VRIJE UNIVERSITEIT — Amsterdam, The Netherlands

MASTER IN BUSINESS ADMINISTRATION (1986)
VRIJE UNIVERSITEIT — Amsterdam, The Netherlands

ASSOCIATION OF PROFESSIONAL CONTROLLERS
The Netherlands — member since 1993

BOARD MEMBER
METAL WORKS

Computer proficiency: SAP/R3; MAPICS; Windows; Microsoft Office: Word, Excel, PowerPoint, Project, Outlook; Internet research.

Bill Raymond, CFA

285 Andover Street
Lawrence, MA 01746

billraymond@alumni.mit.edu
978-624-1210

Experienced Portfolio Manager who achieves consistent results and deals well with volatility. Adept at balancing performance, customer satisfaction, and new business development. Sought-after writer, convention speaker, and regularly quoted analyst in the media. Enthusiastic and aggressive MIT Economics graduate and CFA.

Currently Senior Vice President, performing several major functions within organization: Money Market Portfolio Manager, Fixed Income Credit Analyst and Portfolio Manager, Economic Analyst and Marketer. Launched $1 billion fund.

PROFESSIONAL EXPERIENCE

BOSTON INVESTORS, INC.   <u>Senior Vice President</u>   Boston, MA   **1984–Present**

Promoted to Senior Vice President in recognition of ongoing performance and dedication. Perform 5 major positions with little/no backup support and minimal supervision for this investment-counsel firm.

Money Market Portfolio Manager   1986–Present

- Manage all aspects of retail and institutional Money Market Portfolios with assets of nearly $1 billion.
- Developed and launched institutional 2a-7 fund that grew to $1 billion in 3 years.
- Created proprietary systems and models resulting in consistent 2nd quartile gross performance, despite wild volatility of assets in extremely tough market.
- Analyze markets to determine best areas in which to invest.
- Evaluate buy/sell ideas and execute trades to maximize fund.
- Ensure portfolios continuously comply with SEC and IRS regulations and internal guidelines.
- Complete credit research for all corporate credits used in portfolios.

Fixed Income Credit Analyst and Portfolio Manager   1987–Present

- Successfully evaluate and determine creditworthiness of companies in the financial sector.
- Rigorously find and analyze published data about companies.
- Seek out and interact with information providers.
- Attend several annual conferences with key company and industry presentations.
- Make buy/sell recommendations for fixed income portfolios.

Mortgage-Backed Securities Analyst and Portfolio Manager   1987–1998

- Determined value within the mortgage-backed and asset-backed markets.
- Made buy/sell recommendations for fixed income portfolios and executed trades.

Economic Analyst   1984–Present

- Solely responsible within company to analyze and report on economic trends and events.
- Write 1–2 four-page <u>Boston Investors Staff Letters</u> per year for extensive distribution to over 750 clients and news media. Letter has been largest source of new clients.
- Write and produce comprehensive quarterly 20-page publication: <u>Economic Outlook</u>, complete with commentary, graphs, and economic trends, that is distributed to clients and staff.
- Give interactive multimedia presentations at staff and client meetings.
- Report, track, and analyze political developments and potential impact on markets for internal staff.
- Quoted by numerous newspapers and wire services as an expert on market response to political changes, economic indicators, and market movements.

Strategy: *Convey the "multiple hats" worn by this CFA who spent 18 years with a small investment-counsel firm. Demonstrate his important ability to bring in new business.*

Bill Raymond, CFA   **Page 2**

<u>Marketing</u>   **1986–Present**

- ◆ Create original fixed income marketing materials for marketing department to use with clients.
- ◆ Compose written explanations of performance and process for several critical marketing materials per quarter.
- ◆ Provide perspective, data, and other information during business presentations to potential clients.
- ◆ Presented speeches at major industry conferences such as IBC and Fabozzi to build brand awareness. Recent topics:
    - "Creating and Maintaining an Effective Credit Research Process"
    - "Building Blocks of Money Market Securities"
    - "Creating and Maintaining an Effective Credit Research Process"
    - "Government Securities"
    - "Anomalies in the Short-Term Markets"
- ◆ Requested by Columbia business professor to address Business School classes on financial topics.

<u>Money Market Portfolio Manager</u>   **1985–1987**

- ◆ Executed buy and sell orders for firm's individual and institutional clients.
- ◆ Obtained best execution of orders with minimal market impact.
- ◆ Managed trade settlement and dispute resolution.

EDUCATION, CERTIFICATIONS & MEMBERSHIPS

EDUCATION:	MASSACHUSETTS INSTITUTE OF TECHNOLOGY, Cambridge, MA
	A.B. in Economics, 1982
CERTIFICATIONS:	Chartered Financial Analyst (CFA), 1989
MEMBER:	Bond Analysts Society of Boston
	Boston Security Analysts Society

COMMUNITY ORGANIZATIONS

THE CHILDREN'S MUSEUM OF LOWELL   **Lowell, MA**   **2001–Present**

<u>Vice President, Board of Directors</u> and <u>Chairman, Capital Campaign Committee</u>

Recruited to join and lead effort to create area non-profit museum due to experience in fund raising and organizational development. Museum targeted to open Fall 2003 in a historic mill building that also serves as the headquarters for the Lowell National Historical Park. Capital Campaign goal: $2 million.

THE FRIENDS OF MIT RUGBY   **Cambridge, MA**   **1987–Present**

<u>Chairman</u> (1997–Present), <u>Vice Chairman</u> (1993–1997), <u>Treasurer</u> (1987–1993)

One of 8 co-founders of an organization that provides financial and logistical support for the MIT Rugby Club. As Chairman, revamped board to improve productivity and results. Raised over $250,000 as endowment to ensure future of organization.

MIT RUGBY CLUB   **Cambridge, MA**   **1987–Present**

<u>Assistant Coach</u> (1983–1984, 1991–1993)

Served as part-time assistant coach on teams that won one National Championship, appeared in 2 "Final 4s," and reached the "Final 16" once.

DENIZ CELIK

8100 Harrison Avenue
Roseland, NJ 07068
(973) 974-5232
deniz_celik@yahoo.com

Financial Services New Business Manager

PROFESSIONAL SUMMARY

Creative business leader with five years' management experience and seven years in financial services. Background includes successful management of teams of business professionals. Track record in driving innovation in process redesign and in creating and implementing organizational solutions that positively affect the bottom line. Proficient in using technology to solve company-wide challenges. Organized, detail-oriented, bilingual.

PROFESSIONAL EXPERIENCE

ADP, Roseland, NJ   1997–2001

New Business Manager (1998–2001)

Managed a team of six, ensuring an accurate and timely installation of new retirement plans and the conversion of existing ones. Provided ongoing training and supervision of the team. Supported the Senior Vice President in his reports to the CEO regarding new business. High interaction with the sales team. Attended sales meetings with prospective clients and produced timelines for the conversion process.

- Assisted in designing and developing procedures for a new product. By streamlining the process, efficiency was increased by 60%.
- Invented "commitments log" for the team, a calendar listing all outstanding client commitments. With the help of this tool, the new business department did not miss a single deadline in two years. This tool assisted the team in becoming proactive rather than reactive.
- Assisted the accounting department in clearing up logs of assets received. Discovered over $75,000 in additional billable fees.
- Designed a new billing process for the team that increased the department's billings by 30% per month and also allowed an initial billing of $200,000 for the missed prior months.
- Created timeline and status log to streamline the conversion process. Increased communication both within the department and with the sales team, and assisted sales team in setting expectations of operations.

Retirement Plans Senior Conversion Specialist (1997–1998)

Responsibilities included attending post-sale meetings with clients, conversion processing and on-going administration of new retirement plans, timely investment of plan assets, and advising clients and their employees on plan-related issues. Trained new team members and assisted them in their duties.

- Converted company's own 401(k) plan with minimum days lost in the stock market. This conversion saved the company $50,000 a year in administrative costs alone.
- Developed conversion process operational procedures that were later enhanced with the help of technical writers and are still being used today in training new employees. Streamlining the conversion procedure increased efficiency and communication within the department.

Strategy: *Create a strong resume that highlights the candidate's skills in managing teams, record of driving innovation, and ability to use technology to solve problems.*

DENIZ CELIK

Page Two

NATIONWIDE FINANCIAL SERVICES, INC., Columbus, OH   1995–1997
Pension and Systems Administrator
As a pension administrator, processed all daily activities of 30 retirement plans, interacted with clients, and worked closely with the mutual fund companies to ensure timely investments and liquidations. Supervised four administrative assistants and trained new employees. As a systems administrator, resolved daily computer-related issues and interfaced with hardware and software consultants to ensure an efficient and effective work environment.

- Designed an Excel spreadsheet for trust accounting, which reduced the chance for human error and increased productivity by 20%. This document became the template for company trust accountants.
- Assisted in the system conversion to Quantech; its faster and more flexible report-writer tools improved production by more than 50%.
- Created a new filing system for trust statements. With proper archiving, consolidated two filing rooms into one, which increased efficiency and work space in the office.

KOLATAN HOLDING CORPORATION, Ankara, Turkey   1993–1995
Marketing Assistant
Assisted the Director in administrative duties and prepared reports of findings and conclusions based on proposals received from various operating units. Projects involved mainly health care and tourism.

EDUCATION

Bachelor of Science in Management, Ankara Technical University, Ankara, Turkey, 1995

Certificate of English Language in Business, London University, London, England, 1990

Professional Development Training:

Employees Retirement Income Security Act Seminar, 2000
Quantech Advanced Users Training, ADP, 1999
Pension Administrator Certificate of SPARK (Society of Pension Administrators and Record Keepers), ADP, 1998
Quantech Beginners Training, Nationwide Financial Services, Inc., 1997

COMPUTER SKILLS

Proficient in the use of MS Excel, MS Word, MS Project, Lotus 1-2-3, Ami Pro, Novell Networking 3.12, Report Writer, various Internet browsers, TimeSheet and Timeslips Professional, SQL, Quantech, Pentabs, Trustmark, Pentax Government Forms, RIA, and OS/2 Voice Response applications.

LANGUAGE SKILLS

Fluent in both English and Turkish

■ ■ ■

GERALD BERGER

5001 Woodlake Lane
Charlotte, NC 28222

Home: 704-123-1234 Office: 704-123-1234
gerald.berger@westover.com

GLOBAL BUSINESS / RELATIONSHIP MANAGER

Contract Negotiations • Business Development

A decisive financial analyst skilled at hedging risk, dispersing exposure, and identifying major gaps in profitability forecasts, communication infrastructure, information sharing, and business processes.

Background in corporate and investment banking, commercial property management, and international business practices. Qualifications include:

- "At-risk" business financial analysis
- International currency, letters of credit, and credit agreements
- Software and technology systems evaluation
- Competitive and market analysis, specifically in China
- Bond and stock transfers, debt and equity trusts, and financial accounting (GL)
- MBA, Global Business Management, China concentration, Wake Forest University, 2001

Recognized as a negotiator and persuasive presenter who listens well and breaks down barriers — engendering trust and confidence in a positive and fair outcome.

PROFESSIONAL HIGHLIGHTS

WESTOVER BANK (formerly Universal Union National Bank), Charlotte, NC   1995–present

Capital Markets Portfolio Analyst, AVP (1998–present)
Corporate & Investment Banking Loan Administration

Manage relationships with brokers, client CEOs and COOs, and other financial institutions to track, analyze, and sell loans and collect fees for a portfolio of over 200 companies in forest products, textile, and utility groups. Specialize in "special situation" client base at risk of bankruptcy.

As an internal liaison among Operations, IT, and Customer Relations:
- Consulted with IT designers to fine-tune and streamline the database system that tracks corporate loans and ensures accurate capture of fees. Modeled and tested all contingencies to deliver an error-free system that eliminated duplicate information and paperwork and improved the processing time tenfold.
- Researched and recovered over $150k in unpaid fees for utilities department.

Corporate Trust Debt Services Manager, AVP (1995–1998)

Interfaced with bond administrators, upper management, and operations to oversee the accuracy and timeliness of $1 billion per month in bond payments. Managed 19 analysts.

- Promoted to Bank Officer after one year.
- Discovered embezzlement by former Senior Trust Officer, leading to recovery of over $7 million of bearer bonds.
- Evaluated and recommended software/technology infrastructure proposals, working with software vendors and internal analysts. Resulted in a $1+ million software contract.

Continued....

Strategy: *Support this candidate's goal of transitioning to international management by emphasizing his recent MBA degree in global business management, noteworthy international experiences in academia, and domestic financial background.*

GERALD BERGER, page two

APEX MANAGEMENT, Charlotte, NC   1991–1995
Property Manager
   Managed a $20 million, 400-unit property, the company's largest. Led a staff of eight employees.
   - Consistently exceeded budgeted net operating income.
   - Brought delinquent rent to zero within three months on a property that had never achieved zero delinquents for previous five years.
   - Selected (out of 77 managers) to test and evaluate new property-management software.

THE CAROLINAS S&L, Daysville, NC   1989–1991
Branch Manager

INTERNATIONAL EXPERIENCE

BABCOCK SCHOOL OF MANAGEMENT, China   June–August 2001
East Asia Management Program Fellow

   Unable to ignore the enormous opportunity for global commerce with China — volunteered for this business/academic experience traveling across China from Beijing to Shanghai to Hong Kong.

   - Focused on the challenges and risks of entering into a developing market in the face of cultural and economic barriers as well as political and legal constraints.
   - Acquired an understanding of Chinese business practices — their need for control, technology, and capital; their appreciation of American technical/financial expertise; and their complex system of bartering and negotiating between government and corporate officials.
   - Concluded that it is worthwhile and necessary for American companies to expend the resources to assess and predict the profitability and risks involved in Chinese commerce in order to reap the potential and protect the interests of all concerned.

SOFFLE INTERNATIONAL, Inc., Charlotte, NC   March–June 2002
A leading French construction company ranked in the top ten internationally.

Financial Analyst/Consultant
   Analyzed the viability and risks of further expansion into the Chinese market. Evaluated construction material and equipment costs, quality control, credit financing, labor development issues, economy, demand, competition, and political/legal factors.

   - Recommended that SI refocus its business model and utilize its 15-year presence in China to function as a consultant to the Chinese construction industry and to other foreign companies seeking to supply the industry. This would leverage SI's ability to find new niches and to develop Chinese alliances, creating competitive advantages for future construction opportunities.

EDUCATION

Master of Business Administration, 2002
Concentration in Global Business Management
WAKE FOREST UNIVERSITY, Babcock Graduate School of Management, Winston-Salem, NC

Bachelor of Arts, 1988
Economics and Business Administration
LENOIR-RYNE COLLEGE, Charlotte, NC

RESUME 79: MARTIN BUCKLAND, CPRW, JCTC, CEIP, CJST; OAKVILLE, ON, CANADA

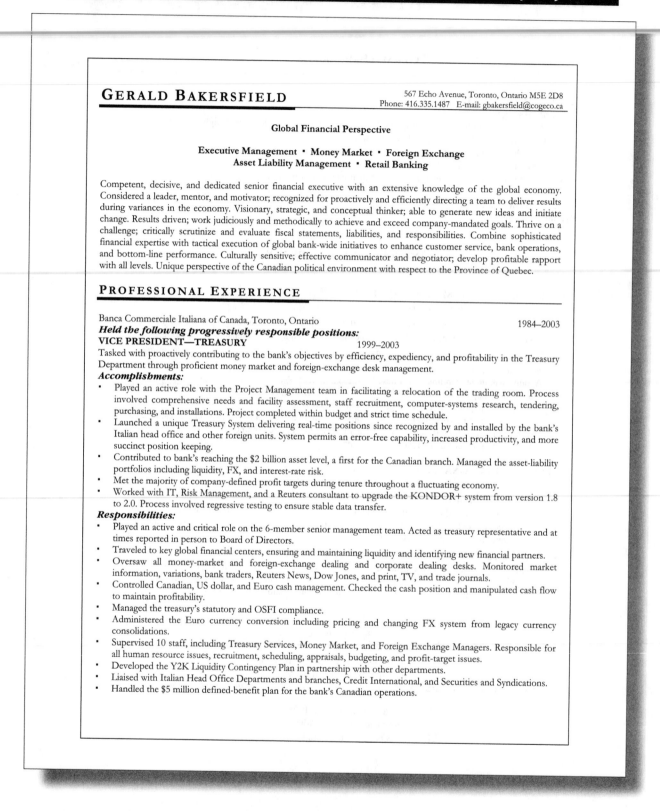

GERALD BAKERSFIELD

567 Echo Avenue, Toronto, Ontario M5E 2D8
Phone: 416.335.1487   E-mail: gbakersfield@cogeco.ca

Global Financial Perspective

**Executive Management • Money Market • Foreign Exchange
Asset Liability Management • Retail Banking**

Competent, decisive, and dedicated senior financial executive with an extensive knowledge of the global economy. Considered a leader, mentor, and motivator; recognized for proactively and efficiently directing a team to deliver results during variances in the economy. Visionary, strategic, and conceptual thinker; able to generate new ideas and initiate change. Results driven; work judiciously and methodically to achieve and exceed company-mandated goals. Thrive on a challenge; critically scrutinize and evaluate fiscal statements, liabilities, and responsibilities. Combine sophisticated financial expertise with tactical execution of global bank-wide initiatives to enhance customer service, bank operations, and bottom-line performance. Culturally sensitive; effective communicator and negotiator; develop profitable rapport with all levels. Unique perspective of the Canadian political environment with respect to the Province of Quebec.

PROFESSIONAL EXPERIENCE

Banca Commerciale Italiana of Canada, Toronto, Ontario   1984–2003
Held the following progressively responsible positions:
VICE PRESIDENT—TREASURY   1999–2003
Tasked with proactively contributing to the bank's objectives by efficiency, expediency, and profitability in the Treasury Department through proficient money market and foreign-exchange desk management.
Accomplishments:
- Played an active role with the Project Management team in facilitating a relocation of the trading room. Process involved comprehensive needs and facility assessment, staff recruitment, computer-systems research, tendering, purchasing, and installations. Project completed within budget and strict time schedule.
- Launched a unique Treasury System delivering real-time positions since recognized by and installed by the bank's Italian head office and other foreign units. System permits an error-free capability, increased productivity, and more succinct position keeping.
- Contributed to bank's reaching the $2 billion asset level, a first for the Canadian branch. Managed the asset-liability portfolios including liquidity, FX, and interest-rate risk.
- Met the majority of company-defined profit targets during tenure throughout a fluctuating economy.
- Worked with IT, Risk Management, and a Reuters consultant to upgrade the KONDOR+ system from version 1.8 to 2.0. Process involved regressive testing to ensure stable data transfer.
Responsibilities:
- Played an active and critical role on the 6-member senior management team. Acted as treasury representative and at times reported in person to Board of Directors.
- Traveled to key global financial centers, ensuring and maintaining liquidity and identifying new financial partners.
- Oversaw all money-market and foreign-exchange dealing and corporate dealing desks. Monitored market information, variations, bank traders, Reuters News, Dow Jones, and print, TV, and trade journals.
- Controlled Canadian, US dollar, and Euro cash management. Checked the cash position and manipulated cash flow to maintain profitability.
- Managed the treasury's statutory and OSFI compliance.
- Administered the Euro currency conversion including pricing and changing FX system from legacy currency consolidations.
- Supervised 10 staff, including Treasury Services, Money Market, and Foreign Exchange Managers. Responsible for all human resource issues, recruitment, scheduling, appraisals, budgeting, and profit-target issues.
- Developed the Y2K Liquidity Contingency Plan in partnership with other departments.
- Liaised with Italian Head Office Departments and branches, Credit International, and Securities and Syndications.
- Handled the $5 million defined-benefit plan for the bank's Canadian operations.

Strategy: *Expand on the candidate's sound and diverse international money-market experience in the top section, with accomplishments making up the bulk of the resume.*

GERALD BAKERSFIELD   PAGE 2

ASSISTANT VICE PRESIDENT—TREASURY   1997–1999
Accomplishments:
- Oversaw the introduction of the KONDOR+ system, which significantly improved accountability, instant market analysis, pricing of products, and maintenance of positions. Recognized by the senior management team as an integral component of productivity and reporting improvements and streamlined operations.
- Actively addressed a critical business-development issue by leading a team tasked with designing and building a new trading room. Completed on time and within strict budget.

Responsibilities:
- Worked judiciously in partnership with Executive Vice President to support the department operations, priorities, objectives, and tactical plans.
- Guided the policy and procedure development to support the regulatory authority requirements.

SENIOR DEPARTMENT MANAGER   1990–1997
- Promotion recognized as the first Canadian management position to be filled by a non-Italian citizen.
- Selected by senior banking peers to fulfill the Director, Financial Markets Association of Canada (formally FOREX of Canada), position for one year.
- Facilitated the complex centralization of the corporate currency exchange, eliminating the retail responsibilities and permitting better management over the foreign-exchange and money-market clientele.
- Instrumental in raising the Canadian asset level to $1 billion Canadian for the first time.
- Implemented the Bank of Canada zero-reserve environment.

MONEY MARKET TRADER/FX TRADER   1984–1989
- Actively managed the asset and liability gap positions; developed trading relationships to provide access to liquidity.
- Handled customer activity, providing information and booking money-market/FX transactions.

Continental Illinois of Canada, Toronto, Ontario   1981–1984
Held the following two positions:
POSITION KEEPER/TRADER
AUDIT OFFICER

Royal Canadian Mounted Police, Regina, Saskatchewan   1981
CONSTABLE
- Successfully completed initial training. Posted to Maple Ridge, British Columbia.

EDUCATION

Strong proponent of continuing education. Relevant financial courses include:

- Canadian Treasury Functions	- Bank of Montreal, Toronto
- Treasury Functions	- Banca Commerciale Italiana, Milan
- Futures	- Dean Witter (Carr Futures), Toronto
- Asset Liability Management	- Risk Conferences Limited

Sheridan College, Oakville, Ontario   1981
CERTIFICATE—Business Administration
Accounting and Finance Major

COMMUNITY INVOLVEMENT

Participated in the Terry Fox run for 17 of the last 21 years. Raised $15,000 in total, $3,500 in highest year.

ARTHUR SALAZAR

1234 N. Carpenter Lane
Los Angeles, California 90069

(323) 555-1234
artsalazar@email.com

INVESTMENT SERVICES FINANCIAL EXECUTIVE
Financial Planning / Budget Management / Internal Reporting / General Accounting
Project Management / Financial System Technology / Leadership / Relationship & Consensus Building

❑ Highly motivated, results-driven financial professional with 14 years' experience developing, presenting, and implementing value-added recommendations for improvement. Strong analytical, technology, and communication skills with a track record of achievements in financial planning and project management.

❑ Strong leadership and team-building skills with ability to coordinate cross-functional groups to accomplish objectives and meet critical deadlines in a fast-paced, high-growth, dynamic environment. Committed to high ethical standards. Consumer, shareholder, and employee focused.

MBA / Big Six CPA Experience

PROFESSIONAL EXPERIENCE

U.S. INVESTMENTS CORPORATION, Los Angeles, CA • 1990 to Present
Achieved fast-track promotion to positions of increasing responsibility for industry-leading financial-services and e-commerce provider with diverse product offerings including discount securities brokerage, mutual funds, electronic brokerage, and bank-like products. Annual revenues grew from $300 million to $2 billion.

Director, Planning and Analysis (1997 to Present)
In charge of corporate financial planning, budget process, and evaluation/implementation of information technology upgrades utilized by 100+ analysts. Directed staff of seven; interfaced on regular basis with 200+ co-workers at all corporate levels; reported directly to Corporate Controller / VP of Finance.
  • Led company's annual operating-plan process, managing continuous process improvements to support high growth cycle and migration to a decentralized planning and budgeting business unit.
  • Developed spreadsheet models to support financial targets and strategic allocation of funds to business units. Consolidated budgets into financial statements; delivered high-level presentations.
  • Orchestrated new planning process and launched investment-analysis guidelines supporting a highly volatile environment.
  • Spearheaded acquisition and implementation of new integrated planning, reporting, and analysis tool that generated productivity improvements in finance groups across multiple divisions. Concept was enthusiastically endorsed by user community, and vendor selection was adopted as corporate standard.
  • Implemented Windows-based state-of-the-art financial software application, replacing proprietary mainframe budgeting application. Accomplished complex conversion within three-month window.

Manager, Revenue Reporting (1997 to 1998)
Analyzed and prepared periodic reports of customer-segment revenues to support business diversification. Managed revenue-reporting definitions and databases, ensuring company-wide consistency and efficiency. Completed numerous special projects for Controller and CFO encompassing project tracking, contingency planning, and internal billing.
  • Coordinated company-wide effort to develop corporate definitions for customer-related data and published first definitions manual. Successfully achieved consensus among cross-functional team of support managers.
  • Managed information technology team in developing revenue databases to support common definitions throughout company. Served as springboard for a later data warehousing project.

Strategy: *Capture the reader's attention at first glance with important highlights: executive-level experience, an MBA, and a Big 6 CPA background. Use the Professional Experience section to show consistent promotions and quantifiable achievements.*

ARTHUR SALAZAR • PAGE TWO

U.S. INVESTMENTS CORPORATION, continued

Manager, Financial Systems (1994 to 1996)
Orchestrated corporate-wide resource management reporting system used by accounting and cost-center managers for financial reporting and variance analysis.
- Managed monthly data production, distribution, and quality control in addition to user training and customer service. System received widespread praise by users for reliability and flexibility.

Senior Financial Analyst/Accountant (1990 to 1994)
Evaluated accuracy of financial analysis on investment proposals. Analyzed budget variances. Prepared top-down corporate estimates, consistently achieving goal of less than 2% variance in net income. Developed complex variable-compensation and breakeven-analysis models.

PRICE WATERHOUSE, Los Angeles, CA • 1988 to 1990
Auditor
Participated in financial audits across diverse industries including manufacturing, broadcasting, and banking. Prepared corporate tax returns.

EDUCATION

MBA; Concentration in Finance; UNIVERSITY OF CALIFORNIA, Los Angeles, CA; 1988
B.S. Accounting; BOSTON COLLEGE, Chestnut Hill, MA; 1986
CPA; State of California; 1990

SKILLS

Proficient in multiple business applications including Microsoft Office (Word, Excel, PowerPoint), Hyperion Pillar and OLAP (Budgeting & Analysis), PeopleSoft (General Ledger), Windows, Outlook.

Bilingual English/Spanish.

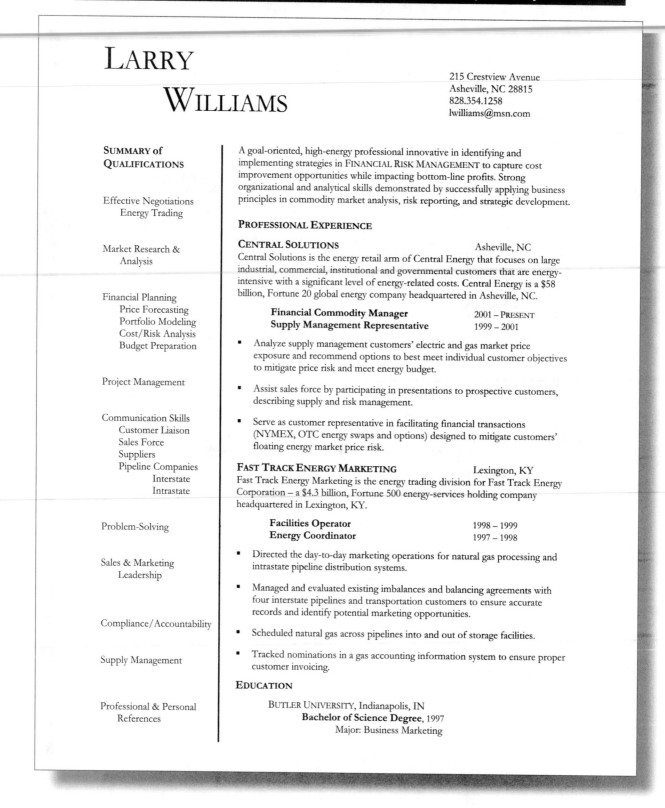

LARRY
WILLIAMS

215 Crestview Avenue
Asheville, NC 28815
828.354.1258
lwilliams@msn.com

SUMMARY of QUALIFICATIONS

Effective Negotiations
Energy Trading

Market Research & Analysis

Financial Planning
Price Forecasting
Portfolio Modeling
Cost/Risk Analysis
Budget Preparation

Project Management

Communication Skills
Customer Liaison
Sales Force
Suppliers
Pipeline Companies
Interstate
Intrastate

Problem-Solving

Sales & Marketing
Leadership

Compliance/Accountability

Supply Management

Professional & Personal
References

A goal-oriented, high-energy professional innovative in identifying and implementing strategies in FINANCIAL RISK MANAGEMENT to capture cost improvement opportunities while impacting bottom-line profits. Strong organizational and analytical skills demonstrated by successfully applying business principles in commodity market analysis, risk reporting, and strategic development.

PROFESSIONAL EXPERIENCE

CENTRAL SOLUTIONS   Asheville, NC
Central Solutions is the energy retail arm of Central Energy that focuses on large industrial, commercial, institutional and governmental customers that are energy-intensive with a significant level of energy-related costs. Central Energy is a $58 billion, Fortune 20 global energy company headquartered in Asheville, NC.

Financial Commodity Manager	2001 – PRESENT
Supply Management Representative	1999 – 2001

- Analyze supply management customers' electric and gas market price exposure and recommend options to best meet individual customer objectives to mitigate price risk and meet energy budget.

- Assist sales force by participating in presentations to prospective customers, describing supply and risk management.

- Serve as customer representative in facilitating financial transactions (NYMEX, OTC energy swaps and options) designed to mitigate customers' floating energy market price risk.

FAST TRACK ENERGY MARKETING   Lexington, KY
Fast Track Energy Marketing is the energy trading division for Fast Track Energy Corporation – a $4.3 billion, Fortune 500 energy-services holding company headquartered in Lexington, KY.

Facilities Operator	1998 – 1999
Energy Coordinator	1997 – 1998

- Directed the day-to-day marketing operations for natural gas processing and intrastate pipeline distribution systems.

- Managed and evaluated existing imbalances and balancing agreements with four interstate pipelines and transportation customers to ensure accurate records and identify potential marketing opportunities.

- Scheduled natural gas across pipelines into and out of storage facilities.

- Tracked nominations in a gas accounting information system to ensure proper customer invoicing.

EDUCATION

BUTLER UNIVERSITY, Indianapolis, IN
Bachelor of Science Degree, 1997
Major: Business Marketing

Strategy: *Create an eye-catching format that, in a matter of seconds, shows skills that are essential in the energy and utilities industry.*

CHAPTER 12

Resumes for Manufacturing, Operations, and Senior/Executive Management

- Materials Manager
- Purchasing and Supply-Chain Manager
- Logistics Manager
- Operations Executive
- Manufacturing Executive
- Plant and Operations Executive
- Manufacturing and Operations Executive
- Administrative Manager
- Public Relations Executive
- Senior Executive (Chief Executive Officer, Chief Operations Officer, President)

Andrew Daniel Tripp, CPM, CPIM

2003 Lane Street, Beaufort, NC 28516   (252) 504-1223   andrewdanieltripp@aol.com

Career Focus

Materials Manager position using my organization and planning skills to achieve the goals of the company.

Professional Profile

- Materials Management
- Customer Service
- Planning / Coordinating
- Staff Development
- Strategic Planning

- ERP Implementation
- Production / Distribution
- Training
- Certified ISO Auditor
- Inventory Reconciliation

- Shipping / Receiving
- Conflict Resolution
- Purchasing / Negotiating
- MRP / Logistics
- Manufacturing

Career Highlights

Castles, Inc., Beaufort, NC   1995 to present

$100 million international employee-owned company that produces computer racking, shelving, and cable-management products.

ERP Project Manager—Since 1/2000

- Manage the implementation and operation of the Enterprise Resource Planning System.
- Develop project plans, resource requirements, and system specifications.
- As part of the core company-wide implementation team, train users at a variety of site locations and serve as Team Leader.

Materials Administration Supervisor—1998 to 2000

- Supervised purchasing, planning, inventory control, and ERP systems and implementation.
- Planned purchases of all metals, handled negotiations, wrote contracts, and procured capital equipment.
- Coordinated and reconciled physical inventories; maintained Bill of Material structures and the Inventory Item Master.
- Implemented JIT programs with key suppliers, reducing inventory levels and increasing turns from 14 to 18 per year.
- Developed automated available-to-promise order entry/capacity scheduling computer system, eliminating manual activities and providing real-time order ship-date commitments to customers.

Warehouse Supervisor—1996 to 1998

- Managed all warehouse and shipping activities including budgeting, hiring, and employee training and development.
- Directed materials-planning activities.
- Planned and executed the delivery of raw materials for production using MRP and Kanban concepts.
- Developed cycle-counting program that was implemented at all facilities and achieved inventory accuracy of 99.0%.
- Served as Chairman of the local plant ESOP Committee, Chairman of the State ESOP Programs Committee, Vice-President of the Carolinas ESOP Chapter, and member of the National ESOP Strategic Plan Committee.
- Planned and executed the ESOP Southeast Chapter Conference and was a key presenter.

Senior Planner—1995 to 1996

- Coordinated start-up activities, including decisions concerning product-line transfers from California to North Carolina and installation of materials and engineering databases for support.

Strategy: *Position this individual for advancement in his company by quantifying his achievements and highlighting the breadth of his experience.*

Andrew Daniel Tripp, CPM, CPIM
Page 2

Classic Faucets Company, Morehead City, NC   **1983 to 1995**

Production Control Supervisor—1993 to 1995
- ▶ Executed the master production schedule and managed shop orders.
- ▶ Supervised 6 Production Schedulers.
- ▶ Coordinated activities with purchasing, engineering, and customer service.
- ▶ Participated as a member of the supply-chain management team.

Warehouse Supervisor—1989 to 1993
- ▶ Managed warehouse, shipping, and receiving activities and developed budgets.

Planner/Buyer—1985 to 1989
- ▶ Planned and purchased raw and MRO materials needed for production.
- ▶ Determined supply sources using cost analysis and supplier-selection criteria.
- ▶ Conducted supplier certification reviews and analyses.

Warehouse Attendant/Production Operator—1983 to 1985
- ▶ Assembled products, filled orders, loaded trucks, and delivered materials to production.
- ▶ Maintained inventory records and supplier data to support the supply-chain management program.

Education and Professional Certification

National Association of Purchasing Management (NAPM)—Certified 5/2000
American Production and Inventory Control Society (APICS)—Certified 3/99
Specialized training in Demand Flow Technology, Human Relations, Materials Management, and ERP—1985 to 1995
Carteret Community College, Morehead City, NC—30 hours toward BS Manufacturing Operations Management

Computer Skills

Windows, Lotus 1-2-3, Excel, Word, WordPerfect, Paradox, and various manufacturing systems.

RESUME 83: DEBORAH S. JAMES, CPRW; ROSSFORD, OH

RICHARD K. TOBER
1010 Schreier Road • Rossford, OH 43460
Residence: 419-666-4518 • Mobile: 419-666-6224 • E-Mail: rktober@netzero.net

SENIOR INTERNATIONAL SUPPLY CHAIN MANAGEMENT / PURCHASING EXECUTIVE
Transportation & Logistics • Production Planning • Packaging

Performance-driven Six Sigma Black Belt Senior Executive offering 15 years' comprehensive achievements within Supply Chain Management, Purchasing, and Production Planning. Leveraged business acumen across diverse cultures and economies. Developed performance-based, low-cost solutions through aggressive negotiation with new and existing suppliers and use of outsourcing. Solid history utilizing out-of-the-box approaches, adapting to new business environments, and negotiating win-win agreements. Recognized for ability to incorporate innovative management techniques that result in enhanced business practices, increased productivity, and profits. Forged strong business relationships focused on teamwork, service level, and cost containment. Fluent in German, Spanish, and Mandarin.

AREAS OF EXPERTISE

- **Strategic Supplier Development**
- **Change Management**
- **Planning & Development**
- **Operations Management**
- **Creative Problem Solving**

- **Inventory Management**
- **Cost Optimization and Control**
- **Import / Export Operations**
- **International Operations**
- **SAP Implementation**
- **Supplier Consolidation**

- **Quality Assurance**
- **Leadership / Team Building**
- **Supply Chain Analysis**
- **Relationship Management**
- **Project Management**

MBA, Finance • George Washington University, Washington, DC
BS, Industrial Engineering • Clemson University, Clemson, SC

CAREER BACKGROUND

MOSER CHEMICAL, Toledo, OH
Leading international science and technology company with a presence in more than 150 countries. Provides innovative chemical, plastic, and agricultural products and services to essential consumer markets.

MANAGER, DOMESTIC / INTERNATIONAL SUPPLY CHAIN (1998–2002)
Chlorinated Organic Business Unit ($650 million in sales / $65 million Supply Chain Budget)

Introduced supply-chain initiatives by restructuring business-wide domestic and international operations and spearheading contract negotiations. Oversaw 30 direct reports in managerial roles throughout the world; reported to division Vice President.

Career Highlights:

- Delivered $18 million in cost savings over three-year period primarily through use of inter-company supply-chain teams involving strategic suppliers and strategic customers.
- Achieved benchmark pricing for drumming-related activities, resulting in outsourcing of all activity in North America and shutdown of two packaging lines in Europe and Germany.
- Developed cross-cultural relations with international team members; supervised seven-person planning team with members from the US, Germany, Hong Kong, and Brazil. Team integrated operations of 10 plants at five sites on three continents, with production of more than 2 billion pounds per year.
- Installed and commissioned a keg-packaging line that centralized the filling of 15-gallon stainless-steel returnable containers and included a container-tracking system.

Strategy: *Highlight transferable supply-chain management and purchasing skills and showcase his ability to lead international cross-functional teams.*

`RICHARD K. TOBER

Residence: 419-666-4518 • Mobile: 419-666-6224 • E-Mail: rktober@netzero.net

GLOBAL BUSINESS PLANNER AND PROJECT MANAGER FOR CHEMICALS (1994–1998)

Career Highlights:

- Led international teams in the establishment and implementation of business planning and monthly forecasting policies and procedures, enabling an across-the-board inventory reduction of 65% and releasing $25 million in working capital.
- Conducted an in-depth worldwide supply-chain study analyzing all work processes between product manufacturer and delivery to customer. Study served as basis to reengineer and streamline supply chain and identified low-hanging opportunities for additional cost savings.
- Pioneered use of domestic contract terminals for primary storage, achieving lowest terminal costs within Moser and release of capital money associated with terminal projects.
- Increased domestic process capability of distribution system to meet increasing quality requirements for products, reducing product contamination defects from one per hundred orders to less than one per thousand orders.
- Established worldwide supply-chain teams with all strategic suppliers, strategic service providers, and strategic customers both domestically and internationally.
- Achieved largest single-lane-rail rate reduction in Moser's history by developing a water-compelled alternative, saving Moser over $1 million per year and customer $2 million per year.
- Implemented and monitored SAP R2 start-up and maintenance.
- Won *"Supplier of the Year Award"* on three separate occasions.

BUSINESS OPERATIONS MANAGER FOR CHEMICALS (1987–1994)

Career Highlights:

- Optimized use of raw materials in short supply by identifying intermediate products that could be alternatively purchased and diverting short products into higher value-added opportunities. Purchased up to 70,000 MT per year of intermediate products.
- Maintained supply-demand balances.
- Resolved domestic and international logistics and product-quality problems.

PROFESSIONAL TRAINING & DEVELOPMENT

International Relations • International Finance

Stepping Toward Quality • Quality 2000 • Improving Vendor Relations • Project Management

Six Sigma • Green Belt / Black Belt Training

Statistical Analysis Techniques • Managing Difficult People • Train the Trainer

Dale Carnegie – "Enhancing Communications"

COREY MARTIN PETERS
222 Alexander Street, Bridgewater, NJ 08807
(908) 575-7716 Home ▪ cmpeters@excite.net

Logistics / Transportation Management Executive
Supply-Chain Management ▪ Third-Party Logistics ▪ Distribution-Center Management

Versatile and well-qualified logistics professional with experience in regional management of commercial logistics and transportation systems, ensuring continuous process improvement and revenue gains. MBA in Supply Chain Management. Decisive leadership in strategic planning and development, P&L management, full-service lease and rental services, and project management.

Solid analysis, leadership, and problem-solving skills combined with motivational team building that elicits high levels of productivity. Strong record of cost reductions and demonstrated success in:

☑ Integrated Logistics Management
☑ Carriage / Fleet Management
☑ Staff Development / Management

☑ Strategic Planning / Process Improvement
☑ Inventory Optimization / Inventory Planning
☑ Asset Management / Vendor Alliances

PROFESSIONAL EXPERIENCE

TRANS-GLOBAL SYSTEMS, INC., Tampa, FL (corporate worldwide headquarters) 1994–present
Logistics and transportation solutions leader. Top third-party logistics provider of full-service leasing and commercial rentals and integrated logistics services worldwide. Annual revenues of $8 Billion.

Manager, Tri-State Commercial Rentals / Asset Manager (1999–present)
Full P&L responsibility for $19 million, 600-truck rental fleet in Tri-State Commercial Business Unit. Assist GM in managing $56 million Logistics, Dedicated Contract Carriage, and Full-Service Lease Operations for 1800-truck fleet with 200+ employees. Manage 12 direct reports. Oversee operations and logistics support, sales/revenues, expenses, financial metrics and tracking, purchasing, strategic planning and market development, forecasting, customer relations, and human resources.

ACCOMPLISHMENTS

Leadership and Process Improvement
✓ Key player (asset manager) on turnaround management team that transformed one of the worst-performing customer business units into one of the top 10 in the company in 2001.

✓ Obtained critical buy-in from all stakeholders, developing and cultivating win-win partnerships with internal and external customers, to achieve remarkable levels of cooperation and trust. Successfully motivated and led integrated logistics support for effective asset management and disposal, as well as outstanding customer relationship management.

Revenue Improvement and ROI
✓ Generated $15 million (20% increase) in revenues from 600-unit rental fleet in 1999 and 2000. Achieved consistent track record of revenue increases (up to 30%) and margin improvement (up to 700 basis points) in every position held, from branch rental manager to current position.

✓ Maintained 88% rental utilization rate for optimum revenue-producing capability by tracking operations daily. Closely managed the in-service and out-service processes for leasing operations to ensure maximum ROI (no more than 2% of fleet not earning revenue).

Page 1 of 2

Strategy: *Use functional headings to segment accomplishments and showcase the breadth of these results. Pepper the summary with industry keywords.*

COREY MARTIN PETERS

Page 2

(908) 575-7716 Home ▪ cmpeters@excite.net

Cost Reductions

✓ Successfully managed operating costs despite seasonal fluctuations in business. Maintained fixed costs at 35% of rental revenue and running costs at 10% of revenues (totaling $195,000 monthly).

✓ Reduced costs and increased revenues through effective asset management, including strategic planning of purchases and equipment disposal. Developed in-service and out-service processes that eliminated most costly vehicles first, as well as the ones with the most sales potential.

✓ Cut losses in unbilled physical-damage repairs in half by initiating cost-reduction measure to track physical damage repairs and re-bills through to the final billing process.

Team Building and Communications

✓ Maintained favorable customer relations with diverse accounts, from small businesses to Fortune 500 key accounts, including UPS, Coca Cola, Baskin-Robbins Mid-Atlantic Distribution Center, Federal Express, Kraft Foods, Daimler-Chrysler, and Wal-Mart.

✓ Developed future management and sales leaders by utilizing participative management techniques. Team has initiated new processes and solutions for cost reduction and sales improvements.

✓ Developed vendor relationship with body shops, outside maintenance shops, and transfer services at the local level and negotiated favorable terms and conditions for contracts.

Rental Representative—Northwest Philadelphia (1997–1999)

▪ Spearheaded turnaround of stagnant business unit, setting records for revenue and margin output. Generated $7.8 million in revenues for 1997 and 1998, averaging 48% profit margin.

▪ Key player in 210-truck fleet management with full responsibility for rental receivables. Utilized P&L accounting and database-management knowledge to conduct multiple logistics operations.

Rental Representative—Piscataway (1995–1997) and Edison (1994–1995)

▪ Revitalized failing commercial rental and fleet-management business units, increasing operational efficiency and ROI through strategic utilization planning and process-improvement initiatives.

▪ Increased revenues by 77% within two years. Set branch revenue record of $2.2 million in 1997. Key team member in district that achieved first-place finish for margin percentage gains in 1996.

DIGITALCOM, INC., Morristown, NJ   1993–1994

Account Executive. Managed corporate accounts for telephone equipment and services provider. Maintained customer accounts and developed new business despite highly competitive industry.

PATHMARK SUPERMARKETS, Bridgewater, NJ   1987–1992

Manager, Seafood Department. Managed and motivated team to surpass goals, ranking as 2nd most profitable department in the company. Raised year-over-year margins and revenues by 13%.

EDUCATION

MBA—Supply Chain Management, University of Pennsylvania, Philadelphia, PA—December 2001
Bachelor of Science—Business Administration, Rider University, Lawrenceville, NJ—1992

Carole Meriweather Komack

122 Caribou Court, Princeton, NJ 08540
(609) 203-5555 • ckomack@comcast.net

Operations / Management Executive
Administrative Management ▪ Project Management ▪ Sales and Marketing ▪ PR

☑ Proactive, results-oriented Operating Executive with 20 years of progressive experience and expertise in **leadership and problem-solving** for start-up, early-stage growth, and Fortune 500 companies. Strong strategic and tactical planning, organization, and general management qualifications.

☑ Keen understanding of business priorities…a genuine team player committed to managing operations and projects flawlessly while contributing to **business-development and revenue-producing** activities.

☑ **Cross-functional communications** and interpersonal skills. Easily interface with high-profile business clients, manufacturers, distributors, consultants, staff, vendors, governmental agencies, media, and others.

☑ Versatile, innovative, and loyal **management professional** able to see the "big picture" while staying on top of all the details. Recognized for consistent success in developing the systems, processes, and procedures to streamline corporate operations, increase revenues, and enhance profit performance.

PROFESSIONAL EXPERIENCE

PERSONAL PRODUCTS, INC., Princeton, NJ   1997–present
Operations Manager / Business Development
Promoted to start-up international product-development and licensing business (spin-off from previous employer, Engineering Pros). Full operations management responsibility with budget sign-off of $100,000.

Operations / Project Management
▪ Key player in building highly successful business (ranked #2 nationally in personal appliances) through active role in product planning and design, off-shore manufacturing and distribution channels, operations, marketing and sales, new product launches, client relationship management, and media / public relations.

▪ Designated point person for problem-solving issues with manufacturers, international distributors, attorneys, and CPAs, as well as high-profile clients. Utilize highly developed multi-tasking and communication skills, as well as finely tuned diplomacy and acquired expertise in Asian culture nuances.

▪ Spearheaded and maintain the administrative and legal structure for this international business. Developed and transitioned manual financial record-keeping system to computerized financial systems.

Business Development / Sales and Marketing / Revenue Enhancement
▪ In less than 10 months, developed initial product offering that represented 100% of company revenues for the first two years and continues to generate revenues.

▪ Played instrumental role in bringing five products to market in five years and capturing Revlon as key national account. Assisted in obtaining critical patents / licensing agreements and negotiated favorable vendor contracts. Products currently distributed by six big-box chains.

▪ Initiate and proactively pursue royalty-payment collections, contributing $400,000 annually to revenues.

Cost Reduction and Avoidance
▪ Saved two production days per month for two engineers, as well as $4,000 in monthly expenses, by changing from New York City corporate and patent attorneys to local attorneys. Realized 10% savings in annual corporate income taxes by sourcing new CPA, expert in international and corporate tax rules.

- continued -

Strategy: *Segment recent accomplishments into functional areas to highlight broad operations and management experience.*

Carole Meriweather Komack
(609) 203-5555 • ckomack@comcast.net   Page 2

ENGINEERING PROS, Princeton, NJ   1988–1997
Operations Manager / Executive Liaison to President
Key contributor to the rapid growth of this engineering consulting group, which specialized in technology transfer and development as well as litigation support. Sole administrative/operations management authority.

Operations / Project Management
- Reorganized chaotic office-management systems, which were jeopardizing confidential documents, and introduced standardized tracking systems for cash flow, revenues, and operating expenses. Independently oversaw administrative management, daily operations, client relations, media / PR, and accounting.

- Initiated and managed transition from manual to computerized record-keeping system, which increased operations efficiency by 80% and eliminated the need for three full-time employees. Authored company's first policies and procedures manual, capturing front-end and back-end operations processes.

Business Development / Client Relationship Management
- Developed and managed effective public-relations efforts as well as client relationship-management strategies (including high-profile meetings and special events), which laid the groundwork for securing and retaining major government contracts (Departments of Army and Defense, FAA, The National Security Agency) as well as contracts with the entertainment industry and international clients.

REYNOLDS PAINE ADAMS INC., New York, NY   1985–1987
Supervisor, Insurance Licensing Department
Oversaw daily operations of mission-critical department for NY stock-brokerage headquarters and 43 domestic branch offices, maintaining 9,200 state licenses for 800 account executives. Supervised staff of 12.

- Established centralized licensing activities in the New York headquarters office, reviewing and updating all licenses nationally within six months. Streamlined licensing process from three months to three weeks.

- Built cooperative relationships with each state's Insurance Department, streamlining procedures for receiving new and renewed licenses, which enabled 50% reduction in staff. Met regularly with insurance companies and Insurance Commissioners to proactively solve intricate insurance-licensing issues.

THE KENT GROUP, INC., Beverly Hills, CA & New York, NY   1982–1985
Insurance Licensing Administrator
- Promoted from Account Executive to key administrative management role in NYC home office. Established and managed Licensing Department for home office and four branch offices, representing 600 agent and broker licenses in 50 states, 250 broker surety bonds, and commission agreements with 300 insurance companies. Restructured and streamlined complex licensing procedures.

- Collaborated with marketing in establishing new niches for group insurance sales. Secured previously withheld commissions by obtaining new corporate and individual licenses.

EDUCATION
Bachelor of Science, Economics, Rutgers State University, New Brunswick, NJ
Continuing Education: Zenger-Miller Frontline Leadership Program (including Achieving Organizational Goals, Managing Individual Performance, Communication Skills, Greater Productivity, and Managing Change).

PROFESSIONAL ASSOCIATIONS
American Management Association (AMA)   American Business Women's Association (ABWA)
American Society of Association Executives (ASAE)   National Association for Female Executives (NAFE)

COMPUTER SKILLS
Windows 98 / NT, MS Office 2000, MS Word, MS Excel, MS PowerPoint, MS Access, MS Outlook, Adobe Photoshop, QuickBooks Pro 2001, Internet Explorer, email.

Joseph E. DiCarlo

44 Sampson Rock Road
Milford, MA 01757
res. 508.555.1212 • fax 508.401.1212 • cell 508.631.0202
jedicarlo@mindspring.com

EXECUTIVE PROFILE

- Highly accomplished manufacturing executive qualified for COO/Divisional–Operations–General Manager's position with company demanding expertise in all aspects of operations management, P&L, manufacturing, engineering, and new product design/launch.
- Solid track record of successful experience includes optimizing productivity, improving profitability, and successfully turning around declining operations. Innovative and creative problem-solving skills.
- Performance-, process-, and results-driven in commitment to quality and continuous improvement.

PROFESSIONAL EXPERIENCE

BOSTON METAL-TECH, INC. • Revere, MA   1988–Present
Vice President, Operations (1990–Present)
Direct overall operations of one of the nation's largest surface-finishing contractors, with accountability for manufacturing, laboratory, quality, engineering, new product development, production control, tooling, safety (workers' comp/health insurance), and regulatory affairs; company employs up to 900 across 3 shifts in 4 locations. Support a dynamic customer base comprising 650 active accounts globally; strategic accounts include such customers as Boeing, ATT, L'Oreal, Compaq, and Ford Motor Company.

Select Accomplishments ...

- Increased sales by $3MM over 2 years; led research and development team launch of electroplating on liquid-crystal polymer substrates.
- Produced $800K in annual sales through development/installation of plating process to clean and chrome-plate highly polished aluminum writing instrument components.
- Achieved key cost-saving objectives through following initiatives:
  – Realized annual savings of $600K through conversion of premium workers' compensation plan to self-insured program; launched Safety Committee, training programs, and rewards programs. Total consecutive days accident-free: 3,100.
  – Orchestrated development of paint-manufacturing software system that eliminated nonusable product and yielded annual material/labor savings of $125K–$180K.
  – Led research/development of electroplating treatment process: Saved $95K annually.
  – Implemented just-in-time delivery and renegotiated terms/prices with suppliers; result: 11%–15% reduction in chemical-procurement costs.
- Recipient, MCE Perfect Compliance (4 years); Environmental Achievement Award.

As **Director of Engineering** (1988–90), key accomplishments included the following:
- Identified key projects in area of regulatory compliance and established comprehensive, proactive program; Boston Metal-Tech falls under purview of many regulatory agencies.
- Reengineered alternate fuel boiler; result: $400K annual savings via recycling of energy and reduction in heating oil; avoided hazardous-waste shipping/exposure to liability.
- Engineered and launched thermal-oxidizer program for VOC destruction/energy recapture.
- Collaborated with MIS to automate 80% of regulatory-reporting process; result: reduced quarterly hours from 500 to 50 and improved accuracy while assuring regulatory compliance.

Strategy: *Diminish job duties to allow a strong focus on measurable achievements across multiple areas of operations.*

Joseph E. DiCarlo   Page Two

ADAPTIVE TECHNOLOGIES, INC. • Billerica, MA   1987–88
Manufacturing Engineering Manager
Directed Manufacturing and Industrial Engineering Groups for contract manufacturer (consignment and turnkey PC board and computer-systems assembly and testing); developed and managed Documentation Control Department. Managed 3 engineers and 4 associate engineers; coordinated technical support instrumental in assisting sales force with marketing of services. Provided labor and material costing for all production-quote estimates.

Select Accomplishments ...

- Designed and executed layout of 65,000-sq.-ft. manufacturing facility.
- Improved operational productivity by 18% through launch of team development programs; ergonomic workstation improvements increased efficiency 5%–20%.
- Streamlined manufacturing support operations by standardizing all processes, systems, and procedures; result: 98% on-time delivery of product.
- As a result of key value-engineering initiatives, reduced labor and material costs by 16% for product-handling changes, saved $50K annually from development of wave solder zero-defects program, and produced $30K annual savings through implementation of semi- and automatic component-performing equipment.

DIGITAL EQUIPMENT CORPORATION (now Compaq) • Waltham, MA   1983–87
Manufacturing Engineer, Special Systems Division
Implemented process equipment and assembly/test procedures for mechanical, PCB, cable, and systems configuration. Managed introduction of new electro-mechanical/PCB products and process equipment into manufacturing. Directed and trained process engineers in industrial engineering, product costing, and facilities layout.

Select Accomplishments ...

- Managed project team for renovation and layout of 30,000-sq.-ft. manufacturing and office facility; implementation resulted in annual savings of $180K.
- Key projects implemented included: automatic costing system, bar coding, and new Electro Static Discharge (ESD) Control Program.
- Developed X-Bar and Control Limit Charts for manufacturing operations.

EDUCATION

MASSACHUSETTS INSTITUTE OF TECHNOLOGY • Cambridge, MA
- **Bachelor of Science, Industrial Engineering** (1983 Honors Graduate)
- Alpha Pi Mu Industrial Engineering and Tau Beta Pi Engineering Honor Societies

CONTINUING EDUCATION ... Successfully completed numerous professional management, environmental, compliance, OSHA, and Haz-Mat training courses throughout career.

AFFILIATIONS / CIVIC

AMERICAN MANUFACTURING ASSOCIATION
- **Board of Directors** (1997–Present); **Vice President** (1995–97)

MASSACHUSETTS COUNCIL OF MANUFACTURERS — **Vice President** (2000–2001)
MILFORD PARK & RECREATION DEPARTMENT — **Soccer Coach** (1999–Present)

WILLIAM T. PARKERSON

35 Sunderland Drive
Cedar Grove, NJ 07009   E-mail: parkersonw@compuserve.com

Home: (732) 599-6694
Fax: (732) 599-4481

PLANT / OPERATIONS / GENERAL MANAGEMENT EXECUTIVE

Multi-site manufacturing plant/general management career building and leading high-growth, transition, and start-up operations in domestic and international environments with annual revenues of up to $680 million.

Expertise: Organizational Development • Productivity & Cost Reduction Improvements • Supply Chain Management • Acquisitions & Divestitures • IPOs • Plant Rationalizations • Safety Performance • Customer Relations • Change Agent

CORE COMPETENCIES

Manufacturing Leadership—Strong P&L track record with functional management experience in all disciplines of manufacturing operations • Developing and managing operating budgets • Spearheading restructuring and rationalization of plants and contracted distribution facilities • Initiating lean manufacturing processes, utilizing SMED principles • Establishing performance metrics and supply-chain management teams.

Continuous Improvement & Training—Designing and instituting leadership enhancement training program for all key plant management • Instituting Total Quality System (TQS) process in domestic plants to promote the business culture of continuous improvement • Leading ISO 9001 certification process.

New Product Development—Initiating plant-based "New Product Development Think Tank" that developed 130 new products for marketing review, resulting in the successful launch of 5 new products in 2000.

Engineering Management—Overseeing corporate machine design and development teams • Developing 3-year operating plan • Directing the design, fabrication, and installation of several proprietary machines • Creating project cost-tracking systems and introducing ROI accountability.

PROFESSIONAL EXPERIENCE

BEACON INDUSTRIES, INC., Maspeth, NY (1994–Present)
Record of continuous promotions to executive-level position in manufacturing and operations management despite periods of transition/acquisition at a $680 million Fortune 500 international manufacturing company. Career highlights include:

Vice President of Manufacturing (1997–Present)

Senior Operating Executive responsible for the performance of 7 manufacturing/distribution facilities for company that experienced rapid growth from 4 plants generating $350 million in annual revenues to 14 manufacturing facilities with revenues of $680 million. Charged with driving the organization to becoming a low-cost producer. Established performance indicators, operating goals, realignment initiatives, productivity improvements, and cost-reduction programs that consistently improved product output, product quality, and customer satisfaction.

Achievements:

- Selected to lead corporate team in developing and driving forward cost-reduction initiatives that will result in $21 million savings in 3 years through capital infusion, process automation, and additional rationalizations.

- Saved $13 million annually by reducing fixed spending 11% and variable overhead spending 18% through effective utilization of operating resources and cost improvement initiatives.

- Cut workers' compensation costs 40% ($750,000 annually) by implementing effective health and safety plans, employee training, management accountability, and equipment safeguarding. Led company to achieve recognition as "Best in Industry" regarding OSHA frequency and Loss Workday Incident rates.

- Reduced waste generation 31%, saving $1 million in material usage by optimizing manufacturing processes as well as instituting controls and accountability.

- Enhanced customer satisfaction 3% during past year (measured by order fill and on-time delivery percentage) through supply-chain management initiatives, inventory control, and flexible manufacturing practices.

- Trimmed manufacturing and shipping related credits to customers from 1.04% to .5% of total sales in 1999, representing annual $1.8 million reduction.

- Decreased total inventories 43% from 1997 base through combination of supply-chain management, purchasing, master scheduling, and global utilization initiatives.

- Rationalized 3 manufacturing plants and 6 distribution facilities, saving $6 million over 3 years.

Strategy: *Bring out core competencies with a detailed introduction, then support these areas of strength with significant achievements listed with the chronological work history.*

WILLIAM T. PARKERSON – (732) 599-6694 – Page 2

General Manager, Northeast (1994–1997)

Assumed full P&L responsibility for 2 manufacturing facilities and a $20 million annual operating budget. Directly supervised facility managers and indirectly 250 employees in a multi-line, multicultural manufacturing environment. Planned and realigned organizational structure and operations to position company for high growth as a result of acquiring a major account, 2 new product lines, and 800 additional SKUs.

Achievements:

- Reduced operating costs by $4.5 million through consolidation of 2 distribution locations without adverse impact on customer service.
- Accomplished the start-up of 2 new manufacturing operations, which encompassed a plant closing and the integration of acquired equipment into existing production lines for 2 new product lines; achieved without interruption to customer service, 2 months ahead of target, and $400,000 below budget.
- Increased operating performance by 15% while reducing labor costs by $540,000.
- Reduced frequency and severity of accidents by 50% in 3 years, contributing to a workers' compensation and cost-avoidance reduction of $1 million.
- Decreased operating waste by 2% for an annual cost savings of $800,000 in 2 manufacturing facilities.
- Negotiated turnkey contracts for 2 distribution warehouses to meet expanded volume requirements.
- Maintained general management and administrative cost (GMA) at a flat rate as sales grew by 25% annually over 3 years.

ROMELARD CORPORATION, Detroit, MI (1980–1994)
Division Manufacturing Director (1989–1994)

Fast-track advancement in engineering, manufacturing, and operations management to division-level position. Retained by new corporate owners and promoted in 1994 based on consistent contributions to revenue growth, profit improvements, and cost reductions. Scope of responsibility encompassed P&L for 3 manufacturing facilities and a distribution center with 500 employees in production, quality, distribution, inventory control, and maintenance.

Achievements:

- Delivered strong and sustainable operating gains: Increased customer fill rate by 18%; improved operating performance by 20%; reduced operating waste by 15%; reduced inventory by $6 million.
- Justified, sourced, and directed the installation of $10 million in automated plant equipment.
- Implemented and managed a centralized master schedule for all manufacturing facilities.
- Reduced annual workers' compensation costs by $600,000.
- Created Customer Satisfaction Initiative program to identify areas of concern; implemented recommendations, significantly improving customer satisfaction.

Prior Positions: Manufacturing Manager (1987–1989); Plant Manager (1986–1987); Engineering Manager (1984–1986); Plant Industrial Engineer (1980–1984).

EDUCATION & PROFESSIONAL DEVELOPMENT

Bachelor of Science in Manufacturing Engineering
Syracuse University, Syracuse, NY

Continuing professional development programs in
Executive Management, Leadership, and Finance

JEFFREY K. HUNTINGDALE

70 Lookdown Arrow Street • Wichita, Kansas 67226 • (306) 698-2563 • huntjk@slscom.com

SENIOR MANUFACTURING & OPERATIONS EXECUTIVE
Start-up, Turnaround, and High-Growth Manufacturing Operations

QUALIFICATIONS SUMMARY

High performance, results-driven Senior Executive with a career demonstrating visionary leadership, expertise, and distinguished performance in business startup, turnaround, and operational management of multi-site, national, and international manufacturing operations. A catalyst for change, combining tactical execution of strategic initiatives with strong leadership of cross-functional staff and development of key alliances to capture and enhance overall quality, productivity, business, and bottom-line financial performance.

CORE COMPETENCIES

- Strategic Planning & Execution
- Analysis & Problem Resolution
- Team Performance Optimization
- Process Analysis & Reengineering
- Productivity & Performance Improvement
- Vendor Selection & Negotiations
- Quality Control Leadership
- Supply Chain Management
- Cost Reductions & Profit Growth
- Purchasing & Materials Management

EMPLOYMENT HISTORY

SMITHVILLE, INC., WICHITA, KANSAS   1995 to Present

Rapid promotion through increasingly responsible positions, implementing manufacturing-improvement strategies to capture cost reductions and deliver strong revenue gains.

Chief Executive Officer (1998 to Present) **Vice President—Operations** (1996 to 1998)

Senior operating executive with full responsibility for strategic planning, development, and operational management within this motor-vehicle parts-manufacturing company. Scope of accountabilities encompasses management of all manufacturing processes; quality assurance; purchasing; warehouse safety and government compliance; and shipping/receiving. Establish and build strategic alliances with vendors, outsourced processors, and key customers to reduce expenses and drive profitability. Responsible for staff recruitment, training, and support and cross-functional team leadership and development. Identify and implement continuous-improvement measures including lean manufacturing, TQM, and cycle-time reduction.

☑ Entrepreneurial drive and vision demonstrated through set-up and development of successful international motor-vehicle fabrication subsidiary, Smithville Motors.

☑ Accelerated annual sales from $8 million to $150 million; grew Wichita premises threefold; optimized staffing levels through development of successful local/international manufacturing subsidiaries, aggressive turnaround leadership, process redesign and optimization, and implementation of strategic staffing initiatives.

☑ Captured 65% reduction in overhead through consolidation of departments.

☑ Optimized productivity 45% through development and implementation of weekly performance-monitoring and reporting methodologies.

Continued...

Strategy: *Bring out the candidate's most relevant experience, beginning with core competencies and highlighted by strong achievements throughout his career.*

JEFFREY K. HUNTINGDALE   Page 2

☑ Secured net savings in excess of $120,000 per year through material waste/cost reduction.

☑ Decreased accidents almost 90% through introduction of formal Safety Program.

☑ Authored and received state funding grants totaling $66,000 for employee training.

☑ Pioneered creation and implementation of quality-assurance system as per standards approved by major commercial automotive-industry companies.

Quality Assurance Manager (1995 to 1996)

Diverse role, developing and implementing sound quality-assurance procedures, with accountabilities spanning Material Manager, Shipping-Receiving Supervisor, and Compliance Officer functions.

MORSEN PTE, KHAN YUNIS, ISRAEL   1990 to 1995

Recruited to spearhead all facets of motor-vehicle manufacturing company start-up, with fast-track promotion to VP role.

Vice President (1991 to 1995) ***Director of Planning & Development*** (1990 to 1991)

Planned, developed, and implemented start-up initiatives including building, infrastructure, equipment, and staffing; researched, assessed, and wrote project feasibility studies. Interfaced with key organizations, consulates, and embassies. Created and executed manufacturing quality assurance. Developed marketing materials to promote company on both national and international levels. Oversaw all administrative and manufacturing operational functions; recruited, supervised, and supported 60 cross-departmental personnel.

☑ Secured $10 million in funding through development of alliances with key organizations.

☑ Orchestrated start-up and core operational strategies; developed solid foundations that facilitated company growth.

☑ Pioneered benchmarking manufacturing methodologies.

EDUCATION

MBA — Wichita State University   1990

Bachelor of Science, Electrical Engineering (BSEE) — Wichita State University   1988

PROFESSIONAL MEMBERSHIPS

Wichita Area Chamber of Commerce

COMPUTER LITERACY

• MS Windows • DOS • MS Excel • MS Access • Outlook Express • CMES (quality software)

DARLENE FORD

1209 Conduit Road, Petersburg, VA 23805 • Tel: 804-504-5666 • Mobile: 804-725-2783
Email: dford@msn.com

ADMINISTRATIVE / BUSINESS MANAGEMENT
DISTRICT MANAGEMENT / OFFICE MANAGEMENT / OFFICE ADMINISTRATION

RESULTS-ORIENTED PROFESSIONAL with over 10 years' broad-spectrum experience planning and directing senior-level business administrative affairs. Possess outstanding capacity for leadership and problem solving. Combine strong strategic-planning, organizational, and communication skills with an innate ability to direct high-level projects simultaneously. Deliver high performance under stress, with strong ability to focus. Extensive communication and interaction with top-level officers and Board Members as well as federal, state, and local officials. Relocating to Sarasota, Florida.

Core competencies include:

- Strategic Planning & Leadership
- General Business Management
- Purchasing / Negotiations
- Inspection, Analysis & Research
- Problem Identification & Resolution

- Staff Training & Development
- Customer Service, Support & Communications
- Organizational Reengineering / Revitalization
- Quality Assurance & Performance Management
- Accounts Payable / Receivable / Payroll

GENUINE LEADER WITH OUTSTANDING INTERPERSONAL SKILLS

VALUE OFFERED

- **PROJECT MANAGEMENT:** Manage and direct all phases of complex projects from conception to fruition. Excellent follow-through skills. Organized, efficient, and precise, with strong liaison skills.

- **PURCHASING:** Directed procurement process encompassing up to $300,000 in equipment and supplies.

- **PUBLIC RELATIONS:** Excellent ability to communicate on all levels from staff to "C" level. Strive for outstanding Customer Relationship Management. Extraordinary ability to build trust and defuse tense and difficult situations.

- **MANAGEMENT / LEADERSHIP:** Participative Manager with "open-door policy." Excellent capacity to motivate and impact team relations to form cohesive and productive team.

- **COMPUTER LITERACY:** Exceptional PC skills including Microsoft Office, Word, Excel, and PowerPoint; legacy programs including industry-specific software such as Caselle (government software), Accounts Receivable, GL, and Connect Trace.

SHARP — RESOURCEFUL — QUICK LEARNER, READY TO FACE CHALLENGES

SELECTED ACHIEVEMENTS

- **Received Achievement Award in Operator Certification** — 1998, 1999, 2000, 2001, 2002.
- **Spearheaded development** and implementation of innovative meter-reading process that increased productivity from 19 days to only 1–2 days. Saved substantial revenues in payroll and labor.
- **Championed expansion** of water reservoir from 300,000 to 570,000 gallons, increasing fire protection for approximately 165 homes.
- **Aligned forces** with neighboring city to utilize our water supply, thereby **resolving water deficits** caused by low water pressure that had created fire hazards within the city.

Strategy: To enable an industry switch, deemphasize utilities-industry background and use the first page to highlight skills, value, and selected achievements.

DARLENE FORD   PAGE 2

PROFESSIONAL EXPERIENCE

Petersburg City Improvement District, Petersburg, VA — 1987–present

DISTRICT MANAGER / OFFICE ADMINISTRATOR (1991–present)
DISTRICT CLERK / MANAGEMENT TRAINEE (1989–1991)
CLERK (1987–1989)

Fast-track promotion through several positions with advanced accountability. Recruited to each successive position based on consistent contributions to productivity, excellence, and efficiency improvement. Career highlights include:

Manage and direct all aspects of Water Distribution and sewer collection, including administrative initiatives and supervision of staff of 25. Provide financial and operational support. Liaison between district engineers, attorneys, and Petersburg city, state, and county agencies. Communicate and consult on behalf of the Board of Trustees to resolve issues, deliver materials, clarify information, and strategically plan and make recommendations to seek viable solutions to District problems. Recommend and administer approval for all contractor repairs and construction.

- ◆ Negotiate complex, formalized legal agreements and contracts for District.
- ◆ Develop and implement high-level administrative documents including: owner and tenant agreements, employee policy and procedural manual, purchasing policies, leave and benefit policies, and Government Records Access Management Act policy.
- ◆ Formulate and institute **annual budget of $850,000** and coordinate yearly audit process.
- ◆ Manage and direct entire payroll process and all facets of account procedures.

Colonial Heights Trucking Corporation, Chester, VA — 1984–1987
CORPORATE SECRETARY
Managed all aspects of office administration to include accounts receivable/payable and supervision of office clerks and receptionists for trucking company. Developed contracts and finalized taxes, licensing, and insurance for all company vehicles.

EDUCATION AND PROFESSIONAL DEVELOPMENT

Bachelor of Science in Business Management, 1991
Richard Bland College, Petersburg, Virginia

Continuing education through classes, workshops, and seminars – 3 CEUs annually
Connect Software, Trace Meter Reading System, and Caselle Government Software
Water Distribution Certification level 4 — highest in Virginia

TEACHING APPOINTMENTS

Back Flow Incident and Prevention, 2002
City Water Conference – Taught class on Management Techniques, 2001

PROFESSIONAL AFFILIATIONS

Member, City Water Association of Virginia
Member, American City Water Association

— References will be furnished upon request. —

ELAINE KENNEDY

4736 Grande ▪ Dallas, Texas 75205
Home: 214-523-7488 ▪ Cell: 214-917-7582 ▪ ekennedy@aol.com

SENIOR PUBLIC RELATIONS EXECUTIVE

Award-winning, forward-looking leader with over two decades' senior management experience. Attested ability to assess and tackle critical situations and follow through to best outcome. Vision for high-return media opportunities and strategies that strengthen organizational market position and enhance revenue growth. Possess exceptional ability and knowledge to lead PR campaigns and issue-management programs across multiple industries. Strong ability to influence thinking of others, forge strategic relationships, and build consensus. Agile in multitask environment with wide scope of activities. Skillfully lead cross-functional teams to achieve corporate, branding, and marketing goals.

AWARDS

Dallas Ad League Award: Regional Hospital Print Ad Campaign
Matrix Award: Venture Capital Conference for Ernst & Young
Matrix Award: Client Marketing Brochure
Regional Emmy: Best Newscast

CORE COMPETENCIES

- ❑ Strategic Planning & Positioning
- ❑ Corporate Identity & Reputation Management
- ❑ Promotions & Events Planning
- ❑ Media Relations & Scheduling

- ❑ Product & Brand Strategy
- ❑ Crisis Communications & Issues Management
- ❑ Multimedia Advertising & Placement
- ❑ P&L Management

EXECUTIVE EXPERIENCE

Ricklear Studios, Dallas, TX **1994–Present**

Lead PR team to consistently maintain million-viewer-strong audience for Emmy-nominated television series for $500M television-programming company of 250 employees.

PUBLIC RELATIONS DIRECTOR (1998–Present)

Direct in-house senior PR team and activities of selected partner PR firms in LA and NY in multiple product/brand marketing strategy support. Develop PR plans across full spectrum of marketing activities for $200M annual sales, including product launch, brand license, multimedia advertising, and customer communications. Exercise full P&L responsibility. Counsel president and CEO on critical-issues management, media response inquiries, and corporate strategies. Corporate spokesperson, controlling all media relations.

- ■ Doubled advertising equivalency results to $3M in 24 months and reduced PR operating budget by $500,000 annually.
- ■ Staged high-impact event that drew 20,000 consumers and demonstrated toy brand's sustained popularity to world press, retailers, and business partners for FAO Schwarz 2001 International Toy Fair kick-off.
- ■ Secured placements on *The Today Show, Rosie, Good Morning America,* and others by convincing national broadcast media producers of product's national value.
- ■ Produced over 50 promotional videos, ranging from high-end film pieces to video news releases.
- ■ Conceived, designed, and launched Electronic Press Room for company's corporate website.

Strategy: *Design the resume to showcase achievements without mentioning the name of the children's program, which might affect her credibility for "serious" PR and promotional opportunities.*

ELAINE KENNEDY

Home: 214-523-7488 ▪ Cell: 214-917-7582 ▪ ekennedy@aol.com

Page Two

Ricklear Studios, Continued

MEDIA RELATIONS MANAGER (1994–1997)

Managed and coached PR staff in media placement of award-winning television programming brands and products. Responsible for $100,000 annual, multi-project budget.

- Developed publicity launch model that produced 30-minute ticket sellouts in most major cities for international live tour.
- Orchestrated 20-million-viewership public-service announcement for Governor George Bush.
- Secured coveted placement of stories, articles, and appearances in *USA Today, LA Times, NY Times, CBS This Morning, Today,* and *Donahue* through strong leadership of PR multimedia advertising team.
- Produced and directed over 40 promotional videos.

Communication Counsel of America (CCA), Dallas, TX   1990–1994

Public-relations firm providing crisis and issue management strategic-response guidance to multibillion-dollar clients, such as US Department of Energy, Westinghouse, Rocky Flats Nuclear Facility, British Petroleum–Alaska, and Syntex Pharmaceuticals.

CONSULTANT

Independent consultant brought in to manage high-stakes and sensitive PR projects. Advised on and developed client crisis strategies. Prepared executives on oral presentations for large government contracts. Developed technical witnesses for regulatory and legislative appearances. Trained companies in strategic negotiation techniques with communities and stakeholders for effective corporate goal attainment.

- Netted upwards of $1B in government contract awards, $750M in estimated CCA new-client presentations, and FDA hearings that achieved over-the-counter approval for Aleve, through careful preparation of Westinghouse, Coopers & Lybrand, and Procter & Gamble executives for high-stakes oral presentations.
- Created positive media and stakeholder relations for US Department of Energy in release strategy of National Environmental Impact Statement for Nuclear Defense Facilities.

Kennedy Communications, Dallas, TX   1988–1990

Public relations, issues management, and marketing firm, serving multibillion-dollar clients such as Hitachi Semiconductor, Campbell Travel, and Conoco Oil Company.

PRESIDENT

- Raised positive community response for Conoco Oil Company $25M community settlement.
- Developed TQM Quality Circles program for Hitachi.

Lewis & Partners, Dallas, TX   1984–1988

$20M ad agency serving multimillion-dollar clients such as Ernst & Young; American Eagle Airlines; Donaldson, Lufkin & Jenrette; and Olivetti USA.

GROUP VICE PRESIDENT, PUBLIC RELATIONS

Founded and directed PR group, recruiting, training, and directing staff of 10. P&L responsibility. Oversaw consumer and B2B work. Billed $1M in annual fees.

- Established consistent emergency responses and elevated public confidence by authoring Issues Management Plans for regional restaurant chain and American Eagle Airline Service.

EDUCATION

Bachelor of Journalism, University of Texas at Austin

WILLIAM E. EVANS

321 Pembroke Road
Bedford, VT 13111   wevans@aol.com

Home: 333.477.4747
Cell: 333.555.7272

SENIOR EXECUTIVE PROFILE

President / CEO / COO / Senior Vice President / General Manager / Consultant / Coach
Start-Up Entrepreneurial Ventures / Turnaround Businesses / High-Growth Organizations
Industrial Products & Technologies / US & International Markets

Accomplished Business Executive with 20+ years' experience driving profitable growth in challenging, competitive markets. Decisive, solutions-focused, and results-oriented—expert in building and revitalizing a company's organizational infrastructure, products, technologies, processes, measurement systems, and sales/marketing strategies to optimize results. Strong leadership, communication, creative, and analytical skills.

EXECUTIVE LEADERSHIP COMPETENCIES

Strategic Planning & Growth	Mergers, Acquisitions, Joint Ventures & Alliances
Revenue/Market Growth & Profit Improvement	Value-Added Products & Customer Relationships
Executive Sales, Marketing & Business Development	Organizational Leadership & Development
Multi-Site Operations	Performance Reengineering
P&L Management	Product Management
Interim Management	Manufacturing / Operations
Government Relations	Competitive Product Positioning

PROFESSIONAL EXPERIENCE

MEREDITH RESOURCES, Bedford, NH   1995–Present
Company provides interim project-management services to clients. Work encompasses internal or spin-off ventures for clients in markets that do not yet exist or are in early stages of definition.
OWNER

Launched company to lead and direct clients' staff in researching market and competition, creating strategy, advancing technology and product development, devising marketing plans, establishing sales channels, and developing and implementing manufacturing or service sources. Engagements have included leading entire companies with up to 125 employees diffused over multiple sites in North America, Europe, and Asia.

Challenge: Re-engineer a strategically disadvantaged electromechanical switch-manufacturing business unit based in the United Kingdom.

Result: Created and implemented a global strategy to transition an unprofitable product-manufacturing division into a profitable contract-manufacturing services business. Strategy included:
- Winning contracts with several Agilent Technologies global business units.
- Increasing annual bookings from an unprofitable $7 million to a profitable $36 million within nine months.
- Launching operations in North America and Malaysia that opened channels for a fourfold expansion of business.

Challenge: Transition a novel internally developed software cost center to an externally marketed product, develop external sales, and recruit a synergistic process-controls company to purchase the product line.

Result: Researched market; created a strategy; directed the product development, product launch, and technical support for a real-time process-control product for the food and beverage, pulp and paper, utilities, environmental monitoring, and mission-critical chemical-processing markets.
- Supported and created over 35 installations and developed $43.5+ million in new sales within 18 months.
- Led a team of 25 sales, marketing, development, service, and technical-support professionals.

Strategy: *Use the Challenge, Action, and Results format (see page 25) to portray this individual as "the solution" to multiple business problems.*

WILLIAM E. EVANS **PAGE TWO**

MEREDITH RESOURCES, continued...

Challenge: Commissioned to advise and lead a $60 million German manufacturer of precision thermal controls for appliances, building technologies, and industrial-automation systems markets in entering the North American market.

Result: Created a comprehensive strategic plan for a proposed product launch. Plan included identifying technical requirements, assessing market potential, creating marketing/sales channels, implementing customer service/support and finance, and planning manufacturing operations.

RAYMOND ENTERPRISES, Hanover, CT 1992–1995
A $60 million manufacturing company engaged in development and manufacturing of electromechanical products for domestic and international industrial and defense industries.
PRESIDENT 1993–1995
DIRECTOR OF STRATEGIC PLANNING & BUSINESS DEVELOPMENT 1992–1993

Promoted to *President* to oversee manufacturing, finance, engineering, marketing, sales, and human resources. Full P&L responsibility. Supervised 400 people.
As *Director of Strategic Planning*, worked closely with Group President to develop strategic plans, interface with corporate lobby group, form business relationships with strategic partners, and mentor operating executives on creating business models in emerging growth markets.

Challenge: Turn around strained relationship with Department of Defense, stabilize sales, and find new commercial growth markets.

Result: Worked with Department of Defense to reverse negative issues and created a positive working relationship. This guaranteed continued business for the company and avoided certain bankruptcy. Also, company was turned into a model defense contractor.

Challenge: Launch a new product with features that extended well beyond the then-conventional computer memory systems.

Result: Replaced all of competitor's products with company's new products in all new fighter aircraft development and upgrades. Increased sales 30% in two years and won multimillion-dollar contracts for converting older technology to new products on the NASA space shuttle and the International Space Station.

Challenge: Capture a lifetime contract from the U.S. Navy for the Tomahawk Cruise Missile Program — winning contract would give company twice the market share and a 25% revenue increase.

Result: Crafted a strategic alliance with GM Hughes Missile Systems by reducing Raymond's price and negotiating an order with GM CLCD for developing a needed safety product using Raymond missile-targeting technology. The contract was won and the competition eliminated. Also, won a contract from GM for a solution to a potential safety-liability problem of a sensing system.

SEIBERCO, INC., Braintree, MA 1984–1992
Inventor, developer, and manufacturer of a novel DC servo motor and related electronic digital-control product line.
COFOUNDER / CEO / PRESIDENT

Launched business after raising $1.5 million in venture capital. Developed the product and recruited 20 professionals to sell and build out the product line. Company expanded after receiving an additional $3 million in venture capital, with annual revenues reaching $2 million, and was eventually bought by a Japanese competitor.

Challenge: Create the greatest advancement in DC motor technology in 25 years.
Result: Built sales to over $2 million with an unknown product in a market that did not yet exist.
Challenge: Design a new classification for brushless DC motors (Sensorimotor) that eliminated the need to have an expensive feedback device.
Result: 50% reduction in cost, giving a significant competitive advantage and capital to develop and sell the systems.
Challenge: Develop marketing strategy for new product within the Zero Defects Manufacturing business.
Result: Utilized adaptive-control techniques, allowing customers to build self-tested automation systems for parts assembly. One builder adopted this technology and became the largest customer, providing over 50% of revenue in the early stages.

WILLIAM E. EVANS   **PAGE THREE**

EG&G CORPORATION, Waltham, MA   1980–1983
Company manufactured DC motors and electronic controls, selling them to OEMs of business machines and computer peripherals worldwide. Annual sales were $18 million.
VICE PRESIDENT, SALES AND MARKETING / VICE PRESIDENT OF CONTROL SYSTEMS BUSINESS UNIT

Hired to head worldwide sales and marketing. Held full P&L responsibility for the division, including strategic planning, financial performance, personnel, resources, and daily business operations.

Challenge: Create an international distribution sales force consisting of 20+ major distributors.
Result: Increased revenue 50% within the first year.
Challenge: Obtain special training in strategic planning based on process developed by Bruce Henderson of Harvard's Business School.
Result: Received a fundamental tool set to develop product and business solutions.

Previous employment: *Sales, Engineering,* and *Product Management* positions with large multinational companies selling industrial-control systems.

EDUCATION

BS, *Mechanical Engineering*, BRADLEY UNIVERSITY, Peoria, IL
Workshops in *Strategic Planning, Mergers and Acquisitions,* and *Market Data Collection* — Boston Consulting Group

AFFILIATIONS

Member, Intelligent Transportation Society of America
Member, Board of Directors — Intelligent Controls, Inc., Saco, ME
Member, Board of Directors — Technic, Inc., Rochester, NY
Member, Board of Directors — Synkinetics, Inc., Lowell, MA
Member, Board of Management — Hermann Kohler Electric GmbH, Nuremberg, Germany
Consultant — various North American business interests

Own four patents in the field of electromagnetics and one for a remote tire-pressure-monitoring system for automobiles.

Paul C. Carter

104 Devonshire Rd.   paulcarter@mcast.net   Home: 313-822-5259
Grosse Pointe Park, MI 48230   Cellular: 313-505-4040

PRESIDENT / CHIEF EXECUTIVE OFFICER
Industrial Manufacturing Environments

Entrepreneurial-oriented executive presenting a formidable record leading global business development, manufacturing, and strategic planning teams within manufacturing environments. Recognized for skill at turning around poorly performing divisions, guiding successful start-ups and/or joint ventures, and establishing strategic alliances. Accustomed to interacting and working closely with C-level executives across industry and cultural lines.

Areas of Expertise

- Strategic / Tactical Planning
- Start-up / Turnaround
- Business Planning
- P&L Management
- Mergers and Acquisitions / Joint Ventures
- Due Diligence / Negotiations
- Operations / General Management
- Sales and Marketing

- Organizational Design
- Continuous Improvement Practices (5S, Statistical, Process Mapping, One-Piece Flow)
- Computer-Integrated Manufacturing
- Quality Control / Assurance
- Facilities / Plant Design
- Staff Development and Supervision

CAREER HIGHLIGHTS

THOMPSON-GENERAL AUTOMOTIVE — Dearborn, MI
(Global manufacturer of primarily body-sealing systems, NVH control systems, and fluid-handling systems, with sales in excess of $1.6 billion.)
DIRECTOR, STRATEGIC PLANNING, 2001–2003
DIRECTOR, BUSINESS DEVELOPMENT, 2000–2001

Selected to stay on as director of strategic planning following merger of General Products Company and Thompson Tire & Rubber. Continued with same areas of oversight, which encompassed mergers and acquisitions, strategic planning, and new ventures. Additionally involved in planning, communications, and competitive intelligence. Worked closely with CEO on M&A, made board-level presentations, and held P&L oversight for new ventures.

Key Accomplishments:

- Actively involved in all aspects of sale of General to Thompson, which delivered premium to shareholders of 80% of trailing stock price.
- Cut business-development costs 40% for FY2002 by prioritizing and delaying or canceling certain projects.
- Successfully managed divestiture of Holt Industries, a plastics business selling product primarily to appliance industry.
- Generated proceeds well in excess of book value, despite continuing losses, following divestiture of plastics facility in Winnsboro, SC.
- Conducted strategic evaluation of European company for NFS Control Systems Division, which subsequently led to an alliance vs. joint venture or acquisition.
- Guided shift of two emerging ventures from technology to market development, greatly increasing credible sales prospects while significantly reducing overall spending.
- Established corporate strategy, which resulted in the creation of four SBUs. Process entailed completing a strategic-planning process, developing performance targets linking strategy and operating plans, and performing portfolio-valuation process for each unit.
- Greatly improved profitability of poorly performing plastics SBU during temporary assignment as VP/General Manager in 1999. Attained cost savings of 10% and achieved annualized sales of $85 million during six-month turnaround period.

Strategy: *Create an accomplishment-rich resume that is laden with auto-industry "buzzwords" for this senior executive who wants to remain in that industry.*

Paul C. Carter

104 Devonshire Rd.   Résumé–Page Two   Home: 313-822-5259
Grosse Pointe Park, MI 48230   paulcarter@mcast.net   Cellular: 313-505-4040

CAREER HIGHLIGHTS, continued

TELDYN *(Unit of Global Intertech)* — Minneapolis, MN
(Leader in compact fluid power components and systems, serving marine, automotive, recreational vehicles, medical, and general industry markets. Acquired by Parker Jamison in 2000.)
PRESIDENT, 1996–2000

Fully accountable for P&L of $42 million standalone unit, with complete oversight of marketing, sales engineering, product development, finance, human resources, manufacturing, and employee base of 300.

Key Accomplishments:

- Grew the company from $24 million to over $40 million within three years by developing key accounts, expanding sales to several European customers, and securing limited number of government contracts.

- Implemented quality operating system, product-development and strategic-planning processes, and new accounting and MRP systems to facilitate and support growth of company.

- Won large contract for outboard-motor hydraulic trim systems from Mercer Marine, resulting in becoming the sole supplier to Mercer. Laid foundation for long-term relationship through the establishment of pricing structure and integration of technical efforts.

- Achieved significant operational improvements by reorganizing manufacturing operations, hiring key operational personnel, and implementing continuous-improvement practices (5S, statistical methods, process mapping, one-piece flow).

- Increased sales and regained business by creating compensation program that rewarded sales force on individual performance to forecast, rather than on total company sales.

- Integrated U.S. operations of a company acquired by Teldyn's parent company.

HURON AUTOMOTIVE COMPONENTS — Benton Harbor, MI
(Start-up Michigan Motor/Cogwell International joint venture company to develop, market, and manufacture interior features for the automotive industry.)
PRESIDENT, 1993–1996

Accountable for P&L, organization design, 10-year strategic plan, five-year business plan, and implementation of world-class business practices (including self-directed work teams).

Key Accomplishments:

- Directed formation of start-up venture including preliminary identification of joint-venture partner and negotiation of final agreement.

- Developed organizational plan and oversaw recruitment of 150 management, technical, and production associates.

- Negotiated modern labor agreement with UAW.

MICHIGAN MOTOR COMPANY — Dearborn and Saline, MI
(Global automotive company.)
SUPERVISOR, ADVANCED MANUFACTURING PLANNING, PLASTIC, AND TRIMS PRODUCTS, 1991–1993

Charged with developing manufacturing strategy for $3.5 billion division, with 13 sites throughout North America and Europe. Devised methods to improve manufacturing efficiencies, created facilities plans for European expansion, and identified initiatives to support growth of newly formed division.

Key Accomplishments:

- Implemented cross-divisional manufacturing cycle-time reduction program.

- Developed plan for initial manufacturing facility in Europe, which involved site selection, plant design, and organizational design.

- Led team redesign of 1.6-million-square-foot instrument panel manufacturing facility.

- Developed divisional Computer Integrated Manufacturing strategy and led implementation of organization to develop key applications.

Paul C. Carter

104 Devonshire Rd.
Grosse Pointe Park, MI 48230

Résumé—Page Three
paulcarter@mcast.net

Home: 313-822-5259
Cellular: 313-505-4040

CAREER HIGHLIGHTS, continued

MICHIGAN MOTOR COMPANY *(continued...)*
SUPERVISOR, ADVANCED MANUFACTURING ENGINEERING, 1990–1991
PROCESS DEVELOPMENT ENGINEER, 1984–1990

Led advanced group focused on initiatives to streamline instrument-panel manufacturing via flow-through manufacturing and improved product design at $350 million plant. Fully involved in process design, project management, and software development for automated systems.

Key Accomplishments:

- Developed and implemented automated manufacturing cells and factory-floor automation.
- Reduced lead time from 13 days to 1 by integrating entire manufacturing process.
- Completed broad array of process-development activities including computer simulation, robotic assembly applications development, design for manufacturability studies, and product-design feasibility activities.

Prior professional experience:

CARTER & CARTER ENTERPRISES, INC. — Houston, TX
(Printing and graphic arts organization.)
PRESIDENT, 1982–1984

NATIONAL SUPPLY COMPANY (division of Armco Steel) — Houston, TX
(Major supplier of oilfield equipment, worldwide.)
ASSOCIATE PRODUCT ENGINEER, 1981–1982

FEDERAL MOGUL CORPORATION — Southfield, MI
(Large manufacturer of industrial products for transportation industry.)
MANUFACTURING ENGINEER, 1980–1981

EDUCATION

MICHIGAN STATE UNIVERSITY — East Lansing, MI
MBA, GENERAL MANAGEMENT, June 1992
BS, MECHANICAL ENGINEERING, June 1980

PROFESSIONAL DEVELOPMENT
- AMA, Management Course for Presidents
- AMA, Mergers & Acquisitions
- Goldratt Institute, Theory of Constraints
- Numerous in-house classes at Ford

STEVEN T. LOCASSIO

Sales • Marketing • Infrastructure

Entrepreneurial Change Agent
Chief Revenue Architect

EXECUTIVE SUMMMARY

Senior-level executive experienced in building and nurturing multimillion-dollar divisions through accelerated growth, mergers, and turnarounds. Directly responsible for 100%+ gross profit increases. Hold an MBA in Management.

- Most recently President / COO of Temp Solutions' $500 million Private Label Services division, servicing the temporary staffing industry nationwide. Last five-year, year-average growth: sales 15%, gross profit 20%, net income 22%.

- Build or energize sales channels while creating new revenues and clients from widening business lines. Make marketing and product divisions 100% client-focused and accountable, then reengineer corporate vision to become more nimble and responsive.

- Meld relentless desire to succeed with dynamic leadership and business acumen to produce extraordinary results. Have survived and thrived in down- and up-markets, through the full market cycle. Have managed divisions / teams in multiple corporate mergers and directed the attendant change management and staff / culture integration.

- Intimately understand the challenges of an uncertain marketplace and maximize corporate potential through innovative business process changes, cost containment, quality control, and outstanding customer care. Lead and motivate individuals and teams to perform in any environment.

- Successfully merge disparate acquisition or departmental cultures, strategically funneling activities to create new revenue streams. Bridge the communications gap between business and tech teams, marrying technology to business need and creating profit rather than resource drain.

EMPLOYMENT

TEMP SOLUTIONS, PRIVATE LABEL SERVICES DIVISION, LAKE SUCCESS, NY　　　**1988 TO PRESENT**

Corporate Entity (M&A)	Executive Position	Date
Temp Solutions	*President / Chief Operations Officer*	1998 to Present
Technix	*President*	1997
On Staff	*President*	1996
Blue Sky Staffing	*Assistant Vice President, Sales & Marketing*	1989 to 1996
Power Hire	*Director, Sales & Marketing*	1989
Green Light Staffing	*Director, Sales & Marketing*	1988
USA Employment Services	*Manager, Sales & Marketing*	1988

With $7 billion in sales, Temp Solutions is the third largest staffing-services company in the world and is the latest owner of firm that originated with the USA Employment Services parent company, founded in 1966 and acquired six times after 1988.

Since 1988, conceptualized, built, and then led company's nationwide Private Label Services division and its three groups (nearly $500 million in sales) with performance steady at 20% profitability ratios despite six acquisitions / mergers in ten years.

Groups included: 1) the Temporary Management Resource (TMR) and Franchise divisions, providing turnkey support in sales, marketing, operations, finance, training, and administration to temporary staffing services, and 2) the Resource Funding Group (RFG), providing payroll financing and back-office support to independently owned and operated temporary staffing services.

Managed full P&L for RFG at $300 million in sales, TMR at $100 million in sales, and Franchise at $100 million in sales. Achieved 50% operational expense margins against gross profit, yielding operational margins of 50%.

Directed general operations for the three groups. Supervised national sales operations and divisional support services. Delivered marketing development and strategies. Supported all front-end growth and back-office services / customer care.

Reported to CEO. Direct reports included Vice President of Marketing, Director of Sales, Vice President of Operations, and Vice President of Finance.

Five Lorraine Court, Patchogue, NY 11772 • phone: 631-555-5555 • fax: 631-000-0000 • locassio21@aol.com

Strategy: *Make a clear value proposition for a highly accomplished executive with a complicated work history (multiple mergers and acquisitions within the same company).*

STEVEN T. LOCASSIO

page two of two

CAREER DEVELOPMENT / TEMP SOLUTIONS, continued

PERFORMANCE MILESTONES

Have delivered a proven track record of profitable cradle-to-grave sales / marketing and business-building success using diversified range of business expertise and knowledge—design, development, and implementation of customized sales and marketing / advertising strategies as well as creation of operational infrastructure to support front-end growth and back-end services.

- Created, launched, and managed the *largest payroll-funding and back-office service in the U.S. employment industry*, surpassing first-year sales plan by 100%.
- Grew new payroll business to current *$300 million in annual sales and $7.5 million in annual operating income* by mounting 13 years of aggressive yet cost-effective sales strategies and marketing campaigns.
- *Achieved $500 million in sales within 13 years* by designing and implementing sales initiatives, territorial structures, and marketing campaigns for all PL service divisions.
- Produced *$60 million in annual sales within 36 months* by identifying financially untapped day-labor market and creating operational infrastructure and computer systems to support and service this market.
- *Increased sales 30%* by identifying, tapping, and developing a new niche marketplace, the business-services industry, for the TMR division.
- *Achieved 120% increase in gross sales* and transformed sister *division's stagnant existing marketplace into a profitability target market by expanding servicing capabilities to address* entrepreneur marketplace.
- *Delivered operational expense margins of 50%* by streamlining systems / procedures without reducing overall quality.
- *Reduced data-entry functions and decreased operation expense by $250,000* by developing strategies for providing private-label services division clients the ability to process payroll on-site.
- Recently negotiated *$50 million sales / $2 million gross profit contract that generated $1 million* in operating income.
- *Grew consolidated gross profits from $15 million to $20 million* (Resource Funding Group and Temporary Management Resource Group) through territory expansion, sales force revision / revitalization, value-added services creation, and new market-niche penetration.

EARLY EMPLOYMENT

CLIMATE TECHNOLOGIES, HICKSVILLE, NY
District Manager, Carrier Building Service Division

1985 to 1988

Built business from $30 million to $40 million and overachieved objectives each year. Managed $20 million in new equipment and contract sales, five district sales managers, five branch offices, and 50 sales representatives.

GRUMAN SYSTEMS, INC., BETHPAGE, NY
Sales Representative, Home and Building Control (H&BC) Division

1982 to 1985

Marketed energy-management systems in metro New York and New Jersey. Consistently exceeded goals; attained over 110% of quota in 1982–1984 as well as Rookie of the Year in 1982, Salesperson of the Quarter nine times, Director's Club in 1983, and President's Club in 1984.

EDUCATION & PROFESSIONAL DEVELOPMENT

MBA in Management, Hofstra University, Uniondale, NY (1991)
BS in Management and Marketing, Adelphi University, Garden City, NY (1982)

- Member: American Staffing Association, National Technical Staffing Association, National Association of Personnel Services
- Annual participant in American Staffing Association's Panel of Industry Experts
- Authored several trade journal articles in *Contemporary Times, Temporary Digest,* and *Staffing Industry*

Five Lorraine Court, Patchogue, NY 11772 ● phone: 631-555-5555 ● fax: 631-000-0000 ● locassio21@aol.com

PHILLIP S. KRAEMER

100-A Frederick Road
Baltimore, Maryland 21043
pskraemerk@earthlink.net

Home: 443-820-7773
Office: 301-776-7878
Cell: 443-820-7774

SENIOR MANAGEMENT EXECUTIVE—CEO
Expertise in Driving Growth, Revenues, Competitive Position, Profitability & Value

EXECUTIVE PROFILE

Consummate Management Executive—True Visionary & Entrepreneur
Startup, Growth, Turnaround & Performance Improvement Expert
Corporate Development Strategist—Deal-Maker

High-powered executive with a results-charged career in the startup, growth, and profitable leadership of dynamic enterprises doing business in domestic and international markets. Offer high-caliber management qualifications, acute marketing instincts, experience-backed judgment, and excellent timing. Strong orientations in technology and finance. Expert in identifying opportunities or creating them from a seed concept. Accustomed to and effective in high-profile executive roles, making high-stakes decisions and overcoming complex business challenges. Talented leader with an interactive, motivational, decisive management style. Assertive, competitive, intuitive, and innovative—an achiever of exceptional rather than expected results.

CAREER HIGHLIGHTS

- Led profitable private and public companies—from startup through growth into multibillion-dollar businesses spanning diverse industries—with operations and market reach in domestic and international arenas. Achieved 35+% margins and triple-digit ROI.

- Managed cross-border operations and staffs spanning 20+ countries—Japan, China, South America, Europe, Middle East, and Soviet Republic—established strong business relationships and political contacts in six major countries. Built, mentored, and led teams of talented managers and provided indirect management to cross-functional, multinational workforces in excess of 1,750 employees.

- Structured, negotiated, and consummated high-dollar corporate transactions, financings, and deals—M&A, IPO, JV, convertible preferred stock, equity and debt financings, equipment financings, divestitures—ranging in value from $2 million to $2+ billion. Led all post-acquisition business transition and integration initiatives.

- Secured multiple contract wins with Fortune 50 and Fortune 100 corporations.

PROFESSIONAL EXPERIENCE

SAFFRON SYSTEMS, Baltimore, MD   1994 to Present

PRESIDENT & CEO

Top-ranking executive for an IT startup that has grown from $0 to $2+ billion in annual revenue and operations in 26 countries. Hold full P&L accountability for every aspect of operations—vision, strategic planning and direction, finance, business development, sales and marketing, technology R&D, product/service launch, technical services, customer relations, and key-account management. Built and continue to lead a core management team of 53 (including 22 Country Managers) and provide indirect oversight to a multinational workforce of 1,750+ employees. Authorities and accountabilities include:

LEADERSHIP ACHIEVEMENTS
- Raised $650+ million in funds—acquired $400 million through personal and professional relationships—raised $200 million after the dot.com crash.
- Authored and executed the business plan and succeeded in growing the company from startup to a multinational global technology enterprise and recognized industry leader.

BUSINESS DEVELOPMENT SUCCESSES
- Led the capture team in a strategic alliance to win $1+ billion contract over five years with $3+ billion in projected residual revenue over subsequent three years—Saffron's share represented 40% of total contract value.
- Captured major share in all competitively important vertical markets—positioning company as #1 or #2 in the market.

Strategy: *Use subheadings to steer readers through the core functional areas of the candidate's experience and multiple achievements without compromising readability.*

PHILLIP S. KRAEMER

SAFFRON SYSTEMS — PRESIDENT & CEO—*Continued:*

KEY ACCOUNTS & RELATIONSHIPS
- Established a global base of business of 7,000+ corporate, institutional, military, and government accounts—AOL Time Warner; Sony; Sears; Wal-Mart; Ford Motors; Toyota; Harvard Medical School; University of Maryland Medical Center; US Navy; US Army; GSA; and numerous others.
- Personally developed, solidified, and managed strategic relationships with the C-level executives of Microsoft, Apple, Cisco, IBM, EDS, DoD, and others.

TECHNOLOGY INNOVATIONS & PROJECTS
- Chief Architect for total systems design. Continue to provide technical and managerial oversight to major projects and products—including new software releases.
- Originator of the concept, content, and graphic design of the corporate website—managed the installation of high-end eCommerce/CRM features that improved customer accessibility, service levels, and satisfaction.

CORPORATE DISTINCTIONS
- Distinguished by Fortune Magazine—"Top 25 Technology Companies," April 2002.
- Recognized in Baltimore Magazine—"Top 10 Fastest Growing Companies in Maryland," 1995 (#1), 1997 (#2), 1999 (#2), 2000 (#1), and 2001 (#2).

RESTIN-10, Hunt Valley, MD   1982 to 1994

PRESIDENT/CEO

Acquired a troubled, privately owned specialty design and manufacturing company and grew it into a dynamic, publicly traded, multi-site operation with sales and distribution in domestic and international markets. Provided P&L oversight to all aspects of operations—headquarters, three US manufacturing plants, two off-shore facilities, three warehouse operations, and 12+ sales offices. Mentored and provided leadership to the Executive Committee, directed the activities of other cross-functional senior managers, sat on the Board of Directors, managed investor relations, and served as spokesperson to the media.

CORPORATE DEVELOPMENT & LEADERSHIP SUCCESSES
- Led the company through successful IPO (1989) and continued to grow the company by as much as 40% year-over-year until its sale to foreign investors in 1994. Delivered triple-digit ROI to stakeholders.
- Energized a stagnant organization suffering from serious customer-service, productivity, and quality issues. Introduced lean manufacturing methodologies, mapped core business processes, and improved employee morale.
- Won buy-in and commitment from the key department heads for the dramatic change in vision and leadership.

OPERATIONAL PERFORMANCE RESULTS
- Conceived and executed an aggressive turnaround and restructure that focused on financial discipline, performance excellence, and culture change.
- Converted $8+ million loss on $22 million in sales (YE 1982) to $39 million profit on $109 million in sales (YE 1991).
- Acquired ISO 9000 Certification.

BUSINESS DEVELOPMENT ACHIEVEMENTS
- Grew annual sales revenue from $22 million to $109+ million, restructured the sales organization and distribution channels, penetrated international markets, and captured 65+% market share in key vertical sectors.
- Led the conceptualization, development, and rollout of 26 new products (commercialized three new products within 10 months of assuming leadership), halting a 3-year period without product innovation (1979 to 1982).

EDUCATION

Harvard MBA
Six Sigma Black Belt

PROFESSIONAL & CIVIC AFFILIATIONS

President, Inner Harbor Business Association, Baltimore, Maryland
Chairman, Policy and Ethics Committee, Association of Approved GSA Suppliers
Chairman, Scholarship Committee, Harvard Business School Alumni Association
Certified Trainer, Six Sigma
Member, Board of Directors, Boy Scouts of America
Eagle Scout, Boy Scouts of America

APPENDIX

Internet Career Resources

With the emergence of the Internet has come a huge collection of job search resources Here are some of our favorites.

Dictionaries and Glossaries

Outstanding information on key words and acronyms.

Acronym Finder	www.acronymfinder.com
AltaVista's Babelfish Foreign-Language Translation Service	http://babelfish.altavista.com/
ComputerUser High-Tech Dictionary	www.computeruser.com/resources/dictionary/dictionary.html
Dave's Truly Canadian Dictionary of Canadian Spelling	www.luther.ca/~dave7cnv/cdnspelling/cdnspelling.html
Dictionary of Investment Terms	www.county.com.au/web/webdict.nsf/pages/index?open
Duhaime's Legal Dictionary	www.duhaime.org
High-Tech Dictionary Chat Symbols	www.computeruser.com/resources/dictionary/chat.html
InvestorWords.com	www.investorwords.com
Law.com Legal Industry Glossary	www.law.com
Legal Dictionary	www.nolo.com/lawcenter/dictionary/wordindex.cfm
Merriam-Webster Collegiate Dictionary & Thesaurus	www.m-w.com/home.htm

National Restaurant Association Restaurant Industry Glossary	www.nraef.org/pdf_files/ IndustryAcronymsDefinitions- edited-2-23.pdf
Refdesk	www.refdesk.com
Technology Terms Dictionary	www.computeruser.com/
TechWeb TechEncyclopedia	www.techweb.com/encyclopedia/
Verizon Glossary of Telecom Terms	www22.verizon.com/wholesale/glossary/ 0,2624,0_9,00.html
The Virtual Reference Desk-Dictionaries	http://thorplus.lib.purdue.edu/ rguides/guides.html
Washington Post Business Glossary	www.washingtonpost.com/ wp-srv/business/longterm/ glossary/index.htm
Webopedia: Online Dictionary for Computer and Internet Terms	www.webopedia.com
Whatis?com Technology Terms	whatis.techtarget.com
Wordsmyth: The Educational Dictionary/Thesaurus	www.wordsmyth.net

Job Search Sites

You'll find thousands and thousands of current professional employment opportunities on these sites.

GENERAL SITES

6FigureJobs	www.6figurejobs.com
All Star Jobs	www.411jobs.net
America's CareerInfoNet	www.acinet.org/acinet
America's Job Bank	www.ajb.dni.us
BestJobsUSA	www.bestjobsusa.com/index-jsk-ns.asp
BlackWorld Careers	www.blackworld.com/careers.htm
Canada WorkInfo Net	www.workinfonet.ca
CareerAge	www.careerage.com
CareerBuilder	www.careerbuilder.com
Career.com	www.career.com
CareerExchange.com	www.careerexchange.com
Career Exposure	www.careerexposure.com

The Career Key	www.careerkey.org/english
Careermag.com	www.careermag.com
CareerShop	www.careershop.com
CareerSite.com	www.careersite.com
Contract Employment Weekly	www.ceweekly.com
Digital City (jobs by location)	home.digitalcity.com
EmploymentGuide.com	www.employmentguide.com
Excite	http://careers.excite.com
FlipDog	www.flipdog.com
For Work	www.4work.com
Futurestep	www.futurestep.com
GETAJOB!	www.getajob.com
Help Wanted	www.helpwanted.com
HotJobs.com	www.hotjobs.com
It's Your Job Now	www.ItsYourJobNow.com
JobBankUSA	www.jobbankusa.com
JobHuntersBible.com	www.jobhuntersbible.com
Job-Hunt.org	www.job-hunt.org
JOBNET.com	www.jobnet.com/philly
JobsOnline	www.jobsonline.com
Job Source	www.jobsource.com
JobWeb	www.jobweb.com
Kiwi Careers (New Zealand)	www.careers.co.nz
Monster.com	www.monster.com
MonsterTRAK	www.monstertrak.com
NationJob Network	www.nationjob.com
NCOA MaturityWorks	www.maturityworks.org
Net Temps	www.net-temps.com
Online-Jobs.Com	www.online-jobs.com
The Riley Guide	www.rileyguide.com
Saludos Hispanos	www.saludos.com

SIRC Internet Resume Center	www.inpursuit.com/sirc
TrueCareers	www.careercity.com
US Resume	www.usresume.com
Wages.com	www.wages.com.au
WorkTree	www.worktree.com

ACCOUNTING CAREERS

American Association of Finance and Accounting	www.aafa.com
CPAnet	www.CPAnet.com
SmartPros Accounting	www.accountingnet.com

ARTS AND MEDIA CAREERS

Airwaves MediaWeb	www.airwaves.com
Auditions.com	www.auditions.com
Fashion Career Center	www.fashioncareercenter.com
Playbill (Theatre Jobs)	www.playbill.com/jobs/find
TVJobs.com	www.tvjobs.com

EDUCATION CAREERS

Academic360.com	www.academic360.com
Chronicle of Higher Education Career Network	www.chronicle.com/jobs
Council for Advancement and Support of Education	www.case.org
Education Jobs.com	www.educationjobs.com
Education Week's Marketplace Jobs Online	www.edweek.org/jobs
Education World	www.education-world.com/jobs
Jobs.EduFind.com	www.jobs.edunet.com
Teaching Jobs	www.teaching-jobs.org/index.htm
University Job Bank	www.ujobbank.com

HEALTH CARE/MEDICAL/PHARMACEUTICAL CAREERS

| Great Valley Publishing | www.gvpub.com |
| Health Care Recruitment Online | www.healthcareers-online.com |

HealthJobSite.com	www.healthjobsite.com
Health Leaders	www.HealthLeaders.com
HMonster	myh.monster.com
J. Allen & Associates (physician jobs)	www.NHRphysician.com
MedHunters.com	www.medhunters.com
Medzilla	www.medzilla.com
Nursing Spectrum	www.nursingspectrum.com
Pharmaceutical Company Database	www.coreynahman.com/ pharmaceutical_company_database.html
Physicians Employment	www.physemp.com
RehabJobsOnline	www.rehabjobs.com
Rx Career Center	www.rxcareercenter.com

HUMAN RESOURCES CAREERS

HR Connections	www.hrjobs.com
HR Hub	www.hrhub.com
Human Resources Development Canada	www.hrdc-drhc.gc.ca/common/ home.shtml
Jobs4HR	www.jobs4hr.com

INTERNATIONAL CAREERS

EscapeArtist.com	www.escapeartist.com
International Career Employment Center	www.internationaljobs.org
LatPro	www.latpro.com
OverseasJobs.com	www.overseasjobs.com

SALES AND MARKETING CAREERS

American Marketing Association	www.marketingpower.com
Job.com	www.job.com/jobsearch/ index.cfm?tid=search.cfm&us=226& catbox=53
MarketingJobs.com	www.marketingjobs.com
Rollins Search Group	www.rollinssearch.com

SERVICE CAREERS

Chefs at Work	www.chefsatwork.com
Culinary Jobs	www.pastrywiz.com/talk/job.htm
Escoffier On Line	www.escoffier.com
Foodservice.com	www.foodservice.com

TECHNOLOGY/ENGINEERING CAREERS

American Institute of Architects	www.aia.org
American Society for Quality	www.asq.org
Brainbuzz.com IT Career Network	www.brainbuzz.com
CareerShop	www.careershop.com
Chancellor & Chancellor Resources for Careers	www.chancellor.com/fr_careers.html
ComputerWork.com	www.computerwork.com
Computerworld Careers Knowledge Center	www.computerworld.com/careertopics/careers?from=left
Dice	www.dice.com
IDEAS Job Network	www.ideasjn.com
IEEE-USA Job Service	jobs.ieeeusa.org/jobs/services/
Jobserve	www.jobserve.com
National Society of Professional Engineers	www.nspe.org
Quality Resources Online	www.quality.org
Resulte Universal	www.psisearch.com
Techies.com	www.techies.com
Techsource	www.techsource.org/index.htm

GOVERNMENT AND MILITARY CAREERS

Federal Jobs Net	www.federaljobs.net
FedWorld	www.fedworld.gov
FRS Federal Jobs Central	www.fedjobs.com
GetaGovJob.com	www.getagovjob.com
GovExec.com	www.govexec.com
HRS Federal Job Search	www.hrsjobs.com

Military Career Guide Online	www.militarycareers.com
PLANETGOV	www.planetgov.com
USAJOBS (United States Office of Personnel Management)	www.usajobs.opm.gov

LEGAL CAREERS

FindLaw	www.findlaw.com
Greedy Associates	www.greedyassociates.com
Legal Career Center	www.attorneyjobs.com

SITES FOR MISCELLANEOUS SPECIFIC FIELDS

AG Careers/Farms.com	www.agricareers.com
American Public Works Association	www.pubworks.org
AutoCareers.com	www.autocareers.com
BrilliantPeople.com	www.brilliantpeople.com
CareerBank.com	www.careerbank.com
CEOExpress	www.ceoexpress.com
CFO.com	www.cfonet.com
Environmental Career Opportunities	www.ecojobs.com
Environmentalcareer.com	www.environmental-jobs.com
Find A Pilot	www.findapilot.com
International Seafarers Exchange	www.jobxchange.com
Logistics Jobs	www.jobsinlogistics.com
MBACareers.com	www.mbacareers.com
RAI: The Executive Search Firm	www.raijobs.com
Social Work Jobs	www.socialservice.com
Vault	www.vault.com

Company Information

Outstanding resources for researching specific companies.

555-1212.com	www.555-1212.com
Brint.com	www.brint.com
EDGAR Online	www.edgar-online.com
Experience	www.experiencenetwork.com
Fortune Magazine	www.fortune.com
Hoover's Business Profiles	www.hoovers.com
infoUSA (small-business information)	www.infousa.com
Intellifact.com	www.igiweb.com/intellifact/
OneSource CorpTech	www.corptech.com
SuperPages.com	www.bigbook.com
U.S. Chamber of Commerce	www.uschamber.com/
Vault Company Research	www.vault.com/companies/ searchcompanies.jsp
Wetfeet.com Company Research	www.wetfeet.com/asp/ companyresource_home.asp

Interviewing Tips and Techniques

Expert guidance to sharpen and strengthen your interviewing skills.

About.com Interviewing	www.jobsearch.about.com/business/ jobsearch/msubinterv.htm
Bradley CVs Introduction to Job Interviews	www.bradleycvs.demon.co.uk/ interview/index.htm
Dress for Success	www.dressforsuccess.org
Job-Interview.net	www.job-interview.net
Northeastern University Career Services	www.dac.neu.edu/coop.careerservices/ interview.html

Salary and Compensation Information

Learn from the experts to strengthen your negotiating skills and increase your salary.

Abbott, Langer & Associates	www.abbott-langer.com
America's Career InfoNet	www.acinet.org/acinet/select_ occupation.asp?stfips=&next=occ_rep

Bureau of Labor Statistics	www.bls.gov/bls/wages.htm
CareerJournal (The *Wall Street Journal*)	www.careerjournal.com/salaries/index.html
Clayton Wallis Co.	www.claytonwallis.com
Consultant Salaries	www.cob.ohio-state.edu/~fin/jobs/mco/salary.htm
Economic Research Institute	www.erieri.com
Health Care Salary Surveys	www.pohly.com/salary.shtml
Janco Associates MIS Salary Survey	www.psrinc.com/salary.htm
JobStar	www.jobstar.org/tools/salary/index.htm
Monster.com Salary Info	salary.monster.com/
Salary and Crime Calculator	www.homefair.com/homefair/cmr/salcalc.html
Wageweb	www.wageweb.com
WorldatWork (formerly American Compensation Association)	www.worldatwork.org

INDEX OF CONTRIBUTORS

The sample resumes in chapters 4 through 12 were written by professional resume and cover letter writers. If you need help with your resume and job search correspondence, you can use the following list to locate a career professional. Many, if not all, of these resume professionals work with clients long-distance as well as in their local areas.

A note about credentials: Nearly all of the contributing writers have earned one or more professional credentials. These credentials are highly regarded in the careers and employment industry and are indicative of the writer's expertise and commitment to professional development. Here is an explication of each of these credentials.

Credential	*Awarded by*	*Recognizes*
CBC: Certified Behavioral Consultant	The Institute for Motivational Living and Target Training International	
CCM: Credentialed Career Master	Career Masters Institute	Specific professional expertise, knowledge of current career trends, commitment to continuing education, and dedication through *pro bono* work
CCMC: Certified Career Management Coach	Career Coach University	Training and expertise in career coaching
CECC: Certified Electronic Career Coach	Professional Resume Writing and Research Association	Expertise in job-search-related Internet technology and electronic communications

(continues)

Credential	Awarded by	Recognizes
CEIP: Certified Employment Interview Professional	Professional Association of Resume Writers and Career Coaches	Expertise in interview preparation strategy
CERW: Certified Expert Resume Writer	Professional Resume Writing & Research Association	Advanced expertise in resume writing
CIPC: Certified International Personnel Consultant	National Association of Personnel Services	Expertise in staffing and placement
CJST: Certified Job Search Trainer	Career Masters Institute	
CMP: Career Management Practitioner	International Association of Career Management Professionals	
CPC: Certified Personnel Consultant	National Association of Personnel Services	Expertise in staffing and placement
CPRW: Certified Professional Resume Writer	Professional Association of Resume Writers and Career Coaches	Knowledge of resume strategy development and writing
CPS: Certified Professional Secretary	Professional Secretaries International	Expertise in business communication
CRW: Certified Resume Writer	Professional Resume Writing and Research Association	Successful passage of all requirements of the Certified Resume Writer examination
CSS: Certified Search Specialist	Search Research Institute	Advanced knowledge of personnel law, recruitment, and placement
CTMS: Certified Transition Management Seminars	William Bridges and Associates	Comprehensive training program on transitions
CTSB: Certified Targeted Small Business	Individual states	Qualifying small business
CWDP: Certified Workforce Development Professional	National Association of Workforce Development Professionals	
Ed.S.: Educational Specialist in Counseling	Accredited university	Graduate-level education

Credential	Awarded by	Recognizes
GCDF: Global Career Development Facilitator	Center for Credentialing & Education, Inc.	Advanced certification for career development professionals
JCTC: Job and Career Transition Coach	Career Planning and Adult Development Network	Training and expertise in job and career coaching strategies
IJCTC: International Job and Career Transition Coach	Career Planning and Adult Development Network	Training and expertise in job and career coaching strategies
LPC: Licensed Professional Counselor	Individual states	Master's in counseling plus three years of supervised counseling experience
MA: Master of Arts degree	Accredited university	Graduate-level education
MAT: Master of Arts in Teaching	Accredited university	Graduate-level education
MBA: Master of Business Administration degree	Accredited university	Graduate-level education
M.Ed.: Master of Education degree	Accredited university	Graduate-level education
MFA: Master of Fine Arts degree	Accredited university	Graduate-level education
MS: Master of Science degree	Accredited university	Graduate-level education
M.S.Ed.: Master of Science in Education	Accredited university	Graduate-level education
NCC: National Certified Counselor NCCC: National Certified Career Counselor	National Board for Certified Counselors (affiliated with the American Counseling Association and the American Psychological Association)	Qualification to provide career counseling
NCRW: Nationally Certified Resume Writer	National Resume Writers' Association	Knowledge of resume strategy development and writing
Ph.D.: Doctor of Philosophy degree	Accredited university	Post-graduate education

Kim Batson, CCMC, CJST
Netconnect Associates
704-228th Ave. NE, PMB 234
Redmond, WA 98074
Phone: (800) 756-7836
Fax: (425) 836-0824
E-mail: kim@careermanagementcoaching.com
URL: www.careermanagementcoaching.com

Janet L. Beckstrom, CPRW
Owner, Word Crafter
1717 Montclair Ave.
Flint, MI 48503
Toll-free: (800) 351-9818
Fax: (810) 232-9257
E-mail: wordcrafter@voyager.net

Marian Bernard, CPS, CPRW, JCTC, CEIP
Principal, The Regency Group
6 Morning Crescent
Aurora, Ontario L4G 2E3
Canada
Phone: (905) 841-7120
Fax: (905) 841-1391
E-mail: marian@neptune.on.ca
URL: www.resumeexpert.ca

Debi Bogard
Principal, Career Formulas
11835 Carmel Mountain Rd., Ste. 1304-175
San Diego, CA 92128-4609
Phone: (858) 592-9406
Fax: (858) 592-7271
E-mail: careerformulas@san.rr.com
URL: www.careerformulas.com

Rima Bogardus, CPRW, CEIP
President, Career Support Services
P.O. Box 2026
Garner, NC 27529
Phone: (919) 779-9772
E-mail: rima@careersupportservices.com
URL: www.careersupportservices.com

Arnold G. Boldt, CPRW, JCTC
Arnold-Smith Associates
625 Panorama Trail, Bldg. 2 #200C
Rochester, NY 14625
Phone: (716) 383-0350
Fax: (716) 387-0516
E-mail: Arnie@ResumeSOS.com
URL: www.ResumeSOS.com

Kathryn Bourne, CPRW, IJCTC
President, CareerConnections
5210 E. Pima St., Ste. 130
Tucson, AZ 85712
Phone: (520) 323-2964
Fax: (520) 795-3575
E-mail: Ccmentor@aol.com
URL: www.BestFitResumes.com

Carolyn Braden, CPRW
President, Braden Resume Solutions
108 La Plaza Dr.
Hendersonville, TN 37075
Phone: (615) 822-3317
Fax: (615) 826-9611
E-mail: bradenresume@comcast.net

Martin Buckland, CPRW, JCTC, CEIP, CJST
President, Elite Resumes
1428 Stationmaster Ln.
Oakville, Ontario L6M 3A7
Canada
Toll-free: (866) 773-7863
Phone: (905) 825-0490
Fax: (905) 825-2966
E-mail: martin@aneliteresume.com
URL: www.AnEliteResume.com

Diane Burns, CPRW, CCM, IJCTC, CEIP, CCMC
President, Career Marketing Techniques
5219 Thunder Hill Rd.
Columbia, MD 21045
Phone: (410) 884-0213
E-mail: diane@polishedresumes.com
URL: www.polishedresumes.com

(Ms.) Freddie Cheek, M.S.Ed., CPRW, CWDP, CRW
Cheek & Cristantello Career Connections
4511 Harlem Rd., Ste. 3
Amherst, NY 14226
Phone: (716) 839-3635
Fax: (716) 831-9320
E-mail: fscheek@adelphia.net
URL: www.CheekandCristantello.com

Annemarie Cross, CEIP, CPRW, CRW, CCM
Advanced Employment Concepts/A.E.C. Office
Services
P.O. Box 91
Hallam, Victoria 3803
Australia
Phone: +613 9796 4464
Fax: +613 9796 4479
E-mail: success@aresumewriter.net
URL: www.aresumewriter.net

Jean Cummings, M.A.T., CPRW, CEIP
President, A Resume for Today
123 Minot Rd.
Concord, MA 01742
Toll-free: (800) 324-1699
Phone: (978) 371-9266
Fax: (978) 964-0529
E-mail: careers@AResumeForToday.com
URL: www.AResumeForToday.com

Norine T. Dagliano, CPRW
Principal, ekm Inspirations
616 Highland Way
Hagerstown, MD 21740
Phone: (301) 766-2032
Fax: (301) 745-5700
E-mail: ndagliano@yahoo.com

Laura A. DeCarlo, CCM, CPRW, JCTC, CECC, CCMC, CERW
President, A Competitive Edge Career Service
1665 Clover Circle
Melbourne, FL 32935
Toll-free: (800) 715-3442
Phone: (321) 752-0880
Fax: (321) 752-7513
E-mail: getanedge@aol.com
URL: www.anexecutiveedge.com

Deborah Wile Dib, CCM, NCRW, CPRW, CEIP, JCTC, CCMC
President, Advantage Resumes of New York
77 Buffalo Ave.
Medford, NY 11763
Toll-free: (888) 272-8899
Phone: (631) 475-8513
Fax: (501) 421-7790
E-mail: 100kPLUS@advantageresumes.com
URL: www.advantageresumes.com

Kirsten Dixson, JCTC, CPRW, CEIP
President, New Leaf Career Solutions
P.O. Box 963
Exeter, NH 03833
Phone: (866) 639-5323
Fax: (888) 887-7166
E-mail: info@newleafcareer.com
URL: www.newleafcareer.com

Nina Ebert, CPRW
President, A Word's Worth
25 Oakwood Dr.
New Egypt, NJ 08533
Phone: (609) 758-7799
Fax: (609) 758-7799
E-mail: keytosuccess@magpage.com
URL: www.keytosuccessresumes.com

Debbie Ellis, CPRW
President, Phoenix Career Group
Danville, KY
Toll-free U.S. + Canada: (800) 876-5506
Worldwide: (859) 236-4001
E-mail: debbie@phoenixcareergroup.com
URL: www.PhoenixCareerGroup.com

Joyce L. Fortier, MBA, CPRW, JCTC, CCM, CCMC
President, Create Your Career
23871 W. Lebost
Novi, MI 48375
Toll-free: (800) 793-9895
Phone: (248) 478-5662
Fax: (248) 426-9974
E-mail: careerist@aol.com
URL: www.careerist.com

Art Frank, MBA
President, Resumes "R" Us
1991 Diamond Ct.
Oldsmar, FL 34677
Phone: (727) 787-6885
Fax: (727) 786-9228
E-mail: AF1134@aol.com
URL: www.powerresumesandcoaching.com

Gail Frank, NCRW, JCTC, MA, CEIP, CPRW
President, Frankly Speaking: Resumes That Work!
10409 Greendale Dr.
Tampa, FL 33626
Phone: (813) 926-1353
Fax: (813) 926-1092
E-mail: gailfrank@post.harvard.edu
URL: www.callfranklyspeaking.com

Judy Friedler, NCRW, CPRW, JCTC, CCM
President, CareerPro International
34 Blantyre Rd.
Buffalo, NY 14216
Phone: (866) 433-6033
Fax: (212) 202-4882
E-mail: info@rezcoach.com
URL: www.rezcoach.com

Roberta F. Gamza, JCTC, CEIP, CJST
President, Career Ink
Louisville, CO 80027
Toll-free: (877) 581-6063
Phone: (303) 955-3065
Fax: (303) 955-3065
E-mail: roberta@careerink.com
URL: www.careerink.com

Louise Garver, CMP, JCTC, CPRW, CEIP
President, Career Directions, LLC
P.O. Box 587
Broad Brook, CT 06016
Toll-free: (888) 222-3731
Phone: (860) 623-9476
Fax: (860) 623-9473
E-mail: TheCareerPro@aol.com
URL: www.resumeimpact.com

Wendy Gelberg, M.Ed., CPRW, IJCTC
President, Advantage Resumes
21 Hawthorn Ave.
Needham, MA 02492
Phone: (781) 444-0778
Fax: (781) 444-2778
E-mail: WGelberg@aol.com

Susan Guarneri, MS, NCC, NCCC, LPC, CPRW, IJCTC, CEIP, CCM, CCMC, CPRW
President, Guarneri Associates/Resumagic
1101 Lawrence Rd.
Lawrenceville, NJ 08648
Phone: (609) 771-1669
Fax: (609) 637-0449
E-mail: Resumagic@aol.com
URL: www.Resume-Magic.com

Michele J. Haffner, CPRW, JCTC
Advanced Resume Services
1314 W. Paradise Ct.
Glendale, WI 53209
Toll-free: (877) 247-1677
Phone: (414) 247-1677
Fax: (414) 247-1808
E-mail: michele@resumeservices.com
URL: www.resumeservices.com

Peter Hill, CPRW
Distinctive Resumes
1226 Alexander St. #1205
Honolulu, HI 96826
Phone: (808) 306-3920
Fax: (877) 273-9493
E-mail: distinctiveresumes@yahoo.com
URL: www.peterhill.biz

Gayle Howard, CPRW, CRW, CCM
Founder/Owner, Top Margin Resumes Online
P.O. Box 74
Chirnside Park, Melbourne 3116
Australia
Phone: +61 3 9726 6694
Fax: +61 3 9726 5316
E-mail: gayle@topmarginonline.com
URL: www.topmargin.com

Lynn Hughes, MA, CPRW, CEIP
A Resume and Career Service, Inc.
3402 A 34th St.
P.O. Box 6911
Lubbock, TX 79493
Phone: (806) 785-9800
Fax: (806) 785-2711
E-mail: lynn@aresumeservice.com
URL: www.aresumeservice.com

Deborah S. James, CCMC, CPRW
President, Leading Edge Resumes and Career Services
1010 Schreier Rd.
Rossford, OH 43460
Phone: (419) 666-4518
Fax: (419) 791-3567
E-mail: djames@leadingedgeresumes.com
URL: www.leadingedgeresumes.com

Billie P. Jordan
Advantage Resumes and Career Services
2362 Belgrade Swansboro Rd.
Maysville, NC 28555
Toll-free: (877) 563-2509
Phone: (910) 743-3641
Fax: (910) 743-0435
E-mail: bjordan1@ec.rr.com
URL: www.benchmarkresumes.com

Michelle Kennedy, CPRW
President, Scribble Ink, Ltd.
P.O. Box 1375
Port Washington, NY 11050
Phone: (516) 767-7465
E-mail: info@scribbleink.com
URL: www.scribbleink.com

William Kinser, CPRW, JCTC, CEIP
President, To The Point Resumes
4117 Kentmere Square
Fairfax, VA 22030-6062
Phone: (703) 352-8969
Fax: (703) 352-8969
E-mail: resumes@tothepointresumes.com
URL: www.tothepointresumes.com

Myriam-Rose Kohn, CPRW, IJCTC, CCM, CEIP
President, JEDA Enterprises
27201 Tourney Rd., Ste. 201
Valencia, CA 91355-1857
Phone: (661) 253-0801
Fax: (661) 253-0744
E-mail: myriam-rose@jedaenterprises.com
URL: www.jedaenterprises.com

Joanne Kowlowitz
The Executives' Job Search Strategist
P.O. Box 4194
St. Johnsbury, VT 05819
Phone: (802) 684-3803
E-mail: writejob1@aol.com

Cindy Kraft, CCMC, CCM, CPRW, JCTC
President, Executive Essentials
P.O. Box 336
Valrico, FL 33595
Phone: (813) 655-0658
Fax: (813) 685-4287
E-mail: careermaster@exec-essentials.com
URL: www.exec-essentials.com

Ric Lanham, CCM, CECC, CRW
General Manager, R.L. Stevens & Associates, Inc.
8888 Keystone Crossing, Ste. 950
Indianapolis, IN 46240
Phone: (317) 846-8888
Fax: (317) 846-8949
E-mail: rlanham@rlstevens.com
URL: www.interviewing.com;
www.myexecutiveweb.com/rlanham

Rolande L. LaPointe, CPC, CIPC, CPRW, CRW, IJCTC, CCM, CSS
President, RO-LAN Associates, Inc.
725 Sabattus St.
Lewiston, ME 04240
Phone: (207) 784-1010 or 782-3327
Fax: (207) 782-3446
E-mail: Rlapointe@aol.com

Lorie Lebert, CPRW, IJCTC, CCMC
President, The Loriel Group—Coaching ROI/Resume ROI
P.O. Box 267
Novi, MI 48376
Toll-free: (800) 870-9059
Phone: (248) 380-6101
Fax: (248) 380-0169
E-mail: Lorie@DoMyResume.com
URL: www.DoMyResume.com

Diana C. LeGere
President, Executive Final Copy
P.O. Box 3731
Petersburg, VA 23805
Toll-free: (866) 754-5465
Fax: (626) 602-8715
E-mail: executiveresumes@yahoo.com
URL: www.executivefinalcopy.com

Kim Little, JCTC
President, Executive Resume Pro
1281 Courtney Dr.
Victor, NY 14564
Phone: (585) 742-2467
Fax: (585) 742-1907
E-mail: info@executiveresumepro.com
URL: www.executiveresumepro.com

Denise Lupardo
President, Denise's Office Support and Resumes
22961 Mullin Rd.
Lake Forest, CA 92630
Phone: (949) 581-7901
Fax: (949) 581-7961
E-mail: Success@ResumeRelief.com
URL: www.ResumeRelief.com

Nick Marino, MA, CPRW, CRW, CACM, CEIP, USN-Ret.
President, Outcome Resumes and Career Service
710 Aurora Dr.
Bishop, TX 78343
Phone: (361) 584-3121
Fax: (512) 857-0782
E-mail: outcomerez@earthlink.net
URL: www.outcomeresumes.com

Peter S. Marx, JCTC
3208 Wallace Ave.
Tampa, FL 33611
Phone: (813) 832-5133
E-mail: marxps@aol.com

Jan Melnik, CPRW, CCM
President, Absolute Advantage
432 Higganum Rd.
P.O. Box 718
Durham, CT 06422
Phone: (860) 349-0256
Fax: (860) 349-1343
E-mail: CompSPJan@aol.com
URL: www.janmelnik.com

Doug Morrison, CPRW
President, Career Power
2915 Providence Rd., Ste. 250-B
Charlotte, NC 28211
Phone: (704) 365-0773
Fax: (704) 365-3411
E-mail: dmpwresume@aol.com
URL: www.careerpowerresume.com

Helen Oliff, CPRW and Certified Executive Coach
TURNING POINT
2307 Freetown Ct., #12C
Reston, VA 20191
Phone: (703) 716-0077
Fax: (703) 997-0506
E-mail: helen@turningpointnow.com
URL: www.turningpointnow.com

Debra O'Reilly, CPRW, JCTC, CEIP
President, A First Impression/ResumeWriter.com
16 Terryville Ave.
Bristol, CT 06010
Toll-free: (800) 340-5570
Phone: (860) 583-7500
Fax: (860) 585-9611
E-mail: debra@resumewriter.com
URL: www.resumewriter.com

Sharon Pierce-Williams, M.Ed., CPRW
President, The Resume.Doc
609 Lincolnshire Ln.
Findlay, OH 45840
Phone: (419) 422-0228
Fax: (419) 425-1185
E-mail: TheResumeDocSPW@aol.com
URL: www.TheResumeDoc.com

Ross Primack, CPRW, CEIP, GCDF
Connecticut Works
55 South St.
Bristol, CT 06010
Phone: (860) 314-2592
Fax: (860) 584-4798
E-mail: rossprimackcprw@hotmail.com

Anita Radosevich, CPRW, IJCTC, CEIP
President, Anita's Business and Career Services
315 W. Pine St., Ste. 5
Lodi, CA 95240
Phone: (209) 368-4444
Fax: (209) 368-2834
E-mail: anita@abcresumes.com
URL: www.abcresumes.com

Teena Rose, CPRW, CEIP, CCM
President, Resume to Referral
7211 Taylorsville Rd., Office 208
Huber Heights, OH 45424
Phone: (937) 236-1360
Fax: (937) 236-1351
E-mail: admin@resumetoreferral.com
URL: www.resumebycprw.com

Jennifer Rydell, CPRW, CCM
Principal, Simplify Your Life Career Services
6327-C SW Capitol Hwy., PMB 243
Portland, OR 97239-1937
Phone: (503) 977-1955
Fax: (503) 245-4212
E-mail: simplify@spiritone.com
URL: www.simplifyyourliferesumes.com

Janice M. Shepherd, CPRW, JCTC, CEIP
Write On Career Keys
2628 E. Crestline Dr.
Bellingham, WA 98226-4260
Phone: (360) 738-7958
Fax: (360) 738-1189
E-mail: janice@writeoncareerkeys.com
URL: www.writeoncareerkeys.com

Debbie Sherrie, CPRW
Right Management Consultants
710 Jefferson Dr.
Charlotte, NC 28270
Phone: (704) 364-1441
Fax: (704) 365-8892
E-mail: dsherrie@bellsouth.net

Igor Shpudejko, CPRW, JCTC, MBA
President, Career Focus
23 Parsons Ct.
Mahwah, NJ 07430
Phone: (201) 825-2865
Fax: (201) 825-7711
E-mail: ishpudejko@aol.com
URL: www.CareerInFocus.com

Kelley Smith, CPRW
President, Advantage Resume Services
P.O. Box 391
Sugar Land, TX 77487
Phone: (877) 478-4999
Fax: (208) 275-7193
E-mail: info@jobsearchpartner.com
URL: www.jobsearchpartner.com

Lisa LeVerrier Stein, CPRW, CEIP, JCTC
Principal, Competitive Advantage Resumes and
Career Coaching
1421 SE 14th Ct.
Deerfield Beach, FL 33441
Toll-free phone: (800) 750-5690
Phone: (954) 571-0313
Toll-free fax: (800) 656-2712
E-mail: lisalev@attbi.com; ds2@justice.com
URL: www.jobcoaching.com;
www.lawyerresumes.com

Billie Ruth Sucher, MS, CTMS, CTSB
President, Billie Ruth Sucher and Associates
7177 Hickman Rd., Ste. 10
Urbandale, IA 50322
Phone: (515) 276-0061
Fax: (515) 334-8076
E-mail: betwnjobs@aol.com

Patricia Traina-Duckers, CPRW, CRW, CEIP
President, The Resume Writer
P.O. Box 595
Edison, NJ 08818-0595
Phone: (732) 239-8533
Fax: (732) 906-5636
E-mail: sales@theresumewriter.com
URL: www.theresumewriter.com

Ilona Vanderwoude, CCMC, CJST, CEIP
Career Branches
P.O. Box 330
Riverdale, NY 10471
Phone: (914) 376-4217
Fax: (646) 349-2218
E-mail: ilona@CareerBranches.com
URL: www.CareerBranches.com

Vivian VanLier, CPRW, JCTC, CEIP, CCMC
Advantage Resume and Career Services of
Los Angeles
6701 Murietta Ave.
Valley Glen (Los Angeles), CA 91405
Phone: (818) 994-6655
Fax: (818) 994-6620
E-mail: vvanlier@aol.com
www.CuttingEdgeResumes.com

Deborah J. Walker, CCMC
Principal, Alpha Advantage, Inc.
Vancouver, WA 98683
Toll-free phone: (888) 828-0814
Phone: (360) 260-4965
E-mail: Deb@AlphaAdvantage.com
URL: www.alphaadvantage.com

INDEX

Cover Letter Magic

Wendy S. Enelow and Louise M. Kursmark

The top professional resume and cover letter writers share their secrets for turning a boring cover letter into a knockout that gets noticed!

Perfect for job seekers at all levels. A before-and-after look at more than 150 sample cover letters from a variety of occupations and levels of employment. An excellent resource that shows why particular techniques work and what makes a powerful cover letter.

ISBN 1-56370-732-2 / Order Code LP-J7322 / **$16.95**

Seven Steps to Getting a Job Fast

Michael Farr

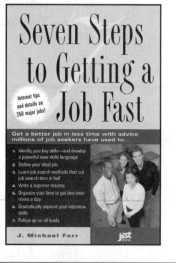

This book points the way for millions of unemployed people who seek quick, solid advice on the shortest distance to their next jobs. Best-selling author Mike Farr distills his time-tested job search techniques in this brief, results-oriented book. Includes advice on using the Internet in your job search.

ISBN 1-56370-888-4 / Order Code LP-J8884 / **$8.95**

Insights for the Journey

Navigating to Thrive, Enjoy, and Prosper in Senior Management

John Lucht

An exquisitely written gem of a book! Lucht combines his own startlingly original insights with a fun-to-read review of management principles. (Hardcover)

ISBN 0-94278-531-2 / Order Code LP-VP5312 / **$19.95**